# The Theory of Reasoned Action:

# Its Application To Aids-Preventive Behaviour

INTERNATIONAL SERIES IN EXPERIMENTAL SOCIAL PSYCHOLOGY

Series Editor: MICHAEL ARGYLE, University of Oxford

New Series Editor from Volume 29: W. PETER ROBINSON, University of Bristol

*Other titles in the series include:*

HOLLIN and TROWER
Handbook of Social Skills Training Volume 1
Handbook of Social Skills Training Volume 2

RUTTER
Communicating by Telephone

BULL
Posture and Gesture

FURNHAM
Lay Theories: Everyday Understanding of Problems in the Social Sciences

SCOTT and SCOTT
Adaption of Immigrants

LIVINGSTONE
Making Sense of Television

REHM and GADENNE
Intuitive Predictions and Professional Forecasts

STRACK, ARGYLE and SCHWARZ
Subjective Well-Being

FORGAS
Emotion and Social Judgements

ALBERT
Genius and Eminence, 2nd Edition

WALKER
The Psychology of Gambling

LIEBRAND, MESSICK and WILKE
Social Dilemmas: Theoretical Issues and Research Findings

SCHNEIDER
Childrens Social Competence in Context

WILSON and GALLOIS
Assertion and its Social Context

# The Theory of Reasoned Action:

# Its Application To Aids-Preventive Behaviour

Edited by

DEBORAH J. TERRY, CYNTHIA GALLOIS and MALCOLM McCAMISH
University of Queensland, Australia

PERGAMON PRESS
OXFORD • NEW YORK • SEOUL • TOKYO

| U.K. | Pergamon Press Ltd, Headington Hill Hall, Oxford OX3 0BW, England |
|------|---|
| U.S.A. | Pergamon Press, Inc., 660 White Plains Road, Tarrytown, New York 10591-5153, U.S.A. |
| KOREA | Pergamon Press Korea, K.P.O. Box 315, Seoul 110-603, Korea |
| JAPAN | Pergamon Press Japan, Tsunashima Building Annex, 3-20-12 Yushima, Bunkyo-ku, Tokyo 113, Japan |

First edition 1993

**British Library Cataloguing in Publication Data**
A catalogue record for this book is available from the British Library.

**Library of Congress Cataloging in Publication Data**
The theory of reasoned action: its application to AIDS-preventive behaviour/ edited by Deborah J. Terry, Cynthia Gallois, and Malcolm McCamish. -- 1st ed.
p. cm. -- (International series in experimental social psychology; v. 28)
Includes bibliographical references.
1. AIDS (Disease)--Prevention--Congresses. 2. Safe sex in AIDS prevention--Congresses. 3. Health behavior--Congresses. 4. Health attitudes--Congresses. 5. Australia. I. Terry, Deborah J. II. Gallois, Cynthia. III. McCamish, Malcolm. IV. Series.
[DNLM: 1. HIV Infections--prevention and control--Australia--congresses. 2. Sex Behavior--Australia--congresses. 3. Knowledge, Attitudes, Practice--congresses. WD 308 T396 1993]
RA644.A25T46   1993
616.97'9205--dc20
DNLM/DLC

ISBN 0-08-041932-1-

*Printed and bound in Great Britain by BPCC Wheatons Ltd, Exeter*

# Contents

PREFACE                                                           ix

LIST OF CONTRIBUTORS                                              xiii

INTRODUCTION BY MARTIN FISHBEIN                                   xv

**1. The Theory of Reasoned Action and Health Care
Behaviour**                                                        1

Deborah Terry, Cynthia Gallois, and Malcolm McCamish

**2. Applying the Theory of Reasoned Action to the Prediction
of AIDS-Preventive Behaviour**                                    29

Virginia J. Lewis and Yoshihisa Kashima

**3. Influences on Condom Use among Undergraduates:
Testing the Theories of Reasoned Action and Planned
Behaviour**                                                       47

Joe Nucifora, Cynthia Gallois, and Yoshihisa Kashima

**4. Predicting AIDS-Preventive Behaviour among
Adolescents**                                                     65

Susan M. Moore, Doreen A. Rosenthal, and Jennifer Boldero

**5. Attitudes Towards Condoms and the Theory of Reasoned
Action**                                                          81

Michael W. Ross and Mary-Louise McLaws

**6. The Theory of Reasoned Action as Applied to AIDS Prevention for Australian Ethnic Groups**    93
Ken Rigby, Biruta Dietz and Stuart Sturgess

**7. Extending the Theory of Reasoned Action: The Role of Health Beliefs**    117
Peta Warwick, Deborah Terry, and Cynthia Gallois

**8. Self-Efficacy Expectancies and the Theory of Reasoned Action**    135
Deborah Terry

**9. Theory of Reasoned Action and the Role of Perceived Risk in the Study of Safer Sex**    153
Perri Timmins, Cynthia Gallois, Deborah Terry,
Malcolm McCamish and Yoshihisa Kashima

**10. Application of the Theory of Reasoned Action to the Measurement of Condom Use among Gay Men**    169
Mary-Louise McLaws, Brian Oldenburg and Michael W. Ross

**11. A Theory Based Intervention: The Theory of Reasoned Action in Action**    185
Malcolm McCamish, Perri Timmins, Deborah Terry and
Cynthia Gallois

**12. The Theory of Reasoned Action and Problem-Focused Research**    207
Yoshihisa Kashima and Cynthia Gallois

**13. On the Need to Mind the Gap: On-Line versus off-Line Cognitions Underlying Sexual Risk Taking**    227
Ron S. Gold

**14. Flaws in the Theory of Reasoned Action**    253
Susan Kippax and June Crawford

EPILOGUE    271

REFERENCES     277

AUTHOR INDEX     315

SUBJECT INDEX     323

# Preface

When AIDS first appeared in Australia in late 1982, the response from the community, particularly the gay community, was immediate; AIDS councils were soon set up in every major city in the country to deal with education, prevention, and support for people with AIDS. Government bodies were somewhat slower to act, but by the end of 1985, the Australian Government had established priorities, policy formulation was underway, and some programs were in place.

Since the first Australian death from AIDS in 1983, the pattern of infections, largely in the gay community but with some cases resulting from contaminated blood products, identified us as what WHO was later to classify as a Pattern I country (i.e., a country where the majority of people are infected with HIV are gay or bisexual men). Australia is perhaps the only remaining classic Pattern I country in the world. With more than 16,000 notifications of HIV infection as of 30 September, 1992, the very large majority, more than 80%, have been infected through male homosexual or bisexual contact. Eight percent of notified infections have been through injecting drug use (one-third of whom have also had male-to-male sexual contact), heterosexual contact accounts for just over 5%, while those infected through contaminated blood or blood products, including haemophiliacs, account for a further 5.2%. With infected women forming less than 5% of the case load, the number of paediatric cases where transmission has occurred from an infected mother is understandably low, less than 0.5%. Similarly, the number of reported diagnoses for those between the ages of 13 and 19 is just over 2% of the total. Thus, the changing epidemiology of other Pattern I countries (see Lewis & Kashima, this volume) is almost imperceptible in Australia.

While it would be wrong and indeed dangerous to underestimate the potential threat to injecting drug users, certain groups of heterosexuals and young people, it is important to acknowledge the important place prevention has had on the Australian health agenda. Australia was the first country in the world to establish universal screening of the national blood supply. Through a variety of national committees, AIDS was successfully removed from the party-political agenda, so that a number of otherwise controversial preventive initiatives could be funded, often at the community level. The early establishment of outreach programs including needle exchanges, accompanied by the necessary legislative changes which facilitated their use (for example, disallowing possession of used injecting equipment as evidence of drug use), has meant that Australia has by Western standards only a minor infection problem among injecting drug users. Similarly, the establishment and continued funding of community groups of men who have sex with men, sex workers, and injecting drug users has meant that a social climate advocating the prevention of HIV transmission within and by the peer group has been able to develop. This has had the effect that consistently over the past five years, notified infections have fallen below predicted levels.

Thus, there has been from the first a strong focus on HIV prevention, and on the social and psychological variables that lead to safer or unsafe sexual behaviour. The focus on prevention has meant that social psychologists have been very active in research on HIV since the mid-1980s. Australia has a large land mass but a relatively small population, and the opportunities to exchange ideas have supported the high level of research activity. Most work has been theory-based, and the theories of reasoned action (TRA) and planned behaviour (TPB) have been strong forces, as the chapters in this book show.

The origin of this book was a symposium on HIV/AIDS held at the 1991 Australian Social Psychology Conference, at which it became apparent that several research groups were working independently on HIV prevention and safer sex from perspectives closely related to the theory of reasoned action, or from perspectives directly challenging it. The contributors to the book come from four of the six Australian states, and represent the range of social-psychological research on HIV prevention in this country. We realised that the work going on provided an opportunity to present a body of research on one topic (safer sex) conducted in one country over a relatively short time period, all of which is informed by TRA, but which involves a number of different behaviours and different populations.

As a result, the theme of the book is TRA and safer sex, and the various chapters indicate the great complexity of research issues in this area, as well as giving an account of the ways in which TRA can be tested and applied. About half the chapters present tests of TRA, and attention is paid to methodological issues in an area where experimental research is generally not possible or reasonable. In a few cases, TRA is tested directly against other models. Several chapters also examine the theoretical characteristics of TRA, their relevance to the context of safer sex, and challenges to the theory. Finally, some extensions to the basic TRA model, resulting from research on safer sex, are suggested and evaluated.

This book could not have come about without the help of many people and organisations. In addition to the authors who contributed chapters, we would like to note that research in several of the chapters involving the editors was supported by Australian Commonwealth AIDS Research Grants (to Gallois, Kashima, & McCamish; Gallois & McCamish; Terry & Galligan). We would also like to thank the Psychology and Chemistry Departments of The University of Queensland for their support. We are grateful to our other colleagues and students for their help with the research, and particularly to Patricia Garcia-Prieto, John Gardner, Linda Tonge, Gloria Hynes, and Jeff Pittam for help with production of the manuscript. The Editor of the series, Michael Argyle, provided very valuable comments on the book, and Lesley Williams at Pergamon was most helpful at the production end. Finally, we would like to thank Martin, Jeff, and Victor for their patience and tolerance during the final stages of producing the manuscript.

**Plan of the Book**

The chapters in the book present a range of the social-psychological research on safer sex conducted in Australia over the past few years, along with several theoretical and review chapters informed by the theory of reasoned action. After an Introduction and commentary by Martin Fishbein, the first section sets the stage. First, Terry, Gallois, and McCamish introduce TRA and its role in the prediction of health behaviour; next, Lewis and Kashima review recent research on HIV/AIDS and safer sex. Two chapters, by Nucifora, Gallois, and Kashima (Chapter 3) and Moore, Rosenthal, and Boldero (Chapter 4) present tests of TRA and TPB in the prediction of condom use among heterosexual adolescents in Brisbane and Melbourne, and come to somewhat different conclusions. In Chapter 5, Ross and McLaws review research on attitudes to condoms since the 1940s, including the role of TRA in this research. Finally, in Chapter 6, Rigby, Dietz, and Sturgess show the role of TRA in examining safer sexual practices among several immigrant groups in Australia.

In the second part of the book, several chapters present empirical work extending TRA and comparing it to other approaches to health behaviour. In Chapter 7, Warwick, Terry, and Gallois compare the performance of TRA and the health belief model in predicting condom use. Chapter 8, by Terry, examines the role of self-efficacy in safer sex, and explores the conceptualisation of control in TPB. Finally, Timmins, Gallois, McCamish, Terry, and Kashima look at the role of perceived personal risk of HIV infection, which recent researchers have tended to play down.

The last six chapters show the wider picture, indicating the role of TRA in application, as well as challenging its capacity to explain safer sex convincingly. In Chapter 10, McLaws, Oldenberg, and Ross illustrate the application of TRA in measuring and examining condom use among gay men in Sydney, the Australian epicentre of the AIDS epidemic. Chapter 11, by McCamish, Timmins, Gallois, and Terry, reviews interventions promoting safer sex and shows the important role TRA can play here. In Chapter 12, Kashima and Gallois examine criticisms of TRA on both theoretical and metatheoretical grounds. The next two chapters challenge the metatheoretical basis of TRA and its extensions in the area of HIV/AIDS: Gold (Chapter 13) from the perspective of cognitive psychology, and Kippax and Crawford (Chapter 14) from the framework of social constructionism. Finally, in the Epilogue, the editors draw out some of the major themes of the book.

We would like to make a note regarding terminology. At the request of the publishers, throughout this book we have used the term 'safer sex' to refer to sexual behaviour that is currently believed to minimise the transmission of HIV (and other sexually-transmitted diseases as well). In Australia, the term of choice is 'safe sex;' this term is advocated in preference to 'safer sex' by the Australian National Committee on AIDS, the advisory body to the Australian Federal government. 'Safe sex' is contrasted to 'unsafe sex,' or practices currently believed to be unsafe with regard to HIV transmission. Even though we have deferred here to wider usage in the English-speaking world, we and the other chapter authors belive that 'safe sex' is the better term. Readers may wish to consider this usage, particularly in the light of the strong focus in Australia on prevention of HIV.

This book represents the first systematic attempt to cover the field of safer sex research in Australian psychology. It also represents one of the few attempts to review and integrate empirical tests of one of the most widely used theoretical models in the health context. In addition, it indicates the many ways in which TRA has informed work on safer sex, as well as its potential for the future. We hope you enjoy the book, and that you will you find it informative as well as challenging.

Deborah Terry Cindy Gallois Malcolm McCamish

# List of Contributors

Jennifer Boldero, PhD, Lecturer in Psychology, The University of Melbourne, Melbourne, Australia.

June Cra School of Behavioural Sciences, Macquarie University, Sydney, Australia.

Biruta Dietz, BA (Hons), Postgraduate Student, Institute of Social Research, School of Social Studies, University of South Australia, Adelaide, Australia.

Cynthia Gallois, PhD, Reader in Psychology, Department of Psychology, The University of Queensland, Brisbane, Australia.

Ron Gold, PhD, Senior Lecturer in Educational Psychology, Department of Education, Deakin University, Geelong, Australia.

Yoshihisa Kashima, PhD, Lecturer in Psychology, Department of Psychology, La Trobe University, Melbourne, Australia.

Susan Kippax, PhD, Associate Professor of Psychology, School of Behavioural Sciences, and Director, Macquarie Unit of the National Centre for HIV Social Research, Macquarie University, Sydney, Australia.

Virginia Lewis, BA (Hons), Postgraduate Student, Department of Psychology, La Trobe University, Melbourne, Australia.

Malcolm McCamish, PhD, Lecturer in Chemistry, The University of Queensland, Brisbane, Australia.

Mary-Lou McLaws, PhD, Lecturer in Epidemiology, School of Health Services Management, University of New South Wales, Kensington, Australia.

Susan Moore, PhD, Senior Lecturer in Educational Psychology, Monash University, Melbourne, Australia.

Joe Nucifora, BA (Hons), Department of Psychology, The University of Queensland, Brisbane, Queensland.

Brian Oldenburg, PhD, Senior Lecturer in Public Health, Department of Public Health, University of Sydney, Sydney, Australia.

Ken Rigby, PhD, Associate Professor and Director of Institute of Social Research, School of Social Studies, University of South Australia, Adelaide, Australia.

Doreen Rosenthal, PhD, Professor and Director of the Centre for Study of Sexually Transmitted Diseases, La Trobe University, Melbourne, Australia.

Michael Ross, PhD, Senior Research Fellow, Albion AIDS Centre, Division of Medicine, Prince of Wales Hospital, Surry Hills, Australia.

Stuart Sturgess, BA (Hons), Postgraduate Student, Institute of Social Research, School of Social Studies, University of South Australia, Adelaide, Australia.

Deborah Terry, PhD, Lecturer in Psychology, Department of Psychology, The University of Queensland, Brisbane, Australia.

Perri Timmins, BSc. (Hons), Research Associate, Department of Psychology, The University of Queensland, Brisbane, Australia.

Peta Warwick, BA (Hons), Department of Psychology, The University of Queensland, Brisbane, Queensland.

# Introduction by Martin Fishbein

It is now more than 25 years since the theory of reasoned action was first introduced (Fishbein 1966, 1967 a,b,c). Developed largely in response to the frustration resulting from repeated failures to predict behaviour from traditional measures of attitude (i.e., Thurstone, Likert, Guttman and semantic differential scales), the theory grew out of my earlier work examining the relationships between beliefs and attitudes.

As a young graduate student, I learned my social psychology in an exciting and stimulating atmosphere. Two new books had just been published, and both changed the face of social psychology: Leon Festinger's (1957) *Theory of cognitive dissonance* and Charles Osgood's (Osgood, Suci & Tannenbaum 1957) *The measurement of meaning*. My advisor, Burt Raven, like many other social psychologists, was excited and intrigued by Festinger's book, and he wanted to test an aspect of Festinger's theory of forced compliance. In order to do this, he designed an experiment in which the dependent variable was to be subjects' beliefs in the existence of Extra Sensory Perception (another hot topic of the times). Thus, my first task as a new graduate student was to find a scale to measure this belief. Much to my surprise, I learned that no such scale existed. Moreover, I also discovered that there were no 'belief' scales. In fact, the word 'belief' rarely appeared in the social psychological literature. In searching various text book indices, I either found no reference to beliefs or, at best, the index would say something like 'Belief — see attitude.' This reflected the prevailing tripartite view of attitude as a complex concept consisting of a cognitive, a conative, and an affective component. Beliefs, at best, were viewed as a component of attitude, and the general consensus was that any change in belief (or cognition) was essentially equivalent to a change in attitude. To put this somewhat differently, it was assumed that beliefs and attitudes were highly correlated.

Fortunately, Osgood had already identified evaluation as a (if not the) major dimension of meaning; and he had eloquently argued (and demonstrated) that semantic differential measures of the evaluative component of meaning could also be viewed as measures of attitude. It was a relatively small step from there to figure out that if one could measure a person's attitude toward a concept by having respondents rate it on a series of evaluative bipolar adjective scales (e.g., good/bad; wise/foolish; harmful/beneficial; pleasant/unpleasant), one could also measure 'beliefs in the existence of an object' by having respondents rate the concept on a series of probabilistic bipolar scales (e.g., probable/improbable; likely/unlikely; existent/nonexistent; possible/impossible).

This led to the development of an instrument (the A–B Scale) to independently measure beliefs and attitudes (see Fishbein & Raven, 1961). Preliminary research utilising this instrument clearly indicated that, rather than being correlated, these two constructs were relatively independent. For example, while many people who believed in the existence of ESP felt it was 'good,' an almost equal number judged it to be 'bad.' The same was true among those who didn't believe in ESP — beliefs had little influence on attitudes. Since this finding was incompatible with the commonly held view that beliefs were a component of attitude, it became important to explain this inconsistency.

Fortunately, the explanation was fairly simple — while the A–B scale had measured beliefs in the existence of an object, the literature had primarily considered beliefs about an object; that is, beliefs that defined or described the attitude object; that linked the attitude object to other objects or attributes. Thus the next step was to demonstrate that one could use the belief scale to measure beliefs about an object and to show that these beliefs were related to attitude. This problem became the central focus of my doctoral dissertation.

Based largely on Irving Maltzman's learning theory approach to imagination and thought, and utilising learning theory concepts and principles (such as a habit-family-hierarchy of responses, classical conditioning, and mediated generalisation; see Fishbein, 1967c), I was able to develop and empirically demonstrate the validity of what has now come to be known as a compensatory, expectancy-value model of attitude (Fishbein, 1963). Simply stated, the model suggests that a person's attitude toward any object is a function of his or her beliefs about the object (i.e., beliefs that the object has certain characteristics, qualities and attributes) and the evaluative aspects of those beliefs (i.e., the evaluation of those characteristics, qualities and attributes). Generally speaking, the more one believes that an object has 'good' characteristics, qualities and attributes, the more one will 'like' (or have a positive attitude toward) the object. Similarly, the more one believes that an object has 'bad' characteristics, qualities and attributes, the more one will 'dislike' (or have a negative attitude toward) the object.

Mathematically, this could be expressed by the following equation:

$$A_o = \mathrm{E}b_i e_i$$

where $A_o$ = the person's attitude (A) toward some object 'o'

$b_i$ = the person's belief about the likelihood that 'i' is associated with 'o'; that is, the probability that 'o' is related to some characteristic, quality or attribute 'i';

$e_i$ = the evaluation of 'i';

and $N$ = the number of salient beliefs the person holds about 'o'.

In this equation, a person's attitude toward an object is operationally defined by taking the product of the person's belief that a particular attribute is likely to accompany an attitude object and the person's evaluation of that attribute, summed across all salient attributes the person associates with the attitude object (this model is described in more detail in the next chapter).

Two key points about this model should be made:

(1) The notion of salient beliefs is based on the concept of a habit-family-hierarchy of responses. That is, based on learning theory principles, it was assumed that only beliefs in the hierarchy (i.e., a person's salient beliefs) would contribute to a person's attitude. Although one could measure the strength of an individual's salient beliefs on a scale from 0 to 1 (and thus follow traditional probability theory), I wanted a model that could be used cross-sectionally. This led to the notion of 'modal salient beliefs;' that is, those beliefs that were elicited most frequently (i.e., were most salient) within a given population. But switching from an idiosyncratic to a cross-sectional measurement model meant that some respondents could disbelieve that an object possessed or was associated with a given attribute. And, according to Fritz Heider's (1958) balance theory, if a person believed that some object was *not* associated with a negative attribute, this should contribute positively toward his or her attitude toward the object. In order to capture this psychology of the double negative, the measurement model specified that, at least in cross-sectional research, both beliefs and their evaluative aspects should be assessed on bipolar scales that were scored from -3 to +3.

As will be seen in Kashima and Gallois (this volume), this methodology has recently come under attack. Largely as a result of Evans' (1991) demonstration that cross-products are not invariant with respect to scoring systems, several mathematical approaches have been suggested to arrive at estimated attitude scores (i.e., the sum of probability beliefs times evaluations) that are invariant to measurement. In addition, several investigators have examined the predictive validity of the model using different (e.g., unipolar vs. bipolar) scoring systems. Although some 'invariant' solutions are statistically elegant, it should be noted that the search for 'the best fitting model' is both inappropriate and atheoretical. Indeed, any measurement model that cannot capture the psychology of the double negative violates the theory upon which the model is based. In addition, it should also be pointed out that this invariance problem was discussed at length in some of our writings describing the expectancy-value model (see e.g., Fishbein, 1967b; Fishbein & Ajzen, 1975).

(2) Somewhat along the same lines, it is important to recognise that the mathematical model of the relationship between beliefs and attitude was never intended to be viewed as a model of process, but only as a computational model to capture the output of a process that occurred automatically as a function of learning. That is, as one learned new beliefs about an object (i.e., learned to associate new characteristics, qualities or attributes with the attitude object), some of the evaluation associated with the characteristic was assumed to become associated with the attitude object through principles of conditioning and mediated generalisation. Thus, as Kashima and Gallois also point out, the mathematical expression of the model is *only* a computational representation and not an algorithmic description.

At the same time, however, the model did have important implications for understanding and changing attitudes. Clearly, if one's attitude toward an object is based upon the set of beliefs one holds about an object and the evaluative aspects of those beliefs, one should be able to change attitude by changing the beliefs that one holds (i.e., by changing existent beliefs or introducing 'new' salient beliefs) and/or by changing the evaluative aspect of those beliefs. While support for this hypothesis (and for the expectancy-value model in general) improved our understanding of the relations between beliefs and attitudes, it did not lead to a corresponding improvement in our ability to predict behaviour from attitude.

Indeed, with the possible exception of U.S. voting behaviour (where one's attitude toward a candidate turns out to be a relatively good predictor of whether one will or will not vote for that candidate), neither a direct (e.g., semantic differential) measure of attitude toward an object, nor an indirect, belief-based estimate of that attitude was able to account for very much of the variance in a given behaviour with respect to that object.

And, as the number of studies reporting the failure of attitude to predict specific behaviours grew, there were an increasing number of calls to eliminate or ignore the attitude construct (see, e.g., Abelson, 1972; Wicker, 1969) as a factor underlying behaviour. Unfortunately, there were no real suggestions for other general constructs that could account for substantial amounts of variance in a given behaviour. Just as traditional measures of attitude and values often failed to predict specific behaviours, so too did measures of personality and a host of demographic variables. In fact, even in animal experiments where the investigator has total control over the animal's environment, where she or he can directly manipulate needs or drives (e.g., by varying the number of hours of food or water deprivation) and where he or she can vary both the amount and the schedule of reinforcement the animal receives, one could usually account for only about 10% of the variance in the animal's behaviour. Thus, there was a growing consensus that behavioural prediction was very difficult, if not impossible.

I am a firm believer in the proposition that everyone is entitled to at least one "Ah Ha!" experience in his or her life. And it was at this point in time that I had mine. It occurred to me that if one really wanted to know whether someone would or would not perform a given behaviour, the simplest, and probably the most efficient thing one could do was to ask that person whether he or she was or was not going to perform that behaviour. And, as one might expect, people turned out to be very good predictors of their own behaviour. So behavioural prediction was not very difficult; people who intend to perform a given behaviour typically do perform that behaviour. Thus, if one wants to predict whether a given individual will (or will not) perform a given behaviour, one should assess the individual's intentions to perform that behaviour. Unfortunately, although this 'solution' to the behavioural prediction problem does lead to accurate prediction, it is not very satisfying psychologically!

But once one realises that, if properly assessed, people's intentions to perform a behaviour are very good predictors of behavioural performance, then the problem changes from one of behavioural prediction to one of understanding and predicting intention. And this is the primary purpose of the theory of reasoned action. That is, given that one has demonstrated that a given intention will predict some behaviour of interest, the theory tries to explain the factors underlying that intention. Thus, in contrast to an often voiced criticism of the theory (which, as you will see, is repeated in several chapters in this volume), the theory is not constrained to considering only intentions to perform volitional behaviours. Indeed, in developing the theory, I tried to develop a general theory of intention; and I assumed that the factors underlying intentions to perform specific behaviours under one's volitional control were no different from those underlying intentions to perform behaviours that were not under one's volitional control. Moreover, I assumed these same factors were also the critical determinants of intentions to engage in a class of behaviours (e.g., to practice safer sex, to exercise) and of intentions to reach a given goal (e.g., to stay healthy, to lose weight).

What I did recognise, however, was that while intentions to perform behaviours under one's volitional control led to highly accurate prediction of behavioural performance, intentions to engage in behaviours *not* under one's volitional control often led to poor prediction. Similar to this, intentions to reach a given goal were also found to be relatively poor predictors of goal attainment (largely because goal attainment — e.g., losing weight, getting pregnant within a given time period, getting an A on an exam) also was most often *not* under one's volitional control. And, to complicate matters further, intentions to engage in a class of behaviours (e.g., to exercise, to practice safer sex) also turned out to be relatively poor predictors of whether one would or would not perform any behaviour within that class (e.g., jog 20 minutes every day, always use a condom). Thus, although the theory was designed to explain all types of intentions, it recognised that only intentions to engage in volitionally controlled behaviours would lead to accurate behavioural predictions.

Fortunately, it seemed to me then, and it still seems to me now, that most behaviours of interest to behavioural scientists are, in fact, largely under volitional control. While we are also often interested in goal attainment and/or motivating people to engage in classes of behaviour (e.g., to diet, to exercise, to practice safer sex), I have always felt that we can best get people to achieve goals by increasing their intentions to perform one or more behaviours that will maximise the likelihood of goal attainment, and that we are much better off focusing in on one or two behaviours in a behavioural category than in trying to increase a person's intentions to essentially engage in all behaviours in that category.

Since the theory is well-described in several chapters in this book, I will not review it here. I do, however, want to point out that, just as the expectancy-value model was heavily influenced by Irving Maltzman's learning theory approach to imagination and thought and by Fritz Heider's balance theory, the theory of reasoned action also has its own intellectual roots. Based largely on Don Dulany's (1968) theory of propositional control, the theory of reasoned action was also influenced by Burt Raven's (1965) work on power and social influence and Harry Triandis' (1964) work on the behavioural component of attitude. In addition, I want to again acknowledge the contributions of Icek Ajzen. As my student, friend, co-author and colleague, Icek has helped to shape the theory. While I am still not fully convinced of the validity of his recent extension of the theory of reasoned action to a theory of planned behaviour (see, e.g., Ajzen, 1985, 1991), I am delighted to see that he and others (including several authors in this volume) are building upon the theory in their attempts to predict, understand and explain human behaviour.

And at this point, it may be appropriate for me to make some general comments about the theory and to suggest some things for you to think about as you read this book.

First, as I mentioned at the start of this introduction, the theory of reasoned action is now over 25 years old. In a recent review of the literature, Fishbein, Albarracin, and Ajzen (in preparation) identified well over 600 articles based on the theory, with over 200 direct tests of at least some aspects of the model (i.e., they contained at least one attitudinal measure, one normative measure, and either a measure of intention or a measure of behaviour). These studies have attempted to predict or explain a wide variety of behaviours, including such things as wearing safety helmets (Allegrante, Mortimer & O'Rourke 1980); smoking marijuana (Pomazal & Brown, 1977); voting (Bowman & Fishbein, 1978); eating at fast-food restaurants (Brinberg & Durand, 1983); smoking cigarettes (Fishbein, 1980); drinking alcohol (Schlegel, Crawford & Sanborn 1977); entering an alcohol treatment program (Fishbein *et al.,* 1980); using birth control pills (Jaccard & Davidson, 1972); breast feeding (Matheny, Picciano & Birch 1987); donating blood (Pomazal & Jaccard, 1976); wearing seat-belts (Stasson & Fishbein, 1990); condom use (Fisher, 1984); church attendance (King, 1975); and sexual behaviour (Fishbein, Chan *et al.,* 1992).

But of all the behaviours studied, I can think of no better use of the theory of reasoned action than for it to be employed in the battle against AIDS. The AIDS epidemic is certainly one of, if not the, major problems facing the world today. Fortunately, it is not who one is, but what one does, that determines whether one will or will not be exposed to HIV, the virus that causes AIDS. Thus, the battle to prevent AIDS is a behavioural battle. It is both a challenge and a rallying call to all behavioural scientists. We must find ways to reduce the likelihood that people will engage in behaviours that put them at risk for AIDS and/or increase the likelihood that they will engage in safe or 'safer' behaviours. The more one understands the determinants of these behaviours, the more likely one is to design effective programs to influence them. It is both a pleasure and an honour to know that researchers around the world are using the theory of reasoned action as a framework to help them discover these determinants, and more important, that they are using this information to design theory-based interventions. It may be an old cliché, but if the theory can help to save even one life, I will feel that my work has been amply rewarded.

I think that one of the main reasons for the theory's longevity (in addition to the fact that it does often explain a considerable and statistically significant amount of variance in intentions and behaviours), is the fact that it is comprised of a relatively small set of theoretically interrelated concepts, each of which has been operationally defined. Yet one of the most common criticisms of the theory is that 'additional variables' should be considered. Indeed, as you will see in the present volume, there are calls to separately measure evaluation and affect, to include partner norms, behavioural norms, and personal norms, and, following Ajzen (1985, 1991), to add perceived behavioural control and/or measures of self-efficacy. In addition, investigators have 'expanded' the theory by including past behaviour, perceived risk, and 'control conditions.'

I doubt very much if the theory would have survived had it originally contained all of these variables. Theories that include "everything but the kitchen sink" do not typically last very long. Not only are they often untestable, but rarely do they spell out the inter-relations among all the variables. And, at least to me, stringing together a long list of variables in a regression equation does not make a theory. This is not to say that the theory of reasoned action cannot be improved upon; nor do I doubt that there are other variables that may be relevant in a given content domain. But other variables are most likely to 'work' when inappropriate measures of the theory's constructs are obtained. That is, when the key constructs of the theory are not appropriately assessed, they cannot be expected to account for as much variance in intentions and/or behaviour as when they are appropriately measured. Under these circumstances, it is not surprising to find that 'other' variables account for some of this unexplained variance. Thus, in reading the chapters in this book, I would suggest that you consider the extent to which the authors have, in fact, obtained appropriate measures of the theory's constructs. For example, consider whether there is (or is not) correspondence between beliefs, attitudes, norms, intentions and behaviour, and then compare the results of studies with 'good' and 'poor' correspondence.

But appropriate measurement does not reduce the impact of all 'other' variables in all studies. At least in a given content domain, some of these other variables may be important. For example, perceptions of what important others do (what Nucifora *et al.,* this volume, refer to as behavioural norms), as opposed to beliefs about the normative proscriptions of these referents (i.e., what they say), do appear to account for additional variance in intentions. But should these be considered different variables, or, as Fishbein, Bandura *et al.* (1992) have suggested, shouldn't both of these measures be viewed as indicants of a single normative construct that captures perceived social pressure to perform or not perform the behaviour in question?

Similarly, although there is some evidence that affective measures of attitude (e.g., pleasant/unpleasant; enjoyable/unenjoyable) sometimes account for variance in intention and behaviour over and above that accounted for by evaluative measures (e.g., wise/foolish; harmful/beneficial), one should ask whether one wants multiple attitude measures or if these different measures are best viewed as indicants of a single attitudinal construct that captures all possible meanings of 'good/bad' and/or 'like/dislike' (see Fishbein, Bandura *et al.,* 1992; Chan & Fishbein, in press).

There is also growing evidence that, at least with respect to behaviours not under one's volitional control, Bandura's (1989) construct of self-efficacy may be an important determinant of intention and/or behaviour. While Ajzen's (1985) original conception of perceived behavioural control (PBC) appeared to be closely related to self-efficacy, his more recent writings have reduced PBC primarily to a judgement of whether performing the behaviour is 'easy' or 'difficult'. Unfortunately, this essentially equates PBC with an affective measure of attitude. That is, there is considerable evidence that judgements of 'easy/difficult' are highly correlated with judgements such as 'pleasant/unpleasant' and 'enjoyable/unenjoyable'. Thus, when a direct measure of attitude includes affective as well as evaluative scales, one would not expect PBC to contribute to prediction. Terry (this volume) provides data relevant to this issue.

In addition to suggesting 'other' variables, several other questions about the theory are raised in this volume. One of the major questions concerns the relative weights of the attitudinal and normative components as determinants of intention. According to the theory of reasoned action, the relative weights of these two components will vary as a function of both the behaviour under consideration and the population being studied. Thus for example, while sexually experienced U.S. male college students' intentions to use a condom were found to be primarily under normative control, this same intention was found to be primarily under attitudinal control in a sample of sexually experienced Mexican male college students (Fishbein, 1990). It is important to recognise that some behaviours may be entirely under attitudinal control, while others may be entirely under normative control. Thus, in contrast to the conclusion drawn by some investigators, (including some in this volume), the theory has not 'failed' if either the attitudinal component or the normative component does not contribute significantly to the prediction of intention.

Unfortunately, which component will be the most important determinant of a given intention and/or behaviour remains an empirical question. And, because the theory does not specify the conditions under which attitudes or norms will be most important, at least some investigators (again including some in this book), have suggested that this makes the theory non-falsifiable. In contrast to this view, I would simply like to point out that the theory would be falsified (at least in a given content domain) if a simultaneous consideration of appropriate measures of attitudes and norms failed to predict an appropriate measure of the corresponding intention. To the best of my knowledge, this has not yet occurred.

Finally I'd like to turn to one other issue raised in this book. Gold (this volume) suggests a distinction between on-line and off-line cognitions, and he argues that the theory of reasoned action fails to take on-line cognitions into account. This strikes me as a potentially important distinction that deserves further consideration. In reading Gold's chapter, you might want to consider what, for example, would be the difference in a respondent's beliefs about using a condom with a new partner, if he or she were asked to indicate the beliefs they held at the time they last engaged in unprotected sex with a new partner (on-line cognitions) or if they were asked to indicate their current (off-line) beliefs about performing this same behaviour. Would we in fact find marked differences in these two sets of beliefs? And, assuming that such differences were obtained, how much additional variance will such 'on-line' cognitions account for, given the success of 'off-line' cognitions in predicting condom use (see Chapters 3, 7, 8 and 9)?

But enough about theoretical issues. What is important about this book is not its focus on the theory of reasoned action, but its focus on identifying factors that may help us to understand why people engage in behaviours that put them at risk of exposure to HIV and/or why they do not engage in behaviours that would reduce their risk. Even more important, the book suggests how this information can be utilised to design effective interventions to reduce risky and to increase 'safer' behaviours. The theory of reasoned action is just one of many tools that may be used to focus research efforts. I have always believed that a theory is only useful if it stimulates and guides research on important issues. The chapters in this book are a clear indication that the theory of reasoned action is serving its purpose. Given my own involvement in AIDS prevention research (see, e.g., Fishbein, 1990; Chan & Fishbein, in press; Fishbein, Bandura *et al.*, 1992; Fishbein, Chan *et al.*, 1992; Fishbein & Middlestadt, 1989; Fishbein, Middlestadt & Hitchcock, 1991), it is personally gratifying to see other investigators using the theory as a framework for their research in this area.

More important, several of the chapters in this book provide clear and compelling evidence that, when properly applied, the theory of reasoned action does help one to identify the factors underlying the decision to perform (or not perform) at least one 'safer sex' behaviour, namely, condom use. But it is important to recognise that 'condom use' is not a single behaviour but a behavioural category. As I've pointed out elsewhere (e.g., Fishbein *et al.*, 1991), using a condom for vaginal sex with one's main partner is a different behaviour from using a condom for vaginal sex with an occasional or new partner. Similarly, using a condom for vaginal sex with a new partner is a different behaviour from using a condom for anal sex with this same partner. Moreover, while using a condom is a behaviour for men, it is a goal for women. What this implies is that intentions to 'use a condom the next time I have sex' should be a better predictor of men's condom use behaviours than of women's condom use behaviours. This also suggests that while it is appropriate to develop interventions to increase men's intentions to use condoms, interventions directed at women should focus on increasing their intentions to engage in behaviours that will increase the likelihood that their partners will use condoms (e.g., increasing their intention to ask, or tell, their partner to use a condom; increasing their intention to hand their partner a condom before undressing or getting into bed).

The ultimate test of the utility of the theory of reasoned action will rest upon its ability to guide the development of effective behaviour change interventions. While, as pointed out above, several chapters in this book demonstrate the theory's utility in identifying factors underlying decisions to engage (or not engage) in AIDS-related behaviours, the present volume only holds out the promise of effective interventions. Perhaps the next step for the Editors of this book is to compile a volume describing tests of the theory 'in action'; by presenting a number of studies evaluating the effectiveness of theory-based interventions.

# 1

# The Theory of Reasoned Action and Health Care Behaviour

DEBORAH TERRY, CYNTHIA GALLOIS and MALCOLM MCCAMISH

*The Univerisity of Queensland, Brisbane, Australia*

It is now widely recognised that, by adopting a healthy lifestyle, people can actively contribute to their state of health (Taylor, 1991). In recent years, researchers have been concerned with identifying the factors that influence people's willingness to engage in health care behaviour (i.e., actions that promote well-being and help prevent disease). This research has been motivated by the realisation that knowledge of the determinants of health care behaviour has implications for the general understanding of health behaviour, as well as the development of intervention programs to encourage people to engage in health-promoting practices. In overall terms, research into the determinants of health care behaviour is significant both for the well-being of individuals and for the collective well-being of a community. The more willing and able people are to protect themselves from preventable illnesses, the more resources the community will have available to be channelled into other areas. Moreover, it can be assumed that, via the effects of modelling and normative influence, collective well-being will have a positive impact on future community health.

Researchers have focused on a range of different health care behaviours. They have, for instance, considered the determinants of behaviours that reflect a healthy lifestyle, including participation in a regular exercise program, adherence to a healthy diet and the avoidance of potentially harmful health habits (e.g., smoking, the consumption of large amounts of alcohol and the use of illicit drugs). Attention has also been focused on people's willingness to use contraceptives (mainly the contraceptive pill and condoms), to engage in dental health behaviours, to participate in screening programs (e.g., pap tests for cervical cancer) and to vaccinate against infectious diseases. As a consequence of the emerging threat of HIV infection, more recent research on health care behaviour has focused on safer sex behaviours (including condom use and having sex in a monogamous relationship).

1

One of the major goals of health research has been to identify the factors that distinguish people who choose to engage in health care behaviours from those who adopt less healthy lifestyles. In this respect, Fishbein and Ajzen's (1975; Ajzen & Fishbein, 1980) theory of reasoned action has been particularly influential. The theory has been demonstrated to be useful across the range of health care behaviours identified above. More recently, a number of researchers have suggested that it may be useful in the context of safer sex behaviour (see Fisher & Fisher, 1992). The application of the theory of reasoned action to the explanation of variation in people's willingness to engage in safer sex behaviour is the central theme of this book.

In the present chapter, a detailed description of the theoretical basis of the theory of reasoned action and its recent extension, the theory of planned behaviour, is provided. Methodological issues involved in testing the usefulness of the two models are also discussed in some detail. Prior to describing the theory of reasoned action, the past literature on the determinants of health care behaviour is reviewed, as is the health belief approach to the study of health care behaviour. In the next chapter, Lewis and Kashima discuss issues of relevance to HIV/AIDS. Specifically, the next chapter describes the epidemiological and social context of the epidemic, reviews previous research on AIDS-prevention, and discusses a number of issues that are relevant when applying the theory of reasoned action to the study of safer sex behaviour.

## Determinants of Health Care Behaviour

In an attempt to identify the determinants of health care behaviours, researchers have considered the extent to which a large number of different variables can explain variation in people's willingness to engage in such behaviours. Much of this research has focused on demographic variables. Age, for instance, appears to have a curvilinear relationship with people's willingness to engage in health care behaviours. Adolescents and young adults engage in more risky health behaviours than either children or older adults (Taylor, 1991). Children, in general, have little choice in lifestyle issues, a factor which presumably accounts for their comparatively low level of health risk behaviours. For adolescents and young adults, feelings of invulnerability (see Elkind, 1967, 1985) combined with the desire for a range of different life experiences may explain the heightened incidence of risky health behaviours at this stage of the lifespan, while older persons presumably adopt a more healthy lifestyle than their younger counterparts because feelings of invulnerability dissipate, they gain more responsibilities and they become more aware of their health problems (Taylor, 1991).

There is evidence of age differences in people's preferences for different sexual practices. In a comprehensive study of gay men, Kippax, Connell, Dowsett and Crawford (in press) found that older gay men preferred penetrative anal sex, while younger men preferred non-penetrative sex. In a similar vein, research with heterosexuals suggests that adolescents are more likely than young adults to prefer non-penetrative sex, a pattern of results that possibly reflects a developmental progression to full sexual maturity. To modify the safety of people's sexual practices, educational programmes need to acknowledge age-related preferences for different sexual practices.

Gender has also been linked to health care behaviour. In general, females are less likely to smoke than males (Taylor, 1991; Waldron, 1988). In comparison with males, they also consume less alcohol, pay more attention to their diet, take more vitamins and engage in more dental care behaviours (see Waldron, 1988). Males are, however, more likely than females to engage in regular exercise (Rodin & Salovey, 1989). Such gender differences have been interpreted as being consistent with traditional norms for sex-role appropriate behaviour (Rodin & Salovey, 1989; Waldron, 1988). It is considered appropriate for women to take care of their physical appearance, while a greater latitude of freedom is typically allowed to men in terms of such behaviours as alcohol consumption (Waldron, 1988). To date, there has been a lack of compelling evidence of gender differences in people's willingness to adopt different safer sex strategies (Gallois, Statham & Smith, 1992). There may, however, be subtle gender differences in beliefs about safer sex (e.g., females may have different beliefs about the costs and benefits of condom use) and constraints to successful behavioural enactment (e.g., females may lack the necessary assertion skills to ensure that a condom is used) that need to be acknowledged by education programmes.

Researchers have also considered the role that socio-economic status plays as a determinant of preventive health behaviour. In this respect, there is evidence of a positive relationship between socio-economic status and the incidence of a range of different health care behaviours, including adherence to a regular exercise programme (Rodin & Salovey, 1989), willingness to make preventive visits to a dentist and participation in vaccination programs (Coburn & Pope, 1974; Kirscht, 1983). Such results presumably reflect the fact that, as a consequence of better education, people with higher socio-economic status are likely to be knowledgeable about health issues. They also may have greater access to health care facilities than people with lower socio-economic status (Coburn & Page, 1974). Other research has demonstrated that there are ethnic differences in people's willingness to engage in health-promoting behaviours (e.g., Gotllieb & Green, 1988). These differences should, however, be interpreted with caution, given that ethnicity is confounded with social class (Rodin &

Salovey, 1989).

There is evidence of effects of social class on sexual behaviour. Men from a working class background, for instance, are more likely to have extra-marital affairs than middle-class men (Argyle, 1993). In research on safer sex, the possible effects of social class have typically been ignored. Researchers have tended to study accessible populations that, because of the socio-economic status of researchers, are characterised by a middle-class bias. Future research needs to broaden the focus of research activity on safer sex, given that the salient beliefs and norms about safer sex are likely to be divergent across different groups at risk for HIV (e.g., homeless youth, bisexual men).

In addition to demographic variables, there is evidence that a range of other variables influence health care behaviour. There is, for instance, strong evidence linking peer influence (Grube, Morgan, & McGree, 1986; Leventhal & Cleary, 1980) and family modelling (Sallis & Nader, 1988) to smoking behaviour among adolescents. Family factors have also been found to be influential in the context of safer sex. In a study of older adolescents, Peterson and Feeney (1993) reported that subjects' habitual style of conflict resolution with their parents influenced both their willingness to discuss AIDS and safer sex with a sexual partner and the extent to which they felt confident in their ability to perform safer sex strategies. Other researchers have considered the role that individual difference variables may play in health care behaviour. In particular, interest has centred on the proposal that people who believe that they have control over their health will engage in more health care behaviours than people who attribute their state of health to external factors. Research has provided some support for this supposition. Internal health beliefs have been linked to seat belt use (Williams, 1972), breast self-examination (Lau, 1988) and contraceptive use (Lundy, 1972). Such beliefs have also been found to relevant in the context of safer sex. Terry, Galligan and Conway (in press), for instance, found that people with internal control beliefs were more likely than people with external control beliefs to behave in accord with their intentions to have sex in an exclusive relationship and discuss their partner's sexual and i.v. drug use history.

## Theoretical Models of Health Care Behaviour

Although research examining the correlates of health care behaviour has been informative, such research is limited because in general it has not been theory-based. Most of the studies have examined the effects of only one or two variables. It is, thus, difficult to integrate the findings into a coherent model of the determinants of health care behaviour. Moreover, the failure to consider the effects of a range of different predictors of health care behaviour may mean that some of the findings in earlier literature are spurious. To provide further insight into the basis of variation in people's willingness to engage in health care behaviours, it is necessary to develop models that specify sets of theoretically-derived predictors of health care behaviours. The health belief model (Rosenstock, 1974a,b) and Fishbein and Ajzen's (1975; Ajzen & Fishbein, 1980) theory of reasoned action have been particularly influential models in this context. Both of these models consider the underlying cognitive factors that may explain variation in health care behaviour. Such factors are likely to be important determinants of such behaviours, given that they reflect people's beliefs about the behaviour, rather than their more generalised background features and personality dispositions (Ajzen, 1988). Prior to discussing the theory of reasoned action (the focus of the present book) in detail, the health belief model is described.

## The Health Belief Model

The health belief model (Rosenstock, 1974a,b) has been widely used to predict health behaviours from knowledge of a person's beliefs and attitudes. The model proposes that readiness to take preventive health action arises from an evaluation of the level of threat associated with a disease (assessed with measures of the perceived susceptibility to the disease and its severity), as well as an analysis of the costs and benefits of taking the action. Specifically, the model is made up of four components. The *perceived susceptibility* dimension reflects the individual's perception of vulnerability or risk of contracting the disease, while *perceived severity* refers to the individual's beliefs about the seriousness of consequences associated with that disease. The positive outcomes of performing the preventive health behaviour, including estimates of risk reduction and feelings of security, are seen as the *perceived benefits* of taking the action, and are typically weighted against the potential negative aspects, the *perceived barriers* of performing the preventive behaviour, including estimates of physical, psychological, financial and other costs incurred in performing the behaviour. Modifications to the original model have included the addition of self-efficacy (Rosenstock, Strecher & Becker, 1988), internal or external cues to action (Rosenstock, 1974b) and salience of health to the individual (Rosenthal, Hall, & Moore, 1992).

There is evidence that health belief variables successfully predict a range of different health behaviours, including dietary compliance (Becker, Haefner, Mainman, Kirscht & Drachman, 1977), calcium intake (Wurtel, 1988), breast self-examination (Kelly, 1979; Hallal, 1982) and vaccination (Cummings, Jette & Rosenstock, 1978). In their review of the health belief model, Janz and Becker (1984) observed that support for the model was evident in both retrospective and prospective designs. Moreover, they found some support for the role of each of the four dimensions of the health belief model (severity, susceptibility, benefits and barriers) in the prediction of health behaviour. Across a range of different behaviours, the dimension of perceived barriers emerged as the most important component of the health belief model. The evidence linking the susceptibility and benefits dimensions of the model to health behaviour was also strong, although the strength of support for each of the dimensions was dependent on the type of behaviour under consideration. Perceived susceptibility had a stronger effect on preventive health behaviours than on sick role behaviour (health behaviours engaged in after diagnosis of a particular medical condition), while the reverse was true for perceived benefits. Overall, the evidence in support of the proposed effect of perceived severity was weaker than for the other components of the model (particularly for preventive health behaviours).

In a more recent meta-analysis, Harrison, Mullen and Green (1992) found weaker support for the health belief model. Only 16 of 147 studies met their criteria of inclusion—that is, that they were based on original data collected from adults; included the four variables of susceptibility, severity, benefits and costs, related the variables to actual behaviour rather than to attitudes or intentions and reported reliability of the measures. The model's performance was generally poor. Harrison *et al.* found that, for any one dimension of the model, 10% was the largest proportion of variance explained in actual behaviour. They questioned whether the model's key variables were able to discriminate between, and therefore apply differentially to, a variety of health behaviours. In using such well-specified criteria they felt that they had given the model its best opportunity to perform well. In accord with Harrison*et al.*'s pessimistic findings, recent studies examining the utility of the health belief model in the prediction of safer sex behaviour have failed to find convincing support for the model (for a review of this research, see Lewis & Kashima, this volume; also Warwick*et al.* this volume).

The lack of convincing support for the health belief model may, in part, be a reflection of the fact that researchers have failed to operationalise the components of the health belief model consistently (Cummings*et al.* 1978; Wallston & Wallston, 1984). Furthermore, when developing measures of the components of the health belief model, there has been a lack of consideration given to the characteristics of the target population. The latter shortcoming of previous research may partially account for the fact that the health belief model has more utility in predicting health behaviours among people of higher socioeconomic status who are knowledgeable about health-related matters, than among other groups of people (see Taylor, 1991). In this respect, the fact that the model in its original form failed to take into account social influences on health behaviour may also be relevant.

An additional characteristic of the health belief model that may account for its lack of utility in the prediction of safer sex is its focus on health or disease outcomes. Although engaging in safer sex is a strategy that can be used to avoid the transmission of HIV and other sexually transmitted diseases, it is difficult to reduce the behaviour to the same status as other health behaviours, such as having a pap test or receiving a vaccination against influenza. The latter behaviours are discrete health behaviours that, beyond the time and temporary discomfort involved in engaging in them, have little impact on a person's life. In contrast, engaging in safer sex may mean making changes that have an impact on an important aspect of people's relations with others.

In comparison to the health belief model, Fishbein and Ajzen's (1975; Ajzen & Fishbein, 1980) theory of reasoned action has been empirically more successful in its predictions (Reid & Christensen, 1988; Lierman, Young, Kasprzyk & Benoliel, 1990). Moreover, although the theory has been employed as an explanatory model in the health context (e.g., breast self-examination, weight loss behaviours, modification to smoking and drinking), it is not restricted to use in this context. The predictors in the model allow consideration of the role of both health beliefs (e.g., the perceived effectiveness of condom use as a safer sex strategy) and more general beliefs about the consequences of performing a particular behaviour (e.g., beliefs concerning the consequences of suggesting to one's partner that safer sex strategies be used). The theory also acknowledges the role of normative influence on behavioural choice, an influence that is likely to be important in the context of safer sex, given the co-operative nature of the behaviour. For these reasons, the theory of reasoned action may form an appropriate theoretical basis for research into the determinants of safer sex, a suggestion that is explored further in the following chapter. In the remainder of the present chapter, the theoretical underpinnings of the theory of reasoned action and its recent extension, the theory of planned behaviour, are described. Consideration is also given to the methodological issues that need to be addressed when operationalising the two models.

## The Theory of Reasoned Action

### Theoretical overview

The central premise of the theory of reasoned action is that people make behavioural decisions on the basis of a reasoned consideration of the available information (see Fishbein & Ajzen, 1975; Ajzen & Fishbein, 1980; Ajzen, 1988). The theory can, therefore, be regarded as a deliberative processing model, to the extent that behavioural decisions are seen to be the consequence of the person's systematic consideration and deliberation of the information available to him or her (Fazio, 1990). When deciding upon a course of action, the model proposes that people do not act spontaneously (as proposed in other models of social behaviour; see Fazio, 1990; Tesser & Shaffer, 1990), but reflect upon the consequences of performing the behaviour, as well as their beliefs about what other people expect them to do. From this perspective, people are assumed to be "rational actors" (Tesser & Shaffer, 1990), who make reasoned behavioural decisions.

For many behaviours, the assumption that people make reasoned behavioural decisions is noncontroversial. People are likely to systematically consider the information available to them when, for instance, they make the decision to engage in a regular exercise program or when they decide to take the oral contraceptive pill. It may, however, be more difficult to accept this position in relation to behaviours that are more proximally related to sexual encounters, including the decision to use a condom or engage in nonpenetrative sex (both behaviours are safer sex options). A number of researchers have argued that sex is influenced by non-rational factors (see Gold, this volume; Kippax & Crawford, this volume). Nevertheless, sexual behaviours need not necessarily be regarded as unreasoned behaviours. In his typology of love styles, for instance, Sternberg (1986) proposes that people make some "rational" choices about who they love. There is also a considerable amount of evidence to suggest that people's attitudes and beliefs do predict their use of condoms (see Ross & McLaws, this volume). Perhaps even more surprising is the fact that there is evidence that people use the withdrawal method successfully as a contraceptive (e.g., Greeks in Australia; see Callan, 1985). This type of evidence suggest that the rational basis of the theory of reasoned action does not preclude its application to safer sex behaviour. The fact there is some evidence for the efficacy of the theory in this context validates this assertion (see e.g., Nucifora *et al.*, this volume; Warwick *et al.*, this volume).

In accordance with the deliberative underpinning of the model, the theory of reasoned action hypothesises that the causal antecedents of behaviour are a logical sequence of cognitions (Ajzen & Fishbein, 1980; Fishbein & Ajzen, 1975) (see Figure 1). According to the model, the immediate determinant of behaviour is the person's *intention* to perform it. The determinants of people's intentions are, in turn, proposed to be the favourability of their *attitude* towards the behaviour and the extent of perceived normative pressure to perform the behaviour (*subjective norm*). The model further proposes that people's attitudes toward a behaviour are a function of their beliefs concerning the consequences of performing the behaviour (*behavioural beliefs*), weighted by the value placed on each of the consequences (*outcome evaluations*), while the subjective norm is proposed to be a function of people's perception of the pressure from

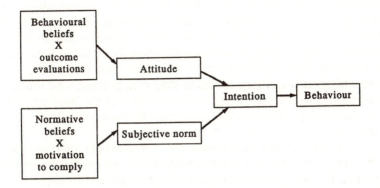

FIG. 1. The theory of reasoned action.

others to perform the behaviour (*normative beliefs*), weighted by their *motivation to comply* with these others. These proposed relationships are discussed in detail below.

*Intention–Behaviour Relationship*

As shown in Figure 1, the theory of reasoned action proposes that a person's decision to engage in a particular behaviour is influenced by the extent to which the person intends to do so. Behavioural intentions reflect the extent to which the person is motivated to perform the behaviour or, in other words, the person's willingness to perform it (Ajzen, 1988). Because motivation typically precedes action, an intention to perform a behaviour is regarded as the most proximal determinant of behaviour (Ajzen, 1988).

According to Fishbein and Ajzen (1975), there should be a strong relationship between a person's intentions and his or her behavioural response. There is considerable support for this proposal. In his review of a sample of studies that have examined the effects of intentions on actual behaviour, Ajzen (1988) found that the correlation between a person's intentions and subsequent behavioural actions ranged from .72 to .96. Behaviours considered included co-operative choices in a laboratory game (Ajzen, 1971), contraceptive behaviour (Ajzen & Fishbein, 1980), having an abortion (Smetana & Adler, 1980) and voting choice (Ajzen & Fishbein, 1980). In a meta-analysis of much larger body of literature (87 studies), Sheppard, Hartwick and Warshaw (1988) also found evidence to support the proposed intention–behaviour link. The average correlation (weighted by the number of subjects in each study) between intentions and actual behaviour was .53. As further evidence of an intention–behaviour link, Ajzen (1988) noted that the effects of intentions are typically stronger than the effects of attitudes, a pattern of results that supports the proposed role of intention as the immediate antecedent of behaviour. Recent research has provided some evidence of an intention–behaviour link in the context of safer sex (see Lewis & Kashima, this volume, for a review of some of this research; also other chapters in this volume, including Nucifora *et al.*; Terry).

Fishbein and Ajzen (1975) described three factors that may weaken the intention–behaviour relationship. First, the relationship between intentions and behaviour is weakened if the measures of intention and actual behaviour are not obtained at the same level of specificity. For example, a measure of the person's general intention to engage in HIV-preventive behaviour is likely to have only a weak relationship with his or her intention to use a condom with a regular partner. This type of proposal accords with Ajzen and Fishbein's (1977) principle of compatibility, which states that the relationship between any two variables strengthens as a function of the extent to which they are assessed along compatible dimensions. Specifically, Ajzen and Fishbein argue that the measurement of the two variables should accord in terms of the action (e.g., buying a condom, discussing condom use with one's partner, or actually using it), target (e.g., ribbed or non-ribbed condoms), context (e.g., with a casual or a regular partner) and time (e.g., on the next sexual encounter or every sexual encounter during the next month, the next three months, or whatever) of performing the behaviour (see Fishbein & Middlestadt, 1989, for additional examples). A change in one of these dimensions reflects a redefinition of the behaviour under consideration (Fishbein & Middlestadt, 1989). If this occurs, the intention–behaviour relationship will be weakened, because of the failure to evaluate the person's behaviour along the same dimensions as his or her intentions. For example, a researcher cannot necessarily expect to find a strong relationship between a person's intention to use a condom on his or her next sexual encounter and whether the person uses a condom on every sexual encounter during the next month.

A second factor that may weaken the intention–behaviour link is the instability of a person's intentions. In the face of unanticipated events, a person's intentions may change (Ajzen, 1988). For instance, a person who intends to use a condom on every sexual encounter may start a relationship with someone who does not wish to use condoms. The person may, therefore, change his or her intentions, which means that the relationship between the earlier intention and subsequent behaviour is weakened. The longer the lapse of time between a person's indication of his or her intentions and the assessment of behavioural actions, the more likely it is that a person's intentions will change (Ajzen, 1988).

The third factor identified by Fishbein and Ajzen (1975) that may influence the strength of the intention–behaviour link is the extent to which the behaviour is under volitional control. A central assumption of the theory of reasoned action is that intention is an accurate predictor of behaviour only when the person can perform the behaviour at will or, in other words, is able to perform the behaviour if he or she wishes to do so. Many behaviours fall into this category. For example, if a person decides to do so, he or she can go for a jog, watch a film, use sunscreen, or attend church (see also Ajzen, 1988). Other behaviours are not so easily performed. Even if the person is motivated to perform a behaviour, successful behavioural enactment may not occur if the person lacks the requisite skills or resources to perform the behaviour, if its execution is dependent on other people, or if obstacles or barriers prevent a person acting in accord with his or her intention (Ajzen, 1988; Sheppard *et al.,* 1988).

Safer sex should be regarded as a behaviour that is not completely under a person's volitional control. A range of different control factors may weaken the link between a person's intention to engage in safer sex and his or her actual behaviour. The person's partner may not wish to use a condom, he or she may lack the assertion skills to insist that one is used, or a condom may not be available. If the behaviour is not completely under the person's volitional control, then it is assumed that the strength of the relationship between behavioural intentions and actual behaviour will be attenuated (Ajzen, 1985, 1987, 1991; Ajzen & Madden, 1986). There is some support for this proposal. In their meta-analysis of studies testing the theory of reasoned action, Sheppard *et al.* (1988) found that the intention–behaviour relationship was stronger for the prediction of specific behaviours than for goals (e.g., having a child in the next three years). Behavioural goals are less likely to be under volitional control than specific behaviours, because successful attainment of them usually entails some uncertainty (Sheppard *et al.,* 1988). For instance, despite being motivated to have a child within a specified period of time, a couple may not be able to do so because of factors outside their control (i.e, fertility problems). The issue of volitional control and behavioural prediction has been addressed in Ajzen's (1985, 1987, 1991; Ajzen & Madden, 1986) theory of planned behaviour (this extension to the theory of reasoned action is described below).

*Determinants of Intention*

The second major prediction of the theory of reasoned action is that a person's behavioural intentions are influenced by two conceptually distinguishable components, namely, attitude and subjective norm. This latter component refers to the extent of perceived social pressure to perform the behaviour, whereas the attitudinal component of the model reflects how favourable or unfavourable a person feels towards performing the behaviour. In specifying both personal and social determinants of behavioural intentions, Fishbein and Ajzen (1975) provide a bridge between the emphasis placed by psychologists on the role of attitudes as determinants of behaviour and research on group processes, which has highlighted the importance of normative influences on behaviour (see Brown, 1988; Fishbein & Ajzen, 1975).

According to the theory of reasoned action, people are more likely to intend to perform a behaviour when they have a favourable view towards doing so and perceive normative support for performing the behaviour. It is, however, acknowledged by Fishbein and Ajzen (see also Ajzen, 1988) that the relative importance of the effects of the two antecedent variables varies as a function of the behaviour under consideration, as well as the population being studied. For some groups of people or some behaviours, attitudes may be the primary determinant of intentions, whereas for other behaviours or other groups of people, intentions may be normatively controlled.

There is considerable support for the proposed effects of attitudes and norms on behavioural intentions. In his review of a number of tests of the theory of reasoned action, Ajzen (1988) reported that multiple correlations between the predictor variables (attitudes and subjective norms) and behavioural intentions ranged from .73 to .89. Sheppard *et al.* (1988) similarly found support for the proposed effects of attitudes and subjective norms on behavioural intentions. In their meta-analysis, the frequency-adjusted multiple correlation between the two predictors and behavioural intentions was .66. In Ajzen's (1988) review of the literature, it is obvious that the relative importance of the two variables varies from study to study. Overall, however, the effect of the attitudinal component tends to be stronger than the normative component, suggesting that people pay more attention to their personal evaluations of the behaviour than to the perceived expectations of others (see also Ajzen, 1991; for further consideration of the role of norms in the theory of reasoned action, see Kashima & Gallois, this volume). In several chapters in this book, researchers take up the issue of the relative importance of norms and attitudes in the prediction of safer sex. This is a context in which behavioural intentions do appear to be under normative control, a pattern of results that has clear implications for the development of safer sex intervention programmes (see McCamish *et al.*, this volume)

As is evident from Figure 1, the effects of attitude and subjective norm on actual behaviour are proposed to be mediated via their effect on behavioural intention. In other words, after control of the effects of intention, the attitudinal and normative components of the model should have no impact on actual behaviour. Although there is some support for this proposal (e.g., Terry *et al.*, in press), other researchers (e.g., Manstead, Proffitt & Smart, 1983; Bentler & Speckart, 1979) have found that attitudes have direct effects, as well as indirect effects, via intention, on behaviour. As Liska (1984) has pointed out, such results can probably be attributed to the weakening of the intention–behaviour relationship that is likely to occur as the time period between the assessments of the two variables increases. In comparison to behavioural intentions, a person's attitudes are likely to be more stable; hence, as the intention–behaviour relationship weakens, the direct effect of the more stable attitudinal component strengthens (Liska, 1984).

## Determinants of Attitude and Subjective Norm

The theory of reasoned action also identifies determinants of both attitudes and subjective norm. The person's attitude towards the behaviour is proposed to be influenced by his or her beliefs about the consequences (i.e., costs and benefits) of performing a behaviour (e.g., using a condom is likely to reduce one's risk of contracting HIV/AIDS, destroy the spontaneity of sex, prevent pregnancy, reduce sexual pleasure) and the person's evaluation of each of the consequences (e.g., reducing the risk of contracting HIV/AIDS is a highly desirable outcome; destroying the spontaneity of sex is moderately undesirable). In representing the effects of these beliefs on a person's attitude, Fishbein and Ajzen (1975) adopt an expectancy-value model of attitude, which proposes that a person's attitude is influenced by his or her beliefs about the consequences of the behaviour, weighted by the person's evaluation of these consequences. According to the expectancy-value formulation, a person will have a positive attitude towards performing the behaviour if he or she believes that performing the behaviour will lead to mostly positive outcomes; that is, positive outcomes are considered likely, while negative outcomes are considered unlikely (Ajzen, 1988).

Like attitudes, people's norms are considered to be belief-based. According to the theory of reasoned action, subjective norm is proposed to be function of people's beliefs concerning the extent to which other people would want them to perform the behaviour (normative beliefs) weighted by their motivation to comply with each of the referents. More specifically, normative beliefs reflect the person's judgements about whether other people (e.g., sexual partner, friends, parents, medical professionals) would think that it was a good idea to perform the behaviour. In determining the strength of perceived normative pressure to perform a behaviour, the person's desire to behave in accord with the views of the particular referent is taken into account. Even if a referent is perceived to think that it is a good idea for the subject to use a condom for sexual intercourse, this information will have little influence on the person's subjective norm, if he or she is not motivated to comply with the referent's wishes. In general terms, people who believe that most significant others, with whom they are motivated to comply, wish them to perform the behaviour are likely to perceive normative pressure to do so (as assessed by the measure of the subjective norm) (Ajzen, 1988). On the other hand, people will perceive pressure not to perform the behaviour if significant others are judged not to approve of their performing the behaviour.

Fishbein and Ajzen (1975) focus on a person's *salient* beliefs. For any one behaviour, people typically have many beliefs (for instance, the average person is likely to be able to generate a large number of beliefs about safer sex). However, on the basis of evidence that there are limitations to the amount of information that people can process at any one time, Fishbein and Ajzen proposed that only the person's salient beliefs about the consequences of performing a behaviour influence his or her attitude. In the case of subjective norm, Fishbein and Ajzen also highlight the importance of considering the beliefs that are salient to the person, in this case by identifying the important referents that could influence the person's decision to engage in the behaviour. These referents are likely to vary as a function of the behaviour under consideration. For instance, people's perceptions of their partner's wishes are especially influential in the formation of their intentions to engage in safer sex (see Nucifora*et al.*, this volume), a pattern of results that is not likely to be evident in behavioural contexts. The salient beliefs for a particular behaviour are also likely to vary from population to population. In relation to safer sex, the salient referents for gay men may be different from those of heterosexual men. Fishbein and Ajzen, thus, recommend that researchers elicit the modal salient beliefs for the population of interest prior to conducting the research project.

The research literature has provided some support for the proposed belief-based structure of attitudes and norms. In his review of the literature, Ajzen (1988) found that, when researchers correlated belief-based measures (computed as the product of scores on the relevant antecedents of the variable in question) of attitudes and norms with direct measures of these variables, the correlations were moderately high (ranging from .60 to .85). Other researchers have found only moderate correlations. The failure to elicit the salient beliefs for the particular population under consideration may account for these results, as may other methodological factors (Ajzen, 1991; see Kashima & Gallois, this volume for a further discussion of this point). The lack of stronger relations between the belief-based and direct measures of attitudes and norms may also be because global estimates of attitude or subjective norm are unlikely to be able to represent the complexity of beliefs underlying either type of variable (Bagozzi & Burnkrant, 1979). Moreover, responses to specific belief items are likely to be more considered than responses to global questions, which may further weaken the link between belief-based and direct measures of attitudes and norms.

### *Use of Belief-Based Measures*

The use of belief-based measures of attitude and subjective norm allows the researcher to explain, as well as predict, behaviour. If a researcher finds, for instance, that both attitudes and norms influence behavioural intentions, then to further explain the basis for these effects the researcher can examine the underlying belief structure influencing the two components of the model. Specifically, the people who intend to perform the behaviour of interest can be compared with those who do not intend to do so on each of the components of the belief-based measures of attitudes and norms (see Ajzen, 1988; Ajzen & Fishbein, 1980; Fishbein & Stasson, 1990).

An example of this procedure is provided by the data collected for the study described in Chapter 8. In this study, the behavioural criterion was condom use on the next sexual encounter. As predicted by the theory of reasoned action, both attitudes and norms predicted intentions. To examine these results further, a series of analyses of variance were performed, with behavioural intentions (dichotomised on the basis of a median split) as the independent variable. Analyses were performed separately for the behavioural belief items, the evaluation items, the normative belief items and the motivation to comply items.

These analyses revealed that young heterosexuals intending to use a condom on their next sexual encounter differed from non-intenders on the behavioural beliefs. In other words, they differed in terms of their beliefs about the likely consequences of condom use. There was, however, no significant difference between the intenders and the non-intenders on the evaluation of these outcomes (outcome evaluations). For the behavioural beliefs, additional analyses revealed that the intenders were more likely than the non-intenders to believe that condoms would help protect against HIV/AIDS, other sexually transmitted diseases and pregnancy. This result suggests that intenders were using condoms for several reasons, including both prophylaxis and contraception. They were also more likely to consider that promoting a more honest and open relationship with one's partner would be a likely benefit of using a condom on their next sexual encounter, and they were less likely than non-intenders to consider that a reduction in sexual pleasure would be a likely cost of doing so.

Results of the analyses on the normative belief and motivation to comply items revealed that differences between the groups were evident on the normative belief items, but not on the motivation to comply items. Specifically, subjects intending to use a condom differed from non-intenders on their perceptions of whether other people would want them to perform the behaviour. Additional analyses revealed that subjects intending to use a condom on their next sexual encounter were more likely than the non-intenders to perceive that a range of different referents (close friends, other friends and peers, parents and siblings) would want them to use a condom on their next sexual encounter.

This type of analysis shows quite clearly how further understanding can be gained about the determinants of behavioural choice by obtaining belief-based measures of attitude and subjective norm. As well as assisting in the explanation of behaviour, such results have clear implications for the development of intervention programs to encourage people to engage in the desirable behavioural choice. In the example provided above, the researcher would recommend that intervention programs target beliefs both about the consequences of performing the behaviour and the expectations of others, rather than people's evaluations of the outcomes or their willingness to comply with the wishes of others.

The use of belief-based measures of attitudes and norms also allows comparisons among different groups of subjects to be made. In a study of the determinants of safer sex behaviour, Gallois, Kashima*et al.* (1992) found that heterosexual women, heterosexual men and gay men differed in their beliefs about the consequences of their behaviours, their evaluations of these possible consequences and their normative beliefs. Gay men, for instance, rated themselves as more likely to contract HIV than heterosexual men did. Gay men also felt others (except partners and peers) would approve less of their behaviours. In comparison to gay men and heterosexual women, there was also evidence that heterosexual men worried more than other subjects about doing something their partner might not like. Once again, these results suggest clear recommendations for prevention programmes. They also demonstrate the usefulness of obtaining belief-based measures of attitudes and norms.

*The Role of External Variables*

In its original form, the theory of reasoned action is a parsimonious model of behavioural preference, in that it comprises only a small number of predictor variables. Other external variables that may influence a person's decision to engage in a particular behaviour are proposed to have only indirect effects on behaviour via their effects on attitudes and norms. As an example, males may be more willing to engage in some behaviours than women (e.g., use condoms as a safer sex strategy). According to the theory of reasoned action, gender will not directly predict people's propensity to engage in such behaviours, but reflect in gender differences in either attitudes towards the behaviour and/or perceptions of normative pressure to perform it. In a similar vein, the effects of other demographic variables, wider-based belief structures and personality dispositions are proposed to influence behavioural preferences via their effects on attitudes and norms; Warwick *et al.* (this volume) and Timmins*et al.* (this volume) present studies on safer sex behaviour examining the role of external variables in the theory of reasoned action.

For the most part, researchers have focused on demographic variables and personality dispositions as external variables that may influence attitudes and norms. An additional external variable that may be influential in this respect is the basis for a person's decision to engage in a particular course of action. For instance, in relation to condom use it may be useful to know whether the primary basis for the person's decision to engage in the behaviour is contraception or prophylaxis. A person who uses a condom primarily for contraceptive purposes is likely to perceive different costs and benefits of performing a behaviour than is a person who is primarily motivated to ensure protection from sexually transmitted diseases. Different salient referents may also influence each person's decision to engage in the behaviour. For instance, religious groups may be relevant to a person's decision to use a condom for contraceptive purposes, but may not be a salient referent for the person who is deciding whether to use a condom for prophylaxis.

## Methodological Issues

Ajzen and Fishbein (1980) specified a clear set of guidelines for the operationalisation of the components of the model. Comparison of results from different studies is difficult if researchers do not follow the recommended guidelines for the operationalisation of the model. In their guidelines, Ajzen and Fishbein specify the steps involved in constructing a questionnaire to test the theory of reasoned action. They also provide example items and appropriate response formats for measuring each of the components of the model, and describe the type of items that can be used in pilot work to elicit salient outcomes and referents. An overview of these guidelines is provided below.

### Defining the Population and Behavioural Criterion

Prior to constructing the questionnaire, researchers need to define the population of interest. Initially, researchers are likely to make this type of decision on both theoretical and pragmatic grounds. For example, a researcher may choose to conduct a study of safer sex on a sample of gay men, because HIV prevention is a current concern of this group and because he or she has access to this population. However, having made a decision about the population of interest, researchers need to conduct pilot work among the members of the chosen group to ascertain if there are within-group differences that should be considered in the research.

In the context of a study of gay men, for instance, the researcher needs to ascertain whether there are relevant differences among the group as a function of age, social class, ethnicity, religion, or residence (i.e., rural or urban). If this is the case, then the questionnaire needs to incorporate items that can reflect the differences among the group, and allow meaningful within-group differences to be made. In a wider study (for instance, incorporating both gay men and heterosexuals), the importance of doing pilot work to isolate differences among the group in terms of beliefs etc. becomes even more paramount, given the likelihood that both gender and sexual orientation are likely to influence people's beliefs and norms about safer sex.

Having identified the population of interest, Ajzen and Fishbein (1980) recommend that the researcher define the behavioural criterion. This will typically require specifying at least the action component of the behaviour, as well as the time frame (for some behaviours, the context and target are also relevant). As an example, research on safer sex could focus on condom use (action) on the person's next sexual encounter (time). This behaviour criterion is a clear example of safer sex. Moreover, the use of a short time frame minimises the problems of recall and distortion of memory that may characterise studies conducted over longer time periods. In some situations, researchers may wish to specify the behaviour further, for instance, by focusing on the use of a particular type of condom (target) with a specific type of partner (regular, casual, or new partner) (context). Preliminary pilot testing can be used to specify the behavioural criteria of interest (see Madden, Ellen & Ajzen, 1992). In a complex behavioural domain such as safer sex, this may be a useful procedure, given that populations are likely to differ not only in their beliefs about a behaviour, but also in their preferred strategies for prevention of STDs and HIV infection. For example, there is evidence that gay men are more likely than heterosexuals to engage in non-penetrative sex as an HIV-preventive behaviour (Gallois, Kashima*et al.*, 1992). A study of the determinants of this behaviour could provide considerable insight into safer sex among gay men; however, it may not be as useful among heterosexuals.

After identifying the behaviour of interest, Ajzen and Fishbein (1980) recommend that the researchers define the corresponding predictor variables (intention, attitude etc.). In doing so, researchers need to adhere to the principle of compatibility (Ajzen & Fishbein, 1977). Specifically, the measures of all components of the model should be assessed at the same level of specificity (i.e., if the behaviour of interest is using a condom on the next sexual encounter, then the measures of intention, attitude, and so on, should refer explicitly to condom use on the next encounter).

Table 1.1. *Operational Definitions and Example Items of the Components of the Theories of Reasoned Action/Planned Behaviour*

| Variable | Operational definition | Example item[*] |
|---|---|---|
| Intention | Subjective probability judgement of how the person intends to behave. | I intend too use a condom on my next sexual encounter. |
| Attitude | Evaluation of the favourability of the target behaviour. | My using a condom on my next sexual encounter would be... |
| Subjective norm | Subjective judgement concerning the perceived pressure to perform or not perform the beahviour. | People who are important to me think that I should/should not use a condom on my next sexual encounter. |
| Behavioural belief | Perceived likelihood that the behaviour will lead to certain outcomes (costs and benefits). | How likely do you think the following consequences will be if you, or your partner, wears a condom the next time you have sexual intercourse? |
| Outcome evaluation | Evaluation of each of the outcomes (costs and benefits). | How pleasant or unpleasant do you feel each of the following consequences would be... |
| Normative belief | Perceived likelihood that specific referents want the person to perform the behaviour. | How likely is it that each of the following people would think that you, or your partner, should use a condom the next time you have sexual intercourse? |
| Motivation to comply | Willingness to comply with the expectations of the specific referents. | In general, how much are you willing to do what the following people want you to do? |
| Perceived behavioural control | Perceived ease or difficulty of performing the behaviour. | For me, or my sexual partner, to use a condom the next time we have sexual intercourse will be... |
| Control belief | Perceived presence of the necessary resources and opportunities to perform the behaviour. | I, or my partner, have the necessary skills to use a condom on our next sexual encounter. |
| Perceived power | Perceived power of control factor to facilitate or inhibit behaviour. | How much effect would the following factors have on whether you, or your partner, use a condom on your next sexual encounter? |

[*] Response formats provided in text.

*Behavioural Intention*

Ajzen and Fishbein (1980; see also Fishbein & Ajzen, 1975) operationally defined intention as the person's subjective probability judgement of how he or she intends to behave (see Table 1 for a summary of operational definitions of the components of the theories of reasoned action/planned behaviour and example items). Items assessing behavioural intention thus need to assess the strength of the person's intention on an appropriate probability dimension. In their standard questionnaire, Ajzen and Fishbein (1980) recommend that an intention statement (e.g., "I intend to use a condom on my next sexual encounter") be rated along a 7-point (-3) "unlikely" to (+3) "likely" response. Although probability judgements are usually made on a zero to one basis (i.e., a unipolar scale), Ajzen and Fishbein recommend the use of a bipolar scale to assess intentions, because respondents need to be able to indicate that the statement is not true (i.e, that they do not intend to perform the behaviour). To develop a reliable measure of intention, researchers may wish to use more than one item to assess the variable. Interspersed throughout the questionnaire, other items could assess the strength of intention to perform the behaviour on, for instance, (-3) "definitely, do not intend" to (+3) "definitely, do intend" scales.

*Attitude*

Fishbein and Ajzen (1975) operationalise attitude as the person's evaluation of the target behaviour or, in other words, his or her feelings of favourability or unfavourability toward performing the behaviour. Ajzen and Fishbein (1980) noted that a variety of standard measures (e.g., Guttman scale or Thurstone scale) can be used to assess a person's attitude. The semantic differential technique developed by Osgood and his colleagues (Osgood, Suci & Tannenbaum, 1957) is, however, particularly recommended for this purpose, given that this technique yields a relatively direct measure of a person's attitude (Ajzen, 1988) and can be used across a wide range of attitude domains (Osgood *et al.*, 1957). The semantic differential technique employs a series of adjective pairs on which subjects are required to evaluate the behaviour in question (e.g., "My using a condom on my next sexual encounter would be:" good to bad; unpleasant to pleasant). The adjectives are rated on bipolar continua, to allow both negative and positive evaluations to be made. Scores on each set of adjective pairs range from -3 to +3. Subjects are, thus, able to indicate both the direction and strength of their attitude toward the behaviour. Total attitude scores can be computed by summing or averaging across the complete set of items.

On the basis of a large number of factor analyses of semantic differential scales, Osgood *et al.* (1957) concluded that the adjective pairs typically used in research appear to assess three underlying dimensions: evaluation (e.g., bad to good), potency (e.g., weak to strong), and activity (e.g., passive to active). To assess a person's attitude, it is necessary to use items that assess the evaluative dimension. As noted by Fishbein and Ajzen (1975), some items will consistently appear to assess evaluative tendencies; however, other scales will assess different dimensions, depending on the context under consideration. To ascertain whether items are assessing an evaluative dimension, Fishbein and Ajzen recommend that researchers factor analyse responses to their semantic differential items, and use only those items that appear to load on the evaluative factor.

## Subjective Norm

Subjective norm is operationalised as the person's subjective judgement concerning whether significant others would want him or her to perform or not to perform the behaviour. As such, it represents a global judgement—across all salient referents—of perceived pressure to perform the behaviour. An example item to assess subjective norm is: "People who are important to me think that I:(-3) "should not" to (+3) "should" use a condom on my next sexual encounter." Once again, the reliability of a measure of subjective norm can be improved by using more than one item to assess the variable. Researchers can, for example, ask subjects to indicate their perceptions of significant others' reactions to their performance of the behaviour on an (-3) "disapprove" to (+3) "approve" bipolar scale.

## Belief-Based Measures of Attitude and Subjective Norm

Ajzen and Fishbein (1980) regard the identification of the behaviour of interest and the development of the measures of intention, attitude and subjective norm as sufficient to facilitate a general understanding of the determinants of behaviour. They recommend that belief-based measures be used to provide more detailed information on the cognitive basis of behavioural choice. As noted, Fishbein and Ajzen (1975) point to the necessity of incorporating salient beliefs (i.e., outcomes or referents) into the belief-based measures of attitude and subjective norm. They further point out that the modal salient beliefs are likely to vary from one behaviour to another, and Ajzen and Fishbein (1980) specify the types of questions that should be used to elicit these beliefs. For example, the item: "What do you see as the advantages of using a condom on your next sexual encounter?" can be used to elicit the perceived benefits of performing the behaviour, while the item: "Are there any groups or people who would approve of your using a condom on the next sexual encounter?" can be used to help identify the salient referents for the behaviour. The pilot data need to be collected on a sample representative of the target population. Having collected the data, content coding can be used to identify the most frequently mentioned (modal) costs, benefits and referents, which should then be incorporated into the relevant belief-based measures in the final questionnaire (see McLaws*et al.*, this volume, for a more detailed discussion of pilot work).

Ajzen and Fishbein (1980) operationally define a behavioural belief as the person's subjective judgement of the likelihood that a particular outcome (cost or benefit) will be a consequence of performing the behaviour. These researchers recommend that responses to the items be obtained on bipolar scales, ranging from (-3) "extremely unlikely" to (+3) "extremely likely." Outcome evaluations are operationalised as subjects' evaluations of each of the salient outcomes, and are assessed on bipolar scales, ranging from (-3) "extremely bad" to (+3) "extremely good." To obtain a score on the belief-based measure of attitude, the person's scores on each of the corresponding behavioural belief and outcome evaluation items are multiplied and then summed across the complete set of items.

The use of bipolar scales to assess evaluation is widely accepted, given that people can have either negative or positive evaluations of a particular outcome (see Fishbein & Ajzen, 1975). For behavioural beliefs, the use of bipolar scales has been questioned. Ajzen and Fishbein (1980) justify the use of this type of response format on two counts. Firstly, the particular belief statements are not elicited for each subject individually. For this reason, the person has to be given the opportunity to indicate that he or she believes that a particular outcome is an unlikely consequence of performing the behaviour (even though representative members of the population identified it as a probable consequence of performing the behaviour), which necessitates the use of a bipolar scale. Secondly, the use of a bipolar scale to assess behavioural beliefs means that both likely positive consequences and unlikely negative consequences have a positive impact on a person's attitude (both combinations of beliefs yield a positive value) (Ajzen & Fishbein, 1980). This is reasonable, given that a person is likely to have a positive attitude towards a behaviour if he or she believes that it is likely that it will be accompanied by positive outcomes, and that it is unlikely that negative outcomes will occur.

Normative beliefs are operationally defined as the person's perception of whether specific referents would want him or her to perform the behaviour under consideration (Ajzen & Fishbein, 1980). Normative beliefs are, therefore, similar to subjective norm, although they focus on specific referents and groups, rather than reflecting a general consideration of the expectations of important others (as in subjective norm). Ajzen and Fishbein suggest that "normative" beliefs should be assessed in a similar manner to the subjective norm, where the respondent indicates the extent to which he or she perceives that each of the salient referents or groups would think that the person should perform the behaviour (e.g., "My parents think: (-3) "I should not" to (+3) "I should" use a condom on my next sexual encounter").

The motivation to comply component of the belief-based measure of the subjective norm is operationalised as the person's willingness to comply with the expectations of the specific referents. Because people are unlikely to be motivated to do the opposite of what they perceive significant others want them to do, Ajzen and Fishbein (1980) recommend that the motivation to comply items be assessed on a unipolar scale. These researchers suggest the use of the item: "Generally speaking, how much do you want to do what your parents think you should do?" (1) "not at all" to (7) "very much" to assess motivation to comply. As for the belief-based measure of attitude, the corresponding measure of subjective norm is computed as the sum of the products of the corresponding normative belief × motivation to comply items.

*Behaviour*

Finally, assessment of behaviour should take place at a later time than the assessment of the other components of the model (i.e., attitude, subjective norm and intention). The period of time between the two phases of data collection needs to encompass the time period specified in the measures of Time 1. For instance, if the researcher is interested in predicting sexual behaviour over a six week period, then behaviour should be assessed after the six week period has passed. Direct observation of behaviour is desirable; however, because many behaviours are performed in private (e.g., using a condom), it may, in some instances, be necessary to rely on self-report (Ajzen & Fishbein, 1980). The accuracy of self-report is enhanced if subjects are not required to report on behaviour over a long period of time, and if it is clear that all data are confidential. Actual behaviour is typically scored as a dichotomy (i.e., the subject either performed or did not perform the behaviour in question). In some instances, it may be appropriate to use a measure that reflects the extent to which the behaviour has been performed (e.g., the proportion of times that a condom was used) (Ajzen & Fishbein, 1980; see for example, Boyd & Wandersman, 1991).

## The Theory of Planned Behaviour

### Theoretical Overview

As noted previously, the theory of reasoned action proposes that intention to perform a particular behaviour is an accurate predictor of actual behaviour only when the behaviour is under the person's volitional control (Fishbein & Ajzen, 1975). If the behaviour is not completely under the person's control—for instance, if its execution is dependent on other people or the person lacks the appropriate skills to perform the behaviour—then it is assumed that the strength of the relationship between behavioural intention and actual behaviour will be attenuated (Ajzen, 1988; Ajzen & Madden, 1986). In an attempt to extend the theory of reasoned action to situations where the behaviour is not completely under the person's control, Ajzen (1985; 1987, 1991; Ajzen & Madden, 1986) proposed the theory of planned behaviour (see Figure 2). Essentially this model states that if a behaviour is likely to be influenced by factors outside the person's control, then to predict behaviour accurately the extent to which the behaviour is under the individual's volitional control needs to be considered (Ajzen, 1987, 1991; Ajzen & Madden, 1986). As Ajzen and Madden further point out, although a measure of the actual controllability of the behaviour would be desirable, it is difficult to obtain adequate measures of actual control. External factors that prevent a behaviour occurring are often unanticipated, while the absence of the appropriate skills to perform the behaviour may not be evident until after the person has attempted to perform the behaviour. Ajzen and Madden (1986), thus, favour the use of measures of perceived control as proxy measures of actual control.

Ajzen and Madden (1986) formulated two versions of the theory of planned behaviour. In the first version it was proposed that perceived behavioural control would emerge as a significant predictor of behavioural intentions (after the effects of attitudes and norms were controlled). This proposal is based on the assumption that if a person doubts the extent to which the behaviour is controllable, then the person is unlikely to be motivated to perform the behaviour. In this version of the theory, the effect of perceived behavioural control on actual behaviour is assumed to be mediated via its effect on intentions. In the second version of the theory of planned behaviour, it is proposed that perceived behavioural control will have both indirect (via intentions) and direct effects on behaviour. As Ajzen and Madden (1986) pointed out, the proposed direct effect of perceived behavioural control on actual behaviour is based on the assumption that performance of a behaviour is dependent not only on the extent to which the person is motivated to perform it (intentional component), but also on the extent to which the behaviour is under his or her control (measure of perceived behavioural control used as a proxy

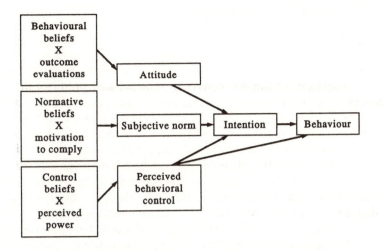

FIG. 2. The theory of planned behaviour.

measure for actual control). According to Ajzen and Madden (1986), perceived behavioural control has a direct effect on behaviour only when the behaviour is not completely under the person's volitional control, and when the measure of perceived behavioural control is an accurate reflection of the degree of actual control the person has over performing the behaviour.

Ajzen and Madden (1986) acknowledged the possibility that the effects of perceived behavioural control on intentions and actual behaviour may be interactive, rather than additive. For instance, it is possible that the relationship between intentions and behaviour will be stronger when the behaviour is perceived to be controllable than under conditions of low perceived control. To perform the behaviour, high scores on measures of both perceived behavioural control and behavioural intentions may be necessary preconditions for the behaviour to occur (Ajzen & Madden, 1986).

There is some empirical support for the second version of the theory of planned behaviour. Perceived behavioural control has been found to influence both behavioural intentions and actual behaviour. Schifter and Ajzen (1985), for instance, reported that, even after the effects of attitudes and norms were controlled, perceived behavioural control emerged as a significant predictor of intentions to lose weight. Ajzen and Madden (1986) reported further support for the proposed effects of perceived behavioural control, although the effects were additive, rather than interactive. Ajzen and Madden's (1986) findings are strengthened by the fact that there was no evidence that the effects of perceived behavioural control were a reflection of subjects' predictions of their ability to be able to perform the behaviour in the future, based on their success at doing so in the past. Control of the effects of past behaviour did not change any of the observed effects of perceived behavioural control. Although Fishbein and Stasson (1990) failed to find any support for the proposed effects of perceived behavioural control on either behavioural intentions or actual behaviour, recent studies have found further evidence to support the inclusion of this variable in the theory of reasoned action (e.g., Beale & Manstead, 1991; Madden *et al.*, 1992; Netemeyer & Burton, 1990; Nucifora *et al.*, this volume).

Ajzen (1988, 1991) proposed that judgements of perceived behavioural control are belief-based. Specifically, he hypothesised that people's perceptions of behavioural control are influenced by their beliefs concerning whether they have access to the necessary resources and opportunities to perform the behaviour successfully (referred to as control beliefs) weighted by the perceived power or effect of the particular control factor. People who perceive that they have access to the important resources considered necessary to perform the behaviour and/or perceive that there will be no major obstacles that interfere with their behavioural attempts are likely to perceive a high level of behavioural control (see Ajzen, 1991).

There is some empirical support for the informational basis of perceptions of behavioural control. Early studies linked judgements of behavioural control to perceptions of the extent to which control factors would inhibit or facilitate behavioural performance (Ajzen & Madden, 1986). More recent research has reported that measures of control beliefs, weighted by the perceived power of the control factor to impede or assist performance of the behaviour, are moderately correlated with global estimates of perceived behavioural control (see Ajzen, 1991). Once again, the fact that the correlations are only moderate may be a reflection of the failure to identify the salient control beliefs accurately.

*Methodological Issues*

In tests of the theory of planned behaviour, Ajzen and his colleagues (see Ajzen & Madden, 1986; Madden *et al.*, 1992; Schifter & Ajzen, 1985) have typically obtained direct measures of perceived behavioural control using multi-item scales, employing a range of different response formats. In the context of condom use, example items include: "For me or my partner, to use a condom on my next sexual encounter would be?" (-3) "very easy" to (+3) "very difficult" and "How much control do you have over whether a condom is used on your next sexual encounter?" (-3) "no control at all" to (+3) complete control."

Like the belief-based measures of attitude and subjective norm, Ajzen (1988, 1991; Ajzen & Madden, 1986) proposed that the belief-based measure of perceived behavioural control should be based on the salient control beliefs for the particular behaviour and population under consideration. Thus, pilot work should be conducted to elicit the salient control beliefs. To elicit such beliefs, Ajzen and Madden (1986) asked subjects participating in a pilot study to list the factors that could prevent them from engaging in the behaviour under consideration. For safer sex, issues such as being highly sexually aroused, drinking or taking other drugs and having sex with a new partner, have all emerged as important control beliefs for gay men (see McLaws *et al.*, this volume) and for others (see Moore, *et al.*, this volume). Subjects can also indicate the factors that could help them to perform the behaviour. The modal beliefs that are identified in the pilot work then form the basis for the measure of control beliefs. Ajzen (1991) recommends that the control beliefs be scored on bipolar scales of likelihood of occurrence ((-3) "extremely unlikely" to (+3) "extremely likely"). He also recommends that the perceived power of the control factor to facilitate or inhibit performance the behaviour be obtained on bipolar scales.

## Summary and Conclusions

In summary, the theory of reasoned action and its recent extension, the theory of planned behaviour, are based on the assumption that when making behavioural decisions, people consider the information available to them. Specifically, it is proposed that the immediate determinant of behaviour is intention, which is proposed to be influenced by the person's attitude towards performing the behaviour and the extent of perceived normative pressure to do so. Personal beliefs about the behaviour under consideration, as well as the person's beliefs about the expectations of others are, in turn, proposed to provide the informational bases of attitudes and subjective norms. In the theory of planned behaviour, it is proposed that the extent to which the behaviour is under volitional control also needs to be taken into account.

This book focuses on the utility of the theory of reasoned action in the context of a current public issue, namely, the goal of encouraging people to engage in safer sex behaviours. In the next chapter, consideration is given to the epidemiological and social context of the AIDS epidemic. Consideration is also given to the specific characteristics of safer sex behaviour that need to be addressed when applying the theory in this context.

# 2

# Applying the Theory of Reasoned Action to the Prediction of AIDS-Preventive Behaviour

VIRGINIA J. LEWIS AND YOSHIHISA KASHIMA

*La Trobe University, Melbourne, Australia*

## Epidemiological and Social Contexts of AIDS Prevention

This chapter discusses how the theory of reasoned action may be applied to the study of HIV/AIDS-preventive behaviour. In this chapter we will review the current behavioural research in HIV/AIDS prevention and examine major issues surrounding the use of the theory of reasoned action in behavioural AIDS research. However, no application of the theory can be free from the context of its use. Prior to discussing the application of the theory, we will first examine the epidemiological and social contexts in which AIDS prevention research must be conducted.

### The HIV/AIDS Pandemic

The Acquired Immune Deficiency Syndrome (AIDS) and the Human Immunodeficiency Virus (HIV) that causes AIDS are epidemic worldwide. HIV may infect an individual, but leave no external signs of illness for a very long period. Studies to date indicate that about 50% of adults infected with HIV will develop AIDS within 10 years of infection, and it is expected that the vast majority of infected persons will develop AIDS eventually. Once activated, HIV attacks the host's immune and nervous system functions, leading to a variety of conditions such as secondary cancers and opportunistic infections, and ultimately death. In developed countries survival time after diagnosis of AIDS is about 1–2 years on average. This is reduced to six months or less in developing countries (World Health Organization [WHO], 1991). The longer survival time after diagnosis of AIDS in developed countries is thought to be related to a better overall quality of health care, as well as the routine use of antiviral drugs and prophylactic drugs for some opportunistic infections (WHO, 1991).

**29**

In late 1992, the World Health Organisation (WHO) estimated that 10–12 million adults and more than 1 million children had been infected with HIV since the start of the pandemic. Of these, over 2 million had developed AIDS, most of whom had died (Merson, 1992). WHO estimates that by the year 2000 there will be 25–30 million cumulative cases of adult HIV infection with 8–10 million cumulative AIDS cases, and 5–10 million cumulative cases of paediatric HIV infection with 4–8 million cumulative AIDS cases, resulting in 30–40 million people having been infected with HIV since the start of the pandemic and 12–18 million of these having died from AIDS (WHO, 1991). Clearly AIDS and HIV represent a human tragedy on a global scale.

HIV is not an easily transmitted virus compared with the viruses that spread such contagious diseases as influenza or the common cold. There are three major modes of HIV transmission. These are unprotected vaginal or anal sexual intercourse between a male and female or two males; direct exposure of bodily fluid to semen, organs, blood, or blood products (principally involving reuse of, or accidental injury with, inadequately sterilised needles and syringes or blood transfusion); and perinatal transmission (in utero, during birth or shortly after, with increased risk due to breast-feeding) (WHO, 1991). While the pattern of HIV transmission varies geographically, the majority of infections worldwide is via sexual intercourse. In fact, 70% of global infections by early 1991 were estimated to have been via vaginal intercourse (WHO, 1991).

While the numbers alone communicate the scale of the direct tragedy that HIV represents, it is in considering the dynamics of the pandemic that the full ramifications of the tragedy are highlighted. During the late 1980s WHO reported that three main patterns of infection described the spread of HIV in the different geographical epidemics. These patterns reflected the broad epidemiological patterns of HIV/AIDS in terms of when the epidemic appeared to start its spread, and the predominant modes of HIV transmission. Pattern I was particularly evident in Western developed countries, where AIDS was initially detected among homosexual males, followed by injecting drug users in the early 1980s. Pattern II was particularly characteristic of sub-Saharan African and Caribbean countries, where reporting of cases began in the early 1980s, and where the virus was, and still is, predominantly heterosexually transmitted. Regions where the spread of HIV did not really begin to be recorded until the late 1980s, so that the overall HIV prevalence was relatively low and the predominant transmission mode not yet established, were called Pattern III regions (WHO, 1991). Because of changing epidemiological patterns (i.e., the rapid spread of heterosexually transmitted HIV) in countries which had been described as Pattern I, WHO later introduced Pattern I/II used to describe countries where the spread of HIV began among homosexual men and injecting drug users, but from the mid to late 1980s, a large and significant proportion of new HIV infections has been due to heterosexual transmission. Pattern III countries have been reclassified as Pattern I or Pattern II as the epidemic has become established in them.

While WHO reports now that the "distinctiveness of these epidemiological patterns has become increasingly blurred" (WHO, 1991), there remains a dynamic to the spread of HIV which varies geographically, even within individual countries. Differences in apparent primary modes of transmission are reported between cities within countries, and countries within the same continent. For example, on the west coast of the U.S.A. about 90% of AIDS cases have been diagnosed in homosexual men, compared with only about 60% on the east coast. Similarly, Scandinavia has reported the vast majority of AIDS cases in homosexual men, while in Spain and Italy less than half of the AIDS cases reported have been in homosexual men. In the West, there is growing concern being expressed that HIV and AIDS will increasingly become diseases of the socially and economically disadvantaged (Mays & Jackson, 1991; Ford & Norris, 1991; Crofts, 1992). It has been suggested that this may be a result of the greater predominance of injecting drug use and other sexually transmissible diseases in minority groups (Crofts, 1992), or perhaps because of a failure to successfully target interventions to the specific cultural context required (Ford & Norris, 1991). Even if it is not the case that AIDS becomes a disease of the underprivileged, the economic cost to Western countries alone is already estimated to amount to several thousand million U.S. dollars or more annually, and a knowledge of the delayed onset of AIDS-related illness and AIDS can only see this cost rise.

In sub-Saharan Africa the predominantly heterosexual transmission has resulted in a male to female ratio of HIV infection of approximately 1:1.2. High rates of STD incidence are suspected to have facilitated spread of the virus (WHO, 1991). Given the large number of women infected, perinatal transmission has become an ever increasing problem. Such a pattern of transmission, whereby the disease affects people particularly in the age range of 15–49, with associated infant mortality increases and life expectancy decreases, is expected to have immense economic, social and political impact (Lule & Gruer, 1991; WHO, 1991). The demographic gains of the past decades in these countries are expected to stall totally, or even to reverse (Merson, 1992). While extensive spread of HIV in South and South-East Asia is still relatively recent, the patterns of STD prevalence and the social and economic climates in some of these countries are similar to Central Africa, leading to the most rapid projected growth rates of HIV infection and AIDS for the South and South-East Asian region (Crofts, 1992; WHO, 1991).

Clearly preventive programs offer the best chance to combat HIV and AIDS, and the nature of the main transmission modes highlights the need for effective behavioural change interventions. The fact that transmission of HIV requires direct bodily fluid interaction, that the behaviours which lead to such transmission appear to be largely within human rather than environmental control, and that there is no effective vaccine against HIV, mean that prevention of infection remains the only effective means to fight the pandemic. WHO stated that "education strategies which modify or eliminate risk behaviours continue to be the primary intervention available to prevent and control the continuing spread of HIV" (WHO, 1991). While transmission of HIV via the sharing of contaminated needles and syringes by injecting drug users is a significant mode of transmission in some countries, the predominance of sexual transmission of HIV globally suggests clearly that encouraging change in sexual behaviour must be the keystone of any program designed to prevent the further spread of HIV. If people can be convinced not to practice the kinds of behaviours that lead to the direct exchange of bodily fluids, then the likelihood of transmission of the virus is reduced. Given the very specific nature of the behaviours that are considered most risky, and the small number of these key behaviours, one might suppose that the outlook for HIV/AIDS prevention was good. Unfortunately, there is far more to changing behaviour than merely informing people of the desirability, however imperative to their health, of making such changes.

## *The Social Context of HIV/AIDS Prevention*

The problem of encouraging behaviour change is one that is familiar to psychologists, being the focus of much of the theory and practice of clinical and social psychology. There is also a vast literature on health behaviour which has focussed on behaviour change in the health context, and the discipline of health promotion aims to design, implement and evaluate interventions ranging from the spread of information via mass media, to practical programs and targeted education programs that encourage health behaviour change. While there is a literature on health behaviour change, it can be argued that the nature of the primary modes of transmission of HIV leads to specific issues in the development of models of behaviour change that can be used in this context. Each of the two primary transmission modes of HIV involves intimate, social interaction between people, within the broader context of social morals.

Transmission of HIV via infected blood has been largely of two kinds—through the receipt of infected blood or blood products in the course of medical treatment and through the sharing of inadequately sterilised needles and syringes while injecting drugs. In almost all countries now medical blood and blood product supplies are successfully screened for HIV (WHO, 1991). However, injecting drug users who share inadequately sterilised injecting equipment continue to expose themselves to the risk of infection. The impact of the moral and political context surrounding the use of drugs which are illicit in most countries is compounded by the group sub-culture of the injecting drug users, which involves individuals and therefore the risky behaviours in a social relationship, introducing a huge array of factors into any attempt to influence behaviour change.

Similar complexity is apparent when considering the most common route of transmission of HIV worldwide—penetrative sexual intercourse. AIDS first appeared in the public discourse as a sexually transmitted disease, and in the West as an STD of homosexual and bisexual men (Adib & Ostrow, 1991), with the associated dilemma of how to approach primary prevention in a complicated moral and political context. On the one hand it is widely accepted that the spread of HIV needs to be halted, however others argue that addressing this aim could lead to the promotion of 'immoral' sexual activity by reducing people's fear of disease. For example, Brandt (1985) parallels the public and medical response to syphilis with the response to HIV and AIDS in the United States. Whereas broad behavioural change was recognised as an effective way to prevent the spread of syphilis by the U.S. Public Health Service (Valdiserri, 1989), the availability of a successful treatment option allowed the issue of public morality and primary prevention to be avoided. Identifying syphilis cases by encouraging widespread public testing, followed with treatment, became the dominant approach to the prevention of the spread of the disease. Brandt (1985) and Valdiserri (1989) argued that the fact that the U.S. public health approach to HIV is based on case identification is a legacy of the campaign used to deal with syphilis. In the context of AIDS, however, it is likely to be ineffective because, unlike treatable syphilis, there remains no effective vaccine or treatment against HIV.

Every country that has had to respond to the HIV pandemic has to deal with the complex social, political and moral context in which they are developing their HIV-prevention strategies. Generally speaking, in the domain of sexual behaviour, most of the research and intervention emphasis has been on encouraging people to want to practise safer sex, with an assumption that, in most instances, the physical means to do so (e.g., condoms and water-based lubricant) are readily available, although increasing the availability of the physical means to some safer sex practices (e.g., distribution of free condoms and lubricant to gay and bisexual men, sex workers, male prisoners and injecting drug users; introduction of condom-vending machines to public lavatories, hotels and even schools) has been a feature of some approaches to HIV/AIDS prevention (Intergovernmental Committee on AIDS, 1992; Mak & Plum, 1991; Siraprapasiri, Thanprasertsuk, Rodklay, Srivanichakorn, & Temtanarak, 1991; Nzila *et al.*, 1991). The latter policies, in particular, have attracted negative reactions from some public commentators, politicians and even health professionals. The continuation of programs that increase the availability of condoms and lubricants will depend on the political beliefs and commitments of the government of the day.

## Current Behavioural Approaches to HIV/AIDS Prevention

As well as the above policy-based programs, the recognition that primary prevention is the best and currently the only way to slow the spread of HIV has led to the accumulation of a large psychosocial and behavioural literature on AIDS-related issues. This literature is basically of three kinds: intervention, descriptive survey, and theory-based studies.

### Intervention Studies

Intervention studies seek to describe, and less often evaluate, a program or campaign that has been designed to prevent the spread of HIV. Prevention campaigns and programs that have been designed, implemented and (sometimes) evaluated are various. Fisher and Fisher's (1992) review of the AIDS-risk reduction literature from 1980 to 1990 included interventions aimed at homosexual and bisexual males, injecting drug users, female prostitutes, STD clinic patients, adolescents, college students and the general public. The interventions ranged from small-group sessions providing information or information and skills (e.g., Valdiserri *et al.,* 1989) to mass media campaigns (Lehmann, Hausser, Somaini & Gutzwiller, 1987). Given the period covered by Fisher and Fisher's review, attention in this chapter is focussed on the literature of 1991–1992, within the developmental context of the pandemic.

In Western countries, because of the U.S. Centers for Disease Control's method of reporting case data, the pattern of the spread of HIV led to the identification of 'high risk groups'. As a consequence, the initial emphasis on prevention and research was aimed at homosexual men, and later at injecting drug users. In addition, basic knowledge and prevention messages were directed at the whole community via mass media. Given the pattern of spread of HIV in the West, a great number of interventions have been targeted at homosexual and bisexual men, including informational discussion groups (Flowers *et al.,* 1991), a workshop-based program called 'Eroticising Safer Sex', currently used in many Western countries (Shernoff & Bloom, 1991) and use of key opinion leaders of targeted populations to spread information (Kelly, St Lawrence, Piaz *et al.,* 1991). During the late 1980s, and into the 1990s, there has been growing recognition that reference to 'high risk groups' diverts attention from the behaviours that are 'risky', and encourages stigmatisation of people against whom much of society is often already prejudiced (Hayes, 1991).

Perhaps this recognition, coupled with ease of access to samples, has led to the increase in research and interventions aimed at adolescents in Western countries. Adolescents have recently been a major target of intervention research on sexual behaviour change, including school-based interventions (Brown, DiClemente & Reynolds, 1991), programs for adolescents in a multi-ethnic context (Ford & Norris, 1991), peer-led interventions aimed at knowledge increase, attitude change and behavioural intention change in American college students (Shulkin*et al.*, 1991; Brown, 1991), use of video-taped information (Lipson & Brown, 1990) and behavioural training to teach assertive strategies to university students (Franzini, Sideman, Dexter, & Elder, 1990).

Whereas Western countries combined general population information and knowledge campaigns with the initial 'risk groups' focus, countries with the pattern of predominantly heterosexually transmitted HIV have placed most emphasis on population-based prevention strategies. Information and education programs directed at the general public have been the primary focus of efforts to control the sexual transmission of HIV in Africa (Moses *et al.*, 1991). As in most Western countries, these programs operate separately from conventional STD-targeted programs, despite the overlap of prevention strategies. Uganda was the first African country to have a well-developed national AIDS control program (Lule & Gruer, 1991), with mass-media messages encouraging safer sex. As with other countries, the dilemma of the social and cultural moral context of AIDS is such that the Ugandan government has argued that widespread promotion of condoms "may not be consistent with local cultural attitudes and practices" (Okware, 1988). In Uganda, the major behavioural options promoted by government public health campaigns and educational programs have included abstinence, fewer sexual partners, monogamy, the establishment of local by-laws prohibiting activities that lead directly or indirectly to the spread of AIDS, alternative income generating activities (i.e., for sex workers) and alternative recreational activities (Moodie, 1992). In Zaire, most national HIV/AIDS control and prevention programs have focussed on educational activities to encourage fewer sexual partners and/or the use of condoms (Kamenga *et al.*, 1991; Bertrand *et al.*, 1991). Programs especially designed to address the issue of relationships between couples with discordant HIV-1 serostatus have been particularly important in Africa where at least 80% of infection is reported to have been acquired through heterosexual contact (Kamenga *et al.*, 1991). There have also been some HIV-infection control programs focussed on sub-populations in which particular risky behaviours are practised more frequently than the general population. Female sex workers in Kenya, for instance, have been targeted with educational campaigns through public and one-to-one counselling (Moses *et al.*, 1991). Similarly, in Zaire, female sex workers have been highlighted as a highest priority group (Nzila *et al.*, 1991).

In their review of the intervention literature, Fisher and Fisher (1992) concluded that most reported interventions have been based on informal conceptualisation, with little or no formal elicitation research in the design stage, have contained only an acknowledgment that a broad focus on information, motivation and behavioural skills is required without subsequent action on that observation, and have contained poor or nonexistent outcome evaluation. Unfortunately, the conclusions of Fisher and Fisher are as applicable to the recent literature as to the earlier period. As they noted, most of the intervention literature is atheoretical and noncumulative, which seriously undermines its usefulness in planning future prevention strategies.

## Descriptive Surveys

Descriptive survey studies report information about variables such as behaviour, knowledge, attitudes or any combination thereof, occasionally with seroprevalence data to indicate the rate of HIV infection within the sample. The nature of the primary modes of transmission of HIV has meant that widespread general population-based surveying of sexual (and illicit drug using) behaviours has been politically difficult to achieve, so that much research uses fairly selective or self-selecting samples. There are few examples of large-scale surveys that contain very extensive information (Bertrand *et al.*, 1991). Populations that have been surveyed recently include homosexual and bisexual men (Weatherburn Hunt, Davies, Coxon, & McManus, 1991), sex workers (Nzila *et al.*, 1991; Mak & Plum, 1991) homosexual and bisexual adolescents from racial minority groups (Rotheram-Borus & Koopman, 1991a), multi-ethnic adolescents (Dusenbury, Botvin, Baker, & Laurence, 1991), adolescents (Moore & Rosenthal, in press), high school students (Skurmick, Johnson, Quinones, Foster, & Louria, 1991), university students (Bruce, Shrum, Trefethen, & Slovik, 1990; DiClemente, Forrest, & Mickler, 1990; Carroll, 1988; Lule & Gruer, 1991), runaway youths (Rotheram-Borus & Koopman, 1991b) and health professionals (Gallop*et al.*, 1991). Many of these kinds of studies report summary statistics, with limited reporting of tests of association between variables.

Without some theory of the process of change, survey research of this kind is only useful at the level of offering preliminary information. The lack of sampling control and the inconsistencies in methodology in terms of the operationalisation of variables do not allow the data to be used as accurate indicators of change. While each study makes recommendations for intervention on the basis of its findings, the lack of a common theoretical foundation for the research undermines the power of any such conclusions.

## Theory-Based Research on HIV/AIDS-Preventive Behaviours

The third kind of behavioural research seeks to be more descriptive and predictive in exploring the reasons for certain behavioural practices and beliefs, and is more likely to be theoretically based in a focussed way, if not broadly model-driven. There have been some attempts at theory-based intervention or manipulation. Other studies rely on multivariate prediction of a key behavioural variable in order to make recommendations for future prevention strategies. There is a great variety in the kinds of theories that have formed the bases for theory-based research on HIV/AIDS-preventive behaviours. Recent research, for example, has shown that perceptions of higher risk of HIV infection are linked to riskier sexual behaviour in adolescents (Moore & Rosenthal, 1991a). In addition, adolescents' self-esteem and self-efficacy have been shown to predict safer sexual behaviour (Rosenthal, Moore & Flynn, 1991). Finally, attitudes to condoms (Sacco, Levine, Reed, & Thompson, 1991), background subject variables (Allender, Senf, Bauman, & Reid Duffy, 1991) and health locus of control (Heaven, Connors & Kellehear, 1992) have been linked to attitude change about safer sex, sexual behaviour, and discriminatory attitudes toward people with HIV/AIDS. While studies of this type have some strengths, the conclusions of Fisher and Fisher (1992) in their review of the AIDS-risk reduction literature on interventions may also be applied to the HIV-related behavioural research. Problems of poor conceptualisation, inadequate elicitation research and a lack of a broad focus characterise this research. Moreover, the non-cumulative nature of much of the research undermines its general usefulness.

Apart from the approaches which focus on the effects of a small number of theoretically-relevant variables, there is a growing body of research that uses more integrated general theories of behaviour such as health belief models, the theory of reasoned action, and self-efficacy theory. This approach holds more promise of offering some cumulative guide to the development of effective behavioural interventions for HIV and AIDS. These theories have in common the premise that the AIDS epidemic can be managed by controlling human voluntary action. They try to point out ways to encourage behaviours that reduce the probability of HIV infection and to discourage behaviours that have high probabilities of transmitting the disease. Most theories of human decision making are based on the premise that people perform behaviours that they consider to be best for themselves. The decision as to the best behaviour is typically evaluated by a combination of probability (subjective or objective—that is, the likelihood of the behaviour effecting certain consequences)—and value (subjective utility or objective value—that is, the value of those consequences).

## Health Belief Model

The health belief model, which was specifically developed in the context of problems in health education and public participation in screening programs, is an endeavour to explore decisions made about volitional behaviours that affect health status (Rosenstock, 1974a; for a description of this model, see Terry, Gallois, & McCamish, this volume). Reviews of applications of health belief models have produced mixed results (see Terry *et al.*, this volume), with some suggesting limited validity (Harrison, Mullen & Green, 1992; Rosenstock, 1974b; Weisenberg, Kegeles & Lund, 1980) and fewer claiming it to be powerful in explaining and predicting health behaviour change (Janz & Becker, 1984).

In the context of AIDS research, the health belief model has not performed any more convincingly than in relation to other health behaviours (see also Warwick*et al.*, this volume). Studies have tended to conclude that one or other of the elements of the model has more predictive power than the others, or that none is particularly useful (Brown *et al.*, 1991). Kirsch and Joseph (1989), in reviewing the model's use with reference to homosexual men, observed that 'rarely has there been a confirmation of the full model; more often different elements are predictive of behaviour.' On the basis of their own attempted application they concluded that 'there was no real instance in which the set of elements together give a coherent picture of what is happening.' Wilson, Lavelle and Hood (1990) reported that the only predictor of intended condom use among Zimbabwean adolescents in probation/remand homes was belief in the effectiveness of the use of condoms. Wilson, Lavelle, Greenspan and Wilson (1991) applied the model to Zimbabwean students and reported that the overall model explained 15% of the variance for men and 12% for women, with different variables contributing significantly to each equation. They concluded that other models needed to be examined, and suggested the possible need for new theoretical formulations attentive to the unique complexities of AIDS. Research in Australia by Rosenthal, Hall and Moore (1992) has reported similarly differential patterns of predictive power for the variables of the health belief model, and concluded similarly that the health belief model is of limited use.

In their analysis of the utility of the health belief model for HIV prevention for adolescents, Brown *et al.* (1991) pointed out the poor demonstrated reliability and validity of measures, and the lack of empirically established relationships among health belief model constructs. There seems to be a low level of sophistication at an operationalisation level in much of the health belief model research. Apart from the methodological problems of the applications of the model, the theory has limitations in the context of sexual behaviour. Several authors have commented on the problem of the application of models based on value-expectancy theories of decision making, or rational volitional control to sexual behaviour (Rosenthal *et al.*, 1992; Kirsch & Joseph, 1989; Brown *et al.*, 1991). The lack of attention to either affective variables or to the potential role of peer group influence has also been criticised. The possibility of a curvilinear rather than linear relationship between perceived severity and behaviour, such that both extremely low and extremely high levels of seriousness inhibit action, has been raised by several researchers as theoretically problematic (Rosenthal *et al.*, 1992). An observed lack of variability in the relationship between severity and behaviour when comparing different health issues (e.g., AIDS, cancer and using child restraints in cars) has also been raised, with the suggestion that the model is not sufficiently discriminating in its applicability to different issues (Harrison *et al.*, 1992).

## *Theory of Reasoned Action*

The theory of reasoned action (Fishbein & Ajzen, 1975; Ajzen & Fishbein, 1980) has been a popular model in the social psychology and general health literatures, and for this reason is a good candidate for structuring a theory-based HIV/AIDS-prevention program. Like the health belief model, this model is based on the general idea that people make decisions to perform behaviours. The theory of reasoned action assumes that in the final analysis behaviours are caused by beliefs (for a general introduction, see Terry *et al.*, this volume). Clearly then, recommended intervention strategies revolve around identifying beliefs that lead to risky or risk-reducing behaviours, and designing interventions to change the former or encourage and maintain the latter.

Despite its general popularity, the model was not used in the HIV/AIDS-prevention area until quite recently. Where the model has been applied in accordance with the authors' recommendations, results are complex. Boyd and Wandersman (1991) compared the theory of reasoned action with Triandis' (1977) theory of attitude–behaviour relations in investigating American undergraduate students' use of condoms. They reported that intentions were best predicted by the behavioural beliefs/evaluations and normative beliefs/motivation to comply components of the model directly, and not through attitudes or subjective norms as indicated in the theory. Boyd and Wandersman also found that additional variables proposed by the Triandis model to explain the intention–behaviour link (past behaviour; facilitating conditions of self-efficacy, perceived control and perceived knowledge; susceptibility and fear of AIDS) almost doubled the amount of variance explained when predicting self-reported behaviour (53% compared with 27%). This issue of the weakness of the intention–behaviour relationship is fundamental to any assessment of the theory of reasoned action, but frequently overlooked, despite existing criticism in the general and health literature (Liska, 1984; Macey & Boldero, 1992; Sutton, 1989).

Some variations are expected on the basis of Fishbein and Middlestadt's (1989) own recommendations for application of the theory of reasoned action. Different predictor variables have been highlighted for different populations. Ross and McLaws (1992) concluded that subjective norms were good predictors of intention to use a condom in their sample of active homosexual men. Macey and Boldero (1992) found that both attitudes and subjective norms predicted intentions for females, but that neither predicted male heterosexuals' intentions to use a condom. Richard and van der Pligt (1991) applied the model extended with measures of self-efficacy, past behaviour and anticipated affective reactions. They concluded that groups should be distinguished in terms of monogamy and gender, reporting that male and female adolescents in a monogamous relationship differed from male and female adolescents in casual relationships, and that within the latter group males and females differed markedly, whereas they did not in the group involved in monogamous relationships.

Apart from differences between target populations, differences in the prediction of a range of behaviours have also been reported. In a well operationalised application of the theory, Terry, Galligan and Conway (in press) applied the theory of reasoned action to predicting three different behaviours: avoiding casual sex, asking a partner about their sexual and drug using history, and engaging in an exclusive sexual relationship. They reported that both attitudes and subjective norms predicted intentions for the first two behaviours, but that neither did for the third. In terms of the intention–behaviour link, the relationship was very weak, once again raising questions about a primary assumption of the model.

Quite commonly, research based on the theory of reasoned action has been inconsistent in its operationalisation of the key components of the model (e.g., the measurement of attitudes: Schaalma, Kok & Peters, 1993; Ross & McLaws, 1992; Richard & van der Pligt, 1991), thus undermining any claims of predictive strength or weakness. The theory of reasoned action remains an attractive model, however, and developments, particularly in the form of extensions, will be discussed below, before returning to a more detailed discussion of issues of application of the model to HIV prevention and sexual behaviour.

## Self-Efficacy Theory

Bandura's notion of self-efficacy (1986, 1989b) has also been employed to explain HIV-related behaviours, both in and of itself (Rosenthal, Moore & Flynn, 1991), and as an addition to the health belief model (Wilson, Lavelle, Greenspan & Wilson, 1991) or the theory of reasoned action (Boyd & Wandersman, 1991; see also Terry, this volume). In short, perceived self-efficacy reflects actors' beliefs about whether they think they can perform a given activity. Bandura, noting the discrepancy between people's HIV/AIDS knowledge and behaviour, suggested that when people lack a sense of self-efficacy, they do not manage situations effectively even though they know what to do and possess the requisite skills. Self-inefficacious thinking creates discrepancies between knowledge and action.

Whereas the theory of reasoned action and the original health belief model deal with situations in which people have volitional control over their behaviours, self-efficacy theory attempts to predict behaviours when volitional control over the behaviours is questionable. It is this complementary nature of self-efficacy theory that has led to its inclusion in revisions and extensions of the health belief model and the theory of reasoned action. Ajzen and Madden (1986) revised the theory of reasoned action by including the notion of perceived behavioural control in their theory of planned behaviour. The concept of behavioural control has links with notions of self-efficacy, in that it addresses the idea that individuals may have, or perceive themselves to have, varying degrees of control over any behavioural situation (see Terry, this volume). This attention to the potential disruptions to the intention-behaviour link in human planning or decision making is reflected in several other models that have recently emerged to address the issue of HIV-prevention research.

### Attempted Integrations of Behavioural Models

Van de Velde and van der Pligt (1991) applied Rogers'(1975, 1983) protection motivation theory and Janis and Mann's (1977) conflict theory to HIV/AIDS-related behaviour, to explore why some people behave in a manner which they know to be contrary to their best interests. The model that they developed also included aspects of the health belief model and the theory of reasoned action, as well as self-efficacy, perceived situational constraints, past behaviour and regrets about maladaptive behaviours. They then used structural equation modelling to predict behavioural intention for heterosexual and homosexual subjects separately.

They concluded that coping-appraisal processes in the form of self-efficacy and response efficacy independently affect intentions to adopt recommended behaviours, but that threat-appraisal processes in the form of perceived severity and vulnerability contribute little to prediction. The coping style variables did not add any explanatory power, but the additional variables (particularly social norms and previous behaviour) were predictive of behavioural intentions. In the case of maladaptive behaviours, situated constraints and cognitive barriers were also predictive of behavioural intentions. The study is a good example of theory-driven research, but there is no development of the results into a more useful composite theory of HIV-prevention behaviour. Clearly there is a great deal of overlap with the theory of reasoned action and the health belief model, and as such this study contributes to the general consideration of the usefulness of behavioural models in HIV-prevention research.

Fisher and Fisher (1992) also drew on the theory of reasoned action, as well as the health belief model and self-efficacy theory, in integrating much of the existing literature on HIV/AIDS interventions. They proposed a general model of AIDS-risk reduction, which they labelled the IMB model according to its primary elements: Information, Motivation and Behavioural Skills. According to Fisher and Fisher, information regarding the means of HIV transmission and specific preventive actions are necessary prerequisites of risk-reduction behaviour. In addition, Fisher and Fisher argued that individuals have to be motivated to translate their knowledge into concrete actions (motivation). In its full enunciation the motivation element of the IMB model is actually the theory of reasoned action, applied as per the recommendations of Ajzen and Fishbein (1980) and Fishbein and Middlestadt (1989), although the relationship between intentions and behaviours is later assumed, so that the IMB model predicts self-reported behaviour directly from theory of reasoned action components. Fisher and Fisher used the term 'motivation' to refer to personal attitudes toward AIDS-preventive behaviours and perceived normative support for such behaviours. They suggested that 'information' and 'motivation' determine whether people acquire skills necessary to carry out their risk reduction measures, and, in conjunction with these skills, determine people's actual HIV-preventive behaviours. At the behavioural skills level, the model identifies a broad range of skills assumed to be universally necessary for the practice of HIV prevention. These are self-acceptance of sexuality, acquisition of behaviourally relevant information, bringing-up/negotiating AIDS prevention with partner, public prevention acts (condom purchasing, HIV testing) and consistent AIDS prevention/self- and partner-reinforcement. In addition to these skills, the need for cultural relevance in application of the model is acknowledged, with the recommendation that elicitation studies be used to identify skills which may be specific to particular target groups. Bandura's self-efficacy theory is also introduced, with possession of a self-belief in one's ability to use the behavioural skills in one's repertoire proposed as a final behavioural skill required in order to engage in preventive behaviours.

As is claimed for the theory of reasoned action, the constructs are regarded as highly generalised determinants of HIV/AIDS-preventive behaviours. The strength of the IMB model lies in the fact that it has taken all three of the more popular general behavioural models and combined them specifically within the context of HIV-prevention research. Unfortunately the two studies that Fisher and Fisher (1992) reported as attempting to test the IMB model offer only limited support for the application of their theory. Performing structural equation modelling with a small sample ($n = 91$) of gay men, the model accounted for 35% of the variance in AIDS-preventive behaviours. Only 10% of the variance in a larger sample ($n = 174$) of university students could be accounted for by the model. As indicated earlier, such variation between populations would be expected under the theory of reasoned action. The amount of variance accounted for, however, is very small given the large number of additional factors, leading to doubts about the models's predictive power and therefore its usefulness as a theory to guide behavioural research.

## *Summary*

The appeal of the theory-based approach is most clearly reflected in the way theories can be used to organise the vast body of existing research and to suggest future directions. Hayes (1991) demonstrated the advantages of the theory-based approach in his application of the health belief model to the discussion of psychosocial barriers to behaviour change. In much the same way that Hayes (1991) used the health belief model as an organisational device to review the literature and recommend action, Gallois, Statham and Smith (1992) used the general components of Fisher and Fisher's model in an elegant review of the literature on women and HIV/AIDS. Both of these are instances of how models can usefully drive interpretation and organisation of the diverse literature, thus providing some accumulation of HIV/AIDS-prevention efforts.

Of those reviewed here, the theory of reasoned action appears to have more promise for providing a general framework for behavioural AIDS research than other behavioural theories. Extensions to the theory are clearly attempting to deal with perceived inadequacies and improve applicability of the model to HIV-prevention research, yet empirical support for such developments is often weak (e.g., Fisher & Fisher, 1992). Some of the extensions may actually obscure the fundamental issues concerning the components and relationships of the original theory. Before such extensions are considered as a theoretical base for research in their own right, there are issues of application of the theory of reasoned action in its original form which should be addressed by any researcher using the model. If the model is not considered at its theoretical level then extensions and revisions may be practical, yet not advance the development of a valid and practical model for predicting behaviour change in HIV/AIDS prevention research.

## Application of the Theory of Reasoned Action to HIV-Prevention

Fishbein and Middlestadt (1989) outlined the theory of reasoned action and recommended strategies for applying it to HIV-preventive behaviours. We will draw attention to some of the general points they raised, and then examine issues more specific to sexual behaviours. As they point out, the theory of reasoned action provides an overview of the proposed relations among a set of general concepts. It is up to users to specify these concepts to suit their local context. While the theory argues that the same small set of theoretical constructs and psychological processes will apply to most behaviours, Fishbein and Middlestadt (1989) remind researchers that "substantive specifics are expected to differ from one behaviour and/or from one population to another." Therefore, the first task for researchers using the theory of reasoned action is to choose a population and a behaviour of interest (see Terry *et al.*, this volume).

On the basis of previous research, it seems likely that there will be a great variety of group differences in the influence of norms and attitudes, (e.g., between homosexual males and heterosexual males, heterosexual males and heterosexual females, sexually experienced and inexperienced people, adolescents and older people, across social class, and among different ethnic groups) (Gallois, Kashima*et al.*, 1992). In the light of Fishbein and Middlestadt's (1989) recommendations, these potential group differences mean that, for effective behavioural research and interventions, specific populations must be targeted. Having identified the population of interest, researchers are advised to examine the target population's salient beliefs (both behavioural and normative) about the behaviour of interest by conducting an elicitation study (see Terry *et al.*, this volume). When the researchers shift their focus from one behaviour to another, or from one population to another, it is recommended that they conduct a new elicitation study.

Some of the criticisms of the theory of reasoned action have ignored the expectation of variability in the prediction of the behaviour of different populations, or of different behaviours themselves. While it may be empirically and intuitively supportable to allow for variation in the role of behavioural or normative beliefs at a theoretical level, there is an issue of the practicality of a model that requires such specificity. Given the large number of sub-populations that need to be individually targeted, as well as the emerging differences between specific behaviours (Terry *et al.*, in press), a question of time and resource limitations to research arises, particularly when taking into consideration the social context of HIV-prevention discussed earlier. The identification of appropriate behaviours, in particular, may be one of the most difficult aspects of applying the theory of reasoned action to sexual behaviour (see Kashima & Gallois, this volume, for more detail on this issue).

A special issue in the area of safer sex concerns the fact that the theory of reasoned action is designed to predict behaviours under volitional control; habitual or automatic behaviours are not within the scope of the theory. Yet some HIV-preventive behaviours in the sexual context are not completely under volitional control. One approach in this case is to shift the focus from these behaviours to others that are under volitional control. For example, if condom use is determined partly by factors outside the control of the actor (e.g., the actor does not have a condom or the partner refuses to use one), the focus of intervention might be directed at behaviours which culminate in condom use, such as buying and carrying a condom or asking a partner to use a condom. This approach would involve identifying a behaviour of interest, which may be found not to be under volitional control, and exploring its determinants in order to identify behaviours that are under volitional control, so that the latter may be targeted.

Clearly this has not been the approach generally observed in the literature. Instead, the extensions to the theory of reasoned action go some way to addressing the issue of non-volitional control of sexual behaviours by adding one or more variables to the models, with Fisher and Fisher's (1992) quite long list of behavioural skills underlining the point. In this approach, factors that prevent the actor from controlling the behaviour of interest are identified. These factors include individual variables such as self-efficacy or perceived behavioural control, situational variables such as condom availability, and the nature of the relationship between the actor and partner (see later chapters in this book for several examples of this approach). Once the factors that inhibit or facilitate behavioural change are identified, interventions may be designed to target these elements of the extended model.

Finally, circumstances that intervene between measured intentions and target behaviours may produce a last-minute change of intentions. These circumstances may be especially likely to occur in the sexual context. Given that a person has a condom available and prior to the situation feels able to introduce the topic of its use into conversation, factors in the immediate context can induce a change in intention (or weakness of will), such that condom use does not follow. Gold, Skinner, Grant, and Plummer (1991; Gold, this volume) raise the concept of situated cognitions and list over 80 thoughts that may interfere with a prior intention at the time of actual behaviour. Kippax and Crawford (this volume) address the issue in terms of culture and interpersonal dynamics in what is frequently an emotionally-charged situation.

In terms of the theory of reasoned action, the problem is one of stability of intention. As such, it has been raised in other health research, including smoking cessation, where the study of 'slip-ups' has focussed on the issue of the impulsive change in intentions (Borland, 1992). One solution is to find relevant predictors of stability of intentions. For instance we (Gallois, Kashima *et al.*, 1992; Kashima, Gallois, & McCamish, 1992) found that past behaviour is a good indicator of the extent to which intentions are stable over time. Other factors, such as the extent to which intentions are well formed (Bagozzi & Yi, 1989), may provide another indication. If there are practical ways to distinguish stable and unstable intentions and factors can be identified that determine the stability of intentions, then intervention programs may be devised not only to influence intentions to adopt HIV risk-reduction behaviours, but also to stabilise such intentions.

## Conclusions

Given the differences in the resources that are available to researchers, educators need to be able to develop and build upon knowledge of behavioural prevention in order to cumulatively identify the best interventions to try in a variety of contexts. If, at an international level, AIDS is not to become a disease of the politically, socially and economically dispossessed even more than it has already, behavioural theorists and practitioners must continue to grapple with the issue of balancing the need for locally refined research and interventions with the need for more universally applicable theories to guide the development of global solutions to HIV and AIDS prevention.

Despite the failure of any one model to address all the difficulties involved in HIV/AIDS-prevention research, the need to have theory-driven research cannot be understated. It is only by having a theory-based approach that there is a chance that the diversity of research can possibly be related back to a general set of ideas, thus allowing for some emergence of general themes over time. As such, the best option for organising the field of HIV-prevention research that emerges from the literature to date seems to be the theory of reasoned action. Yet the theory of reasoned action has its own problems (see other chapters in this book). Practical solutions have been proposed to deal with some of the difficulties related to application, but the underlying principles of the theory must not be overlooked in accepting such an approach.

# 3

# Influences on Condom Use among Undergraduates: Testing the Theories of Reasoned Action and Planned Behaviour

JOE NUCIFORA AND CYNTHIA GALLOIS

*The University of Queensland, Brisbane, Australia*

YOSHIHISA KASHIMA

*La Trobe University, Melbourne, Australia*

Research on the use of condoms among sexually-active university students is timely. Students are recognised as being particularly at risk of infection by HIV, because they are at the age of sexual experimentation and are in constant and continuing proximity with each other (Crawford, Turtle, & Kippax, 1990). As one might expect from an educated section of the population, university students generally possess good basic knowledge on HIV/AIDS issues and the most effective ways of preventing infection. It appears, though, that this knowledge is not being acted upon (Carroll, 1988; Edgar, Freimuth, & Hammond, 1988; Turtle *et al.,* 1989). In the study reported in this chapter, we explored some of the reasons for this discrepancy by searching for the most important predictors of safer sex.

The major model used in this study is the theory of reasoned action (TRA: Ajzen & Fishbein, 1980; Fishbein & Ajzen, 1975) and its extension, the theory of planned behaviour (TPB: Ajzen, 1985, 1988, 1991). TRA proposes a path leading to the performance (or not) of a specific behaviour, where performance is best predicted by the intention to engage in the behaviour. It should be noted that intention is expected to predict behaviour only if the intention has not changed prior to performance of the behaviour (see Terry *et al.,* this volume). Intention, in its turn, is predicted by attitude to the behaviour and subjective norm, or the perceived pressure from significant others to perform the behaviour. Finally, attitude is related to the sum of products of the evaluation of each perceived consequence of the behaviour and the perceived likelihood of the consequence occurring. Similarly, subjective norm is predicted by the sum of products of the perceived pressure from each significant other (normative beliefs) and the motivation to comply with that person.

The theory of reasoned action has shown its utility in predicting a range of behaviours (see Ajzen, 1991; Ajzen & Fishbein, 1980; other chapters in this volume). Not all research into behavioural prediction has supported this model, however. For example, an acknowledged limitation of the theory of reasoned action is the susceptibility of intentions to change (Ajzen & Fishbein, 1980). To overcome this problem, the authors recommend that the intention be assessed as close as possible to the time the behaviour is to occur. It appears that when this intervening time interval is increased, not only does the effect of intention on behaviour weaken, but there is a corresponding increase in the direct effect of attitude on behaviour unmediated by intention. Liska (1984) explained this in terms of the relative stability of attitudes when compared to intentions. On the other hand, Kashima, Gallois, and McCamish (1992; Kashima, Gallois, & McCamish, in press) found that some factors, including past performance of the behaviour, stabilised intentions.

Bagozzi and Burnkrant (1979) showed that behavioural beliefs predicted intention directly, when the influence of attitude was controlled for. In examining this finding, Liska (1984) argued that belief structures are often too complex to be captured by an evaluative dimension like attitude. Others, in particular Triandis (1977), Breckler and Wiggins (1989a), and Ajzen (1991) have argued that attitude does not fully capture the affective influences on intention, and that a separate measure of feelings about the behaviour should be included (see Kashima & Gallois, this volume, for a discussion of this issue). In the study reported in this chapter, we examined the unmediated impact of the belief-based measures of both attitude and subjective norm on intention to use a condom and on condom use. We also included a separate measure of anticipated emotions about condom use, to assess the independent influence of affect.

Miniard and Cohen (1981) further argued that attitude and subjective norm are not causally independent, as implied in the theory of reasoned action, but rather are supported by similar and inter-related beliefs. Their observation was that the reactions of others, assumed to underlie subjective norm, are often considered an important consequence of behaviour, which, in turn, is the basis of the belief-based measure of attitude. Any interdependence that exists between attitude and norms is likely to intensify for co-operative behaviour, as the partner is both involved in the behaviour and is also a very important specific referent. We tried to deal with this issue by considering the perceived norm of the sexual partner separately from other normative beliefs.

Several other normative variables have been proposed as contributors to intention and behaviour, beyond the variables in TRA. One is personal norm. Measures of personal norm assess the person's own expectation about his or her behaviour, and are normally operationalised by request-ing the subject to indicate the likelihood of whether he or she should per-form the target behaviour. Initially, Fishbein (1967a) included this con-struct in his model, but later removed it as it was felt to be merely an al-ternative measure of intention (Ajzen & Fishbein, 1973). Several authors (Schwartz & Tessler, 1972; Budd & Spencer, 1984; Kashima & Kashima, 1988) however, have reported contrary findings (see Kashima & Gallois, this volume). In addition, Grube, Morgan and McGree (1986) argued that behavioural norm, or the perceived behaviour of significant others, is an important social influence on behaviour. They reasoned that the impor-tance of modelling for social behaviours (Bandura, 1982) constitutes a particularly potent determinant of the target behaviour they were study-ing, adolescent smoking (Jessor, 1976; Chassin, Presson, Sherman, Corty & Olshavsky, 1984). In the study reported in this chapter, as well as ex-amining the effects of behavioural norm, we assessed the influence of personal norm on intention after TRA variables had been accounted for.

Kashima *et al.* (1992) also argued for the inclusion of personal norm, behavioural norm, and partner norm, as well as interaction terms between attitude and these normative factors, in predicting intentions. Condom use is a cooperative behaviour that crucially involves the sexual partner. These authors proposed that the influence of the sexual partner is multi-faceted, and suggested three conceptually different types of influence that the sexual partner might have. The first is an effect on the actor's attitude, which should be more negative when the partner finds the behaviour unpleasant. Secondly, the sexual partner's view of the behaviour should strongly influence subjective norm, as he or she represents an important referent for this behaviour. Finally, because safer sexual behaviours are in general conditional on the partner's approval, the actor's belief about the partner acts as a facilitator or inhibitor of the decision to engage in the behaviour. This last type of influence is related to perceived control in the theory of planned behaviour (see below). Kashima *et al.* (in press) found that personal norm was a significant predictor of intention, and that partner norm was the strongest predictor of personal norm. The respondent's sense of obligation to use a condom was translated into the motivation to use one, and this obligation involved the wishes of the sexual partner.

TRA does not account well for behaviour that is not under volitional control. There are many goals that, although planned, do not come to fruition; many of these objectives are obstructed because requisite con-ditions have not been fulfilled. Ajzen's (1985) response to this problem was to adapt the theory to accommodate all behavioural domains. To al-low for influences inhibiting the enactment of intended behaviour, Ajzen introduced a new predictor, the degree of control an individual had over the target behaviour. The most immediate determinant of behaviour was then expressed as the strength of the person's attempt to perform it, given the degree of control the person has. Actual control is thus of pivotal importance, as it indicates the extent to which other behavioural determinants can be predictive of behaviour, but it is difficult to measure. Ajzen recommends the use of the individual's own perception of control over the behaviour as an estimate of this construct (but see Terry, this volume, for a discussion of the relation between perceived behavioural control and self-efficacy).

Ajzen and Madden (1986) suggested two ways the control variable could be operationalised and incorporated into the theory of reasoned action. The first involves a direct link between perceived behavioural control and intention. This path suggests that people who believe they have minimum resources or opportunities to perform behaviour are unlikely to form strong behavioural intentions to engage in that behaviour. The second posits a direct link between perceived behavioural control and behaviour. This path suggests that behaviour is a function of the motivation one has to enact behaviour and the degree of control one has, or believes one has, over the behaviour. Ajzen (1991) reviews research on both these propositions; the studies show some support for the influence of perceived behavioural control on intention and behaviour.

This version of TPB also implies an interaction effect; that is, behaviour is enacted only if both motivation *and* an adequate level of control are present. Schifter and Ajzen (1985), however, found that perceived control significantly predicted both intention to lose weight and actual weight loss, but the interaction of this measure and intention exhibited only a marginally significant effect in predicting weight loss. Ajzen and Madden (1986) reported similar results: a measure of perceived control was a significant predictor of both intention and behaviour, but there was an absence of any significant interaction effects.

On the other hand, Kashima *et al.* (in press) created a variable assessing the extent to which respondents had satisfied necessary behavioural conditions for using a condom, and thus actually had control over this behaviour. They coded subjects as not having a condom readily available, having a condom readily available but no agreement about condom use with the sexual partner, or having both a condom readily available and an agreement with the sexual partner. They found that, unlike the results of Ajzen and his colleagues described above, the interaction of their measure of behavioural control and behavioural intention was a significant predictor of behaviour.

Given all these considerations, we undertook a study to test the major predictions of the theory of reasoned action and the theory of planned behaviour in the context of safer sex. We were especially interested in the additional predictive power provided by adding measures of perceived behavioural control and satisfaction of behavioural conditions as a measure of actual behavioural control. In addition, we wished to examine the variables of personal, behavioural, and partner norms, possible interactions between normative variables and attitude, and the influence of affect in predicting attitude and intention.

## A Study of Condom Use

Following the theory of reasoned action, we expected that condom use would be predicted by intention, that intention would be predicted by attitude and subjective norm, and that attitude and subjective norm would be predicted by their respective belief-based measures. Given the findings of Liska (1984) and Bagozzi and Burnkrant (1979), however, we also explored the prediction that attitude regarding condom use would directly influence behaviour after intention was accounted for, and that belief-based measures of attitude would influence intention after the direct measure of attitude was accounted for. Following the theory of planned behaviour, we predicted that the addition of a measure of perceived control would increase the prediction of intention and behaviour, once measures of the theory of reasoned action had been accounted for. Furthermore, the interaction between intention and perceived control was expected to enhance the prediction of behaviour even further. Similar effects were also expected to appear with the addition of actual behavioural control, measured as satisfaction of behavioural conditions (Kashima *et al.*, in press). Finally, we expected that personal norm, behavioural norm, and partner norm, as well as interactions of attitude with personal norm, behavioural norm, and partner norm, would increase the prediction of intention, after measures of the theory of reasoned action were accounted for.

## Pilot Study

The theory of reasoned action makes it clear that the predictors of intention and behaviour must be relevant not only to the behaviour under investigation, but also to the specific population under study (see Fishbein & Middlestadt, 1989, for a recent discussion of this issue in the area of HIV prevention). In order to achieve this end, it is usually necessary to conduct pilot work (see Terry *et al.*, this volume). In this study, open-ended interviews with sexually-active undergraduate students (13 males and 8 females), aged between 17 and 21 years ($M = 18$), were used to identify the most common beliefs about the use of a condom during sexual intercourse, the relevant significant others who would approve or disapprove of the person using a condom, and the factors that would facilitate or inhibit the use of condoms during sexual intercourse. All respondents in the pilot study were exclusively heterosexual.

A content analysis of responses in the interviews was performed, in which similar responses were grouped together and labelled to capture the essence of the common theme. In addition, items that were salient in past research, but absent in the pilot study, were also included in the main questionnaire. In selecting these items, we made special use of the findings of Gallois, Kashima,*et al.* , (1992) and Kashima *et al.* (in press), who used similar subject samples and conducted similar pilot research.

## Main Study

### Participants

One hundred and sixty sexually-active undergraduate students (72 males and 88 females), aged between 17 and 21 years ($M = 18.4$), volunteered to participate in the main study for course credit. All subjects in this study described themselves as exclusively heterosexual in orientation, and 89 reported that they were in an exclusive and continuing sexual relationship. The follow-up questionnaire was completed by 140 (56 male, 84 female, 81 in continuing relationships) of the 160 respondents who completed the main questionnaire. Comparisons on salient measures showed no differences on the first questionnaire between those subjects who completed the second one and those who did not.

### Procedure

Participants in the study attended an initial session in the laboratory in groups of 10–50 people. During the session, they responded to a structured questionnaire (see below for details of the measures). They were told that in order to gain credit they also had to return a follow-up questionnaire at a later date. They were assured of anonymity and confidentiality. After instructions were given regarding the follow-up questionnaire, subjects began the main questionnaire, and completed it on average in twenty minutes. Subjects were asked to complete the follow-up questionnaire either immediately after the next time they had sexual intercourse or on a specified date (some five weeks after completing the main questionnaire), whichever came first. They were then requested to return the completed questionnaire to a common collection point.

## Measures

### Intention and Behaviour

The target behaviour for this study was: 'you or your partner wearing a condom the next time you have sexual intercourse.' The *intention* to use a condom was measured by three similar items: whether the subject planned to use a condom the next time he or she had intercourse, whether the subject intended to do so, and whether the subject would do so. All items were answered using a 7-point scale, anchored at "no, definitely not... (-3)," and "yes, definitely ... (+3)." Like other multiple measures, these items were interspersed throughout the questionnaire. The three items formed a reliable scale (alpha = .95), so an average score was used.

On the follow-up questionnaire, respondents were asked to 'indicate your intentions to use a condom at the time you completed the first questionnaire '(*memory of intentions* ). They were also asked to indicate their response to the statement 'you, or your partner, wore a condom' by ticking either yes (2) or no (1) (*behaviour* ). Those respondents who had not had sexual intercourse since completing the main questionnaire ($N = 20$) were asked to ignore this question. Responses to the behaviour item indicated that 52% of subjects who had intercourse did use a condom.

### Attitude

These measures were all taken from the initial questionnaire. A direct measure of *attitude* was obtained by means of a set of eight semantic differential-type scales, for the target question, 'you, or your partner, wearing a condom the next time you have sexual intercourse is...' On the basis of a factor analysis of these scales, ratings of five scales loading at .5 or higher on a single factor: favourable–unfavourable, useful–useless, good–bad, exciting–dull and pleasant–unpleasant, were averaged to obtain the direct measure of attitude.

*Belief-based measure of attitude* was determined from ratings of the probability of each of eight behavioural consequences elicited from the pilot study. These were reducing sexual pleasure, interrupting foreplay, reducing the intimacy of sex, delaying your or your partner's sexual climax, being offensive to you or your partner, disposing of a used condom, preventing you or your partner from becoming pregnant, and protecting against a sexually transmitted disease such as HIV. Each consequence was presented as a statement, followed by a 7-point scale anchored by 'extremely unlikely (-3)' and 'extremely likely (+3).' This likelihood rating was multiplied by the desirability of the consequence, which was obtained from a rating of each consequence on a 7-point scale anchored by 'extremely unpleasant (-3)' and 'extremely pleasant (+3).' The eight products of probability and desirability were summed to form the belief-based measure of attitude.

## Affect

The 20 items of the Positive Affect–Negative Affect Scale (PANAS: Watson & Tellegen, 1985) were included on the initial questionnaire. Subjects were asked to indicate the extent they would feel each emotion the next time they or their partner wore a condom for sexual intercourse. Half the PANAS items relate to positive emotions, and include enthusiastic, interested, excited, active, strong, proud, and attentive. The remaining items refer to negative emotions, and include scared, upset, nervous, ashamed, irritable, and hostile. Items were anchored on 5-point scales, from 'very slightly or not at all' to 'extremely.' A factor analysis indicated that a two-factor solution accounted for 34% of the variance, and that the PANAS items loaded as theorised. Therefore, two scores, on positive and negative affect, were obtained by averaging the ratings on relevant items.

## Norms

All normative measures came from the initial questionnaire. Two direct measures of *subjective norm* assessed the perceived degree of social pressure from significant others placed on the respondent to use a condom: how much 'people who are important to you think you should... (anchored from 'think I should not': -3, to 'think I should' +3),' and 'people who are important to you approve... (anchored from 'strongly disapprove:' -3, to ' strongly approve': +3).' These measures, also anchored on 7-point scales, were correlated ($r = .62$), and so were averaged into a single measure. The *belief-based measure of subjective norm* included normative beliefs for 5 significant others: friends, member of your church, parents, brother and/or sister, and your doctor, each rated on a 7-point scale. This rating was multiplied by a measure of the motivation to comply with the referent, rated on a 4-point scale ranging from 'not at all (0)' to 'very much (+3).'

A sixth normative belief about the sexual partner was extracted from the belief-based measure of subjective norm and used independently as *partner norm*. Three items (alpha = .78) were averaged to assess *personal norm* ; each of them asked subjects whether they thought they or their partner should wear a condom for the next sexual intercourse. Once again, these items were answered on 7-point scales.

Respondents were asked to estimate the percentage of times each of the specific significant others would engage in the target behaviour (*behavioural norm* ). A factor analysis of these items yielded two factors: one containing items about the perceived condom use of the respondent's doctor, parents, church associates and siblings, and the second tapping the perceived condom use of friends and the respondent's sexual partner. Items on these two factors were averaged to obtain two measures.

## *Behavioural Control*

The measure of *perceived behavioural control* was an average across six items on the initial questionnaire, selected through a factor analysis, all anchored on 7-point scales: the likelihood of the sexual partner wanting to use a condom next time, having a condom readily available next time, having an agreement to use a condom next time, forgetting to use a condom next time, the amount of control over using a condom for the next sexual intercourse, and the difficulty involved in using a condom for the next sexual intercourse.

On the follow-up questionnaire, the degree of *actual behavioural control* the respondent had over the target behaviour, measured as the satisfaction of behavioural conditions necessary for condom use (Kashima *et al.*, in press), was determined from responses to two items. Subjects scored lowest on this measure (a score of 1) when they reported that they did not have a condom readily available. Subjects who reported having a condom readily available, but who had not made an agreement with their sexual partner regarding the use of a condom, scored a 2 on this measure. Finally, those subjects who reported having a condom readily available and having an agreement with their sexual partner scored highest (3) on this measure.

## Results

A series of hierarchical multiple regression analyses were performed, in order to assess the effectiveness of the theory of reasoned action, the theory of planned behaviour, and the additional constructs in predicting intention and behaviour for condom use. The measure of actual behavioural control assessed the extent of satisfaction of behavioural conditions (condom availability and agreement with the sexual partner) at the time of the subsequent sexual contact. Consequently, this behavioural control measure was used to predict behaviour, but not intention, as measures of intention had been determined at an earlier date.

## *Predictions from the Theory of Reasoned Action*

An initial analysis assessed the association between the belief-based and direct measures of attitude and subjective norm. The correlations

Table 3.1. *Hierarchical Regression Analyses Predicting Intention and Behaviour: Theory of Reasoned Action*

| Criterion | Intention † | | Behaviour ‡ | | |
|---|---|---|---|---|---|
| Predictor | $R^2_{change}(F_{cha})$ | Beta | Predictor | $R^2_{change}(F_{cha})$ | Beta |
| Step 1 | .44(59.70)*** | | Step 1 | .56(149.10)*** | |
| Attitude | | .42*** | Intention | | .75*** |
| Subjective Norm | | .39*** | Step 2 | .02(2.29) | |
| Step 2 | .09(14.46)*** | | Intention | | .66*** |
| Attitude | | .30*** | Attitude | | .15 |
| Subjective Norm | | .23*** | Subjective Norm | | .01 |
| B–B§ attitude | | .12* | | | |
| B–B Sub. Norm | | .33*** | | | |

† $\underline{N}$ = 158.
‡ $\underline{N}$ = 118.
§ B–B Attitude and B–B Sub. Norm refer to the belief-based measures of attitude and subjective norm.
* $\underline{p}$ < .05; *** $\underline{p}$ < .001.

between the two measures of attitude ($r = .40$, $p < .001$) and those for subjective norm ($r = .56$, $p < .001$) supported the prediction that attitudes and subjective norms are determined by weighted behavioural beliefs and normative beliefs (Fishbein & Ajzen, 1975).

In a hierarchical multiple regression to test the influence of the immediate determinants of intention, the direct measures of attitude and subjective norm were entered on the first step. Table 1 summarises the results of this analysis. Consistent with the theory of reasoned action, both attitude and subjective norm contributed significantly to the prediction of intention. In the second step of the hierarchical regression, however, the significant increase in variance following introduction of the belief-based measures of subjective norm and attitude did not support the pathways in TRA. The impact of the belief-based measures of attitude and subjective norm on intention was not wholly mediated by the direct measures of attitude and subjective norm. Thus, the expectancy-value formulation of TRA did not capture attitude and subjective norm completely (see Ajzen, 1991, for a discussion of this issue).

When condom use at the next sexual encounter (behaviour) was the criterion, intention was entered on the first step and the result (see Table 1) showed that intention was strongly linked to behaviour (Fishbein &

Ajzen, 1975). The introduction of attitude and subjective norm on the second step ($R^2_{change} = .02$) and the belief-based measures on the third step ($R^2_{change} = .01$) indicated no significant contribution to prediction of behaviour from either the direct or the belief-based measures of attitude and subjective norm, as expected.

### *Predictions from the Theory of Planned Behaviour*

The measure of perceived behavioural control was added to the hierarchical regression predicting intention. Consistent with TPB, perceived control added significantly to prediction of intention, after attitude and subjective norm were controlled for (see Table 2 for a summary of the results of this analysis).

When actual behaviour was the criterion, the predicted improvement when the two measures of behavioural control were added to the equation did occur. Both perceived behavioural control and actual behavioural control were significant predictors of behaviour, once intention had been accounted for. The direct measures of attitude and subjective norm did not significantly increase the prediction of behaviour when added in the third 'step', nor did the introduction of belief-based measures entered on the final step.

Finally, in separate analyses to test for interaction effects between intention and control measures in the prediction of behaviour, the product of intention and each measure of behavioural control was entered after the main effect of the relevant control measure had been accounted for. To avoid multicolinearity effects between the main effect and interaction terms, products of standardised scores of intention and control measures were used to assess the latter. The interaction of intention and perceived behavioural control was significant ($R^2_{change} = .02$, $F_{change}$ (1, 116) = 4.71, $p < .05$, $\beta = .12$, $p < .05$). Similarly, the interaction of intention and actual behavioural control ($R^2_{change} = .03$, $F_{change}$ (1, 116) = 11.05, $p < .01$, $\beta = .21$, $p < .05$) added significantly to the prediction of behaviour, as proposed by TPB. Thus, the intention–behaviour link was stronger when either perceived or actual control was high than when control was low.

### *Additional Normative Variables*

The additional constructs described above, which have been shown to improve the predictive power of the theory of reasoned action in other behavioural domains, were incorporated in the last set of regression analyses. As the location of these additional variables in the causal path could

Table 3.2. *Hierarchical Regression Analyses Predicting Intention and Behaviour: Theory of Planned Behaviour*

| Criterion | Intention † | | Behaviour ‡ | | |
|---|---|---|---|---|---|
| Predictor | $R^2_{\text{change}}$ $(F_{\text{cha}})$ | Beta | Predictor | $R^2_{\text{change}}(F_{\text{cha}})$ | Beta |
| Step 1 | .44(59.70)*** | | Step 1 | .56(149.10)*** | |
| Attitude | | .42*** | Intention | | .75*** |
| Subjective Norm | | .39*** | Step 2 | .06(9.21)*** | |
| Step 2 | .03(4.96)* | | Intention | | .60*** |
| Attitude | | .39*** | Perceived Control | | .18** |
| Subjective Norm | | .37*** | Actual Control | | .15* |
| Perceived Control | | .14* | | | |

† $\underline{N}$ = 158.
‡ $\underline{N}$ = 118.
* $\underline{p}$ < .05; ** $\underline{p}$ < .01; *** $\underline{p}$<.001.

only be speculative, they were entered simultaneously in the hierarchical regression after known theoretical predictors (belief-based and direct measures of attitude and subjective norms) had been accounted for. As personal norm correlated very highly with intention ($r = .90$), it was excluded from further analyses.

In one analysis, the measures of behavioural norm, partner norm, and the interaction terms of attitude and each of these were considered. When both dimensions of behavioural norm were entered to predict intention, after attitude and subjective norm had been accounted for, only the second dimension (perceived behaviour of friends and the sexual partner) was significant ($\beta = .29, p < .001$). Therefore, only the second behavioural norm variable was included in an analysis with partner norm and the interaction terms.

This analysis showed a significant increment in explained variance after TRA variables were accounted for ($R^2_{change} = .10, F_{change}$ (4, 148) $= 10.26, p < .001$). Beta weights indicated that behavioural norm (.17, $p < .01$) and partner norm (.27, $p < .001$) were significant predictors of intention, but that neither interaction term was significant ($\beta = -.01$ and $-.10$, respectively). The influence of the sexual partner on the respondent's motivation to use a condom was particularly marked, and confirmed the special status of this variable in cooperative behaviour (Kashima *et al.*, in press). The perceived frequency with which sexual partners and peers use condoms also had a strong influence on intention, and confirmed the importance of modelling in shaping the intentions of adolescents and young adults. That the direct measure of subjective norm was now only marginally significant ($\beta = .12$, $p < .09$) indicated that partner norm and behavioural norm accounted for a substantial proportion of the variance of intention that had been accounted for by subjective norm.

The belief-based measure of subjective norm, partner norm, and behavioural norm for friends and the sexual partner all provided significant increases in the variance accounting for intention. Nonetheless, the simultaneous introduction of these measures into a hierarchical regression to predict behaviour did not produce a significant increase in variance, once intention, both measures of control, attitude and subjective norm had been accounted for ($R^2_{change} = .02$, $F_{change}$ (4, 108) = 1.67, ns). This implied that the influence on behaviour of the additional predictors of intention was mediated by intention and behavioural control.

### Affect

A hierarchical multiple regression analysis was conducted to test the prediction that anticipated positive or negative feelings about using a condom would influence intention to use one, beyond the influence of attitude and subjective norm. Results indicated that, once the theory of reasoned action variables were controlled for, positive and negative affect did not produce a significant increment in explained variance ($R^2_{change} = .004$, ns). On the other hand, when they were entered along with partner norm and the belief-based measures of attitude and subjective norm into a regression predicting the direct measure of attitude, both positive affect ($\beta = .20$, $p < .01$) and negative affect ($\beta = .16$, $p < .05$) were significant predictors ($R^2 = .33$, $p < .001$), as were partner norm ($\beta = .30$, $p < .001$) and the belief-based measure of attitude ($\beta = .20$, $p < .01$).

### Discussion

These results provide further support for the theories of reasoned action and planned behaviour. Table 3 presents a summary and indicates support for or challenge to both theories. First, there was a high correlation between behaviour and intention. The theoretical connection between these two constructs has sometimes been pointed to as the weak link in TRA (Ajzen & Fishbein, 1980). When the link is weak, the problem is due primarily to the susceptibility of intentions to change in the interval between the measurement of intentions and the performance of the behaviour. The results of this study indicate that this was not a problem here, as the intentions of these older adolescents to use condoms were stable and were likely to be acted upon, even up to five weeks after the original intention was expressed. Kashima *et al.* (1992) and Gallois, Kashima, *et al.* (1992), both found good prediction from intention to behaviour on condom use and other safer sex behaviours (see also Moore *et al.,* this volume). In fact, in general the relation between intention and HIV-preventive behaviours has been fairly strong (Fisher & Fisher, 1992). Other pathways specified in TRA were also supported. Both attitude and subjective norm were significant predictors of intention. In addition, the significant correlations between the belief-based measures and direct measures of attitude and subjective norm showed that beliefs provide the basis for the formation of attitudes and subjective norms, as Fishbein and Ajzen (1975) proposed.

The act of using a condom during sexual intercourse is not completely under volitional control. The cooperation of another person (the sexual partner) is required. Thus, one would expect that the addition of measures of behavioural control would improve prediction. This was borne out by the results. The measure of perceived control significantly enhanced the prediction of both intention and behaviour. Students were more highly motivated to use a condom, and more likely to actually to use one, if they felt that they had control over this behaviour. Similarly, they were more likely to use condoms if they had planned for this event by having a condom readily available and reaching an agreement with the sexual partner concerning condom use.

Our subjects appeared to have a good idea of the control they could exert over the use of a condom. This may be because a majority of these respondents were in a continuing sexual relationship, and consequently were more likely to have come to a prior arrangement regarding condom use. The addition of the interaction effects of intention by perceived control and intention by behavioural control also added significantly to the prediction of behaviour. Thus, for some respondents at least, the motivation to use a condom is not enough for the behavioural goal to be achieved. It is also necessary that they plan for this event (e.g., by obtaining a condom), or at least that they feel confident that they have control over condom use.

These results also suggest that measures of perceived control and actual control tap different aspects of control, as both measures independently influenced intention. Perceived control has been theorised as strongly related to self-efficacy (Ajzen, 1988, 1991). Actual control, on the other hand, is more related to external factors influencing the performance of behaviour, including the satisfaction of behavioural conditions necessary for it to occur (Kashima *et al.,* in press), and to planning for the behaviour. Whether perceived or actual behavioural control is more important for intentions to be carried out is likely to be largely determined by what the behaviour is and the context in which it occurs. The salient ingredients of control are also likely to differ depending on the context and on normative and cultural factors relevant to the behaviour. An important task for future

Table 3.3. *Summary of Results, Indicating Support for the Theory of Reasoned Action (TRA), the Theory of Planned Behaviour (TPB), or Extensions to These Theories (EXT)*

| Criterion | Predictor and result | Support |
|---|---|---|
| Behaviour | Intention shows strong relationship | TRA |
| | Perceived and actual behavioural control predict independently, after intention is controlled for | TPB |
| | Perceived and actual behavioural control both interact with intention to enhance prediction, after main effects are controlled for | TPB |
| | Attitude and subjective norm do not predict, after intention is controlled for | TRA |
| | Behavioural norm, partner norm, and belief-based attitude and sub. norm do not predict, after TRA variables are controlled for | TRA |
| Intention | Attitude and subjective norm are significant predictors | TRA |
| | Perceived behavioural control predicts, after TRA variables are controlled for | TPB |
| | Belief-based attitude and sub. norm predict, after attitude and subjective norm are controlled for | TPB/EXT |
| | Partner norm, behavioural norm for friends and partner predict, after TRA variables are controlled for | EXT |
| | Anticipated positive and negative affect do not predict, after TRA variables are controlled for | TRA |
| Attitude | Belief-based attitude predicts | TRA |
| | Partner norm predicts | EXT |
| | Positive and negative affect predict | TRA |
| Subjective Norm | Belief-based subjective norm predicts | TRA |

research is to explore the ways in which behavioural control functions in determining whether people do what they intend to do.

There was no support for the direct effect of attitude on behaviour, once intention had been accounted for. The relative stability of intentions in this study is probably the reason why attitude did not directly predict condom use. In other behavioural domains, the relative instability of intentions, in comparison to attitudes, has often resulted in a significant direct attitudinal influence on behaviour (e.g., Liska, 1984). Further research is needed to establish what circumstances must apply for attitude to affect behaviour directly.

Despite the strong empirical support for TRA and TPB, neither theory was completely supported. Contrary to the prediction of Fishbein and Ajzen (1975), the belief-based measure of subjective norm directly influenced intentions after the direct measure of this construct had been accounted for. A possible explanation for this result is that global assessment of subjective norm involves more complex cognitive processing, and could consequently yield less reliable or less sensitive measures, than the assessment of the social pressures exerted by individual referents. Similarly, the significant direct effect of the belief-based measure of attitude on intention provides support for the view that belief structures are too complex to be completely captured by a predominantly evaluative dimension like attitude (Ajzen, 1991; Bagozzi & Burnkrant, 1979).

In two studies (see Warwick *et al.*, this volume; Terry, this volume), Terry and her colleagues also found that the belief-based measure of subjective norm predicted intention after attitude and subjective norm were controlled for. Taken together, these findings show that belief-based measures of attitude and norms, which encapsulate the specific costs, benefits, and reactions of significant others for the participants and the behaviour under study, contribute to the intention to use a condom in a way that is not mediated entirely by simpler measures of attitude and subjective norm. This reinforces Fishbein and Middlestadt's (1989) point that the local characteristics of a population with respect to a particular behaviour must be considered in any attempt to predict intention. It also indicates that education for safer sex needs to take account of the specific features of the target group.

The introduction of additional predictors of intention provides a challenge to the established formulation of the theory of reasoned action. One, personal norm, did not perform as predicted by Budd and Spencer (1984) and Kashima *et al.* (1992). Personal norm appeared in this study to be simply another measure of intention. It may well be that personal norms are distinguishable from intention in other behavioural domains, or for a different group of subjects. For these students, however, the moral imperative to use a condom was easily transferred into the motivation to do so.

That the measure of behavioural norm for doctors, parents, siblings and church members is a poor predictor of intention was perhaps to be expected. The use of condoms as an HIV-preventive measure (or indeed for contraception) might not be perceived by unmarried young people as especially salient for the majority of these referents, because of their involvement in long-standing monogamous relationships. The interaction of attitude and larger social norms did not really influence intention, as researchers on adolescent behaviour have claimed (Grube *et al.,* 1986; Chassin *et al.,* 1984). The impact of the behavioural norm relating to peers and the sexual partner, however, is also proposed by these same authors. The presence of peer models appears to be as influential in shaping intentions to use a condom as subjective norms are.

The impact of affect, as distinct from attitude, was not great for this sample. As Fishbein and Ajzen (1975) propose, affect was significantly related to attitude, but did not predict intention once attitude and subjective norm had been controlled for. The extent to which affect must be considered in predicting intention and behaviour is still a matter for some debate (see Kashima & Gallois, this volume). The behaviour under study is no doubt important; in this case, the belief-based measure of attitude contained many highly emotive elements. In addition, the way affect is measured may have an important impact on the results. In this study, subjects rated the feelings they anticipated when the behaviour was performed. A rating of the emotion they felt when thinking about the behaviour now may have produced different results. Nevertheless, for this group of students, TRA variables seem to be sufficient to capture the impact of affect.

Finally, the social factor that demonstrated the strongest individual influence on intention was the norm of the sexual partner. The expectations of the sexual partner strongly influenced the respondent's intention to use a condom; nor was the influence of the sexual partner restricted to the direct effect on intention. Antecedents to intention, especially attitude, were also affected by partner norm. Additionally, this partner term correlated significantly with the measures of perceived control ($r = .46$) and behavioural control ($r = .40$), which implies substantial influence over these predictors of behaviour as well. The dimension of behavioural norm associated with the sexual partner and friends was also a significant predictor of intentions, which indicates once again how pervasive an influence the sexual partner has in shaping the intentions and behaviour of students about condom use. The impact partner norm has in explaining and predicting the cooperative behaviour of condom use indicates that it should be included as a separate variable for the prediction of all cooperative behaviours.

The impact of partner norm on attitude also supports the research finding that the reactions of others are often an important influence on attitudes. In this study, not only was partner norm correlated with attitude, but many of the items on the belief-based measure of attitude confirmed the importance of the partner. For instance, 'interrupting foreplay,' 'reducing the intimacy of sex,' and in particular, 'being offended by, or offending your partner' all convey the respondent's concern about the partner's reaction to the use of a condom. There is little doubt that in a cooperative behaviour like condom use, belief-based measures of attitude and subjective norm are less likely to be independent. The theories of reasoned action and planned behaviour may need some revision to accommodate the interdependence of these measures in cooperative behaviour.

One possible criticism of our results is that the consistency between the measures of the constructs used is an artefact of asking respondents to assess them all at the same time. The argument is that the respondents are likely to remember their past responses and strive to be consistent when answering subsequent measures. The accurate recall of intentions up to five weeks after the main study, and the strong correlation of intentions and subsequent behaviour over the same period, however, imply that these constructs are stable over time. Nonetheless, research can usefully investigate the extent to which assessing measures at different times influences the internal consistency of the model. In studies that have done this for safer sex and condom use, results have generally shown a good relationship between attitude and subjective norm, intention, and behaviour. For example, Gardner (1992) found strong predictive relationships among these variables when they were measured in three phases at monthly intervals, for the behaviour of sexual intercourse.

Generally, our results support the view that the theory of reasoned action adequately predicts condom use, although the extended TPB model incorporating measures of control improved prediction. Perceived and actual control, in addition, were independent influences on behaviour, reinforcing the logic of constructing measures for both of them. It is also clear that the addition of other factors to these theories further enhances their predictive power. In particular, future researchers should consider including such social factors as behavioural norms and a measure of the perceived social pressure of a partner in any cooperative behaviour. Consideration should also be given to accommodating and exploring the direct influence which belief-based measures have on intention in other behavioural domains. Theory-testing research can be performed to determine the underpinning of these significant additional factors, and to locate them in the causal chain to predict behaviour.

# 4

# Predicting AIDS-Preventive Behaviour Among Adolescents

SUSAN M. MOORE

*Monash University, Melbourne, Australia*

DOREEN A. ROSENTHAL

*La Trobe University, Melbourne, Australia*

JENNIFER BOLDERO

*The University of Melbourne, Melbourne, Australia*

## Adolescent Sexual Behaviour Today

Adolescence is a time of experimentation, of making major strides toward discovery of self. In this search for identity, dealing with sexuality is a crucial task. This is even more true for today's youth than for previous generations because of the difficulty of reaching economic independence in a society where job training is long and often unpaid, and youth employment rates are low. The badge of adulthood gained by earning one's own living does not occur for many young people until well into their 20s, so that adolescents must find other avenues for becoming adult. Loss of virginity is one such avenue and, as we shall see, this milestone is happening earlier, and with greater social sanction, than in the past.

Research suggests that there has been a substantial increase in adolescent sexual activity in recent decades. In the early 1960s, Schofield (1968) found in a major study of 2000 British 15 to 19 year-olds that only 20% of boys and 12% of girls had had sexual intercourse. Ten years later, over 50% of teenagers aged 16–19 years reported that they were not virgins (Farrell, 1978). In two national surveys of young American women, Zelnik, Kantner and Ford (1981) found in 1971 that 30% of 15- to 19-year-old women reporting having premarital sexual intercourse, this number rising to 41% by 1976. Current estimates are that about 60% of 18-year-olds are sexually active, a figure that is consistent across many Western nations, although there is substantial variation between groups (Hofferth & Hayes, 1987; Rosenthal, Moore & Brumen, 1990).

A trend toward earlier sexual initiation as well as increased rates of sexual activity is also evident across most Western countries (Goldman & Goldman, 1988). In Sweden, the average age of first sexual intercourse dropped from 19 to 16 years in forty years. In the United States there has been a similar shift, with a dramatic rise in the 1970s of the number of younger females—especially whites—experiencing sex. In 1981–2, 40% of 17-year-olds in an Australian study reported that they were sexually active (Australian Institute of Family Studies, 1981–2), but by 1988 60% reported they were non-virgins at that age (Goldman & Goldman, 1988). Ford and Morgan (1989) showed that, for British teenagers, about 9% reported their age of first intercourse as 13 years or earlier, 40% as 15 years, and 63% were non-virgins by age 16.

Adolescents are also experimenting more with sexual activity than did their parents. Young people are engaging in a wider variety of sexual behaviours than before, and with more partners. The practice of oral sex (both fellatio and cunnilingus) is now widespread among adolescents, and there seems to be a shift in formerly negative attitudes to these less traditional practices (Moore & Rosenthal). For example, 33% of British teenagers reported they would engage in oral sex with a casual partner (Ford & Morgan, 1989). Among 18-year-old tertiary students in a recent Australian study, 46% of boys and 28% of girls had engaged in oral sex with casual partners, while corresponding figures for regular partners were 56% and 58%, respectively (Rosenthal *et al.*, 1990). In a younger sample of Australian 16-year-olds, Buzwell, Rosenthal and Moore (1992) found the figures for some subgroups were even higher, reaching 100% for homeless boys, with both casual and regular partners. The incidence of anal sex in these two studies was also high for some groups. It was relatively uncommon among the 18-year-olds, but 25% of homeless 16-year-old boys and girls reported that they had engaged in anal intercourse with casual or regular partners (or both). Unprotected anal intercourse is reported by more than 20% of heterosexual teenage girls attending clinics in New York and San Francisco (Moscicki, Millstein, Broering & Irwin, 1988).

Earlier sexual initiation, combined with the worldwide trend for marrying later or not at all, leads to a situation in which it is likely that many if not most young people will experience more than one sexual partner in their teens and early twenties. Sorenson (1973) coined the phrase 'serial monogamy' to describe the common situation among sexually active adolescents of maintaining a relatively regular and faithful relationship with a partner over a period of time, then moving on to a new sexual partner. Relationships may last from a few weeks to a number of years, yet even when they are short-lived they are interpreted by the protagonists as 'steady'. Reiss (1967) described this pattern as 'permissiveness with affection', noting that young people who have a number of sexual partners over their adolescent years are unlikely to describe themselves or their similarly behaved peers as promiscuous, so long as their relationships, while they last, are committed and monogamous.

Our own studies indicate that adolescents are highly approving of sex outside marriage within this caring context, but that casual encounters are certainly not unknown and, in fact, relatively common among certain groups of young people, such as the homeless. Further, casual sexual encounters are more approved of for teenage boys by both girls and boys alike, and teenage girls are more likely to describe as 'steady' or 'regular' relationships that boys perceive as casual (Moore & Rosenthal, 1992; Rosenthal & Moore, 1991). In the same studies, girls expected themselves and their partners to be faithful in long term relationships, and this pattern was consistent across a number of age and ethnic groups tested. Among the boys however, while most (86%) expected their partner to be faithful, expectations for their own behaviour were far less stringent and varied markedly across groups. On average, 75% of young men said they would try to be monogamous in a steady relationship, but for some groups the figure was considerably lower. Taken together, these factors (approval of serial monogamy among teenagers, moderate acceptance of casual relationships and unfaithfulness at least among boys, and the long time span likely between beginning sexual activity and finally 'settling down' with one steady partner), mean that adolescents and young people today are likely to have many more sexual partners on average than did their parents.

Of course caution is necessary in accepting too readily the evidence for increased teenage sexual activity and variety. With attitudes to sex now more liberal than in previous decades, adolescents of today may be more willing to admit to these behaviours than were teenagers from previous generations. Nevertheless the generality of these findings across studies in different countries, using different samples and different data gathering strategies, suggests that real changes have occurred.

Sexual experimentation among adolescents is traditionally considered in a negative light by adults, yet it clearly provides the potential for some developmentally desirable outcomes. Aside from being a pleasurable activity in itself, sex is one of life's most important steps toward independence and can contribute to an individual's sense of self or identity. Experimentation can be considered as part of the training for maturity and participating in adult relationships. Sex can enable people to feel lovable and provides the opportunity to express love, to enhance closeness and sharing and to experience intimacy. But for these positive outcomes to occur, the circumstances must be right. The individual needs to feel ready for sex and not forced or exploited emotionally or physically. Further, it is important that if adolescents engage in sex, they do so safely without unwanted outcomes, such as unplanned or too early pregnancy, or a sexually transmitted disease, particularly HIV/AIDS.

Unfortunately, these ideal conditions for experimentation are frequently not present. Many young people are at risk of AIDS and other STDs because of their sexual activity. Although the number of adolescents among diagnosed HIV cases is low (about 1% in Western countries), more than 20% of people with AIDS are in their 20s. Given the long lead time from infection to symptomatic AIDS, the inescapable conclusion is that many were infected in their teens. Reports from New York indicate that heterosexual transmission of HIV is more widespread among adolescents than adults, leading one researcher to question whether adolescents are the 'next wave' of the AIDS epidemic (Hein, 1989a). There is also evidence of a high incidence of other sexually transmitted diseases among adolescents and young adults. These conditions, though not life threatening, have serious consequences including the potential of infertility or cervical cancer in women.

As we have seen, young people are likely to be sexually active by mid-to-late teens, to engage in high risk sexual behaviours involving penetration and exchange of bodily fluids and to change partners at regular intervals. They are not always faithful to their regular or steady partners. All of these activities could be relatively safe, however, if young people implemented the most basic precaution by using condoms consistently when engaging in penetrative sex. There is clear evidence that this is not happening in Australia, Britain or the United States (e.g., Abrams, Abraham, Spears & Marks, 1990; Hein, 1989b; Kegeles, Adler & Irwin, 1988; Moore & Rosenthal, 1993; Rosenthal *et al.*, 1990; Rollins, 1989; Turtle *et al.*, 1989). Condoms are still used infrequently by many sexually active youth, and not at all by some. For example, in our study of older adolescents aged 17–20 years, only one-third of those who had had intercourse with a casual partner always used a condom, and the proportion dropped to one-fifth for those having sex with a regular partner (Rosenthal *et al.*, 1990). What factors underlie these risky sexual practices?

## The Search for Predictors of Risky Sexual Behaviour

Risky (unprotected) sexual behaviour among adolescents does not occur for the most part as the result of ignorance about HIV, its effects and the role of condoms in its prevention. Early surveys of adolescents' knowledge of HIV transmission (e.g., DiClemente, Zorn & Temoshok, 1986; Strunin & Hingson, 1987) suggested that substantial numbers of teenagers had misconceptions about the ways in which HIV is transmitted and that these misconceptions were most apparent among minority group youths and those who were poorly educated. But by 1988, it seemed that almost all the American youths surveyed had learned the major modes of HIV transmission and misconceptions had largely diminished (Strunin & Hingson, 1992). Australian youth, too, seem well informed about HIV/AIDS, with recent studies showing most adolescents to have reasonable factual knowledge about how HIV is transmitted and the value of condoms as a protection against this virus (e.g., Rosenthal *et al.,* 1990; Turtle *et al.,* 1989).

Several researchers have shown that higher levels of knowledge are substantially unrelated to safer sex practices (Keller, Schleifer, Bartlett & Johnson, 1988; Richard & van der Pligt, 1991; Turtle *et al.,* 1989). In our Victorian study of 18-year-olds, greater knowledge did not result in safer sex (Rosenthal *et al.,* 1990). A recent study of adolescents over one year in the United States (Kegeles, Adler, & Irwin, 1988) yielded the alarming result that knowledge about condoms and their effectiveness as a barrier to HIV transmission did not result in greater intention to use them, nor in greater actual use.

The gap between knowledge and behaviour is consistent with Abbott's (1988) finding that 99% of the young women she surveyed thought that because of AIDS they would need to make behavioural changes, but half of the sexually active sample had made no such changes in actuality. Another study which bears on the knowledge-behaviour link is that of Turtle and her colleagues (Turtle *et al.,* 1989), who gave parallel sets of questionnaires to two groups of students selected at random, one asking about HIV beliefs, the other about sexual behaviours. They found a marked discrepancy between belief and action. For example, 92% of their 'beliefs' group answered 'always' to the question 'Should you use a condom as a safeguard against AIDS in vaginal sex with a casual partner?.' In the 'behaviours' group, only 26% had actually done so. Knowledge about AIDS and HIV transmission is of course a vital first step in protection against the virus, but it appears that knowledge is a necessary, but not sufficient, cause for action.

What about the role of attitudes? With consistent condom use a vital behaviour in limiting the sexual transmission of HIV, it is important to assess adolescent attitudes to this contraceptive, and to examine the relationship between attitudes and use. Among teenagers attitudes to condoms vary. For some, the use of condoms (or in fact any contraceptive) is inconsistent with their moral values, or with the view that sex should be spontaneous and unpremeditated. For others, using a condom implies a lack of trust in one's partner's fidelity or sexual history. Some young people find their use 'messy' or 'unnatural.' Still others say they interfere with the enjoyment of sex, referring to the use of condoms as being akin to 'having a shower in a raincoat' or 'washing your feet with your socks on.' While dislike of condoms is reported by many young people (e.g., Chapman & Hodgson, 1988; Holland, Ramazanoglu, Scott, Sharpe & Thompson, 1991; Worth, 1989), there is evidence that some of these negative attitudes are dissipating, and that the benefits of condoms are being recognised (Chapman, Stoker, Ward, Porritt & Fahey, 1990; Klitsch, 1990; Moore & Rosenthal, 1991c).

Links between attitudes to condoms and their use have been demonstrated, but for the most part correlations are low. Moore and Rosenthal (1991c) isolated four attitudinal dimensions relating to AIDS precautions—antiprecautions, risk denial, abrogation of responsibility and fatalism—and found that these accounted for a significant but small proportion of the variance of condom use (less than 10%) in a sample of 1000 sexually active 17- to 20-year-olds. Richard and van der Pligt (1991) reported that attitudes to condom use were predictive of actual use in a sample of monogamous adolescents but not in a group with multiple sexual partners. They suggest that teenagers who believe themselves to be in a monogamous relationship and who have negative attitudes to condoms assume that they can, with safety, dispense with this precaution, a choice not open to teenagers with multiple partners.

Thus attitudes and knowledge, while important preconditions of adolescent safer sex behaviour, obviously do not tell the whole story. If we are to plan educational and public health interventions to influence condom use, we need to go beyond these two variables. The theory of reasoned action (Ajzen & Fishbein, 1980; Fishbein & Ajzen, 1975) potentially provides a more comprehensive framework for understanding teenagers' sexual behaviour, involving as it does a complex of predictors, which includes but is not limited to attitudes and beliefs (see Terry *et al.*, this volume). Although past studies of adolescent contraceptive use have shown elements of *irrationality* and *non-planning* (Morrison, 1985), we were interested in the question of whether the threat of AIDS has brought to bear a more considered approach among teenagers to their implementation of sexual activity. Further, the theory incorporates not only knowledge (behavioural beliefs) and attitudinal components, but also perceived norms and the motivation to comply with the norms of significant others. In adolescence, parent and peer influences have long been considered by developmental theorists as strong motivators of behaviour. Extrapolating from research on other teenage behaviours to condom use, we can hypothesise that the perceived norms of these salient others will influence the uptake of safer sex among adolescents.

The Fishbein and Ajzen (1975) model also incorporates the role of intention as an important intermediate step between attitudes, norms and behaviours. Two studies of contraceptive use (specifically the birth control pill) by Jaccard and Davidson (1972; Davidson & Jaccard, 1975) have already demonstrated a strong relationship between intention and action among samples of both college women and married women with children. Following Fishbein and Ajzen (1975), we sought to explore among adolescents the role of intention in predicting the use of a specific contraceptive, the condom, which is also a protection against HIV.

Finally, although aspects of the Fishbein and Ajzen (1975) model have been tested in other research (e.g., Barling & Moore, 1990; Kashima, Gallois & McCamish, in press; Pleck, Sonenstein & Ku, 1990) no study has examined the predictions of the model fully in the domain of adolescent condom use. Thus, there is still the question of whether attitudes, subjective norms and intention all have direct effects on condom, use or whether intention alone has a direct effect on behaviour, with the effects of attitudes and subjective norms being indirect, through intention. The study described below, some results of which have been reported elsewhere (Boldero, Moore, & Rosenthal, 1992), addresses these concerns.

### A Test of the Theory of Reasoned Action

Collecting data about sexual behaviour presents difficulties because of our inability to observe directly the behaviour in question, so that we are dependent on self reports. These may be distorted because of respondents' reluctance to reveal such private information, and the social desirability biases to which memory is prone. In the study to be described, we attempted to minimise these problems by ensuring anonymity and focussing our attention on behaviour during a very recent sexual encounter (see Nucitora *et al.*, this volume).

We asked sexually active student volunteers in the 17–20 years age group, recruited by advertisements at a tertiary campus, to respond to a questionnaire about past sexual behaviour. The questionnaire assessed general attitudes to condoms (perceived benefits and disadvantages) using a scale developed by Chapman *et al.* (1990). Also assessed were the variables comprising a test of the theory of reasoned action in predicting condom use as HIV protection. These variables were behavioural beliefs about condoms as protection from HIV/AIDS (behavioural beliefs), the perceived importance of being protected from the disease (outcome evaluation), beliefs about the importance the respondents' families and friends place on using condoms (normative beliefs) and the motivation to comply with the wishes of these referent groups (motivation to comply). These particular referent groups were selected for study, because they have been shown to be important in adolescent decision making about HIV/AIDS precautions (Moore & Rosenthal, 1991b). The behavioural belief and outcome evaluation items were combined in the manner specified by Ajzen and Fishbein (1980) to produce a measure of specific attitudes to condoms as protection from HIV/AIDS, while the normative belief and motivation to comply items were similarly combined to give a subjective norm measure. In addition, this questionnaire measured intention to use a condom during the participant's next sexual encounter (prior intention). Respondents were then given a second questionnaire, in a sealed envelope, which they were instructed to complete and return within 24 hours of the next time they had sex. In this questionnaire, details of the particular encounter were sought, including whether or not a condom was used.

We were aware that many factors have the potential to interfere with an individual's 'good' intentions to use a condom. Ajzen and Madden (1986) and Kashima *et al.* (in press) have discussed this issue in terms of the extent to which the behavioural context allows for individual control. The context in this case includes all events and circumstances which occur immediately before or during the sexual encounter. We considered the following factors as potentially important: type of relationship between the two partners (Rosenthal *et al.*, 1990), the use of drugs or alcohol (Stall, McKusick, Wiley, Coates & Ostrow, 1986), level of sexual arousal (Goggin, 1989), the degree of concern with infection from HIV or other sexually transmissible diseases and the extent to which partners had communicated about condom use (Kashima *et al.*, in press), and, as a necessary condition, whether a condom was actually available during the encounter. Further details of the measures included in each questionnaire are available in Boldero *et al.* (1992).

To encourage honesty, the 223 participants who completed the first questionnaire were asked to return the second questionnaire within six weeks even if they had not had a sexual encounter during that period. Those who did so were paid whether or not they had filled in the survey. Participants used a code name on the two measuring instruments so that these could be matched and to ensure anonymity. Payment was made by an administrative assistant unaware of the nature of the study. She alone had access to the list of names and addresses of participants linked with their code names. As questionnaires were returned, one of the researchers notified the administrator of the code name, so that payment could ensue. It was hoped that this complex system would convince participants that their responses were completely confidential and anonymous, and that this assurance would encourage truthfulness in responding.

In all, 144 participants (49 males and 95 females) completed both parts of the study. There was no difference in the proportion of males and females completing the requirements of the study when compared with those not completing, nor were there any differences in prior intention to use a condom. The final sample were, however, slightly older than the 'drop-outs.'. Age was the only variable measured by Questionnaire 1 on which there was a significant difference between the final sample and the subjects who completed only the first questionnaire.

As a group, participants who completed both questionnaires were moderately sexually experienced (mean number of past sexual partners = 2.8), held relatively positive attitudes to condoms and had strong subjective norms about the value of their use. In addition, the majority (64%) indicated on the first questionnaire that they intended to use a condom during their next sexual encounter (prior intention), 11% indicated that they did not intend to use a condom and the remainder were unsure.

During the specific sexual encounter targeted in the second questionnaire 114 respondents (79%) had a condom available, while 94 (81% of these and 65% of the total sample) reported using it. Direct communication with partners about using condoms occurred for 29% of subjects, while 42% communicated only indirectly. The remaining respondents (29%) did not discuss using a condom, either directly or indirectly. Thus the present sample, for the most part, intended to use a condom, communicated with a partner about its use, had one available and used it.

For 63 respondents, the encounter was with a regular partner (a monogamous relationship of more than 3 months duration), 20 had an encounter with a potentially regular partner (a monogamous relationship of less than 3 months duration) and the remaining 61 respondents had what they described as a casual relationship (with someone whom they had known for a short time or just met). On average, the sample was highly sexually aroused (mean 17.0, possible range 4–20), unaffected by alcohol or drugs (mean 2.6, possible range 2–8) and moderately concerned about HIV and other sexually transmissible diseases (mean 4.7, possible range 2–10).

As we have discussed, the main purpose of this study was to examine the predictive validity of the theory of reasoned action and to assess the effects of situational contextual factors on condom use. Because of this we were interested not only in the factors which predicted actual behaviour, but also in those which predicted intention. As intention can change over time, we assessed it at two points, 'prior intention' in Questionnaire 1, and 'intention in action' in Questionnaire 2. This latter measure gave an indication of the adolescent's intention to use a condom at the beginning of the particular sexual encounter targeted. The prior intention measure, assessed at an earlier time, asked about the participant's next sexual encounter before he or she knew with certainty any of the situational details of this encounter, for example, who the partner would be or whether alcohol would be used.

## Predictors of Intentions and Action

To examine the model we constructed hierarchical regression models in which the factors at the lowest level of the model, namely attitudes to condoms as protection against HIV, general attitudes to condoms and subjective norms, were entered into the first step of the analyses followed by those variables at higher levels. Included in first level analyses were the demographic factors of age, sex and number of previous sexual partners.

The variables next entered were prior intention, communication with a partner about condom use, condom availability, type of relationship between respondents and their partners and concern with HIV and other STDs. The last variables entered (when appropriate) were intention in action and the contextual factors of level of sexual arousal and the effects of alcohol on respondents and their partners. Because respondents had indicated their intentions, in both cases, on a scale ranging across degrees of intention it was possible to use multiple linear regression for these analyses. However for the prediction of actual condom use we used logistic regression because the dependent variable (condom use) was dichotomous (yes or no). In all, three regression analyses were performed, one for the prediction of prior intention, one for the prediction of intention in action, and one for the prediction of actual behaviour.

For prior intention, the model tested included only a single step. The measures of attitudes to condoms as HIV protection, and subjective norms, along with two more general measures of attitudes to condoms (benefits and disadvantages) and the demographic factors of age, sex and number of previous sexual partners, accounted for only 27% of the variance in prior intention, although the regression equation was statistically significant. Of these factors, only the general attitude measures and number of previous sexual partners were independent predictors of prior intention. Strong prior intentions to use a condom were predicted by perceiving greater benefits and fewer disadvantages of condoms and by having a greater number of previous sexual partners. The interesting feature of these results is the failure of both theory of reasoned action concepts (attitudes to condom use as HIV protection and subjective norm) to predict prior intentions. One possible reason for this is that the adolescent respondents for the most part held very positive attitudes towards condoms as HIV protection and had strong subjective norms concerning condom use. As a result there was little variability in measures of these factors. However the fact that general attitude measures were predictive of prior intention highlights the importance of the advantages and disadvantages of condoms in general (not only their HIV-protective function) as determinants of condom use.

The twelve possible predictors of intention in action (those entered in the first multiple regression, together with prior intention, condom availability, type of partner, communication with partner and concern about HIV and STDs) yielded a significant regression equation which accounted for 29% of the variance of this second intention measure. Only two factors, communication with a partner about condom use and prior intention, were significant independent predictors. Those who communicated directly with their partner about using a condom were more likely to hold a strong intention to use one immediately before the sexual encounter, as were those holding a strong intention somewhat prior to the encounter. Interestingly, while the two intention measures were significantly correlated ($r = 0.27$, $p < .05$), only 7% of the variance in the second measure (intention in action) was accounted for by the first measure (prior intention). Thus the respondents' intentions changed over time. One possible reason for this instability in intentions is that the respondents were young, so that their intentions about sexual behaviour may not have been stable or clear because of their developmental status and lack of experience. Another possibility is that, because a high percentage of respondents were not in regular, stable relationships, they may not have established clear patterns of sexual behaviour.

The hierarchical logistic regression analysis showed that prior intention, communication about condom use, condom availability, intention in action, level of sexual arousal and perception of the disadvantages of condoms were all significant predictors of actual condom use. Respondents holding strong intentions both sometime prior to, and immediately before, the sexual encounter were more likely to use condoms as, obviously, were those who had a condom available. Likewise, communicating with a partner directly about using condoms was predictive of their use. Conversely, those who perceived greater disadvantages of using condoms and those who were more sexually aroused were less likely to engage in safer sexual practices.

Taking the results of these three regression analyses, it is possible to construct a picture of both the direct and indirect effects of the components of the theory of reasoned action and situational contextual variables on condom use. This is presented in Figure 1 and demonstrates that sexual arousal, condom availability and communication with a partner about using condoms (all contextual factors) had direct effects on condom use, as did perceiving the disadvantages of condoms, and the two intention measures (prior intention and intention in action). In addition, communication and prior intention had indirect effects on behaviour via their effect on intention in action. General attitudes toward condoms (their perceived benefits and disadvantages) and number of previous sexual partners affected behaviour indirectly through their influence on prior intentions.

Overall, therefore, there was limited support for the theory of reason action in predicting safer sex behaviour with this sample of older adolescents. The only predictor of condom use from the model was intention, there being no direct link between condom use and either attitudes to condoms as HIV protection or subjective norms. Furthermore, neither norms nor the specific attitude measure predicted prior intention or intention in action. However, perceiving the disadvantages in general of using condoms was both a direct and an indirect predictor of condom use, and perceived benefits of condoms also had an indirect effect on behaviour via the effect on prior intention.

Thus, while the present results are consistent with previous studies which have examined aspects of the theory of reasoned action (e.g., Bar-

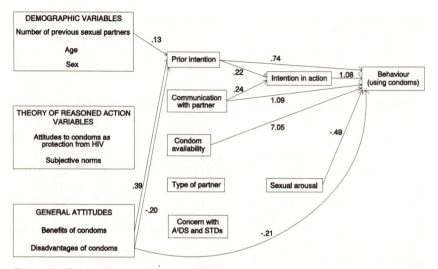

FIG. 1. Predicted and obtained direct and indirect influences on condom use (arrows indicate significant influences). Note: coefficients for the prediction of prior intention and intention in action are beta weights, and coefficients for the prediction of behaviour are regression coefficients from logistic regression.

ling & Moore, 1990; Kashima *et al.,* in press; Pleck *et al.,* 1990), the predictive ability of the model is clearly different from that of other studies, particularly those which have examined the use of other contraceptives. For example, Davidson and Jaccard (1975; Jaccard & Davidson, 1972) found that attitudes to the birth control pill, subjective norms about its use and intention to use it all related strongly to actual use. This was clearly not the case for the use of condoms in the young sample we surveyed. Why was there a difference? Because of their youth and inexperience, these teenagers' intentions about using condoms may not have been stable or well thought out. Their relationships, too, were relatively unstable, with the norms surrounding their sexual encounters unclear because they frequently did not know their partners well enough to predict their reactions to condoms. Equally, it could be that the situation surrounding condom use operates to inhibit rational control. Those studies which have supported the model are of contraceptive behaviour over which individuals have a great deal of personal control, such as the use of the contraceptive pill. Individuals can make a commitment to using the pill well before a sexual encounter, and its use is independent of any specific encounter. Thus it is an action that may be completely private and not involve a sexual partner. Condom use is, however, not a private act and involves partners communicating and, tacitly at least, agreeing about their use. Many young people have considerable difficulty dealing with condoms, either purchasing them, discussing them with a partner, or handling the mechanics of their use (Rosenthal, Moore, & Flynn, 1991). Situational contextual factors are likely to have a greater impact on condom use than on contraceptive pill use and these factors may work to override the effects of norms, attitudes and intentions; that is, those elements that are a significant part of rational decision making.

The fact that contextual factors are important is also highlighted by our finding that there was no one-to-one correspondence between intention and behaviour, even though intention was a predictor of behaviour. This is consistent with the findings of others (Ajzen, 1985; Davidson & Jaccard, 1979; Liska, 1984) who have found changes in intention over time. We found not only that intention changed over time but that the predictive ability of intention increased the closer it was measured to the behavioural episode. The changes in intention probably do not reflect the impact of new information (Fishbein & Jaccard, 1973) but rather the influence of contextual factors, possibly heightened by the lack of stability of intentions and relationships in this youthful sample.

In this study, being affected by alcohol did not influence intention or behaviour and neither did the adolescent's degree of concern about HIV or STDs. These factors may be influential in a sample in which there was a greater range of both alcohol use and HIV concerns. For this group the former was uniformly low and the latter uniformly high (but see Timmins *et al.,* this volume).

Of the other contextual factors we examined, three were significant predictors of condom use. Consistent with the work of Emmons*et al.* , (1986) and Goggin (1989), increased sexual arousal was linked with the non-use of condoms. In addition, the fact that the majority of those participants who changed their intentions shifted from intending to use condoms to having no thoughts of using condoms at the time of the sexual encounter suggests that arousal may operate in a similar fashion to the effects of arousal on other tasks. When arousal is high, the encounter alone becomes the focus and the associated task of condom use receives little or no attention (Norman, 1976; see Gold, this volume).

One method which may eliminate such arousal-induced failure to use condoms is overtraining, a common preventive technique used in other stress-related performance situations (Moates & Schumacher, 1980). Such training could include simulating high (but non-sexual) arousal situations such as competition, then providing practice under such conditions with opening a condom packet and putting a condom on an inanimate object like a cucumber. Another example would be to encourage young men to do sex education 'homework,' such as to practice putting on a condom while by themselves and only moderately aroused. In this way the procedures involved are more likely to become habitual and immune to the interfering effects of high arousal.

Communication with a partner about using condoms was the second important contextual factor. Not only did this factor predict behaviour, but also intention in action. Those respondents who communicated directly with their partners about using condoms had a stronger intention to use one immediately before or during a sexual encounter and were more likely to do so. This is an important finding because it reflects the fact that condom use is a behaviour which involves not just one partner. It also reinforces the importance of certain skills which individuals need, such as broaching the topic of condom use with a partner (Kashima *et al.,* in press; Liska, 1984). Similarly, the obvious finding that having a condom available is a necessary condition of use implies that individuals must be able to purchase condoms and carry them around. Sexually inexperienced adolescents have been found to have moderately high levels of embarrassment about condoms (Pleck *et al.,* 1990; Rosenthal *et al.,* 1991). Skills which overcome such embarrassment must be acquired by adolescents so that they can buy condoms, discuss their use and use them correctly.

It is interesting to consider in some detail the fifteen individuals who intended to use a condom in their next sexual encounter but did not carry through that intention. Not one of the five young men in this group actually had a condom available during the encounter. Interventions to improve the resolve of young men such as these could profitably centre on increasing planning and/or the assertion skills needed to buy and carry a condom. The story is not so simple for the ten females who did not carry out their intention to have safer sex. Seven of these did have a condom available. Why was it not used? None of the variables we measured shed any light on this conundrum, over and above our general findings of non-use being associated with high sexual arousal and low partner communication. We speculate that at least three factors may restrict young girls' use of condoms in this situation. Although willing to use condoms, these girls may be inhibited in initiating discussion about their use, or their partners may override their desire to use condoms, or their levels of arousal may, indeed, preclude carrying out their intention. Each of these possibilities has implications for effective interventions.

### Conclusion: Rational and Non-Rational Factors in Adolescent Condom Use

It is clear that the theory of reasoned action, as interpreted in our study, has only limited explanatory value in the prediction of safer sex practice. Situational contextual features of the sexual encounter, together with the beliefs, values, and assumptions brought to the encounter by adolescents, are very important in making the decision about whether to use condoms and carrying through this decision in the 'heat of the moment.'

It is not surprising that models which explain relatively premeditated, rationally governed behaviours (such as voting or buyer behaviour) fall short of explaining the emotionally charged and multidetermined world of adolescent sexuality. Even when specific decision-making paradigms like the health belief model are applied successfully to health promoting behaviours such as the maintenance of dental hygiene, they have limited value in predicting sexual health promoting activities like condom use (Janz & Becker, 1984; Rosenthal, Hall, & Moore, 1992).

The difficulties inherent in predicting behaviour whose determinants are so complex has been partly recognised by Ajzen and his colleagues in later work (Ajzen & Madden, 1986). Acknowledging that most social acts are not under complete volitional control, Ajzen and Madden modified the theory to incorporate the role of the situational context in which behaviour occurs. In the study described in this chapter, we explored aspects of this situational context when adolescents engage in intercourse, and were able to delineate some of the relevant factors at work in determining condom use.

However, much of the variance of teenage sexual precautionary behaviour still remains unexplained by both components of the theory of reasoned action and the situational variables which we measured. Our belief is that the broader social context of adolescent sexuality must be explored more fully if our predictions of who is at risk sexually are to be improved. This context consists of myths, assumptions, values, ideals and beliefs, some conscious, some subconscious, some rational, some irrational. For each individual, sexual context is unique but can be shared to some extent by one's social, ethnic, age and gender group. It is more pervasive and complex than one-dimensional norms such as those which are assessed by the 'subjective norms' element of the Ajzen and Fishbein model. It includes, but is more than, the perceived attitudes of significant others about condom use and the adolescent's motivation to comply with those referents.

For example, in our interview-based study of the sexual worlds of 16-year-olds, we found that beliefs about love, fidelity, trust and romance, together with perceptions of peers' beliefs about these issues, could influence condom use over and above expressed attitudes to condoms and subjective norms about their use (Buzwell et al., 1992; Moore & Rosenthal, 1992). The three groups of young people in this study (homeless youth, Anglo- and Greek-Australians living at home) constructed their sexual worlds in very different ways. Delineation of the dimensions of these constructions requires that we go back to the adolescents themselves, to discover through in-depth techniques such as interviews and projective tests, how their sexual worlds are interpreted and how these complex constructions impinge on specific behaviours such as condom use (see also Kippax & Crawford, this volume).

We have raised questions about the general applicability of the theory of reasoned action on the basis of our study of condom use intentions and behaviour. However, there are several factors which may limit the generality of our findings. First, the sample consisted primarily of white, middle-class undergraduate student volunteers who perceived the benefits of, expressed positive attitudes towards and, generally, intended to use, condoms. It is unlikely that the general population would be as positive or as homogeneous as this sample. The sampling bias may have reduced the predictive ability of attitudes and subjective norms because of limited variability in responses on these dimensions. Thus it is not possible to conclude that they are not at all important in condom use. Rather, even when individuals have positive attitudes towards and intend to use condoms, there is no guarantee that they will use them.

Second, all measures were assessed using self reports, which have well known limitations in terms of accuracy, honesty of recall and willingness to report socially disapproved behaviour (Catania, Gibson, Chitwood & Coates, 1990). While accuracy of recall was enhanced by requiring respondents to complete the questionnaire within 24 hours of a sexual encounter and honesty encouraged by taking considerable care to ensure that all responses were confidential, it is possible that the incidence of condom use could have been over-reported because of its social desirability. Finally, the measures of both attitudes to condom use and subjective norms about condoms as HIV protection were assessed 'in general,' rather than in relation to the participant's next sexual encounter as recommended by the model. Greater specificity of these measures may have led to their greater predictive power.

However, the study had several advantages over previous research in the area. Not only was the model tested in its entirety but intention was measured twice, enabling an assessment of the influence of time on this variable. The study was able to demonstrate the role of situational contextual factors in predicting condom use, and to show that combining these factors with both attitudes and intentions led to improved prediction of behaviour. But an inescapable conclusion is that the variance accounted for by these factors is low, and we need to explore in more depth the contribution of the broader, social context if we are to predict adolescent condom use with greater accuracy.

# 5

# Attitudes Toward Condoms and the Theory of Reasoned Action

MICHAEL W. ROSS

*Albion AIDS Centre, Division of Medicine, Prince of Wales Hospital, Sydney, Australia*

MARY-LOUISE McLAWS

*University of New South Wales, Sydney, Australia*

## Attitudes Towards Condoms

Predicting AIDS-preventive behaviour, particularly condom use, with a model such as the theory of reasoned action (Ajzen & Fishbein, 1980) must be seen in the context of related research into attitudes and beliefs about condoms. This chapter attempts to review the previous evidence on the influence of attitudes towards condoms, in order to locate the data on the theory of reasoned action within work on determinants of condom use and to conceptualise the application of the theory of reasoned action as part of an attempt to better explain HIV and STD-preventive behaviour. It is important to note that a substantial portion of this work has involved attitudes toward condoms as contraceptives (although a significant amount of work fails to distinguish the use of the condom as STD prophylaxis with contraceptive use). This work is included in the historical perspective as attitudes toward, and beliefs about, condoms have been located within previous discourses and built upon previous perceptions about condoms. Indeed, with heterosexual condom use, it may not be possible to separate STD prophylactic and contraceptive elements. While much of the research cited is atheoretical, it does contribute substantially to an understanding of attitudes and beliefs regarding condoms and condom use which the theory of reasoned action later develops. Prior to reviewing the previous literature on condoms, it must be noted that the term 'attitude' as used in these studies may not necessarily be similar to the definition of attitude adopted by the theory of reasoned action. Nevertheless, an understanding of attitude as more broadly defined will guide any specific definitions of attitude in the context of the application of the theory of reasoned action.

One of the most comprehensive studies examining attitudes towards condoms was carried out by Darrow (1974), who studied 2325 individuals at a California STD clinic with regard to their attitudes toward, and utilisation of, condoms as a prophylactic. His sample had a mean age of 22 years, and two thirds were unmarried. The objections of Darrow's respondents (percentages for each objection in parentheses) were that condoms interfered with sex (25.9%), were unnatural (17.9%), were unsatisfying (16.3%), were messy and uncomfortable (15.7%), irritating (8.2%), unreliable (7.2%), were forgotten (5.2%), unsafe (3.1%), hard to buy (1.6%), didn't work (1.3%), reduced pleasure (1.2%) and against people's religion (1.2%). It can be seen that the problem with condoms was perceived by most respondents in this study as being one of interference and discomfort, rather than of access to condoms.

A review of three studies (Curjel, 1964; Hart, 1974; Wittkower & Cowan, 1944) in military environments points to other reasons for failure to use a condom. Wittkower and Cowan found that most soldiers did not use condoms because they considered infection unlikely (56%), followed by impaired pleasure (17%), influence of alcohol (13%) and lack of availability (10%). Curjel found that lack of availability was the main reason (29%), followed by considering infection unlikely (23%), influence of alcohol (16%), impaired pleasure (13.5%), knowing the partner (6.5%), no fear of STDs (5.5%) and ignorance (3.4%). Hart, in contrast, found that impaired pleasure was the main reason given (35%), with influence of alcohol (25%), lack of availability (22%) and forgetting (12.5%) following. These results all indicate that condoms were judged with respect to prophylaxis, which may well have influenced the reasons given for non-use. It may also be that the main reasons for non-use in the military differ from the most salient reasons among civilians. It is interesting to note, however, that a judgement as to risk of infection appears to be a part of the judgement process, with known partners apparently being considered safe!

The finding that a substantial proportion of the respondents in all these studies had negative attitudes towards condoms may be a reflection of the fact that they were considering the use of condoms for prophylaxis. The use of condoms for this purpose possibly has connotations that engender negative attitudes. Yarber and Williams (1975), for instance, found that university students thought that the condom was the most effective prophylactic against STDs, but were concerned about using them because they implied that there was something wrong with their partner. Yacenda (1974) also notes that it is thought that using a condom implies that the other person is 'dirty.' Such findings suggest that the stigma associated with sexually transmitted diseases affects attitudes toward condoms.

Some of these points are evident in more recent research examining attitudes to condoms as prophylactics for HIV prevention. In an interview-based study, Chapman and Hodgson (1988) found that, while most individuals in a broad series of high-risk heterosexual community-based groups recognised the risk of HIV and believed that condoms prevented infection, there was a strong view expressed that it was insulting or embarrassing to raise the question of condom use, and that there was a silent collusion to avoid the subject. Moreover, the respondents generally felt that condoms were juvenile, unnatural, lacked sensation, interrupted sex and were unreliable, as well as being embarrassing to purchase and unavailable when needed. Interestingly, in contrast to Darrow's (1974) findings, the subjects studied by Chapman and Hodgson (1988) were concerned about a lack of accessibility to condoms, possibly because the subjects in the research were relatively young.

In Chapman and Hodgson's (1988) study, some more subtle beliefs about condoms emerged. There was a consistent story across interview groups of Catholics in condom factories putting pin-pricks in every few condoms, such stories being personalised in many cases, and stories about being asked 'what size?' when purchasing them. Clearly, the myths about condoms are as prevalent and inaccurate as ever, and are used as rationalisations to avoid their use. In general, the attitudes noted in the earlier literature were replicated by Chapman and Hodgson (1988), who suggest that the condom needs to be conceptually repositioned since condom sex is seen as inferior sex.

Although some of the above-mentioned results can be attributed to the use of condoms as a prophylactic, it should be noted that, even when considered in the more socially acceptable role as a contraceptive, a number of studies have found that people have negative attitudes towards condoms. In one such study, Keith, Keith, Bussell and Wells (1975) examined the attitudes of men to contraceptives. They found that all men surveyed were familiar with condoms, that 9% preferred them as a contraceptive method, and that 15% used them all or most of the time for contraception. The main psychological reasons for rejection of condoms included denial, guilt, shame, 'coital gamesmanship,' sexual identity crisis, hostility, masochism, nihilism, fear and anxiety and the availability of abortion.

In a more extensive study, Brown (1984) developed a scale to measure attitudes toward the condom as a measure of birth control. While the purpose of the scale was to assess attitudes toward methods of barrier contraception, it also provided an indication of other attitudes toward condoms. Brown (1984) started with a 55 item pool and reduced this to 40 items on the basis of high and low score criterion groups. Following a factor analysis of these 40 items on data obtained from a sample of male and female college undergraduates, five factors were interpretable. These factors, which accounted for 45% of the total variance, were dimensions measuring: (1) satisfaction with the safety and reliability of condoms as a contraceptive; (2) comfort with condoms; (3) embarrassment; (4) effect of condoms on sexual arousal and excitement; and (5) interruption of sexual activity. While the first factor may be specific to condoms as contraceptives, the remaining factors may be related to attitudes toward condoms which are general and not purpose-related. The high internal consistency of Brown's (1988) scales suggests that her data are stable, as does her finding that there are no sex differences in attitudes toward condoms.

Ross (1988a) used a modified version of Brown's (1984) scale to examine the attitudes toward condoms of homosexually active men. He modified her scale by changing the word 'female' to 'male,' and 'contraception' to 'preventing infection,' as well as adding questions relating to availability, attitudes toward purchase and breakage. He found that after factor analysis, five interpretable factors emerged: (1) seeing condoms as unreliable and unerotic; (2) protecting from infection; (3) availability; (4) interruption of sex; and (5) having a responsibility to use, and feeling comfortable using, condoms. These factors, accounting for 50.7% of total variance, reproduced two of Brown's factors, suggesting that there are both common and specific factors of attitudes toward condom use in homosexually active men. The dimensions common to both homosexual and heterosexual groups appear to relate to interruption of sexual activity, and comfort with condom use. The dimensions in the homosexual group, as in the heterosexual group, appeared to be clear and interpretable, suggesting that there are a limited number of dimensions used to describe attitudes toward condoms. These dimensions had high reliability coefficients and were also significantly associated with condom use during ano-genital intercourse (the responsibility and comfort subscale) and oro-genital intercourse in the homosexual sample, particularly with regard to oral sex (all the subscales with the exception of the protection from infection subscale).

This review of studies on attitudes to condom use reveals that similar attitudes to those seen today were also seen in studies dating from the Second World War, although the emphasis on condoms as prophylactics changed post-penicillin, as it did as a contraceptive in the post-pill period. The advent of HIV/AIDS reactivated a number of latent attitudes toward and beliefs about condoms and for this reason the early research is informative. Much has remained the same with attitudes toward condoms as HIV prophylaxis compared with condoms as STD prophylaxis. With this noted, it must also be stressed that it would be unwise to uncritically take pre-HIV data as still fully generalisable to post-HIV condom use and its associated attitudes and beliefs.

## Attitudes Toward Condoms and Behaviour

Numerous studies have revealed a lack of correspondence between people's attitudes towards condoms, their behavioural intentions and their actual condom use. In the pre-AIDS literature on condoms, the gap between attitudes and behaviour was amply demonstrated by Darrow (1974), who found that when free condoms were offered, less than 30% of his total study population accepted (people who had previously used condoms had highest acceptance, and males higher acceptance than females, ranging from 42.9% of previously experienced males to 16.2% of previously inexperienced females). Contrary to Darrow's hypothesis, acceptance of condoms rose as objections to them rose: objections did not interfere with their use. This suggests that those who use condoms, while aware of their disadvantages, are also aware of the positive reasons for their use. Of particular interest was the finding that persons with a previous STD were less likely to accept free condoms than those who had no previous infections and attended for screening. Darrow suggests that those who attend for screening are probably more concerned about prevention compared with those who attend for diagnosis and cure.

Hart (1974) also reported a lack of consistency between people's attitudes towards condoms and their subsequent behaviour. Hart found that only 22% of the Australian troops he studied, who reported that they had faith in condoms, actually used them. An even lower proportion was reported by Felman and Santora (1981), who gave redeemable vouchers for free condoms to clinic users and found that despite the fact that 78% of their sample said that if they were given free condoms they would use them, only 11% actually picked up the free condoms!

Since the advent of AIDS, studies of attitudes towards condoms and actual condom use have revealed similar results to the earlier research in the area. Kegeles, Adler and Irwin (1988), for instance, looked at changes in attitudes toward, and intention to use, condoms in adolescents over one year in California in 1984–1986. Their sample had a mean age of 16 years, and the majority were sexually active. In general, the respondents placed a high value and importance on using condoms, but over time the females continued not to intend their partners to use condoms, and the male's intention to use them declined, despite an increase in publicity about condoms and their use in preventing transmission of HIV.

More recent work by Chapman et al. (1990) surveyed heterosexual people with more than one opposite sex partner in the past year. They found that three conceptually coherent factors (condom use as a positive action, condom use as a cue to embarrassment and condom use as antithetical to good sex) discriminated between users and non-users. Chapman et al. (1990) suggest that apart from the truism that regular condom users are characterised by stronger affirmations about the necessity for and sense of using condoms with new and steady partners, it was apparent that two levels of 'dialogue' existed in sexually active people concerning condom use with new partners. External dialogue, or what is actually said, is preceded by an often tortuous internal dialogue in the mind of the individual. Their second factor (condom use as a cue to embarrassment) appeared to be similar to such an internal dialogue. They suggest that potential embarrassment often provoked a mutual collusion in not discussing condom use, and that health promotion messages might profitably shape the considerations and attitudes upon which such dialogues are based.

Much of the earlier literature reviewed has been limited to heterosexual or unspecified samples. There are few studies published to date which look at attitudes toward and prevalence of condom use in homosexually active men. In Finland, Valle (1988) found that over a three year period, consistent condom use in homosexually active men increased from 6 to 28%, with an increase from 9.3 to 42.5% of abstention from anal intercourse. However, 28.9% were using condoms not at all or occasionally. Similarly, Detels *et al.* (1989) found in the United States that consistent condom use rose from 3 to 28% in the period 1984–1986, and Ross (1988c) found that condom use was consistent in 23% of his South Australian sample of homosexual men who had insertive sex. Determinants of condom use in this sample included having had an anti-HIV test and associated counselling, being given a free sample condom and membership of gay organisations. The fact that membership of gay organisations was associated with condom use reinforces the findings of Ross and McLaws (1992) that perceived peer support may be another important variable in translating attitudes into behaviour.

Golombok, Sketchley and Rust (1989), in a sample of homosexual men in London, reported that reasons for non-use of condoms during anal intercourse included being in a mutually monogamous relationship in which HIV serostatus was known and concordant (60% of non-users), dislike of condoms because they were uncomfortable, unromantic, or caused a loss of erection (24%) and unavailability or irresponsible behaviour (16%). In a similar study in Australia, Ross (1990a) found that condom non-use during anal intercourse in homosexual men was reported for a number of reasons: steady relationship (33%), alcohol or drug use (8%), partner attractiveness (3%), can't be bothered (10%), known partner or partner thought to be 'safe' (3%), condoms unavailable (19%) and bisexual partners (5%). Silvestre *et al.* (1989) reported on 13 seroconverters in a large longitudinal study, and found that unsafe behaviours leading to seroconversion tended to occur because of strong emotional responses to partners or to a lesser extent mental health or drug-related problems. Taken together, these data suggest that both rationalisations and lack of preparedness, as well as negative attitudes toward condoms and very occasionally psychopathology, are associated with condom non-use in homosexual men.

In a longitudinal study of homosexual men over six months, Ross (1990a) found that items from his Homosexual Attitudes toward Condoms Scale which predicted change to condom use were those from the subscales measuring protection from infection and availability. These data suggest that increasing use of condoms is related to stronger beliefs that condoms may be effective in preventing infection, and to the view that they can be available if one makes an appropriate decision to plan ahead for condom use. The implications of these findings for preventive education include the necessity to reinforce the extent of perceived personal control over the possibility of HIV or STD infection.

The predominant attitudes toward condoms, particularly in terms of prophylactic use, appear to be related to perceptions of impaired pleasure, lack of availability when needed, interrupting sex and being unnatural or unreliable. However, there is also evidence which suggests that there are some positive perceptions of condoms which may balance the negative attitudes, and that attitudes are modifiable. Promotion of condoms by health professionals may play a part in increasing the at present weak relationship between beliefs that condoms are useful in preventing STD transmission and their actual use. As a model of attitude–behaviour relations, the theory of reasoned action may be an appropriate theoretical basis for such research. Not only does it provide a vehicle for examining the role of attitudes towards condoms in predicting intentions to use condoms, it acknowledges the role of social influence in this decision-making process (see Terry, Gallois, & McCamish, this volume). This component of the model is likely to be particularly relevant in the context of condom use, given the fact that a common theme in previous research on attitudes to condoms as prophylaxis has been the partner's interpretation of the suggestion that a condom be used.

## Theory of Reasoned Action and Condom Use

There have been few studies which have directly applied the theory of reasoned action to intention to use condoms. Ross and McLaws (1992) carried out a study of the application of the theory of reasoned action on 173 homosexually active men in South Australia, who were approached in bars or gay organisations, bathhouses or outside cruising areas. Condom use during the past three months was assessed for four behaviours: insertive anal intercourse, receptive anal intercourse, insertive oral intercourse and receptive oral intercourse on a 4-point scale (always, mostly, sometimes, never). Attitude toward using condoms was assessed using a 5-point semantic differential scale in response to the item, 'my attitude toward using condoms is...' ('favourable–unfavourable'), and behavioural intention was measured by a similar scale defined at the poles by the dimensions of 'likely–unlikely' in response to the question, 'I intend to use condoms any time I have unsafe sex in the next two months.' Unsafe sex was defined as 'sex which would be unsafe *if a condom were not worn at the time* ' (emphasis in original). There might be some doubt, however, as to whether oral sex without a condom was considered unsafe by many respondents.

The five items assessing behavioural beliefs about the use of condoms (based on the five dimensions of attitudes toward condoms found by Ross (1988a)) were 'condoms will protect me from infection with the AIDS virus' 'condoms are unerotic' 'condoms are never available when needed' 'condoms interrupt sex' and 'I have a responsibility to use a condom during unsafe sex.' Following each of these items was a 5-point semantic differential scale measuring subjective probability and asking 'How certain are you?' and defined at the poles by the words 'very certain–very uncertain.' Behavioural beliefs about condoms were obtained by multiplying each of the items by the degree of certainty with which it was held and summing the products, as described by Ajzen and Fishbein (1980).

The five items assessing normative beliefs about the degree of support for using condoms from significant others were responses to the question asking the respondent whether others believed that they should use a condom during unsafe sex (steady sexual partners, casual sexual partners, close gay friends, people in the community, family: these classes were identified from pilot interviews). Each of these in turn was followed by the item, 'I generally take (a lot of notice–no notice) of (the class of persons named)' and again scored on a 5-point semantic differential scale. Subjective norms were obtained by multiplying each of the five normative belief items by their associated items on how much motivation there was to comply with these classes of persons, and summing the products. Intentions to use condoms was then regressed on attitude toward condoms and subjective norms.

The resulting model demonstrated that there was a multiple correlation of 0.44 between both subjective norms and attitudes and intentions, with the bulk of the variance being accounted for by the subjective norms rather than attitudes. While this was a cross-sectional study, and causality cannot be implied, these data do confirm that about one fifth of variance in intention to use condoms in this sample of gay men is accounted for by the components of the theory of reasoned action. The reason for a comparatively low proportion of variance accounted for can be attributed to a number of factors: first, there was no distinction made between those with casual partners and those in long-term monogamous relationships, in which it might be presumed that condom use was unnecessary if both partners had been tested for HIV and were concordant in HIV status. Second, and perhaps more important, a significant proportion of the variance will be accounted for by the attitudes and norms of the other partner, and the circumstances of the sexual encounter (for example, condom availability and degree of intoxication).

In an additional analysis, sexual behaviour in the previous two months accounted for approximately 18% of variance in behavioural intentions. The relationship of previous sexual behaviour to intention might be interpreted as indicating that previous behaviour (since condom use is presumably a common behaviour in this sample) is an indicator of intention as well. The comparatively low proportion of variance accounted for by past behaviour suggests that there may be major contextual determinants of condom use, and that the theory of reasoned action accounts for a substantial proportion of the person-based determinants of condom use, but not for the situation-based determinants. Given that condom use involves a person–person–situation interaction, the fact that this model can account for 20% of the variance of intention to use condoms is encouraging, compared with other individual health behaviours (i.e., not involving co-operation with any other person or people) which have been studied using the theory of reasoned action.

These data raised questions regarding additional sources of variance. It was hypothesised that one aspect of self-efficacy in terms of condom use, given that this is a behaviour which takes place between two consenting persons, might be assertiveness. Self-efficacy is an independent predictor of intention in the theory of planned behaviour (Ajzen & Madden, 1986) and assertiveness may be considered an element of self-efficacy. Treffke, Tiggemann and Ross (1992) investigated the relationships among attitudes, assertiveness and intention to use and actual use of condoms in 83 homosexual and 128 heterosexual men in South Australia. While the theory of reasoned action was not directly tested, Ross's (1988a) Attitude toward Condoms Scale was used, along with general assertiveness as measured by the Rathus Assertiveness Inventory, and a specific Condom Assertiveness Scale which measured the degree to which the respondent felt anxious about being assertive regarding condom use in a variety of contexts. Interrelationships among the psychological variables confirmed that intention to use condoms was positively associated with attitudes. Favourable attitudes, in turn, were associated with condom assertiveness in both groups.

The pattern for general assertiveness, however, differed markedly between the two sexual preference groups. For the homosexual men, social assertiveness and condom assertiveness were positively correlated, whereas for the heterosexual group, attitudes toward condoms were negatively correlated with social assertiveness. As expected, actual use and intention to use were highly correlated in both groups (0.93 in the homosexual men, 0.87 in the heterosexual men). It is possible that since condom use in homosexual men is a new behaviour, the social skills have been learned along with the attitudes; however, in the heterosexual men, the skills and attitudes have developed independently. These data most importantly illustrate that while there are similarities between homosexual and heterosexual men, there are also some important differences, particularly in the relationship between general assertiveness and condom assertiveness.

In other research testing the theory of reasoned action in relation to condom use, there has been some support for the inclusion of a measure of self-efficacy. Basen-Engquist and Parcel (1992) used a cross-sectional statewide survey of 1720 Texas ninth graders which tested the applicability of the theory of reasoned action/planned behaviour along with other approaches. They also used 5-point semantic differential scales to measure attitudes, subjective norms, self-efficacy, intention and behaviour, and used a regression model to identify the significant predictors of intention. The path model found that attitude was the major predictor of intention to limit number of partners. Attitudes, norms and self-efficacy together accounted for 36.4% of variance. These same three variables accounted for 17% of the variance in intention to use condoms, and for 19% of the variance in frequency of condom use. These percentages of variance are very similar to those found by Ross and McLaws (1992), and strengthen the suggestion that a substantial proportion of the remaining variance may be accounted for by partner variables. Basen-Engquist and Parcel note that the addition of self-efficacy makes a unique contribution to the theory of reasoned action model, with attitudes and norms related to behaviour only through intention. However, contrary to the findings of Ross and McLaws, they concluded that social norms were a weak predictor of intention and behaviour. This difference is probably due to the vastly different social norms with regard to condom use existing between the gay and heterosexual communities. It may also be due to the fact that Basen-Engquist and Parcel used an adolescent sample, while Ross and McLaws used a significantly older sample (see Nucifora, Gallois, & Kashima, this volume; Warwick, Terry, & Gallois, this volume, for other research that has found support for the role of norms in the prediction of heterosexuals' intentions to engage in safer sex).

In a more recent study, McLaws (1992) found further support for the role of norms in predicting intentions to use a condom. This study tested the theory of reasoned action in a sample of 207 homosexual men recruited in bars, bathhouses and gay dance parties in Sydney, Australia. Her questionnaire contained scales to measure behavioural intention to use a condom, subjective norms, attitudes and behavioural norms. The behavioural norms scale was a new one based on previous qualitative work which suggested that gay men are influenced by the apparent behaviours of their peers, and measured condom use in open relationships or with new partners by the respondent's peers. McLaws found that the final model accounted for 39% of the variance. The three variables which accounted for this variance were attitudes toward condoms, behavioural norms and HIV status. These data suggest that perceptions of what peers think respondents ought to be doing (subjective norms) may be modified to include a perception of what peer behavioural norms are. External variables including age and HIV status were both associated with intention. The data of McLaws are important in that they make a distinction between subjective norms (what the respondent thinks that peers feel that they should be doing, and their motivation to comply with the views of peers) and behavioural norms (what respondents think that their friends are actually doing). Essentially, this distinction can be best envisaged as similar to the distinction between what one's parent thinks about smoking (they may be against it) and what they actually do (they may smoke themselves).

## Summary and Conclusions

The applicability of the theory of reasoned action to condom use appears to have been demonstrated in the studies we have described, and particularly with the addition of self-efficacy into the equation as proposed in the theory of planned behaviour and, at least for homosexual men, the importance of norms. However, it must be noted that unlike most health behaviours which have been examined using the theory of reasoned action that are based on individual decisions, with condom use the decision involves negotiation with another party and thus the fact that the proportion of variance accounted for is lower than in other health behaviours is not surprising. In extending the model, accounting for this external component will need to be included, and this will present the greatest challenge to its extension. In doing so, it may be useful to consider as context the putative partner's attitudes and norms. While this would be practically difficult, it may be feasible to include as a further term in a regression equation the response of the partner. This would, however, involve the construction of putative scenarios and be further removed from the theory of reasoned action.

Although some conclusions can be drawn from the studies described, the paucity of literature testing the theory of reasoned action suggests that these conclusions be treated cautiously and that replications or comparisons with different populations in terms of sexual orientation, age, gender, culture and stage of the HIV epidemic be carried out. In terms of the theory of reasoned action, the balance between attitudes, norms, self-efficacy and contextual variables in predicting intention may vary in terms of some or all of the variables noted above, and it is probably in examining such population and temporal differences that the utility of the theory of reasoned action in accounting for condom use will be best demonstrated.

# 6

# The Theory of Reasoned Action as Applied to AIDS Prevention for Australian Ethnic Groups

KEN RIGBY, BIRUTA DIETZ and STUART STURGESS

*University of Southern Australia, Adelaide, Australia*

In a multicultural society such as Australia's it is to be expected that members of different ethnic groups will be influenced by different social and cultural forces in the way they conduct their relationships with each other. It should not surprise us if people from the different groups act differently in their response to the threat of HIV and AIDS. There is, as we shall see, accumulating evidence that there are various ethno-specific beliefs about what constitutes acceptable and appropriate attitudes and behaviours concerning sex, and what can and should be done to counter HIV infection. In the context of this diversity, in this chapter we ask the question of whether the theory of reasoned action can assist in explaining what people intend to do about HIV to make their lives safer, regardless of ethnic group identification.

## HIV and Ethnic Groups in Australia

Interest in AIDS-related beliefs among ethnic groups in Australia developed in the late 1980s in Australia because it was thought that some groups—particularly those of non-English speaking background (NESB)—were in some respects more at risk from HIV infection than Anglo-Australians. It was maintained by some that people who are not so fluent in the English language would tend not to access or understand information about HIV and AIDS that was available for mainstream Anglo-Australians. Unless they were effectively targeted to receive information in their own community language, people of non-English speaking background would be seriously disadvantaged.

Accordingly, various Commonwealth and State initiatives were undertaken to induce greater awareness of HIV/AIDS in selected ethnic communities. In 1986 the State Government of New South Wales produced information sheets about HIV/AIDS in nine community languages, and then later provided a series of videotapes in sixteen different languages. In 1987 the Victorian State Government began producing and disseminating brochures in sixteen community languages. Since then the Australian Commonwealth Government has played a major role in promoting services designed to raise the awareness of people of NESB of the dangers of HIV/AIDS and how to protect themselves against this disease.

Being less fluent in English is not necessarily the only factor placing people at risk of HIV infection. For example, beliefs of a cultural or religious nature may result in conservative or prejudiced attitudes that will hinder the acceptance of ideas and practices seen as desirable in the fight against AIDS. A number of research projects have been undertaken to examine such questions.

The earliest relevant study in Australia was conducted in NSW by Chown (1986). In this study, 118 people of NESB from nine language groups were interviewed. Unfortunately Chown did not differentiate in his report between the different ethnic backgrounds of the interviewees. Chown's study, based mainly on anecdotes, claimed that there was a widespread denial of the dangers of AIDS to non-Anglo-Australian communities and considerable ignorance and prejudice about AIDS-related issues. No control group of Anglo-Australians was interviewed.

In 1987 the first quantitative study of AIDS-related beliefs was reported following a survey undertaken by Australian Market Research (1987). Responses to questionnaire items by non-English migrants (10% of a sample of 1500) were compared with those of others. From this study it was concluded that the migrants were less knowledgeable about HIV and AIDS than others and more prejudiced against homosexuals and people with AIDS. But again, no distinctions were made between people with different non-English speaking backgrounds.

In 1988 a three year program of research was begun at the University of South Australia in Adelaide to examine the attitudes, beliefs and practices of selected groups of people of NESB in relation to HIV and AIDS. Those groups chosen consisted of two Southern European groups—Italians and Greeks; a northern European group—Polish; and two groups of Vietnamese people, distinguished according to whether they spoke Vietnamese or Chinese. These groups reflected a diversity of origins and sizeable minorities in Adelaide.

In a preliminary study of the groups (Rigby, Anagnostou, Brown, Rosser & Ross, 1988) the methodology involved interviewing people (twenty from each of the five ethnic groups) who were not only well-integrated in the Australian community, but also had strong links with one of the ethnic groups and were able to speak the language. Interviews conducted using bi-lingual workers focussed on the views of the interviewees about the ethnic community they knew best. In particular the interviewees were asked to make explicit comparisons between members of their own ethnic group and people in the Anglo-Australian community generally. A high level of consensus was found among the interviewees reporting upon their ethnic group. It was generally agreed that people in their ethnic community were relatively uninformed about AIDS and reluctant to talk about the subject. It was also suggested that there was less acceptance among people of NESB of homosexual people and people with HIV/AIDS. At the same time the results suggested that it was important to differentiate between ethnic groups. For example, not all groups were seen as having a low degree of concern about the threat of AIDS. Greek people in particular appeared to be highly concerned, significantly more so, according to the judgements of the interviewees, than the Vietnamese. Although these results were suggestive, and in general consistent with previous reports, it could be argued that they reflected stereotypes held by non-representative members of ethnic groups about other mainly less well-educated members of people in their ethnic community.

Subsequently in 1988–9, a larger study was undertaken employing representative samples of people from the selected ethnic groups (Rigby, Brown, Anagnostou, Ross, & Rosser, 1989). In each there were 120 people, composed of 60 male and 60 female respondents. A control group of 202 Anglo-Australians was also employed in this study. Linguistically equivalent interview schedules were developed for each comparison group, containing questions to assess (a) level of concern about HIV/AIDS, (b) knowledge of HIV transmission, (c) acceptance or tolerance of people with HIV/AIDS and (d) level of acceptance of male homosexuals. Level of concern was assessed using a simple 7-point scale from 'not concerned' to 'extremely concerned'. Multi-item scales were used to assess both knowledge and attitudes, and each of the measures was shown to have adequate to good internal consistency as assessed by coefficient alpha.

In general, the results from this second study supported those suggested in the preliminary one. On three of the measures, namely, knowledge of HIV/AIDS, acceptance of people with HIV/AIDS and acceptance of male homosexuals, Anglo-Australians obtained the highest mean scores. There were significant differences between the Anglo-Australian sample and some of the other samples. For example, Anglo-Australians were significantly more concerned about AIDS, more knowledgeable about HIV and more accepting of people with HIV/AIDS and also male homosexuals than either of the two groups of Vietnamese respondents. However, a simple contrast between Anglo-Australians and others was not indicated. In fact, personal concern about HIV/AIDS appeared to be slightly higher among the Greek respondents than among the Anglo-Australians. Italians and Anglo-Australians appeared to be about equally accepting or tolerant of male homosexuals.

From this study, it was apparent that among the selected ethnic groups of NESB, one could not claim homogeneity with respect to beliefs and attitudes relevant to HIV/AIDS. For example, Italians and Poles were found to be significantly more knowledgeable about HIV than the Vietnamese. Poles were more homophobic than Italians. In short, groups of people of NESB differed significantly among themselves, and the differences depended upon what AIDS-related issues were the focus.

Further studies conducted in the state of Victoria (Rigby & Rosenthal, 1990) and in South Australia (Rigby & Dietz, 1991) clearly supported the generalisation that ethnic groups differed among themselves in response to AIDS-related issues. The former included a sample of Arabic-speaking people, not hitherto assessed, who were found to be less positive in their attitudes towards male homosexuals and people with HIV/AIDS than some of the other ethnic groups, notably Italians. In each of these studies, it was also possible to assess whether changes had occurred in AIDS-related beliefs *after* a nationwide Commonwealth Government campaign had been launched to change AIDS-related beliefs and attitudes among people of NESB. There was, in fact, little evidence of change, apart from a tendency for Vietnamese people to be significantly more concerned about AIDS after the campaign in the Victorian study, and both more concerned and more knowledgeable about HIV (post-campaign) in the South Australian study. It should be noted that in both studies levels of concern and knowledge were lowest pre-campaign for the Vietnamese group; consequently, there was more scope for them to change. In general, what these results suggested is that beliefs and attitudes about HIV and AIDS were relatively stable within ethnic groups.

As previously indicated, much of the justification for government action to promote HIV/AIDS education for people of NESB was derived from a belief that ethnic groups of NESB are disadvantaged primarily because they are generally less fluent in English than others. How far such fluency might affect attitudes and beliefs about HIV/AIDS was examined as part of the second South Australian study of Italians, Poles and Vietnamese (Rigby & Dietz, 1991). In this study, it was apparent that English language fluency was related to some, but not all, AIDS-related variables, and for some, but not all, ethnic groups. For example, it correlated positively with rated seriousness of the threat of HIV and AIDS to one's ethnic community for Vietnamese respondents, but not for Italians or Poles. Knowledge of HIV, however, did correlate significantly with English language fluency in each of the three groups, thus providing some justification for the rationale of the information campaigns. Of particular interest to this chapter, significant correlations were found between English language fluency and the measures of attitudes towards condoms for two of the three groups.

## Applying the Theory of Reasoned Action

It was in the context of demonstrated differences in AIDS-related beliefs and attitudes between ethnic groups that a study was undertaken in 1991 by Rigby and Dietz to examine factors thought to be relevant to adopting safer sexual practices. The choice of factors was guided, but not entirely determined, by the theory of reasoned action (Ajzen & Fishbein, 1980; Fishbein & Ajzen, 1975) and the theory of planned behaviour (Ajzen, 1988).

As noted by Terry *et al.* (this volume), the theory of reasoned action proposes that actions are largely determined by relevant intentions, which in turn are influenced by attitudes and subjective norms specific to the intentions. In the application of the theory we stopped short of actions, and dealt only with the prediction of expressed intentions.

### *Intended Safer Sexual Practice*

We assumed that risk reduction as far as HIV transmission is concerned can be achieved by either using a condom during sexual intercourse or maintaining exclusive sexual relations (i.e., with one partner only). Although condoms may occasionally fail to offer adequate protection, it is generally agreed that risk from HIV is greatly reduced by using condoms, and HIV/AIDS educators have rightly emphasised their importance in HIV-prevention campaigns. The advocacy of reliance upon 'exclusive relationships' is more controversial. It has been pointed out that people are sometimes misled into believing that a relationship is exclusive when it is not. Also, a partner who is currently in an exclusive relationship may have been infected with the virus by a previous partner or partners. For these reasons, some HIV/AIDS educators argue that the advocacy of exclusivity in relationships to counter HIV is unwise and they do not recommend it. Nevertheless, in the study we employed both criteria implying safer sexual practice—condom use and exclusivity in relationships—while recognising the dangers involved in making incorrect assumptions about the nature of one's relationships and the HIV status of one's partner.

### *Predictors of Intention to Use a Condom*

Consistent with the theory of reasoned action, independent variables included (a) a measure of attitudes towards condoms and (b) a measure of subjective norm regarding condom use. In both cases, belief-based measures of the variables were obtained. In one version the strength of agreement with relevant belief statements was weighted by the importance or value attached to them. This measure will be referred to as the 'weighted version' and its computation is in accordance with the procedure suggested by Fishbein and Ajzen. However, in addition, an 'unweighted version' of these variables were computed for comparison.

A further variable of interest was included, derived from the theory of planned behaviour (Ajzen, 1988). The latter theory suggests that the extent to which respondents believe they are able to practise a given behaviour, in this case taking appropriate precautions to avoid HIV, should be included as a predictor. Accordingly, a measure of perceived behavioural control was added to the two other predictor variables.

### Predictors of Intention to be in an Exclusive Sexual Relationship

The predictor variables in this case included a measure of attitude towards exclusive relationships. The strength of beliefs about such a relationship were *not* weighted by importance or value associated with them; that is, the measure did not adhere to the procedure suggested by the theory of reasoned action. To this degree, the theory was not fully applied or tested. A second variable was subjective norm in relation to exclusive sexual relationships. Here the weighting procedure was used, but in addition (for comparison) a non-weighted version was obtained.

### Other Independent Variables in the Analyses

Several other variables not suggested by the theory of reasoned action were also included in subsequent analyses. It seemed possible that the age of the respondent may be a factor, as attitudes and beliefs frequently become more conservative with age and more resistant to change. Clearly gender needed to be included, given the possibility of differential sensitivity to the issue of AIDS among men and women. Also, being attached to a partner in a marriage or defacto relationship, as opposed to having no such attachment, may influence how people view the precautions they might take to avoid HIV infection (see Kashima & Gallois, this volume). Finally, as we have seen, fluency in English has been considered to be a significant factor affecting knowledge of HIV and, arguably, community responses to it. The additional variables therefore were age, gender, partner relationship (which we will call 'attachment') and fluency in English.

### The Sample of Ethnic Groups

For this study respondents consisted of groups of 80 people who indicated that they were either of Anglo-Australian, Vietnamese, Polish or Italian background. Given that there is no comprehensive list of people of ethnic background in Australia, sampling was unavoidably by convenience. Interviewees selected for this inquiry were interviewed by people of the same ethnic background and gender as themselves. Interviewers were instructed to contact people of the specified groups who were (a) at least 18 years old and (b) not known previously to them personally (introductions were arranged). It was planned that approximately two thirds of the respondents would be under the age of 30 years, and that within each group there would be exactly equal numbers of males and females (i.e., 40) in each ethnic group.

### Characteristics of the Samples

The percentages of people in each of the ethnic groups under 30 years were as follows: Anglo-Australian 72%; Vietnamese 65%; Polish 58%; Italian 62%; total sample 64%. Percentages who were 'attached' (being married or defacto) were: Anglo-Australian 36%; Vietnamese 49%; Polish 65%; Italian 53%; total sample 51%. Finally, the proportions indicating that they spoke English fluently were as follows: Vietnamese 14%; Polish 28%; Italian 73%. Self-rated ability to read English 'very well' gave these results: Vietnamese 13%; Polish 32%; Italian 80%. These differences reflected what is known about the language skills of the three ethnic communities. Vietnamese, being the most recent arrivals, are least fluent in English; Italians, being a longer settled group, are the most fluent.

### Data Collection Procedure

First, interviewers were trained in the use of an interview schedule for which two versions were provided: one in English and one in the respective community language, either to be used as appropriate. The schedule contained relatively non-intrusive questions relating mainly to attitudes and beliefs about sexual practices. This schedule was used in face-to-face interviews with selected respondents in a one-to-one situation. In addition, a self-administered questionnaire was provided for each respondent to answer privately. This asked more intimate questions about the respondent's AIDS-related behaviours. This questionnaire was answered after the interview was over and placed in a sealed envelope. The questionnaire had been previously coded so that it could be linked to the information provided in the interview. Despite the more intrusive nature of the questionnaire, only a few respondents refused to answer it: one Anglo-Australian, one Italian and two Vietnamese. As with the interview schedule, English and community language versions were available for the questionnaire, as desired. Interviews were conducted wholly or partly in the community language with 98% of the Vietnamese; 86% of Poles and 32% of Italians.

## Operationalising the Key Variables

### Intention to Use Condoms

Scores on this variable were derived from answers to two questions, one asked in the interview and the other in the questionnaire. The interview question was as follows: 'It is difficult to look into the future, but if you were to have a new sexual partner, do you think you would use a condom?'. The questionnaire item read: 'Would you insist that a condom be used with a new or first sexual partner?'. The response categories ranged from 'definitely no' scored as 1, to 'definitely yes' scored as 5. The index of intention to use a condom was the mean of the two scores.

### Intention to be in an Exclusive Relationship

Scores were obtained for this variable from a single question asked in the self-administered questionnaire: 'Because of AIDS some people believe that they will stick to one sexual partner. Is this true of you'? Again a 5-point scale was employed for responses, from 'definitely no' (1) to 'definitely yes' (5).

### Attitude to Condom Use

On the basis of earlier studies on dimensions of attitudes in this area (Bernard, Herbert, deMane, & Farrar, 1989a,b; Sheeran, Abraham, Abrams, Spears, & Marks, 1990), five items were devised to assess beliefs about condom use. These were as follows: (1) condoms are embarrassing to buy; (2) condoms are inconvenient to use; (3) condoms reduce people's pleasure in having sex; (4) condoms give good protection against AIDS; (5) condoms encourage sexually immoral behaviour.

Each item was responded to using a 7-point scale from 'strongly agree' to 'strongly disagree' and scored in the pro-condom direction (item 4 was reverse scored). In addition, an assessment was made of the importance to respondents of the embarrassment, inconvenience, pleasure reduction, protection afforded and encouragement to sexual immorality that might be associated with condom use. Again a 7-point scale was used, scoring responses as 1 for 'unimportant' and 7 for 'extremely important'. As previously discussed, a weighted version of the attitude measure reflected by the sum of the scores for belief strength multiplied by importance was computed. An unweighted version based on the scores on the belief items only was also computed.

*Attitude to Exclusiveness of Partner*

Four items were used for this measure: (1) sticking to one sexual partner for life is very difficult (R); (2) the risk of getting AIDS by changing sexual partners is worth taking (R); (3) it is wrong to have sex with anyone except your regular partner; (4) people are happier if they are faithful to their regular partner.

Each item was scored on a 5-point scale ('strongly agree' to 'strongly disagree'). The items followed by (R) were reverse scored. As there was no 'importance' scale for this attitude measure, only an unweighted version of the measure could be computed.

*Subjective Norm About Condom Use*

To assess normative beliefs respondents were asked how strongly they thought the following were in favour of people using condoms with a new sexual partner to reduce their chances of getting HIV: your friends; your parents; present partner (if any); the church; the media (TV, newspapers, radio). Response categories ranged from 'very strongly in favour' to 'very much against' on a 5-point scale. In addition, to assess motivation to comply, respondents were asked to say how often they would 'take notice of' what the above people or institutions think they ought to do to avoid getting HIV. The categories ranged from 'rarely or none of the time' to 'most or all of the time', scored on a 5-point scale. Two measures of subjective norm were computed: a weighted version, obtained by multiplying scores on the belief items by motivation to comply, and an unweighted version.

*Beliefs About Gender Roles in Carrying Condoms*

It was also decided to include two questions relevant to the possible different roles of men and women as far as potential condom use was concerned. These were not intended to be directly related to the theory of reasoned action, but were expected to shed some light upon pressures to adopt or not to adopt safer practices among men and women in the different ethnic groups. The questions asked, first, 'Do you think it's OK for a woman to carry condoms?.' Then: 'Do you think it's OK for a man to carry condoms?'. Response categories were 'yes', 'no' and 'don't know.'

*Subjective Norm About Exclusive Sexual Partners*

Respondents were asked how strongly selected sources (the same as for subjective norms about condoms) were 'in favour of people sticking to one sexual partner to reduce their chances of getting AIDS.' Both unweighted and weighted versions of this measure were obtained.

## Perceived Control Over Taking Precautions Against HIV Infection

Perceived control was assessed using the following item: 'If you thought it necessary, could you insist that precautions be taken against AIDS when you have sex?' Response categories were: 'yes', 'unsure' and 'no', and were scored as 3, 2 and 1, respectively. Although condoms are not implicated directly in the question, 'taking precautions' was generally understood to be protection by condoms.

## Results

### The Relationship Between Intention to Use a Condom and to Have Sex With One Partner Exclusively

Before examining results for the two methods of safer sex, it is worth noting that intentions to use one or the other were largely independent. The correlations between intention to use a condom with a new sexual partner and the intention to be in an exclusive relationship were as follows: Anglo-Australians .29 ($df = 75$); Vietnamese .18, ($df = 71$); Poles .25, ($df = 74$); and Italians .07 ($df = 77$). The correlation for all respondents was .22, ($p < .01$, $df = 305$). Hence, in general, there was a significant but weak tendency for intentions to practise the two forms of safer sex to be positively associated.

### Comparison of Ethnic Groups on Expressed Intentions to Practise Safer Sex

Whether the four ethnic groups differed in their expressed intentions to use safer sex practices was examined by comparing the proportions of respondents in each group who indicated that they would probably or definitely (these two response categories were combined) (a) insist upon a condom being used with a new sexual partner and (b) stick with one sexual partner. The results are given in Table 1.

Ethnic group differences were evident, particularly with regard to intentions to use a condom, the main contrast being between Vietnamese respondents, among whom less than 50% of each sex indicated an intention (either 'definitely' or 'probably') to use a condom with a new partner, and others. The contrast applied especially to Italian and Anglo-Australian women, more than 80% of whom expressed the intention. Differences in intentions to 'stick with one sexual partner' were less pronounced and confined to men. Again it was the Vietnamese whose responses contrasted with others. Only about one third of Vietnamese men expressed this intention; among Polish men, there were approximately three quarters.

Table 6.1. *Percentages of Respondents in Ethnic Groups Indicating Intentions to Use a Method of Safer Sex*

| Sex | Ethnic group | | | | |
| | Anglo-Australian | Vietnamese | Polish | Italian | Significance of group differences |
| --- | --- | --- | --- | --- | --- |
| Use condom with new partner | | | | | |
| Male | 58 | 38 | 68 | 80 | ** |
| Female | 92 | 49 | 74 | 87 | *** |
| Be in an exclusive sexual relationship | | | | | |
| Male | 59 | 36 | 73 | 48 | * |
| Female | 87 | 62 | 75 | 64 | ns |

Significance level tested by chi-square; in each case, $df = 3$.
*$p$<.05; **$p$<.01; ***$p$<.001.

## Comparison Among Ethnic Groups on the Predictor Variables

### Predictors of Condom Use

Scores on the measures considered relevant to the application of the theory of reasoned action to condom use were compared for each of the four ethnic groups. In Table 2 results are given for the unweighted measures of attitudes to condoms and subjective norm relating to condom use. This is because it was the unweighted versions that were more strongly related to behavioural intentions (see Table 2 below).

From Table 2 it is clear that the ethnic groups did differ significantly in attitudes, subjective norms and perceived capability to take precautions (control). In addition females tended to have more positive attitudes to condom use and to have greater perceived control over taking precautions. Attitudes to condoms were least positive among the Vietnamese; pressure to use condoms was greatest among Anglo-Australians and Italians, as was perceived control.

### Predictors of Intention to be in an Exclusive Sexual Relationship

Here the variables relevant to the theory of reasoned action were (a) attitudes towards an exclusive sexual relationship (only an unweighted version for this measure was available) and (b) subjective norm regarding exclusive relationships (the unweighted version was used, as it provided

Table 6.2. *Mean Scores for Samples of Four Ethnic Groups on Measures Relevant to Condom Use and Exclusive Relationships*

| Measure | Sex | Ethnic group | | | |
| | | Anglo-Australian | Vietnamese | Polish | Italian |
| --- | --- | --- | --- | --- | --- |
| Attitudes to condoms | Male | 19.00 | 16.48 | 18.22 | 18.73 |
| | Female | 20.73 | 19.18 | 18.80 | 20.50 |
| Subjective norm (condoms) | Male | 4.08 | 3.64 | 3.86 | 4.12 |
| | Female | 4.33 | 3.78 | 3.75 | 4.06 |
| Perceived control | Male | 2.79 | 2.45 | 2.58 | 2.88 |
| | Female | 3.00 | 2.67 | 2.72 | 2.87 |
| Attitude to exclusive relationships | Male | 15.23 | 15.79 | 15.97 | 14.95 |
| | Female | 16.90 | 17.95 | 18.18 | 16.87 |
| Subjective norm (exclusive relationships) | Male | 4.11 | 4.19 | 4.30 | 4.37 |
| | Female | 4.45 | 4.69 | 4.49 | 4.51 |

| Measure | ANOVA results: $F$ values and significance | | |
| | Ethnic group | Gender | Ethnic group x gender |
| --- | --- | --- | --- |
| Attitude to condoms | 4.32** | 13.57*** | 0.87 |
| Subjective norm | 4.33*** | 0.46 | 1.16 |
| Perceived control | 6.93*** | 4.83* | 0.63 |
| Attitude to exclusive relationships | 2.27 | 26.69*** | 0.10 |
| Subjective norm | 1.31 | 20.24*** | 1.56 |

*$p<.05$; **$p<.01$; ***$p<.001$.

the better prediction, see Table 3). The mean scores and results of analyses of variance are provided in Table 2.

In contrast to the results for variables relevant to intention to use a condom, no differences in the attitude and subjective norm measures among ethnic groups were found for the variables relevant to exclusive relationships. Significant effects were found, however, for gender, indicating that for both attitudes and subjective norms, females were more positively disposed towards favouring exclusive sexual relationships.

In summary, comparison of scores obtained by ethnic group members on measures relating to condoms showed marked differences among the groups in intentions, attitudes and subjective norms. As far as measures relevant to exclusive relationships were concerned, the differences were much less marked, being confined to males' weaker intentions to be in an exclusive relationship.

## Results for Regression Analyses

### Preliminary Analyses

In preliminary analyses, the set of independent variables for the multiple regression analyses included (a) age group, (b) attachment (married/defacto or not), (c) sex and (d) English language fluency. Self-reports of English language fluency, using a 4-point scale, were generally in agreement with the ratings provided by the interviews. For people of NESB for whom results were available, the Pearson correlation between the two ratings was .78 ($df = 221, p < .001$). Analyses involving English language fluency were conducted only for people of NESB.

Stepwise multiple regression was employed to identify the independent variables that were contributing significantly ($p < .05$) to the prediction of (a) intention to use a condom and (b) intention to be in an exclusive relationship. Only attachment and sex were found to make a significant contribution. Being female was associated with a stronger expressed intention of using a condom with a new sexual partner, and also with the intention to have sexual relationships exclusively with one person. This may appear paradoxical, but it should be noted that the 'new sexual partner' is hypothetical; that is, should there be a new sexual partner. Being attached, that is married or defacto, was likewise associated with an expressed intention to use a condom with a new partner, and also with relating exclusively.

### English Language Fluency

The results for English language fluency were not significant in relation to either of the two dependent variables in analyses including com-

Table 6.3. *Results for Multiple Regression Analyses on Intention to (a) Use a Condom with a New Sexual Partner, and (b) have an Exclusive Sexual Partner*

| | Intention to use a condom (beta coefficients) | |
| --- | --- | --- |
| Predictor variable | Unweighted | Weighted |
| Attitude to condoms | .13*** | .05 |
| Subjective norm (condoms) | .32*** | .28*** |
| Perceived control | .19*** | .24*** |
| Gender | .19*** | .19*** |
| Attachment | -.13* | -.15** |
| Multiple _R_ | .61*** | .57*** |
| Degrees of freedom | 8, 311 | 8, 311 |

| | Intention to have an exclusive relationship (beta coefficients) | |
| --- | --- | --- |
| Predictor variable | Unweighted | Weighted |
| Attitude to exclusive relationship | .15** | .23*** |
| Subjective norm (exclusive relationship) | .29*** | .11* |
| Gender | .08 | .11* |
| Attachment | -.11* | -.14* |
| Multiple _R_ | .47*** | .40*** |
| Degrees of freedom | 7,312 | 7,312 |

Dummy variables were included in the analyses to control for ethnic group membership.
*_p_<.05; **_p_<.01; ***_p_<.001.

bined data for the three groups of non-English speaking background. Nor was fluency significant in analyses for each ethnic group independently. Clearly the view that English language fluency is a factor in adopting safer sexual practices in the selected ethnic groups cannot be sustained on the basis of these results.

*Predicting Intention to Use a Condom*

The results of the analyses predicting intention to use a condom (both weighted and unweighted versions of measures) and the relevant demographic variables are presented in Table 3.

The set including the unweighted versions of the attitude and subjective norm measures accounted for a somewhat larger amount of the variance in intention to use condoms (37% as against 34%) than those with weighted measures. It also produced results that are totally supportive of the predictions: that is, intention to use condoms with a new partner (given that contingency) is positively related to (a) favourable attitudes to condoms, (b) supportive subjective norm about condom use and (c) high perceived control over taking precautions against HIV. This intention is also more likely to be found among females and people who are attached (i.e., married or in a defacto relationship). The differences between the predictive power of the two sets of variables is not great. The main difference is that the unweighted measure of attitude towards condoms is significantly related to intention to use condoms; the weighted measure is not.

*Predicting Intention to be with an Exclusive Sexual Partner*

Results of regression analysis for the two sets of variables (weighted and unweighted) used to predict intention to be with an exclusive sexual partner are also given in Table 3. Again a slightly larger amount of the variance (22%) was accounted for by the set including the unweighted measure of subjective norm, as compared with the set for which the measure was weighted (16%). On this evidence the use of the non-weighted measure of subjective norm seems preferable in predicting intention to be in an exclusive relationship. However, the difference in variance accounted for is again not large. Neither set of variables, in fact, accounted for a substantial amount of variance.

The results were as predicted, with both the attitude and the subjective norm variables being significantly related to intention. As for intention to use condoms, attachment (being married or defacto) was to a small but significant extent associated with intending to be in an exclusive relationship. Although females generally appeared more likely to express an intention to be in an exclusive relationship, the results for gender are significant for the set of weighted variables only.

*Examination of Results for Each Ethnic Group*

The results for individual ethnic groups were based upon much smaller samples and this reduced the power of the analyses considerably. In general, they failed to provide consistent support for the predictions, and suggest that some factors may have different implications for particular groups. These results are given in Table 4.

For intention to use condoms, the three predictors, attitude, subjective norm and perceived control were each associated with the dependent variable as predicted, but for none of the ethnic groups were all three significant. There was, nonetheless, one independent variable, subjective

Table 6.4. *Results for Multiple Regression for Four Ethnic Groups on Intention to (a) Use a Condom with a New Sexual Partner, and (b) to have an Exclusive Sexual Relationship*

| | Intention to use a condom for ethnic groups (beta coefficients) | | | |
|---|---|---|---|---|
| | Anglo-Australian | Vietnamese | Polish | Italian |
| Attitude to condoms (unweighted) | .05 | .12 | .32** | .16 |
| Subjective norm (condoms) (unweighted) | .33** | .41*** | .28** | .26** |
| Perceived control | .31** | .23* | .06 | .37*** |
| Gender | .23* | .07 | .29** | .18 |
| Attachment | .02 | -.25* | -.02 | -.02 |
| Multiple $R$ | .61*** | .62*** | .57*** | .60*** |
| Degrees of freedom | 5, 71 | 5, 64 | 5, 66 | 5, 72 |
| | Intention to have an exclusive relationship for ethnic groups (beta coefficients) | | | |
| | Anglo-Australian | Vietnamese | Polish | Italian |
| Attitude to exclusive relationship | .32*** | -.05 | .16 | .14 |
| Subjective norm (exclusive relationship) | .30** | .34** | .23 | .37*** |
| Gender | .15 | .21 | -.03 | .08 |
| Attachment | -.06 | -.05 | -.07 | -.17 |
| Multiple $R$ | .60*** | .46*** | .35* | .48*** |
| Degrees of freedom | 4, 72 | 4, 69 | 4, 69 | 4, 73 |

These analyses used the unweighted version of the subjective norm variable.
*$p$<.05; **$p$<.01; ***$p$<.001.

norm, that was related as predicted, and significantly so, for each of the four ethnic groups. There is, therefore, highly consistent evidence, from both the total combined sample and the analysis for individual groups, that subjective norms do contribute in this area as the theory predicts. One may also add that for one ethnic group (the Polish) both attitudes and subjective norms independently predicted intention to use condoms, which is consistent with the theory of reasoned action.

For intentions to be in an exclusive sexual relationship, the results provide only limited support for the theory when examined for each ethnic group independently. It was only for the Anglo-Australian sample that there was consistent support for the theory of reasoned action: beta coefficients for both attitude and subjective norm were independently significant. As with the analysis for intention to use a condom, the most consistently significant predictor was the subjective norm measure, the significance level of which failed to reach the .05 level for one group only (the Polish group, for which the $p$ value was .07).

## Subjective Norms and Respondent Intention

Given that normative influences appeared in the analyses to have operated with considerable consistency across the ethnic groups, particularly with respect to condom use, a more detailed examination of such pressures was justified. The judgements of respondents about particular reference sources were examined. There was general agreement about which sources tended to favour condom use strongly and which did not. The range of percentages (across the different ethnic groups) for belief that friends favoured condom use was 60–90; for media, 86–90; for partner, 54–83; for parents, 51–68; and for the church, 31–53. Generally, friends and the media were seen as more positively disposed towards condom use than parents and the church. At the same time, there were some marked differences in judgements between the ethnic groups. Vietnamese and Polish respondents saw their friends and parents as much less favourably inclined to condom use than did Anglo-Australians and Italians. Vietnamese people saw their partners as favouring condom use less than people from other ethnic groups. In short, there was a good deal of cultural diversity in the subjective norms about condom use. By contrast, there was little difference among ethnic groups in judgements about the favourability of sources towards exclusive sexual relationships. There was broad agreement that the sources were *for* exclusive sexual relationships, most obviously in the case of the church (83–94%) and least so in the case of friends (74–78%) and media (71–88%).

The strength of association (and therefore possible influence) between ratings of the sources as favouring the two practices of safer sex and ex-

Table 6.5. *Responses of Ethnic Group Members on Whether it is Acceptable for (a) a Man, and (b) a Woman to Carry a Condom*

| Ethnic group | "OK" for a man | | "OK" for a woman | |
| | Males | Females | Males | Females |
| --- | --- | --- | --- | --- |
| Anglo-Australian | 95% (38) | 100% (40) | 90% (36) | 100% (40) |
| Vietnamese | 85% (34) | 75% (30) | 45% (18) | 44% (17) |
| Polish | 85% (34) | 80% (32) | 75% (30) | 55% (22) |
| Italian | 98% (39) | 93% (37) | 85% (34) | 78% (31) |
| Significance of group differences | ns | <.01 | <.001 | <.001 |

Ns agreeing are given in parentheses.

pressed intended behaviour was also examined. Friends and partners appeared to have most influence. The pattern of correlation, however, suggested differences among ethnic groups. For example, correlations between the respondents' views and those perceived for parents on condom use and exclusive sexual relationships were positive and significant for the Vietnamese group (the correlations being .34 and .42, respectively) but non-significant for Polish respondents ($r = .06$ in each case). Correlations also suggested that the Italian group, but not the Anglo-Australians, may have been significantly influenced by media to adopt condom use: for Italians, $r = .38$, $p < .01$; for Anglo-Australians, $r = .14$, $p < .05$.

## Gender Role and Condom Use

Responses to two questions enabled us to see whether there were ethnic group differences on whether it was considered proper for men and/or women to carry condoms. Percentages of respondents in each ethnic group giving affirmative responses to each question are given in Table 5.

Although there was some disagreement among women of different ethnic groups about whether it is acceptable for a man to carry a condom (with the Vietnamese women least accepting), differences were much more marked on the issue of whether it is acceptable for a woman to do so. Here the judgements of both men and women strongly suggest ethnic group differences, with Vietnamese and Polish respondents least accepting of women carrying condoms. It is notable that a double standard is most evident in the Vietnamese group. These results strongly suggest that in the Vietnamese community it is acceptable for men, but not women, to carry condoms.

## A Partial Replication with Latin-American People in South Australia

A more recent study, undertaken in 1992, has provided further data on the application of the theories of reasoned action and planned behaviour to the prediction of intended condom use, and the possible contribution of English language fluency.

In this study, interview and questionnaire data were collected by bilingual interviewers from 144 people living in South Australia whose ethnic background could be described as Central or South American. Of these, 69 were male and 79 female. Ages ranged from 12 to 50 years, the median age being 24.01 years, with a standard deviation of 7.90. Some 87% indicated that they had been born outside Australia, the highest percentages being from El Salvador (36%) and Chile (29%). Other countries represented were Argentina, Bolivia, Colombia, Guatemala, Honduras, Mexico, Nicaragua, Paraguay, Peru, Uruguay and Venezuela. Apart from a common location in Central and South America, the respondents had in common the ability to speak Spanish: 89% very well. Interviews were mainly conducted in Spanish. For those born in Australia of Latin-American parents, interviews were conducted at least in part in English.

As in the previously reported study, responses to questionnaire and interview items provided measures of intention to use a condom, attitudes to condoms, subjective norm relating to condom use, perceived control over taking precautions, attachment (whether married/defacto or not), age, gender and English language fluency. There were some variations in the operationalisation of variables. Four responses were utilised in obtaining a measure of intended condom use with a new sexual partner: 'yes'; 'probably yes'; 'don't know'; and 'no'. Some 80% of respondents were prepared to answer this question as part of an anonymous questionnaire. Forty-four percent of these respondents gave an unequivocal 'yes' as their answer; 32% indicated that they probably would use a condom.

Attitude to condoms was indexed using four items. These were concerned with: (a) *inconvenience*: 'condoms are a nuisance, I couldn't be bothered using them'; (b) *morality*: 'condoms encourage immoral behaviour'; and (c) and (d) *acceptability of carrying condoms*: 'it's OK for a man/woman to carry condoms.' Responses on the above items were scored in the direction of positive evaluation of condoms. No further questions were asked to provide a means of weighting this variable by perceived importance. Hence an unweighted version was employed in this study.

Measurement of subjective norms about condom use involved six sources about which respondents were asked to say what they believed

Table 6.6. *Results for Pearson Correlations and Multiple Regression Analysis on Intention to Use a Condom with a New Sexual Partner for Latin-American Respondents*

| Predictor variables | Pearson $r$ | Beta coefficients | |
|---|---|---|---|
| | | Step-wise analysis | All variables entered |
| Attitude to condoms | .56*** | .39*** | .34*** |
| Subjective norm | .37*** | .29** | .31*** |
| Perceived control | .46*** | .20* | .24* |
| Gender | .02 | .21* | .20* |
| Attachment | -.12 | - | -.15 |
| English fluency | .27* | - | .03 |
| Age | -.16 | - | .00 |
| Multiple $\underline{R}$ | | .65 | .67 |
| Degrees of freedom | | 4, 92 | 7, 89 |

*$\underline{p}$<.05; **$\underline{p}$<.01; ***$\underline{p}$<.001.

each thought about condom use. The sources were: parents, friends, partner, actors/singers, the church and Latin-American community. Evaluations (on a 5-point scale) were weighted by judgements about how much the respondents thought they had been influenced in their sexual behaviour by the appropriate sources, again using a 5-point scale. Perceived control was assessed by response to the question: 'Do you think you would be able to talk about precautions against AIDS with someone you wanted to make love with?' The categories were 'yes', 'don't know', and 'no.'

Fluency in English was based upon responses to two questions: one relating to speaking, the other reading, both on a 2-point scale, 'very well' and 'not at all well'. Fluency was a general measure: the mean of scores from the two questions. Age (in years), gender and attachment (married/defacto or other) made up the remaining variables used in the multiple regression, the results of which are given in Table 6.

The results are consistent with the theory of planned behaviour; that is, the expressed intention to use condoms with a new sexual partner was predicted independently by (a) attitude to condoms, (b) subjective norm and (c) perceived control. Gender (being female) was also predictive of intentions to use condoms. The amount of variance accounted for is comparable to that reported in previous studies, approximately 45%. Notably, fluency in English, as in the previously reported study, was non-predictive, as were age and attachment.

In a further test of the power of the theoretically relevant variables to predict intention to use condoms, a regression analysis was conducted including a measure of previous use of condoms. A question asked whether the respondent had always, sometimes or never used a condom in the past (13% reported 'always' using a condom; 47% reported 'sometimes'). The results for the stepwise regression showed that four variables were significant ($p < .05$) with the following beta coefficients: attitude to condoms .45; subjective norm .24; previous condom use .22 and gender .19. Perceived control did not yield a significant result in this analysis. From these results it is evident that even when previous relevant behaviour is included in the analysis, the theory of reasoned action is still supported: results for both the attitude and social norm variables were as predicted.

## Review and Appraisal

We have seen that there is strong and consistent evidence that groups of persons in Australia differing in ethnic background respond differently to AIDS-related issues. The differences do not represent a simple contrast between the majority of people of Anglo-Australian background and the minority of others. Ethnic groups of NESB differ among themselves. These differences cover a wide range of issues, including beliefs about HIV and AIDS, HIV transmission, attitudes towards people living with HIV/AIDS and acceptance or rejection of homosexuality. Of particular importance, ethnic groups differ on attitudes towards condoms and, specifically, what they say they intend to do in the future to protect themselves against HIV infection.

We have also seen that the major reason advanced in previous research for differences between ethnic groups on AIDS-related issues is that there are differences in fluency in the English language. The assumption is that inadequacies in access to information about HIV (which in Australia is mainly in English) constitute the problem, to be remedied by more and more brochures, television advertisements and radio announcements in various community languages. This view is plausible; knowledge of HIV, for example, is related to fluency in English, at least for some ethnic groups. The results of these studies, however, do not support the view that differences in English language fluency pose the crucial problem. In fact, as far as intention to use condoms in a future sexual encounter is concerned, English language fluency appears, on the basis of this study, to play a non-significant part. In the light of the failure of this factor to explain why some people are more insistent on using condoms than others, a general theory, like the theory of reasoned action, assumes greater importance.

Before appraising the extent to which the theory of reasoned action helps us to understand the social psychology of adopting safer methods of countering HIV, it should be noted that the complete version of the theory was not applied. For both condom use and exclusiveness in sexual relationships, intention and not action was the dependent variable. Given the high degree of intrusiveness of questions relating to sexual behaviour, and the sensitivity of some ethnic groups, such as Vietnamese, to questions about sex, it is difficult to see how behaviour in this area can be accurately assessed, and it appears that we may have to be content with the proxy of intention.

We should note, too, that in the studies reported in this chapter, the use of variables (attitude and subjective norm) appropriately weighted by theoretically relevant values, was not consistently followed. However, the evidence from results using alternative measures (weighted and un-weighted) suggests that this may not be important in predicting outcomes. Hence this is arguably not a major limitation of this study. The fact that some of the variables used in the replication study were operationalised somewhat differently from the earlier one can be seen as a test of the robustness of the theories. What emerges from the results for different ethnic groups most consistently is that English language fluency is not an effective predictor of intention to adopt safer sexual practices, compared with the variables suggested by the theories of reasoned action and planned behaviour.

Many of the results reported were consistent with predictions. Where all the data for the four ethnic groups from Europe and Asia were used (with dummy variables included for each group) the results are supportive. Attitudes, subjective norm and perceived control each independently figure as significant predictors of intention to use a condom (at least if the non-weighted version of attitude is used). The replication study of Latin Americans provides further support for the theory, again with respect to condom use. Although the amount of variance accounted for in predicting intention to be involved in an exclusive sexual relationship is relatively low, again there is evidence that measures of relevant attitudes and subjective norms can predict intentions to use another method of safer sex.

However, when we examine the results for ethnic groups individually the limitations of the theory become evident. Support for the theory is certainly inconsistent. For intention to use condoms, only subjective norm provides a significant result, as reflected by beta coefficients, for every ethnic group. For intention to be with one sexual partner exclusively, it is only for Anglo-Australians that both attitude and subjective norm measures are significant predictors. It must therefore be concluded that on the basis of results from the studies reported in this chapter, the theories of reasoned action and planned behaviour have limited support only.

The most positive aspect of the results concerns the importance of subjective norms. We can say that an understanding of the pressure on individuals from relevant sources is basic to the devising of effective campaign against HIV and AIDS. The theory of reasoned action helps us to focus attention upon this significant factor, for which significant results were found across a wide range of ethnic groups from Europe, Asia, and Central and South America living in Australia.

# 7

# Extending the Theory of Reasoned Action: The Role of Health Beliefs

PETA WARWICK, DEBORAH TERRY and CYNTHIA GALLOIS

*The University of Queensland, Brisbane, Australia*

## The Health Belief Model

Although there is considerable support for the utility of the theory of reasoned action, both in the context of sexual behaviour and in relation to a range of other behaviours (see Lewis & Kashima, this volume & Terry *et al.*, this volume), other models of health behaviour have also received some empirical support. The health belief model has been influential in this respect. Unlike the theory of reasoned action, the health belief model incorporates variables that indirectly assess the subjective elements of vulnerability and fear arousal associated with most illnesses. To better explain health behaviour, the theory of reasoned action may benefit from a consideration of the unique aspects of the health belief model. In the present chapter, a study that focused on the extent to which health beliefs improve the prediction of safer sex behaviour is described.

The health belief model (Rosenstock, 1974b) proposes that a person's readiness to engage in a preventive health behaviour is influenced by the individual's perception of vulnerability or risk of contracting the disease (percieved susceptibility) and the individual's beliefs about the seriousness of consequences associated with that disease (perceived severity). These two components of the model reflect the level of threat associated with the disease. In addition to threat level, the health belief proposes that a person's willingness to engage in a preventive health behaviour is influenced by the perceived benefits of performing the behaviour weighted against the potential negative aspects of doing so (perceived barriers).

Although not as empirically successful in its predictions as the theory of reasoned action (Reid & Christensen, 1988; Lierman, Young, Kasprzyk & Benoliel, 1990), there is, as noted by Terry *et al.* (this volume), evidence that health belief variables successfully predict calcium intake (Wurtel,

117

1988), breast self-examination (Hallal, 1982), dietary compliance (Becker, Haefner, Mainman, Kirscht & Drachman, 1977), as well as a host of other preventive health behaviours (including participation in screening programs, seeking immunisation, etc.). In their review of the literature testing the utility of the health belief model, Janz and Becker (1984) concluded that there was some evidence linking each of the four components of the health belief model (severity, susceptibility, perceived benefits and perceived barriers) to preventive health behaviour. The review revealed consistent support for the proposed role of the perceived barriers component of the model. There was also evidence linking perceived susceptibility and perceived benefits to preventive health action (the evidence was strongest for perceived susceptibility); however, across the range of studies considered, there was only weak support for the proposed link between the perceived severity of the health condition and people's willingness to engage in the appropriate preventive behaviour.

To date, empirical tests of the health belief model in the context of HIV-preventive behaviour have failed to provide strong support for the model (see also Lewis & Kashima, this volume). In a longitudinal study, Montgomery*et al.* , (1989), for instance, found that the model accounted for only a small amount of variance in homosexual men's willingness to engage in HIV-preventive behaviour. As pointed out by Montgomery *et al.* (1989), the AIDS threat has a number of characteristics that distinguish it from other health threats. In the first instance, the risk of HIV infection is a severe threat. There is currently no vaccination against infection with HIV, nor a known cure for the disease. Second, the recommended behavioural responses to the AIDS threat are more complex than for other health threats. In particular, people need to modify their sexual behaviours, which may not be easy, given that such behaviours are typically influenced by strong emotive and normative influences. In light of the special characteristics of the threat, the health belief model may, therefore, be too simplistic to account adequately for variation in people's propensity to engage in AIDS-preventive behaviour (Montgomery *et al.*, 1989).

More recent studies have replicated the results reported by Montgomery *et al.* (1989). Studies with African-American men (Nathanson*et al.* , 1991) and Hispanics (Porter & Bonilla, 1991) in the U.S.A. both showed that neither susceptibility nor severity were predictors of intended behaviour change. After control of the effects of HIV knowledge and attitudes, the components of the health belief model did not significantly improve the amount of variance explained in HIV-testing behaviour in the U.S.A. (Porter & Bonilla, 1992). Likewise, in a Swiss cohort study, which studied the determinants of condom use during casual sexual contacts (Heusser, Tschopp, Beutter & Gutzwiller, 1992), health belief variables did not emerge as independent determinants of inconsistent condom use. Walter*et al.* , (1992) similarly found that the constructs of the health belief model were not significantly associated with higher risk behaviours in a sample of New York 10th grade students, although Petosa and Jackson (1991) did find some support for the model in the prediction of safer sex intentions among a sample of students, particularly for younger adolescents.

Previous research linking health belief constructs to safer sex behaviour has clearly failed to provide strong support for the utility of the health belief model. Nevertheless, it was considered necessary to examine its utility further given that, unlike the theory of reasoned action, the health belief model does not have clear guidelines about how variables should be operationalised. As a consequence, there are inconsistencies in the way health belief model variables have been defined and measured in previous research (Wallston & Wallston, 1984). These inconsistencies may account at least partially for the weak and unstable relationships often found between health belief model components and behaviour (Lierman *et al.*, 1990).

The operationalisations of the perceived severity and perceived susceptibility dimensions are relatively unambiguous. Most research has targeted these variables simply by asking questions such as 'How serious would it be if....?' or 'How likely is it that....?' (Jette, Cummings, Brock, Phelps & Naessens, 1981). The benefits and barriers components are more difficult to define both conceptually and operationally. In most health belief research, measures of the perceived benefits of performing a particular health care behaviour have focused on the role of positive outcomes and expectations. The components of the benefits dimension, however, seem arbitrarily defined by the researcher's goals. Differences exist as to whether this measure includes only the perceived medical effectiveness of a specific action in reducing the likelihood of disease, or all positive outcomes, psychological as well as medical. A focus only on the medical consequences of an action may mean that salient benefits of the behaviour are neglected, thus reducing the observed effect of the benefits dimension on readiness to engage in health care behaviour. This is particularly likely to occur in relation to safer sex behaviour, where people will presumably consider both the medical and non-medical consequences (e.g., interpersonal and psychological outcomes) of a particular course of action when making behavioural decisions (Montgomery *et al.*, 1989; Ross & McLaws, 1992).

The barriers measure of the health belief model may also cause problems of operationalisation. Most researchers have conceptualised this component of the model as the perceived costs of performing the behaviour. Researchers have typically focused on the tangible costs associated with a particular course of action (such as the physical and financial costs). Like benefits, however, the psychological aspects of the barriers dimension of the model may be relevant to the prediction of safer sex, given that people's perceptions of the difficulty of negotiating safer sex, the potential loss of spontaneity in the sexual relationship and related concerns are likely to have more impact on behavioural decisions than the tangible cost incurred in the purchase of condoms.

In addition to examining further the utility of refined measures of health beliefs as predictors of HIV-preventive behaviour, it is useful to examine whether the components of the health belief model improve prediction of HIV-preventive behaviour, after control of the effects of the components of the more parsimonious theory of reasoned action (the latter model comprises only two direct predictors of intentions, as opposed to the four dimensions of the health belief model). Although both Mullen, Hersey and Iverson (1987) and Hill, Gardner and Rassaby (1985) examined the relative utility of the two models (in both instances, the models explained comparable amounts of variance in health care behaviour), only Hill *et al.* attempted to test an integration of the models. These researchers presented some evidence to suggest that a combined health belief/theory of reasoned action model may improve prediction of intentions to engage in preventive health behaviours; however, these results need to be replicated in the prediction of HIV-preventive behaviour. Moreover, the integration of the two models needs to be tested more systematically, given that in their combined model, Hill *et al.* included only the health belief variables that predicted intentions to engage in both behaviours under consideration (breast self-examination and Pap test).

In order to make predictions concerning the utility of a combined health belief/theory of reasoned action model, one must compare the conceptual structure of the two models. As noted previously, the health belief model includes two intuitively important variables that the theory of reasoned action omits, namely, the dimensions of perceived severity and perceived susceptibility. Fishbein and Middlestadt (1989) acknowledged that the notions of perceived severity and susceptibility are clearly distinguishable from the two central predictors of behavioural intentions in the theory of reasoned action (the person's attitude towards performing a particular behaviour and the perceived level of social pressure to do so). They suggested, however, that like other external variables (such as demographic variables), the effects of susceptibility and severity on behavioural intentions may be only indirect, through their effects on attitudes and norms (e.g., people who judge themselves to be susceptible to HIV may perceive more pressure from others to engage in safer sex behaviours than people with low levels of perceived risk for HIV). This proposal needs to be tested empirically, given that there is evidence that perceived susceptibility, at least, has a direct impact upon people's decisions to engage in health care behaviours (see Janz & Becker, 1984).

Despite the support in the wider literature on health care behaviour linking perceived susceptibility and to a lesser extent perceived severity to health care intentions, it should be noted that there is reason to believe that there may not be a strong relationship between either perceived severity or susceptibility and readiness to engage in HIV-preventive behaviour. As noted, previous research on the determinants of safer sex has failed to support the health belief model. Moreover, perceived severity of AIDS may not be influential in the prediction of HIV-preventive behaviour, because of the almost universal perception that AIDS is a serious threat (Montgomery *et al.*, 1989; Wright, 1990). Once a threat is recognised as being severe, beliefs regarding the severity of an outcome are unlikely to influence behaviour (Weinstein 1989; see also Kruglanski & Khar, 1985). In such cases, behavioural decisions can presumably be better justified in terms of beliefs in personal risk, given that the justification that the outcome (in this case HIV infection) is not severe would be difficult to sustain (see Timmins *et al.*, this volume).

Perceived susceptibility may also have little impact on the decision to engage in HIV-preventive behaviour. Although there is evidence that perceived risk has influenced homosexuals' response to HIV (Becker & Joseph, 1988; Kelly & St. Lawrence, 1988), there is evidence that levels of perceived risk for HIV do not influence heterosexuals' intentions to engage in HIV-preventive behaviour (e.g., Gallois, Kashima *et al.*, 1992; Rosenthal & Moore, 1991). This may be attributable to the fact that, irrespective of actual level of risk, heterosexuals are unlikely to perceive themselves to be at risk for HIV (see Weinstein, 1989). As a consequence of categorising people with HIV as an outgroup, heterosexuals may deny the relevance of the threat of HIV to themselves (Siegel & Gibson, 1988). Denial of personal risk for HIV infection allows the stereotypic beliefs concerning the relationship between attitudes towards homosexuals and the prevalence of HIV to be maintained. If a person accepts that he or she may be personally at some risk for HIV infection, then the boundaries between the ingroup and outgroup are weakened, which has implications for the person's self-concept. Acceptance of the possibility that one trait (potential for contracting HIV) associated with the outgroup may be applicable to a description of oneself means that other associated traits may also be personally relevant.

In contrast to perceived susceptibility and severity, the barriers and benefits dimensions of the health belief model are incorporated in the theory of reasoned action (Fishbein & Middlestadt, 1989). Both the barriers/benefits dimensions of the health belief model and the behavioural beliefs components of the theory of reasoned action assess the perceived costs and benefits of performing a behaviour. However, despite the conceptual differences between the variables, there are a number of differences between the conceptualisation of the role of benefits and barriers in the health belief model and the role attributed to behavioural beliefs in the theory of reasoned action. In the first instance, the benefits and barriers dimensions of the health belief model are proposed to have a direct impact upon behavioural intentions, whereas the effects of behavioural beliefs on intentions are proposed to be mediated by attitudes. Secondly, in the theory of reasoned action, the measures of behavioural beliefs are weighted by the person's evaluation of the pleasantness of each of the outcomes. In contrast, the unweighted scores on the barriers and benefits dimensions of the health belief model are proposed to have an impact on behavioural intentions. The final difference between the notion of behavioural beliefs and the health belief dimensions of benefits and barriers concerns the fact that both the positive and negative aspects of performing the behaviour are assessed in the measure of behavioural beliefs, whereas these two components are considered separately in the health belief model.

On the basis of the conceptual similarity between the benefits/barriers dimensions of the health belief model and the concept of behavioural beliefs, proponents of the theory of reasoned action (e.g., Fishbein & Middlestadt, 1989) would argue that, after control of the effects of a person's attitude towards performing the behaviour, neither benefits/barriers nor behavioural beliefs should directly influence people's intentions to perform the behaviour. For behavioural beliefs, there is support for this hypothesis (e.g., Terry, Galligan & Conway, in press). Research, however, needs to examine further the extent to which this is the case for the benefits/barriers dimensions of the health belief model, given that Hill *et al.* (1985) reported that both attitudes and perceived barriers directly influenced intentions to engage in cancer preventive behaviours (see also Moore *et al.*, this volume). The results reported by Hill *et al.*, suggest that a single evaluative dimension (such as an attitude) may not be able to represent the complexity of beliefs influencing behavioural decisions (Bagozzi & Burnkrant, 1979).

## Predicting Condom Use

The first aim of the study presented in this chapter was to compare the relative utilities of the health belief model and the theory of reasoned action in the context of condom use. Both models regard intention as the immediate precursor of behaviour; thus, there is no difference between the models at this level. The models do, however, differ in their predictions of intention. Although previous studies have found that the models account for comparable amounts of variance in behavioural intentions, it was anticipated that in the context of condom use, the theory of reasoned action would account for more variance than the health belief model. This is because it was proposed that two of the components of health belief model (perceived severity and perceived susceptibility) would not influence readiness to engage in safer sex behaviour.

For the theory of reasoned action, it was proposed that behavioural intentions would be predicted by both attitude and subjective norm, and that the effects of the belief-based measures of these variables would be mediated via their effect on the relevant direct measure (attitude or subjective norm). The health belief model identifies four predictors of behavioural intentions. It was anticipated that, in the context of HIV-preventive behaviour, only two of these variables would affect behavioural intentions (i.e., perceived barriers and benefits of performing the behaviour).

The second aim of the study was to examine whether health beliefs could explain additional variance in behavioural intentions and actual condom use, after control of the effects of the relevant components of the theory of reasoned action. On the basis of the results reported by Hill *et al.* (1985), it was anticipated that barriers may contribute to the prediction of behavioural intentions, after control of the effects of attitudes and norms. Perceived benefits may also have a direct influence on behavioural intentions (not tested by Hill *et al.,* 1985); however, in the context of safer sex, it was expected, as noted previously, that neither perceived severity nor susceptibility would influence intentions to engage in condom use.

## Method

### Pilot Study

As suggested by Ajzen and Fishbein (1980), beliefs about condom use were elicited by asking a series of open-ended questions to 18 (11 male and 7 female) undergraduate psychology students. The questionnaire aimed to determine the most commonly held beliefs about condom use and the important people in the subjects' lives who approved or disapproved of their use of condoms. The most commonly provided responses formed the basis for the measures of behavioural and normative beliefs (see below for example items).

### Subjects

One hundred and thirty-eight sexually experienced undergraduate psychology students, 80 males and 58 females, participated in the study. Subjects were aged between 17 and 21 years, with a mean age of 18.6 years (*S.D.* = 1.10). All subjects described themselves as being exclusively heterosexual. Seventy-eight percent (107) of the 138 initial respondents completed the follow up questionnaire. Scores on the measures of attitudes, subjective norm and intention to use a condom did not distinguish those subjects choosing to complete the second questionnaire from those who did not.

## Design and Procedure

The study was prospective in design. This was to avoid confounding between measures of the predictors and behaviour. The behavioural criterion examined in the present study was condom use on the next sexual encounter. Subjects completed questionnaires at two points in time. The first questionnaire was completed by subjects in groups in the laboratory. It assessed the proposed predictors of condom use (from both the theory of reasoned action and the health belief model). Actual behaviour was assessed at the second wave of data collection. Subjects took a follow-up questionnaire away from the first session, which they returned after their next sexual encounter or after one month, whichever came first.

## Measures

### Theory of Reasoned Action

A direct measure of *attitude* towards using a condom on the next sexual encounter was obtained using six items in semantic differential format (adjective pairs included 'bad–good'; 'wise–foolish'; alpha = .85). Belief-based measures of attitudes were computed as the sum of the products of scores on measures of *behavioural beliefs* and *outcome evaluations*. To assess behavioural beliefs, respondents indicated the likelihood ((-3) 'extremely unlikely' to (+3) 'extremely likely') that 14 different outcomes would be consequences of using a condom on their next sexual encounter. The scale comprised seven costs (e.g., reducing sexual pleasure, reducing the intimacy of sex) and seven benefits (e.g., protecting against sexually transmitted diseases such as HIV, preventing pregnancy). To assess outcome evaluations, respondents were asked to evaluate each of the costs and benefits on a scale ranging from (-3) 'extremely unpleasant' to (+3) 'extremely pleasant.' To assess the subjective norm, a single item assessing whether subjects perceived that significant others would want them to use a condom on their next sexual encounter was obtained ('The people I consider important, think I (or my partner) should wear a condom the next time I have sexual intercourse'). A belief-based measure of subjective norm was computed as the sum of the products of scores on measures of *normative beliefs* and *motivation to comply*. Normative beliefs were assessed by asking respondents the likelihood that salient others (five different referents, including parents, friends, current sexual partner) would think that they should perform the behaviour ((-3) 'extremely unlikely' to (+3) 'extremely likely'), while subjects' motivations to comply were assessed by asking them how willing were they to do what each of the referents wanted them to do ((1) 'not at all' to (4) 'very').

Two items assessed subjects' *intentions* for themselves or their partner to use a condom the next time that they had sexual intercourse (alpha = .97) (e.g., 'How likely is it that you, or your partner, will wear a condom the next time you have sexual intercourse?' (-3) 'extremely unlikely' to (+3) 'extremely likely'). *Actual behaviour* was assessed at Time 2. At this time, subjects indicated whether they or their partner had in fact used a condom on their last sexual encounter. Fifteen of the subjects had not engaged in sexual intercourse in the two weeks after completing the first questionnaire. Valid follow-up data were, therefore, available for 92 subjects. Of these subjects, 64% used a condom on their next sexual encounter.

### Health Belief Model

To assess *perceived susceptibility*, subjects responded to three items designed to assess perceived personal risk of contracting HIV ('What do you think is the risk to you personally of getting the AIDS virus?' (1) 'no risk' to (7) 'very high risk') (alpha = .69). As expected, perceptions of perceived susceptibility were relatively low. Susceptibility scores were, however, not significantly skewed. In contrast, the distribution of scores on the severity item ('Among the diseases I can imagine getting, HIV/AIDS is the:' (1) 'least serious' to (7) 'most serious') was significantly skewed (most people regarded the disease as serious). To reduce the skewness in the data, scores on the item were dichotomised (a score of 2 was assigned if people indicated that HIV/AIDS was the 'most serious' disease; all other ratings were assigned a score of 1).

The measure of *barriers* was computed as the average response to the behavioural belief items (see above) used to assess the negative consequences (costs) of using a condom on the next sexual encounter (7 items; alpha = .64). In a similar vein, a measure of *benefits* was obtained as the average of responses to the positive outcome items in the measure of behavioural beliefs (7 items; alpha = .79).

### Results and Discussion

#### Data Analysis

Preliminary analyses were conducted to determine whether it was necessary to examine the data separately for males and females. Control of the effects of gender in the regression analyses did not change the results reported here. Moreover, entry of gender by predictor interaction terms into each analysis (after entry of the predictor variables) revealed no evidence that the effects of any of the predictors varied as a function of gender. All analyses were, therefore, performed on the pooled sample of males and females.

A series of multiple regression analyses was performed. The first set of regressions assessed the utility of the theory of reasoned action in predicting intentions to use a condom on the next sexual encounter, and predicting actual behaviour. The second set of regressions tested the health belief model's predictive power. The third set of analyses combined the theory of reasoned behaviour and health belief model, in order to examine whether consideration of health beliefs improved the utility of the theory of reasoned action. Prior to performing the regression analyses, bivariate correlations were calculated to assess the strength of the relationship between the belief-based and direct measures of attitude and subjective norm.

## Analyses Testing the Theory of Reasoned Action

### Correlations Between Direct and Belief-Based Measures of Attitude and Subjective Norm

The theory of reasoned action predicts that, as beliefs are inherent in the formation of attitudes and subjective norms, there will be appreciable correlations between the two types of measures. Supporting the theory, there were moderately strong correlations between the belief-based measures of attitude (the product of behavioural beliefs and outcome evaluations) and subjective norm (the product of normative beliefs and motivation to comply) and the direct measures of these variables (attitude: $r = .63$; $p < .001$; subjective norm: $r = .61$; $p < .001$).

### Predicting Intentions

To test the utility of the theory of reasoned action, the direct measures of attitude and subjective norm were entered in the first step of the equation, while the belief-based measures were entered in the second step. After control of the direct measures, it was expected that the belief-based measures would not directly affect behavioural intentions. Consistent with the original theory of reasoned action model, inclusion of the direct measures of attitude and subjective norm contributed significantly to the prediction of intentions (see Table 1). However, contrary to the predictions of Fishbein and Ajzen (1975), the addition of belief-based variables into the model accounted for a significant increase in the variance explained

Table 7.1. *Hierarchical Regression of Components of the Theory of Reasoned Action on Intention*

| Step | Variable | Beta | $R^2$ch. | $F$ch. | $df$ |
|------|----------|------|----------|--------|------|
| (1) | Attitude | .33** | .60 | 96.65** | 2, 131 |
| | Subjective norm | .32* | | | |
| (2) | B-B attitude | .05 | .03 | 5.99** | 2, 129 |
| | B-B sub. norm | .23** | | | |

B-B refers to belief-based measures.
Beta coefficients computed after all variables entered into the equation.
*$p$<.05; **$p$<.01.

in behavioural intentions. When all the variables were in the equation, both attitudes and norms significantly predicted behavioural intentions, as did the belief-based measure of norms. These results suggest that subjects were more likely to use a condom on their next sexual encounter if they had a positive attitude towards doing so, and if they perceived normative pressure to perform the behaviour.

The fact that both the direct and indirect measures of norms emerged as significant predictors of behavioural intentions suggests that the direct measure of subjective norm was not able to reflect adequately the normative influences affecting intentions to use condoms on the next sexual encounter. As Bagozzi and Burnkrant (1979) noted, belief structures are likely to be too complex to be explained entirely by a single global measure, such as the one employed to assess subjective norm. This problem may have been exacerbated in the present study, because the subjective norm measure comprised only a single item. Future research may benefit from using multiple-item measures of this construct.

*Predicting Behaviour*

The effect of intention on actual behaviour was examined in a second hierarchical regression (see Table 2). The measure of intention was entered on the first step of the regression. It accounted for a large portion of the total variance in behaviour. As predicted by the theory of reasoned action, entry of the direct and belief-based measures of attitude and the subjective norm did not significantly increase the amount of variance accounted for in actual behaviour. Intention totally mediated the effects of both measures on behaviour.

Table 7.2. *Hierarchical Regression of Components of the Theory of Reasoned Action on Behaviour*

| Step | Variable | Beta | $R^2$ch. | $F$ch. | $df$ |
|------|----------|------|----------|--------|------|
| (1) | Intention | .87** | .80 | 346.74 | 1, 88 |
| (2) | Attitude | .01 | .00 | <1 | 2, 86 |
|     | Subjective norm | .07 | | | |
| (3) | B-B attitude | -.02 | .00 | <1 | 2, 84 |
|     | B-B sub. norm | .00 | | | |

B-B refers to belief-based measures.
Beta coefficients computed after all variables entered into the equation.
*$p$<.05; **$p$<.01.

It is worth noting that behavioural intentions accounted for a large proportion of variance in actual behaviour, although this result was not unexpected. The study focused on the next sexual encounter, which means that the opportunity for people's intentions to change over time was fairly limited. As noted by Fishbein and Ajzen (1975), when there is a relatively short time period between the assessments of intentions and actual behaviour, a person's intention is likely to remain relatively stable, which strengthens the intention–behaviour relationship. Other factors contributing to the stability of behavioural intentions in the present study could have been the restriction of the sample to sexually experienced subjects, and the fact that the majority of the subjects were in a stable relationship (see Moore *et al.*, this volume; Nucifora *et al.*, this volume).

### Analyses Testing the Health Belief Model

#### Predicting intention

All health belief variables assumed to predict intention were entered in one step, as there was no theoretical reason why any set of variables should be entered prior to any others. The linear combination of these variables accounted for a significant amount of the total variance (see Table 3). The main contributor to this effect was the benefits dimension, although the measure of perceived barriers to performing the behaviour also had a weak negative effect on intention to use a condom on the next sexual encounter (see Table 3).

Table 7.3. *Multiple Regression of Components of the Health Belief Model on Intention*

| Variable | Beta | $R^2$ch. | $F$ch. | $df$ |
|---|---|---|---|---|
| Severity | -.02 | .30 | 13.99** | 4, 133 |
| Susceptibility | .00 | | | |
| Perceived benefits | .50** | | | |
| Perceived barriers | -.14* | | | |

B-B refers to belief-based measures.
Beta coefficients computed after all variables entered into the equation.
*$p$<.075; **$p$<.01.

These results are in accord with predictions, to the extent that neither perceived severity of AIDS nor perceived susceptibility to contracting HIV influenced safer sex intentions. As expected, there was little discrimination among subjects on the severity measure, which presumably accounted for the weak effect of severity on behavioural intentions. Also in accordance with the predictions, most people perceived their level of risk for HIV to be low. This perception of risk is not necessarily inaccurate. Heterosexuals in Australia are currently at low risk for HIV. There is, however, evidence that, even if they are engaging in risky behaviour, Australian samples of heterosexuals do not accurately perceive their level of risk for HIV (Moore & Rosenthal, 1991a; Timmins *et al.*, this volume). In heterosexuals, this denial of personal risk may be a consequence of a perceived association of the disease with the homosexual outgroup.

Contrary to previous research (e.g., Heusser *et al.*, 1992; Montgomery *et al.*, 1989), there was evidence in the present study that both perceived benefits of condom use and, to a lesser extent, perceived barriers to perform the behaviour influenced intentions to engage in safer sex behaviour. The fact that, in this regard, the results of the present study are inconsistent with previous research in the area may be a consequence of the fact that the measures of both dimensions of the health belief model comprised items assessing a range of possible consequences of performing the behaviour. Moreover, the measures of benefits and barriers were based on the salient beliefs of a sample of subjects representative of those who participated in the main study. One criticism of the health belief model has been the lack of attention that has been given to the operationalisation of the measures (Wallston & Wallston, 1984). As well as focusing on a range of potential outcomes of a particular course of action, proponents of the model may benefit from employing Fishbein and Ajzen's (1975; Ajzen & Fishbein, 1980) elicitation methodology to ensure that their measures are tapping the beliefs held by the particular population under consideration. This is particularly relevant to the consideration of the psychological consequences of performing a preventive health behaviour. The researcher's view of such consequences may not accord with the beliefs of the target population.

### Predicting Behaviour

The effects of the health belief variables on behaviour were wholly mediated by intention. Entry of the measure of intention into the equations accounted for a large amount of variance (see analyses reported in Table 2). All the variables in the health belief model were entered on step two of the analysis, but the addition of these variables failed to improve the prediction of behaviour ($R^2_{change} = .01$; $F < 1$).

### Comparison of the Two Models

The previous set of analyses revealed that there was no difference between the models when predicting behaviour, as intention mediated the influence of all variables from each model. This finding supports hypotheses from both models suggesting that readiness to engage in behaviour (intention) is the best predictor of actual behaviour.

For behavioural intentions, the theory of reasoned action accounted for considerably more variance than the health belief model. One could argue, however, that if it incorporated a normative component, the health belief model would perform as well as the theory of reasoned action (i.e., it is possible that the two models represent the attitudinal influences on readiness to engage in health care behaviour equally well). Such a model would, in fact, be in accord with the model that Morin (1988; see Puckett & Bye, 1987) developed to explain variation in homosexuals' response to HIV. He proposed that, in addition to the health belief dimensions, the support of peers enhances the likelihood that HIV-preventive behaviour will be performed.

To test this proposal, a further hierarchical regression analysis was conducted. The measure of subjective norm was entered in the second step of a regression analysis, after control of the dimensions of the health belief model. This analysis revealed that subjective norm accounted for a large amount of additional variance in behavioural intentions ($R^2_{change} = .23$; $F(4,133) = 65.32$; $p < .001$). Even after consideration of the effects of norms, the revised version of the health belief model accounted for a smaller portion of variance in behavioural intentions than the theory of reasoned action ($R^2 = .53$ vs $.63$). This result suggests that the attitudinal factors that are likely to impact on the decision to engage in safer sex are better conceptualised in the theory of reasoned action than in the health belief model, possibly because the latter model fails to directly assess the person's evaluation of performing the behaviour.

### Analyses Testing a Combined Reasoned Action/Health Belief Model

A final analysis was conducted to determine whether the dimensions of the health belief model accounted for any additional variance in behavioural intention, after control of the components of the theory of reasoned action. In this analysis, the direct measure of attitude and both the direct and belief-based measures of norms were entered in the first step (the belief-based measure of attitude could not be entered, because it was constructed from the same items as those used to assess the benefits/barriers dimensions of the health belief model), while the dimensions of the health belief model were entered in the second step. Inclusion of the health belief dimensions explained no additional variance in behavioural intentions, after control of the effects of the components of the theory of reasoned action ($R^2_{change} = .00$; $F(4,126) < 1$). When the order of entry of the variables was reversed, both sets of variables accounted for approximately equal proportions of variance in behavioural intentions (health belief model, step 1: $R^2_{change} = .31$; $F(4,129) = 14.60$; $p < .001$; theory of reasoned action, step 2: $R^2_{change} = .32$; $F(3,126) = 36.35$; $p < .001$). When only the health beliefs were in the equation, both benefits and barriers significantly predicted intentions (as in the previous analysis); however, these effects became non-significant after entry of the measures of attitudes and norms into the regression equation. In other words, the effects of benefits and barriers on intentions were totally mediated through the direct measures of attitude and subjective norm. In support of this conclusion, additional correlational analyses revealed that benefits and barriers were strongly related to subjects' attitudes towards performing the behaviour ($r = .64$; $p < .01$ and $r = -.41$; $p < .01$, respectively). There was also evidence of a link between perceived benefits and subjective norm ($r = .52$; $p < .05$), possibly because some of the benefits accompanying safer sex involve pleasing one's partner (see Kashima & Gallois, this volume).

One additional point concerns Fishbein and Middlestadt's (1989) suggestion that the perceived severity and perceived susceptibility components of the health belief model may also influence the attitudinal and normative components of the theory of reasoned action. The present study provided some support for this supposition, in that the measure of perceived susceptibility was positively correlated with both the direct ($r = .18$;

$p < .05$) and the belief-based ($r = .19$; $p < .05$) measures of norms. These results are not strong, but they suggest that subjects who percieved themselves to be more at risk for HIV perceived stronger normative pressure than others to engage in safer sex. Alternatively, normative pressure may have made them judge themselves as more at risk. There was also some evidence linking perceptions of the severity of HIV to a positive attitude towards condom use ($r = .18$; $p < .05$). Perhaps as a way of supporting their decision to adopt a certain course of action, subjects who perceived the possible consequences of not doing so as extremely severe were more likely to have positive evaluations of performing the behaviour.

### Summary and Implications

In summary, the results of the present study suggest that, in the context of safer sex, the theory of reasoned action is superior to the health belief model. As expected, neither the perceived susceptibility or severity dimensions of the latter model predicted readiness to use a condom. In contrast, the barriers and benefits dimensions of the health belief model did predict intentions; however, analyses of the combined reasoned action/health belief model suggested that the effects of these variables were mediated via their effects on the attitudinal and normative components of the theory of reasoned action. Additional analyses revealed that the perceived severity and susceptibility dimensions of the health belief model may also be related to attitudes and norms, although these results were not strong.

The superiority of the theory of reasoned action cannot be attributed to a meta-theoretical difference between this model and the health belief model. At the meta-theoretical level, the theory of reasoned action and the health belief model are similar, to the extent that both models propose that a rational consideration of underlying beliefs forms the basis for behavioural decision-making. The models differ, however, in relation to the types of beliefs that are proposed to be relevant in this regard. Specifically, the theory of reasoned action proposes that people's beliefs about the expectations of others are likely to influence behaviour, a possibility that is not incorporated into the original formulation of the health belief model. Results of the present study suggest that this difference between the two models accounted for the clear superiority of the theory of reasoned action. The fact that the theory of reasoned action focuses on the person's direct evaluation of the behaviour also appears to be a strength of the model. The present results suggest that perceived benefits and barriers have less explanatory utility than the person's evaluation of the behaviour, possibly because such variables reflect what people believe they should think, rather than their actual attitude towards the behaviour.

The results of the present study are noteworthy, because the study is one of the few direct comparisons of the two major theoretical models that have been used to explain variation in health care behaviour. As noted, the results suggest that the theory of reasoned action is the superior model. There is, however, a necessity for future research to compare the relative utility of the health belief model and the theory of reasoned action in other health contexts. The results of the present study may be specific to condom use, which is a context where normative pressure, particularly from the partner, is likely to be pronounced (see Kashima & Gallois, this volume). When predicting other health behaviours (for instance, in areas where the effects of norms are only weak), the superiority of the theory of reasoned action may not be so marked. Furthermore, the health belief model may perform as well, or better than the theory of reasoned action when the potential health threat is not as severe as HIV, or when feelings of susceptibility do not impact upon people's self-concepts. In such a context, the perceived susceptibility and perceived severity components of the model are likely to have more influence on behavioural intentions than observed in the present study.

Nevertheless, the present study points to a number of shortcomings of the health belief model. The potential utility of the model would be much greater if clear guidelines for the operationalisation of the components of the model were developed. The fact that the theory of reasoned action provides such guidelines is an obvious advantage of the model, as is its clear specification of the proposed links among beliefs, intentions and behaviour. The results of the present research also point to the advantages of doing pilot work to identify the modal beliefs of the population under consideration. The theory of reasoned action acknowledges the specificity of local populations, which not only contributes to its predictive superiority, but also means that the model forms a useful basis for the development of intervention programs (see McCamish *et al.,* this volume).

In terms of applied implications, the results of the present study suggest that safer sex programs and media campaigns may benefit from the knowledge that to influence behaviour they need to target beliefs concerning attitudes towards condom use (e.g. introducing fun and variety into sex, as well as reducing risk for sexually transmitted diseases), rather than focussing on the seriousness of contracting HIV. The role of norms in changing intentions towards condom use is also pivotal. Education programs are likely to benefit from attempts to foster a normative climate that is supportive of safer sex. Such programs may also benefit from encouraging accurate perceptions of personal risk of HIV among heterosexuals. To do this, educators need to counter the view that gay and bisexual men will remain the group most at risk for HIV infection, as well as removing the perceived association between homosexuality and HIV.

# 8

# Self-Efficacy Expectancies and the Theory of Reasoned Action

DEBORAH TERRY

*The University of Queensland, Brisbane, Australia*

According to Bandura's (1977, 1986) social cognitive theory, people's actions are not only influenced by their beliefs concerning the likely consequences of an act, but also by their expectations of personal mastery. Such expectations are referred to by Bandura (1977, 1986) as *efficacy expectancies,* and reflect people's beliefs concerning the likelihood that they will be able to perform a particular behaviour successfully. Self-efficacious thinking cannot be equated with the possession of the requisite skills to perform the behaviour. As noted by Bandura (1986, 1989a,b), successful performance of a behaviour depends not only on the availability of skills, but also on the belief that one will be able to utilise the skills effectively in the appropriate situation. In the absence of the belief that they can successfully perform a behaviour, people will be unlikely to be motivated to perform the behaviour. Moreover, if they do attempt to perform the behaviour, people with low levels of self-efficacy are unlikely to persist in their behavioural efforts.

There is considerable evidence linking levels of self-efficacy to health behaviour (Bandura, 1986; O'Leary, 1985; Strecher, deVillis, Becker, & Rosenstock, 1986). Subjects with high levels of self-efficacy are more likely to engage in health-promoting behaviours (e.g., quitting smoking; dieting) than their counterparts with low levels of self-efficacy (see Strecher *et al.,* 1986 for a review). Additional evidence reveals that people are more likely to comply with the recommendations of persuasive communications if they perceive that they can successfully execute the recommended behaviours (Beck & Lund, 1981; Maddux, Norton & Stolenberg, 1986). The evidence linking perceived self-efficacy to health behaviour is not restricted to correlational support (Taylor, 1991). There is evidence that experimental enhancement of personal efficacy expectations reflects in subsequent behaviour change (see Strecher *et al.,* 1986).

**135**

In the context of HIV prevention, there is evidence that efficacy expectancies or in other words, people's beliefs in their ability to engage in the appropriate behaviours, influence their willingness to engage in such behaviours. McKusik and his colleagues (McKusik, Coates, Wiley, Morin & Stall, 1987), for instance, reported that gay men who were confident in their ability to engage in low-risk sexual behaviours were more likely than others actually to do so. Schaalma, Kok and Peters (in press) similarly found that high levels of self-efficacy predicted heterosexuals' willingness to use condoms. The need to consider the role of self-efficacy in the context of safer sex behaviour is recognised by Fisher and Fisher (1992) in their three-factor conceptualisation of AIDS-preventive behaviour (IMB model). In this model, Fisher and Fisher identify the level of AIDS-related information (I), people's motivation to engage in such behaviours (M) and the presence of the necessary behavioural skills (B) (see Lewis & Kashima, this volume for a more detailed discussion of this model) as the fundamental determinants of AIDS-risk reduction. As noted by Fisher and Fisher, the belief in one's ability to engage in AIDS-preventive behaviour (i.e., self-efficacy) is central to the skill component of the IMB model.

Recently, a number of researchers have suggested the necessity of incorporating self-efficacy expectancies into the theory of reasoned action. In accordance with Bandura's (1977, 1986) social cognitive theory, researchers have justified the inclusion of self-efficacy into the theory of reasoned action on the basis of the necessity of considering people's mastery expectations in the prediction of behaviour. As such, the theory of reasoned action does not incorporate expectations of personal mastery. These beliefs are most clearly related to the attitudinal component of the model; however, the two variables are conceptually distinct. On the one hand, a person makes a judgement concerning his or her ability to perform the behaviour, while on the other, the person evaluates how favourable or unfavourable he or she feels towards performing the behaviour. Although the latter variable may be influenced by efficacy beliefs (a person with low self-efficacy could rationalise his or her reticence to perform a behaviour by evaluating it an unfavourable light), it is unlikely that attitudinal judgements would reduce to efficacy expectancies. Independently of their efficacy expectancies, it can be assumed that, in most instances, individuals are able to evaluate the extent to which performing the behaviour would be a good thing to do.

The inclusion of self-efficacy in the theory of reasoned action is compatible with Triandis' (1977) attitude-behaviour model. Triandis proposed that the likelihood that a person will perform a particular behaviour is increased if certain facilitating conditions are present. As noted by Boyd and Wandersman (1991), perceptions of self-efficacy should act as a facilitating condition. People's feelings of confidence in their ability to perform a behaviour presumably increase the likelihood that they will behave in accordance with their intentions, given that they are likely to persist in their behavioural efforts (see Bandura, 1977, 1986).

Consideration of the role of self-efficacy in the theory of reasoned action is also compatible with the theory of planned behaviour (Ajzen, 1985, 1987, 1991; Ajzen & Madden, 1986), which involves an attempt to extend the theory of reasoned action to situations where the behaviour is not completely under the person's control. In such situations, the theory proposes that to predict behaviour accurately both the person's intention and the extent to which the behaviour is under his or her volitional control need to be considered. As Ajzen and Madden pointed out, adequate measures of actual behavioural control are difficult to obtain; thus, they favour measures of perceived behavioural control as proxy measures of actual control.

According to Ajzen (1988), the notions of perceived behavioural control and self-efficacy are conceptually related. A person who perceives a high level of behavioural control is likely to believe that he or she will be able to enact a particular behaviour successfully. The anticipated presence of barriers that may impede the performance of the behaviour will presumably lessen a person's confidence in his or her ability to perform the behaviour. However, although related, the concepts of self-efficacy and perceived behavioural control should not be regarded as synonymous. Ajzen's (1987, 1991) notion of perceived behavioural control reflects the extent to which the person perceives that both external and internal factors are likely to interfere with performance of the behaviour. However, it can be argued that ratings of self-efficacy primarily reflect the person's judgement of the extent to which internal barriers (e.g., lack of willpower, inappropriate skills) will impede performance of the behaviour. In making efficacy judgements, people will presumably not pay a great deal of attention to external barriers (e.g., condom breakage), given that these factors are less predictable and hence less likely to be cognitively accessible when people make efficacy judgements (see Fazio, 1990, for a discussion on the role of cognitive accessibility in behavioural prediction). Thus, the notions of self-efficacy and perceived behavioural control should be distinguished, given that efficacy expectancies are likely to tap only one component of the domain represented by the construct of perceived behavioural control.

In recent work, Ajzen (1991) has aligned the notion of perceived behavioural control more closely with self-efficacy. Although this step improves the conceptual clarity of the notion of perceived behavioural control, it is problematic, to the extent it means that the rationale for introducing the notion of perceived behavioural control into the theory of planned behaviour does not accord with the conceptualisation of the variable. It will be recalled that, in an endeavour to extend the theory of reasoned action to situations where people cannot perform the behaviour at will, Ajzen

(1987, 1991) incorporated the concept of perceived behavioural control into the theory of reasoned action. Thus, the issue of behavioural control is central to the theoretical basis of the theory of planned behaviour, a focus that is not so clear if perceived behavioural control is reduced to self-efficacy. Although perceptions of self-efficacy can be seen to reflect the extent to which people perceive that they have control over their environment (Bandura, 1989a), these perceptions are based primarily on consideration of control factors that emanate from the person, rather than from external control factors. It is the latter type of factor that is the essence of behavioural control. Many internal control factors (such as willpower, emotions etc.) are potentially under personal control (see Rotter, 1966). Moreover, because people typically have some insight into their personal limitations, external control factors are more likely than internal factors to interfere with people's attempts to behave in accord with their intentions.

Issues of conceptualisation aside, there is some support for the inclusion of the notion of self-efficacy in the theory of reasoned action. In relation to the prediction of behavioural intentions, de Vries, Dijkstra and Kuhlman (1988) found that, even after control of the effects of attitudes and norms, judgements of self-efficacy significantly predicted intentions to quit smoking. In a similar vein, Schaalma *et al.* (in press) found that inclusion of self-efficacy into a regression equation predicting intentions to use a condom explained 12% of additional variance (after control of the effects of attitudes). In a number of tests of the theory of planned behaviour, there is also indirect support for the effects of self-efficacy on behavioural intentions. Measures of perceived behavioural control have consistently improved the explanation of variation in behavioural intentions (after control of the effects of the components of the theory of reasoned action); however, as noted previously, self-efficacy is only one component of the notion of perceived behavioural control.

Evidence linking efficacy expectancies to actual behaviour is more limited. Neither de Vries *et al.* (1988) nor Schaalma *et al.* (in press) measured actual behaviour, although de Vries *et al.* did report a significant relationship between subjects' confidence in their ability to quit smoking and amount of smoking in the immediate past. In their study of condom use, Boyd and Wandersman (1991) failed to find a link between self-efficacy and actual behaviour, as did McCaul, O'Neill and Glasgow (1988). The lack of evidence linking self-efficacy expectancies to actual behaviour is, in fact, consistent with Bandura's (1977, 1986) social cognitive theory of behaviour change. According to Bandura, efficacy expectancies primarily influence people's motivation to engage in a particular course of action.

The present study was designed to examine further the effects of self-efficacy on both behavioural intentions and actual behaviour. Although a number of studies have examined the role of efficacy expectancies in the theory of reasoned action, little research has been conducted in the context of safer sex. This is despite the fact that perceptions of personal mastery about ensuring that a condom is used during a sexual encounter may be low, especially for females. Women may lack confidence in their ability to insist that a condom is used; moreover, they typically have limited control over ensuring that one is actually used.

On the basis of Bandura's (1977, 1986) social cognitive theory, it was proposed that, even after control of the effects of the theory of reasoned action, efficacy expectancies would contribute to the prediction of behavioural intentions but not actual behaviour. It was predicted that subjects would be more likely to intend to use a condom on the next sexual encounter, if they perceived high levels of self-efficacy. In accordance with the recommendations of Bandura (1989b), a domain-specific measure of self-efficacy was obtained. Subjects were required to indicate their efficacy expectancies for the particular behaviour under consideration. Generalised measures of efficacy are unlikely to be useful in the context of the prediction of specific behavioural responses, given that a number of items on an omnibus test may be irrelevant to the particular behaviour of interest (Bandura, 1989b). The reliance on a situation-specific measure of efficacy is also in accord with Ajzen and Fishbein's (1977) principle of compatibility, which states that the relationship between any two variables will strengthen as a function of the extent to which they are assessed along compatible dimensions (see Terry *et al.*, this volume).

The present study was designed to address two additional issues. First, a measure of past behaviour was obtained to determine if the results linking efficacy expectancies to could be explained in terms of past experience at performing the behaviour. Subjects' predictions of their ability to perform the behaviour in the future may simply be a reflection of their success at doing so in the past. If this is the case, control of the effects of the past behaviour should render the effects of self-efficacy on intentions nonsignificant.

Second, a measure of perceived behavioural control unconfounded with efficacy expectancies was obtained to allow consideration of the role of both internal and external control factors in the prediction of behavioural intentions and actual behaviour. In accordance with the original conceptualisation of the theory of planned behaviour, it was anticipated that a measure of perceived behavioural control would influence actual behaviour. Although contrary to the theory of planned behaviour (see Ajzen, 1991; Ajzen & Madden, 1986), it was further proposed that levels of perceived behavioural control (unconfounded with efficacy expectancies) would not influence behavioural intentions. The perception that one's efforts to perform a behaviour may be influenced by external events or people will not generally weaken one's motivation or intention to perform the behaviour (see Terry and O'Leary, 1993). This proposal is compatible with Fishbein and Ajzen's (1975) definition of intention as the extent to which the person is prepared to try and perform the particular behavioural act. A request to indicate the strength of one's willingness to put effort into performing the behaviour implies that one will assume that the external environment will favour the performance of the behaviour. The proposal that perceived behavioural control would not influence the strength of people's behavioural intentions is also compatible with other theoretical models in the area. Sarver (1983), for instance, proposed that the presence of contextual factors that may impede a person behaving in accord with his or her intentions intervenes after determination of the behavioural intention.

## Method

### Pilot Study

Following the procedures suggested by Ajzen and Fishbein (1980), a pilot study was conducted to elicit the salient beliefs for the population concerning the behavioural consequences of condom use and the salient referents for this behaviour. A sample of female ($n = 8$) and male ($n = 11$) undergraduate students participated in the study. They were required to indicate their beliefs concerning: (1) the advantages and disadvantages of condom use and (2) the people/groups who would approve and disapprove of them performing the behaviour. The most frequently occurring responses formed the basis for the development of the measures of behavioural and normative beliefs.

### Design and Procedure

The research was prospective in design. This was to allow a consideration of the extent to which the predictor variables could successfully predict subsequent behaviour. Subjects completed questionnaires at two different points in time. The first questionnaire assessed intentions to use a condom on the next sexual encounter, as well as the person's attitude towards performing the behaviour, the subjective norm, perceived behavioural control, and self-efficacy. Subjects completed the first questionnaire in group sessions. After completing it, they were given a second questionnaire to take away with them. The second questionnaire assessed actual condom use. It was returned after the next sexual encounter or after four weeks (whichever occurred first).

*Subjects*

A sample of 151 undergraduate students completed the first question-naire, of whom 135 (89%) also provided follow-up data. The sample comprised approximately equal numbers of males ($n$ = 72) and females ($n$ = 79). The mean age of participants was 19.19 years (*S.D.* = 1.80). The subjects were sexually experienced; all described themselves as being exclusively heterosexual.

*Measures*

The direct measure of *attitude* comprised ten items in semantic differential format (adjective pairs included 'good–bad'; 'harmful–beneficial'). There were equal numbers of direct- and reverse-worded items. The alpha coefficient for the scale was .87. A belief-based measure of attitude was computed as the sum of the products of scores on measures of *behavioural beliefs* and *evaluations*. To assess behavioural beliefs, respondents indicated the likelihood that 10 different outcomes would be consequences (five costs and five benefits) of using a condom on their next sexual encounter. All items were assessed with 7-point scales ((-3) 'extremely unlikely' to (+3) 'extremely likely'). To assess outcome evaluations, respondents were asked to evaluate each of the costs and benefits on a scale ranging from (-3) 'extremely unpleasant' to (+3) 'extremely pleasant.'

Three items comprised the direct measure of *subjective norm* (e.g., 'People who are important think that I: ((-3) 'shouldn't' to (+3) 'should') use a condom on my next sexual encounter;' alpha = .83). A belief-based measure of subjective norm was computed as the sum of the products of scores on measures of *normative beliefs* and *motivation to comply*. Normative beliefs were assessed by asking respondents the likelihood that salient others would want them to use a condom on their next sexual encounter (7-point response scales: (-3) 'extremely unlikely' to (+3) 'extremely likely'), while subjects' motivations to comply were assessed by asking them, in general, how willing were they to do what each of the referents wanted them to do (7-point response scales: (1) 'not at all' to (7) 'very much').

To assess *self-efficacy,* subjects responded to five items designed to assess their confidence in their ability to ensure that they, or their partner, used a condom on their next sexual encounter (e.g., 'For me to ensure that I or my sexual partner uses a condom on my next sexual encounter would be:? (1) 'difficult' to (7) 'easy.' A measure of *perceived behavioural control* was obtained from subjects' responses to five items (e.g., 'How much control do you have over whether you or your partner wears a condom the next time you have sexual intercourse?' ((1) 'no control' to (7) 'complete control'), which assessed the extent to which they perceived that external factors would interfere with performance of the behaviour (scale scored in high control direction).

A principal components factor analysis with orthogonal (varimax) rotation provided evidence for the distinction between the two measures. A three-factor solution emerged, accounting for 63% of the variance. The five self-efficacy items were the only items to have loadings that exceeded .50 on the first rotated factor, while four of the five perceived behavioural control items were the only items to load above .50 on the second rotated factor. The fifth perceived behavioural control item loaded on the third factor. Because only one item loaded on this factor, it was not interpreted. The 5-item self-efficacy scale and the 4-item perceived behavioural control measures were used in the analyses reported in the present paper. The measures had satisfactory levels of reliability (alpha = .83 and .68 for self-efficacy and perceived behavioural control, respectively). The correlation between the two measures was only moderate ($r = .45$; $p < .01$), thus providing further support for the distinction between the two variables.

To assess *behavioural intention*, subjects responded to two items (e.g., I (-3) 'do not intend' to (+3) 'do intend' for me, or my partner, to wear a condom on my next sexual encounter'). One of the items was reverse-scored; the two-item scale had an alpha coefficient of .92. As a measure of *actual behaviour*, subjects indicated, at Time 2, whether they had used a condom on their last sexual encounter. Of the 135 subjects who provided follow-up data, 25 subjects had not had sexual intercourse since completing the first questionnaire. There were, thus, valid behavioural data available on 110 subjects, of whom 46% did, in fact, use a condom. *Past behaviour* was assessed by asking subjects to indicate whether they had used a condom on their last sexual encounter ((1) 'no'; (2) 'yes').

## Results and Discussion

The first set of analyses examined whether efficacy expectancies improved the prediction of behavioural intentions and actual behaviour, after control of the effects of the relevant components of the theory of reasoned action (attitudes and norms when predicting intentions; intentions when predicting actual behaviour). Additional analyses considered: (a) whether the observed effects of self-efficacy on intentions and behaviour were simply a reflection of past success at performing the behaviour and (b) whether measures of both self-efficacy and perceived behavioural control (unconfounded with efficacy expectancies) predicted behavioural intentions and actual behaviour. Ajzen and Madden (1986) acknowledged the possibility that the effects of perceived behavioural control on intentions and actual behaviour may be interactive (i.e., measures of behavioural control may moderate the effects of the components of the reasoned action). Thus, both additive and interactive effects of self-efficacy and perceived behavioural control were tested.

The final set of analyses considered whether the effects of the predictor variables varied as a function of subjects' gender or whether they were in a current relationship. These analyses were considered necessary, given that the determinants of safer sex behaviour may not be the same for all populations (i.e., males and females; those in a continuing relationship and those not in such a relationship) (Fishbein & Middlestadt, 1989). In particular, it was anticipated that the effects of self-efficacy may vary as a function of gender and relationship status. The effects of self-efficacy may, for instance, be stronger for males than females, given that males typically have more power over whether a condom is used. Moreover, the co-operative nature of sexual encounters may mean that personal efficacy expectancies are more strongly linked to behavioural intentions and actual behaviour when the feelings and attitudes of a person's partner are known (i.e., when the person is in a current relationship) than when the person's next sexual encounter is not going to be with a current partner.

Prior to performing the regression analyses, correlational analyses were conducted to assess the extent to which the belief-based and direct measures of attitudes and norms were related. In both cases, the correlations were significant (subjective norm: $r = .77$; $p < .001$; attitude: $r = .42$; $p < .01$).

## The Role of Self-Efficacy in the Prediction of Intentions and Actual Behaviour

### Regression Analysis Predicting Behavioural Intentions

For the analysis predicting intentions, the direct measures of attitude and subjective norm were entered into the first step of a hierarchical regression procedure. The measure of self-efficacy was entered in the second step of the analysis. This procedure allowed for an examination of whether self-efficacy influenced behavioural intentions, after control of the effects of attitude and subjective norm. To ascertain whether the effects of the belief-based variables on behavioural intentions were mediated via their effects on the direct measures (as proposed by the theory of reasoned action), the belief-based measures of attitude and subjective norm were entered in the final step of the regression equation. It was expected that, after control of the direct measures of attitude and subjective norm, the effects of the belief-based measures would be nonsignificant.

Table 8.1. *Hierarchical Regression of Components of the Theory of Reasoned Action and Self-efficacy on Intention*

| Step | Variable | Beta | $R^2$ch. | $F$ch. | $df$ |
|------|----------|------|----------|--------|------|
| (1) | Attitude | .34** | .58 | 100.23** | 2, 147 |
| | Subjective norm | .19* | | | |
| (2) | Self-efficacy | .21** | .04 | 14.89** | 1, 146 |
| (3) | B-B attitude | -.02 | .03 | 5.90** | 2, 144 |
| | B-B sub. norm | .28** | | | |

B-B refers to belief-based measures.
Beta coefficients computed after all variables entered into the equation.
*$p$<.05; **$p$<.01.

As shown in Table 1, the three steps of the analysis contributed significantly to the prediction of behavioural intentions. When all the variables were in the regression equation, there was evidence linking both attitude and the subjective norm to intentions to use a condom on the next sexual encounter. For subjective norm, there was evidence that both the direct and belief-based measures influenced behavioural intentions. The fact that the belief-based measure of norms significantly predicted intentions provides further support for the conclusion that a global measure of subjective norm is not able to adequately assess the extent of normative pressure from others to engage in safer sex (see Bagozzi & Burnkrant, 1979; also Nucifora *et al.*, this volume; Warwick *et al.*, this volume)

As predicted, after control of the effects of attitude and subjective norm, the measure of self-efficacy explained a significant increment of variance in behavioural intentions. Subjects were more likely to intend to engage in safer sex, not only if they had a positive attitude towards the behaviour and perceived normative pressure to do so, but also if they had confidence in their ability to perform the behaviour. These results replicate the results of other studies, and provide additional support for Bandura's (1977, 1986) social cognitive theory. The results also provide support for the theory of planned behaviour (Ajzen, 1987, 1991), to the extent that the data suggest that perceptions of internal barriers to behaviour (lack of confidence in one's ability to perform the behaviour) weaken behavioural intentions.

The fact that self-efficacy expectancies explained a relatively small amount of variance (4%) in behavioural intentions is partially a function of the conservative nature of the analyses performed. When the measure of self-efficacy was entered into the equation prior to the components of the theory of reasoned action, it accounted for 17% ($F$ (1,149) = 29.69; $p < .001$) of variance in behavioural intentions (the subsequent entry the measures of attitudes and subjective norm accounted for 45% ($F$ (2,147) = 86.55; $p < .001$) of additional variance in behavioural intentions). Although the present analyses employed a conservative procedure to test the role of self-efficacy, it should be noted that other studies have used a similar analytic procedure and have found that efficacy expectancies account for larger amounts of variance in behavioural intentions (e.g., de Vries *et al.*, 1988). The effects of self-efficacy on intentions may be weakened in co-operative behaviours, because people are aware that their attempts to perform the behaviour are likely to be influenced by their partner's feelings and wishes. This awareness may mean that people lack certainty in their perceptions of efficacy. In the context of safer sex, future researchers may benefit from assessing the strength, rather than the level, of self-efficacy (as assessed in the present study). Bandura and Cervone (1983, 1986) have found that the effects of strength of efficacy expectancies are stronger than the effects of level of self-efficacy.

Although the present study did not find strong evidence linking self-efficacy to intentions to engage in safer sex, the results of the study suggest that such expectancies should be considered in safer sex programmes. Clearly, intentions to use a condom will be strengthened if subjects perceive that they will be able to ensure that a condom is actually used on a particular sexual encounter. Education programmes may benefit from increasing people's beliefs in their ability to perform the behaviour by developing the necessary skills to engage in AIDS- preventive behaviour (e.g., self-acceptance of sexuality; raising the topic and negotiating safer sex with partner; assertiveness skills; purchasing and carrying condoms; see Fisher & Fisher, 1992) and by ensuring that people's efficacy expectancies accord with their skills. The use of roleplays and overtraining may help to achieve the latter goal. The results reported by Bandura and Cervone (1983, 1986) suggest that education programmes should focus not only on increasing levels of self-efficacy, but also on increasing people's certainty of their efficacy expectancies.

*Regression Analysis Predicting Actual Behaviour*

For the hierarchical regression analyses predicting actual behaviour, intentions were entered in the first step of the analysis, while the measure of self-efficacy was entered in the second step. The direct and belief-based measures of attitudes and norms were entered in the final step of the equation. The theory of reasoned action proposes that the effects of attitudes and norms on behaviour are mediated via their effects on intentions. It was, thus, expected that, after control of the effects of intentions,

Table 8.2. *Hierarchical Regression of Components of Theory of Reasoned Action and Self-efficacy on Behaviour*

| Step | Variable | Beta | $R^2$ch. | $F$ch. | $df$ |
|------|----------|------|----------|--------|------|
| (1) | Intention | .45** | .37 | 64.14** | 1, 106 |
| (2) | Self-efficacy | .12 | .01 | 1.68 | 1, 105 |
| (3) | Attitude | .10 | .02 | 1.37 | 2, 103 |
|  | Subjective norm | .29* |  |  |  |
| (4) | B-B attitude | -.05 | .02 | 1.71 | 2, 101 |
|  | B-B sub. norm | .25 |  |  |  |

B-B refers to belief-based measures.
Beta coefficients computed after all variables entered into the equation.
*$p$<.05; **$p$<.01.

the effects of both the direct and belief-based measures of attitudes and norms on behaviour would be non-significant.

As predicted by the theory of reasoned action, people were more likely to use a condom on their next sexual encounter if they intended to do so (see Table 2). After control of the effect of intentions, inclusion of self-efficacy into the regression equation did not explain any additional variance in actual behaviour. Consistent with expectations, neither the direct or the belief-based measures of attitudes and the subjective norm significantly incremented the amount of variance explained in actual behaviour. It should be noted, however, that when all the variables were in the equation, there was evidence that subjective norm had a direct effect on behaviour. Because the measures of attitude and subjective norm did not explain a significant amount of variance in actual behaviour, this finding should be interpreted with caution; however, the suggestion of a subjective norm-behaviour link further attests to the central role that norms play in the prediction of safer sex behaviour.

Consistent with expectations, self-efficacy did not predict actual behaviour (after control of the effects of behavioural intentions). These results suggest that the effects of self-efficacy on behaviour are mediated through behavioural intentions. This suggestion was supported by the fact that, when entered into the equation prior to intentions, the measure of self-efficacy significantly predicted actual behaviour ($b = .36$; $R^2_{change} = .13$; $F (1,108) = 16.18$; $p < .001$). Using Ajzen's (1988) terminology, the results of the present study suggest that the presence of internal barriers to behavioural action (low self-efficacy) weaken a person's behavioural intentions, but do not directly influence behaviour (as propsed by Bandura, 1977, 1982).

In this respect, the results of the present study are contrary to the predictions of the theory of planned behaviour. However, as noted previously, Ajzen's (1987, 1991) notion of perceived behavioural control is not synonymous with the concept self-efficacy. A person may be confident in his or her ability to perform the behaviour, yet be aware that external constraints (e.g., unavailability of condom; condom breakage) may interfere with successful execution of the behaviour. As argued previously, external control factors are likely to be more influential in the prediction of behaviour than internal control factors. This issue will be addressed below.

## *Control of the Effects of Past Behaviour*

To ascertain whether the effect of self-efficacy on behavioural intention (observed in the previous analyses) was a reflection of the effects of past behaviour, a further hierarchical regression analysis was performed. In this analysis, the measure of past behaviour (whether subjects had used a condom on their previous sexual encounter) was entered as a covariate in the first step of the regression analyses. As shown in Table 3, the measure of past behaviour had a direct effect on behavioural intentions. Subjects who had used a condom in the past were more likely to do so in the future. This pattern of results is consistent with previous studies in the area. Even after control of the effects of attitudes and norms, past behaviour has been found to predict intentions to engage in a range of different behaviours, including regular exercise (Godin, Valois, Shephard & Desharnais, 1987), class attendance (Fredericks & Dossett, 1983), and condom use (Boyd & Wandersman, 1991). This result is consistent with Triandis' (1977, 1980) attitude-behaviour model. According to Triandis, if a person has performed the behaviour in the past, then subsequent acts of the behaviour are likely to become habitual responses, rather than rational decisions. The results of the present study suggest that behavioural intentions may mediate, in part, the temporal stability in behaviour preference.

## *Effects of Self-Efficacy in the Theory of Planned Behaviour*

In an effort to examine the role of self-efficacy in the theory of planned behaviour, a final set of analyses considered the effects of measures of both self-efficacy and perceived behavioural control (unconfounded with efficacy expectancies) on behavioural intentions and actual behaviour, after control of the effects of the components of the theory of reasoned action. For behavioural intentions, measures of self-efficacy and perceived

Table 8.3. *Hierarchical Regression of Components of Theory of Reasoned Action and Self-efficacy on Intention, Controlling for Past Behaviour*

| Step | Variable | Beta | $R^2$ch. | $F$ch. | $df$ |
|------|----------|------|----------|--------|------|
| (1) | Past behaviour | .45** | .37 | 64.14** | 1, 147 |
| (2) | Attitude | .12 | .01 | 1.68 | 2, 145 |
|  | Subjective norm | .10 | .02 | 1.37 | 1, 144 |
| (3) | Self-efficacy | .29* | | | |
| (4) | B-B attitude | -.05 | .02 | 1.71 | 2, 142 |
|  | B-B sub. norm | .25 | | | |

B-B refers to belief-based measures.
Beta coefficients computed after all variables entered into the equation.
*$p$<.05; **$p$<.01.

behavioural control were entered into the regression equations after the measures of attitude and subjective norm were controlled. For actual behaviour, they were entered into the regression equation after the measure of intention.

The results of these analyses revealed the same pattern of results as obtained in the previous set of analyses. The measure of self-efficacy emerged as an independent predictor of behavioural intentions, but not of actual behaviour, while the measure of perceived behavioural control did not influence either of the outcome variables. Additional analyses revealed no evidence that either self-efficacy or perceived behavioural control moderated the effects of any of the components of the theory of reasoned action.

For behavioural intentions, the results suggest that perceptions of efficacy, but not external control, affect behavioural intentions. The fact that perceived behavioural control did not emerge as an independent predictor of behavioural intentions was consistent with the predictions made in the present study, but inconsistent with the theory of planned behaviour. In the present study, it was proposed that people's intentions would be based on the assumption that the external conditions would facilitate performance of the behaviour; hence, it was anticipated that a measure of perceived behavioural control would not influence behavioural intentions. However, it was proposed that the perceived presence of internal barriers to performance (as reflected in low levels of self-efficacy) would influence intentions. These results suggest that previous evidence in support of a positive relationship between perceived behavioural control and intentions may reflect the fact that measures of this variable have tended to assess efficacy expectancies (e.g., Beale & Manstead, 1991).

The lack of evidence of a link between perceived behavioural control and actual behaviour is more difficult to explain. It is possible that, for complex behaviours (such as sexual behaviours), a measure of perceived behavioural control may not be an accurate measure of actual control (cf. Terry & O'Leary, 1993). Prior to performing a behaviour, actors may not be aware of external factors that may interfere with performance. They may also have difficulty making global judgements about behavioural control, an expectation that is consistent with research into basic social psychological processes showing that people are not very good at making subjective probability judgements (Kahnenman, Slovic & Tversky, 1982). For this reason, more specific measures of perceived behavioural control may be useful. Assessments of the extent to which people have satisfied the necessary preconditions to performing the behaviour (e.g., has a condom available, made an agreement to use one; see Kashima, Gallois & McCamish, 1992; Nucifora *et al.*, this volume) could be employed, as could a planning index (measure of the extent to which the person has planned to minimise the effects of external factors that may interfere with performance, see Schifter & Ajzen, 1985).

In support of the suggestion that more specific measures of control have stronger effects on actual behaviour than global assessments of control, White, Terry and Hogg (1993) found that, in a study of condom use, neither self-efficacy nor perceived behavioural control influenced actual behaviour, although a measure of the extent to which subjects had planned to use a condom every time that they had sexual intercourse during the next month had some effect on actual behaviour. The more subjects had anticipated the external control factors that may interfere with performing the behaviour, the more likely they were to actually perform the behaviour. Nucifora *et al.* (this volume) also found that a measure of actual control (a measure of satisfaction of behavioural conditions) predicted actual behaviour.

## *Effects of Gender and Relationship Status*

To determine whether the effects of the predictor variables were dependent on gender or relationship status, an additional two sets of analyses were performed. In these analyses, one set of interaction terms (either predictor by gender or predictor by relationship status) was entered into each regression equation, after control of the corresponding main effects (relevant components of the theory of reasoned action, self-efficacy, perceived behavioural control, and gender or relationship status). For actual behaviour, both the main effects for gender and relationship status were non-significant, as were the two sets of interaction terms. However, for behavioural intentions, there was evidence of significant main effects of both gender and relationship status. After control of the effects of the components of the theory of reasoned action and the measures of self-efficacy and perceived behavioural control, relationship status accounted for an additional 6% ($F$ (1,146) = 26.25; $p < .001$) of variance, while gender accounted for an additional 2% ($F$ (1,146) = 8.08; $p < .01$) of variance in behavioural intentions. Subjects not in a current relationship were more likely than subjects in a relationship to intend to use a condom on their next sexual encounter. In a stable relationship, people probably use other forms of contraception, and rely on monogamy as a safer sex strategy. There was also evidence that males were more likely to intend to use condoms than females, possibly because men are likely to feel more at ease with condoms than women.

For behavioural intentions, there was some evidence that relationship status moderated the effect of self-efficacy on behavioural intention. Further analyses of the relationship status interaction revealed that the effect of self-efficacy was stronger ($b = .28$; $p < .01$) for subjects in a current relationship, than for those not in a relationship ($b = .09$; ns). People are likely to be even more uncertain of their efficacy expectancies when they are unaware of their partner's attitudes and feelings towards condom use, than in situations where they are in a current relationship with their partner. This uncertainty presumably weakened the self-efficacy-intention link. Safer sex programmes clearly need to focus on strengthening people's perceptions of self-efficacy, particularly if they are not in a current sexual relationship. For such people, the risk of HIV infection may be heightened if they fail to assert their desire to engage in safer sex behaviour.

### Conclusions

In summary, the results of this study provided further support for the theory of reasoned action in the context of safer sex. Both attitude and subjective norm predicted behavioural intentions, while intentions, in turn, predicted actual behaviour. After control of the effects of attitudes and norms, there was some evidence linking efficacy expectancies to subjects' willingness to engage in safer sex behaviour, particularly for subjects in a current relationship. This pattern of results accords with Bandura's (1986, 1989a,b) social cognitive theory and with Ajzen's (1987, 1991) theory of planned behaviour; however, the self-efficacy-intention link was not strong. Because of the co-operative nature of sexual relations, researchers may need to consider the effects of subjects' confidence in their feelings of efficacy. Consistent with predictions, there was no direct effect of self-efficacy on actual behaviour. Although Ajzen (1985, 1988) proposed that the presence of internal barriers to performance will directly influence behaviour, the results of the present study suggest that this source of constraint weakens motivation to engage in a behaviour, but does not influence actual behaviour.

Additional analyses revealed that a measure of perceived behavioural control (unconfounded with efficacy expectancies) did not influence either behavioural intentions or actual behaviour. The lack of a significant relationship between perceived behavioural control and behavioural intention was not unexpected; however, the failure to observe an effect of perceived behavioural control is contrary to the theory of planned behaviour. It is possible that global measures of perceived behavioural control are not able to assess accurately the degree to which the behaviour is controllable, a possibility that should be examined in future research in the area.

Theoretically, the results of the present study suggest that the theory of planned behaviour needs to conceptualise more clearly the construct of perceived behavioural control. The results of the present research suggest that the critical component of the notion of perceived behavioural control is self-efficacy. This conclusion accords with Ajzen's (1991) recent conceptualisation of the notion of perceived behavioural control as self-efficacy; however, as noted previously, this reconceptualisation, although adding some clarity to the theory, should not be accepted too hastily, given that it means that the theoretical basis of the theory of planned behaviour is potentially undermined. Future research needs to further examine the role of situational constraints on behaviour. In the context of complex, socially significant behaviours (e.g., safer sex), such research may need to avoid the use of global estimates of behavioural control, given the clear evidence from research into basic social psychological processes that people are not very good at making subjective probability judgements.

The results of the research provide further evidence for the role of attitudes and norms in the decision to engage in safer sex behaviour. Intervention programmes would clearly benefit from targeting people's beliefs about condom use, and attempting to create a normative climate that is supportive of safer sex. Such programmes should also seek to foster people's belief in their ability to engage in safer sex behaviour, particularly for people not in a current sexual relationship.

# 9

# Theory of Reasoned Action and the Role of Perceived Risk in the Study of Safer Sex

PERRI TIMMINS, CYNTHIA GALLOIS, DEBORAH TERRY AND MALCOLM MCCAMISH

*The University of Queensland, Brisbane, Australia*

YOSHIHISA KASHIMA

*La Trobe University, Melbourne, Australia*

This chapter explores some issues in the literature on perceived risk of HIV infection and the adoption of safer sexual behaviour, within the general framework of the theory of reasoned action (TRA). We argue that the conceptualisation of perceived risk has been inadequate, and we suggest some ways that risk is relevant to the prediction of behaviour from the framework of TRA and its extensions. Some preliminary results are presented as a suggestion to researchers for analysing perceived risk in a more sophisticated and useful way.

It was a virtual truism in the 1980s, given the AIDS epidemic and the accompanying advent of AIDS prevention and education programmes, that the perception of personal vulnerability to HIV is an essential ingredient in the adoption of preventive behaviour, including safer sex. Researchers pointed to the low levels of risk perception among groups of heterosexual young people and gay men, and linked these to normative climates promoting unsafe sex (e.g., Fisher, 1988), denial of risk through the stigmatisation of others (e.g., Siegel & Gibson, 1988), discrimination against people with HIV/AIDS (e.g., Herek & Glunt, 1988) and, most frequently, unsafe sexual behaviour (e.g., Bauman & Siegel, 1987; Kelly & St. Lawrence, 1988; Gallois, Statham, & Smith, 1992).

At present, few if any interventions fail to include awareness of personal susceptibility to HIV (or, more recently, to STDs in general) as an early step in the process of change to safer behaviour. In promoting safer sex, media campaigns have tended to focus on personal risk almost exclusively. In Australia, both mass-media interventions and interventions targeted at specific groups in the community have emphasised the riskiness of certain behaviours (mainly unprotected anal and vaginal intercourse), at least partly in an attempt to change the perception of HIV from a disease that affects 'risk groups' to a disease that results from 'risky behaviours.' One striking example of this approach was the *Grim Reaper* campaign in 1987, arguably the most frightening safer sex message produced on television anywhere. This approach finds an analogue in many other countries, particularly in Europe, although some countries, including Switzerland, Sweden and Denmark, have relied more on the use of humour to get the safer sex message across. In addition, behaviour change programmes based on the health belief model or one of its variants (see Lewis & Kashima, this volume; Terry *et al.,* this volume; Warwick *et al.,* this volume) include perceived personal vulnerability to HIV as a key ingredient. Perhaps the best-known model of HIV prevention in the gay community, the Morin model (Puckett & Bye, 1987), takes this perception as its starting point. For AIDS educators, changing perceived personal risk of HIV infection has been a *sine qua non* of the change to safer sex.

Despite the strong emphasis on perceived vulnerability to HIV in AIDS-education programmes and media campaigns, the research literature has not shown a strong relationship between perceived risk and safer sexual behaviour, for any group studied. For example, Baldwin and Baldwin (1988) found that a self-assessment of vulnerability to infection had little impact on behaviour. In a similar vein, Emmons*et al.,* (1986) found that perceived personal risk of HIV infection was not related to the frequency of anal sex among gay men. In a study of health workers, Brattebo, Wisberg and Sjursen (1990) found that the high level of concern about AIDS among these people was not reflected in their infection control practices.

Not only has perceived personal risk of HIV infection not been consistently related to safe (or unsafe) sexual behaviour, many studies have found very low levels of perceived risk, in spite of years of health campaigns and media messages. This situation has been especially noticeable among young heterosexuals, including university students (see Fisher & Fisher, 1992, for a review), but it is not limited to them. Even gay men, who are aware that the prevalence of HIV is high among their potential sexual partners, have been found to rate their personal risk of HIV infection as low, and perceived risk has not been a consistent predictor of safer sexual behaviour (see Gold, this volume; McCamish *et al.,* this volume; Ross & McLaws, this volume).

Denial of personal risk appears to occur in spite of fairly accurate knowledge of the ways in which HIV is transmitted, and indeed, in spite of the belief that one should practice safer sex. Turtle *et al.* (1989), for instance, found that Australian students were very aware of the need to use condoms for penetrative sex, and believed that they should use them, especially with casual partners. A parallel sample of students, however, reported that they did not often use condoms for sex with either regular or casual partners. Other Australian researchers (e.g., Crawford, Turtle, &

Kippax, 1990; Rosenthal, Moore, & Brumen, 1990) have obtained similar results with high school and university students. The experience in other Western countries has been much the same.

In the face of these discouraging results, many researchers have advocated dropping perceived risk as an important part of HIV prevention programmes, or as a major predictor of sexual behaviour. In their comprehensive model of the prediction of AIDS-preventive behaviour, Fisher and Fisher (1992) include information and knowledge, motivation (represented by the TRA variables of norms, attitudes and intentions), and skills (including a sense of self-efficacy). They do not leave much place for perceived risk, although they acknowledge the importance of risk to HIV prevention.

Others have suggested concentrating on the normative climate in a group (e.g., Gallois, Kashima *et el,* 1992), the social context (e.g., Waldby, Kippax & Crawford, 1990), attitudes to condoms and safer sex generally (e.g., Moore *et al.,* this volume; Ross & McLaws, this volume), and situated cognitions (e.g., Gold, this volume). Given the increasing emphasis on attitudes and norms as predictors of sexual behaviour, the theories of reasoned action and planned behaviour have great appeal, as both theories look mainly to these variables in explaining intentions to perform a behaviour. There is a place for perceived risk in both these theories, which we discuss below, but it is a fairly minor place.

The move away from perceived risk, both in research and now also in HIV-prevention programmes, seems counter-intuitive to say the least. After all, there would be no need for safer sex were it not for the risk of HIV, other STDs, and, in some cases, unwanted pregnancy (this last risk is especially important for heterosexual adolescents, who may not have ready access to other forms of contraception). In addition, although the major concern of educators and researchers at present is with the failure to practise safer sex or the relapse into unsafe practice, gay men have in fact made a massive social change to safer behaviour in the face of an immediate threat (see Herek & Glunt, 1988; Kelly & St. Lawrence, 1988). At the *social* level, it is impossible to deny the pivotal role of risk in safer sex. Therefore, it is important to explain the failure of perceived personal risk to predict behaviour consistently at the *individual* level. In addition, where appropriate, the re-incorporation of perceived risk into more sophisticated models of AIDS-related behaviour is worth consideration.

### Failure of Perceived Risk to Predict Individual Behaviour

There are a number of possible reasons why risk at the individual level is not associated with safer or unsafe sex in any consistent way, only one of which is that perceived risk has no influence on sexual behaviour.

Other reasons include the impact of optimistic bias on risk perceptions, the possibility of bi-directional relationships between perceived risk and behaviour, and the unstudied impact of other variables on risk perceptions (in the sexual arena, these include particularly the influence of the sexual partner). We take up each of these reasons briefly below. All of them add up to the failure to consider the complexities surrounding the perception of personal vulnerability to HIV or other STDs, and the failure to tailor the assessment of risk to the social context of the people being studied (or at whom prevention messages are targeted). In other words, risk may have been considered too much from the researcher's and educator's perspective, and not enough from the perspective of those taking the risks. The data presented later in this paper represent a partial attempt to do this, but we too have been constrained by prevailing operationalisations of perceived risk, so many of our suggestions must be left for future researchers.

### Optimistic Bias

Weinstein (1980, 1982, 1989) has discussed at length the tendency of people to assess their personal risk of any negative event as lower than that of other people. This bias is often thought of in terms of perceived invulnerability among young people, who have little experience of serious illness or death, but optimistic bias is in fact quite general. Weinstein (1980) notes that it is particularly likely to occur in the case of events which are more undesirable, unknown to personal experience, not within an individual's control and associated with strong stereotypes. This is because the need to reduce anxiety associated with very negative outcomes, the need to defend self-esteem, and the use of cognitive heuristics and shortcuts are major contributors to the denial of risk and to optimistic bias.

AIDS has many of the characteristics likely to produce optimistic bias (Weinstein, 1989). AIDS is a dread risk (Slovic, Fischhoff & Lichtenstein, 1979), where perceived severity is so universally high that it does not predict either perceived vulnerability or behaviour. Prevention of HIV infection, however, is constructed as controllable by individuals, who can choose to practise safer sex. Because the disease is perceived as so serious, and because it is associated with stereotypes about homosexuality and drug use (Abrams, Abraham, Spears & Marks, 1990; Buckham, Najman & McCamish, 1990; Siegel & Gibson, 1988), to admit personal risk is a threat to self-esteem. Thirdly, for most heterosexuals and for some homosexual men outside the epicentres of the epidemic and not strongly identified with the gay community, HIV infection is a low-probability event and one where they have little personal experience (i.e., little acquaintance with people with HIV/AIDS).

One consequence of optimistic bias for researchers is that no one is likely to assess his or her own personal risk as high (e.g., Crawford *et al.*, 1990; Wright, 1990). Indeed, many people are likely to see their personal risk as below average, no matter how average is defined. This means that a scale assessing personal risk on, say, a 5-point scale from 'none' to 'extremely high' is not likely to produce sufficient variance to show any relationship between risk and other variables, whatever relationships may really exist; instead, the bulk of responses will probably fall at the 'none' or 'small' end. A partial solution to this problem is to use a longer scale that makes fine discriminations at the extremes (particularly at the low end), although this solution can also open the way to response biases. More importantly, researchers need to be aware that subjects are likely to assess their personal risk as lower than the risk to other people or groups. It is important not to fall into the trap of thinking this response tendency is unique to HIV.

### Bi-Directional Relationship Between Risk and Behaviour

The fact that the influence of perceived personal risk on behaviour is likely to be different for different people provides another reason for the lack of evidence of a link between perceived personal risk of HIV infection and safer sex behaviour. For some people, the perception of high risk leads to a change to safer behaviour; this is the directionality ('perceived risk causes a change to safer behaviour') proposed by the health belief model. No doubt it underlies much of the change to safer sex among gay men (see Bauman & Siegel, 1987). For others, however, perceived risk seems to operate as a rationalisation for behaviour ('behaviour causes perceived risk'). Gold (this volume) has pointed to the tendency of both gay men and heterosexuals in his studies to use stereotypes (the sexual partner does not look like an HIV-positive person) and bargaining (one slip into unsafe behaviour does not count) as strategies to justify unprotected sex. For still others, perceived risk may be an accurate assessment of behaviour; a number of researchers have found that heterosexuals and gay men who assessed their risk as higher were in fact practising less safe sex (e.g., Moore & Rosenthal, 1991c).

Unfortunately for researchers, it is not possible to distinguish these relationships between risk and behaviour by means of a simple assessment of perceived risk. Instead, the perceived antecedents and consequences of behaviour must be explored in detail. To deal with this problem, some researchers have asked subjects for the reasons they assess their own risk as low or high (e.g., Wright, 1990; Moore & Rosenthal, 1991c), using both structured and open-ended measures (as in the case of knowledge tests, it may be important to use open-ended measures, to maximise the extent to which reasons reflect personal experience: see Fisher & Fisher, 1992). The reasons obtained have ranged from safer sex ('I always use condoms for sex'), to the impact of others ('I trust my sexual partner'), to stereotypes ('heterosexuals don't get AIDS'), indicating the complexity of risk assessment (Wright, 1990). To date, there have been few attempts to relate these reasons to actual sexual behaviour, but there is every reason to believe they are related. This is an important endeavour for future research.

### Impact of Unstudied Variables on Perceived Risk

Yet another reason for the lack of relationship between perceived risk and behaviour lies in the way perceived risk is assessed. To measure only perceived personal risk ignores the important influence of social variables on the way knowledge and risk judgements are integrated, and the way they go together (if they do) to influence decisions and behaviour. Kippax and Crawford (this volume) point to the ways in which groups of people work on information that comes their way, to assimilate it to their own culture. This may mean that people who are exposed to the same information end up 'knowing' different things, and using this knowledge in different ways to judge their risk of HIV infection. For example, Kippax and her colleagues found that some gay men were more aware of safer sexual behaviour, whereas others had more knowledge of unsafe behaviour (Kippax, Connell, Dowsett & Crawford, in press). Crawford et al. (1990), similarly, found that heterosexual students could accurately point to behaviours that carry high risk of HIV transmission, but were less certain in their assessment of safe behaviours.

A second variable relevant to risk assessment is the sexual partner. Much research indicates that the partner is one of the most, if not the most, important influences on decisions about sex (see Kashima & Gallois, this volume). A number of studies have also found that subjects believe sexual exclusivity is an effective way of reducing the risk of HIV infection (e.g., Gallois, Kashima, et al., 1992; McCamish, Dunne, Hamilton, & Orth, 1992; Rosenthal et al., 1990), or that activities are less risky with a regular partner than with a casual partner (e.g., Crawford et al., 1990; Turtle et al., 1989; Ross & McLaws, this volume). Indeed, there is strong evidence that gay men use the strategy of having only non-penetrative or protected sex with casual partners, but have unprotected anal intercourse with their lovers, whose HIV-antibody status is known (see Gold, this volume; Kippax & Crawford, this volume; McCamish et al., this volume). Researchers and educators, working from a perspective outside the sexual relationship, have tended to dismiss these perceptions as inaccurate, and have pointed to all the ways in which exclusivity can fail to protect against HIV.

## Theory of Reasoned Action and Perceived Risk

As noted earlier, the theory of reasoned action relies mainly on attitudes and norms to predict intentions and then behaviour. TRA is a value–expectancy theory, and thus it incorporates a cost–benefit analysis of behaviour. Fishbein and his colleagues (Ajzen & Fishbein, 1980; Fishbein & Ajzen, 1975; Fishbein & Middlestadt, 1989) stress the importance of gathering the costs and benefits of a particular behaviour in pilot research on the population under study (see Terry *et al.*, this volume).

If the risk of HIV infection is perceived to be an important cost of unsafe sex, then according to the TRA perspective, risk of infection will appear in pilot work, and will form a part of the belief-based measure of attitude. As such, the perceived likelihood of HIV infection, multiplied by the evaluation of HIV infection, should contribute to the prediction of attitude to the behaviour (e.g., attitude to using condoms for sexual intercourse). Attitude should mediate the influence of this variable, added to the other perceived costs and benefits, on the intention to perform the behaviour. Perceived risk, however, should not perform differently from other perceived costs and benefits; that is, the theory does not postulate a special relationship between perceived risk and attitude or intention.

Fishbein and Middlestadt (1989) also suggest that perceived risk may be related to subjective norm. Presumably, those people who behave in a more risky way come under more normative pressure to make their behaviour less risky. This hypothesis acknowledges the important social aspect of risk in the case of HIV/AIDS and indeed other behaviours, such as smoking, where the social context is central. There is not an obvious way for TRA to incorporate perceived risk directly into the normative side of the model, however. Moreover, for risk to predict subjective norm as well as attitude also weakens the independence between normative and attitudinal variables that is presupposed by TRA (but see Ajzen, 1991, for a review of some challenges to this part of the theory).

Within the framework of the theory of planned behaviour, perceived risk may play an additional role, related to control. While safer sex messages generally promote the view that one can control risk by behaviour, it seems plausible for an actor to believe that personal risk of HIV infection is related mainly to the prevalence of the virus, and thus out of personal control. In this case, perceived risk may be related to perceived control, but not directly to behaviour. Nevertheless, perceived risk may still be related to attempts to gain control over the outcomes of sex. For example, it may predict the satisfaction of conditions necessary for safer sex to take place, such as buying a condom or negotiating with the partner to use one (see Kashima & Gallois, this volume).

## A Study of Perceived Risk and Safer Sex

As part of a larger project on the prediction of safer and unsafe sexual behaviour (Gallois, Kashima, *et al.*, 1992; Kashima, Gallois, & Mc-Camish, 1992; Kashima, Gallois, & McCamish, in press), we assessed the perceived risk of HIV infection and some of its potential predictors (see Timmins *et al.*, 1992, 1993, for more details). In particular, we were interested in the most used and most trusted sources of information about HIV and AIDS, and the impact of these sources on perceived risk. We found that heterosexuals in the study trusted information about HIV and AIDS most if it came from doctors or material produced by the government and the national AIDS council. They received most information, however, from newspapers and magazines. Gay men in the sample trusted the sources from which they received the most information, in particular the gay press and AIDS organisations in the gay community. Nonetheless, for all subjects, the more information they received from friends, the lower was perceived personal risk.

In addition, we gathered data on perceived risk to others (friends and people with the same sexual practices) and related these to perceived personal risk. These variables were strong direct predictors of perceived personal risk; the association for people with the same sexual practices was the strongest of all. Thus for these people, while risk to members of the peer group was related to perceived personal risk, risk based on behaviour appeared to be a more important contributor. This may reflect the impact of media messages stressing that HIV is transmitted by what you do, not by who you are. Equally, it may reflect the fact that sex is still seen as a highly personal activity, where the sexual partner is by far the most important normative influence (Gallois, Kashima, *et al.*, 1992; Kashima *et al.*, in press). Even so, subjects in the study believed that others, even those with the same sexual practices, were at higher risk of HIV infection than they themselves were. The association between perceived risk and acquaintance with people with HIV/AIDS was also examined, and is reported in more detail below.

We were also interested in the extent to which perceived personal risk performed as predicted by TRA and TPB. Thus, we examined the relationships between perceived risk of HIV and other STDs, other costs and benefits of safer sex, attitude, subjective norm, and intention. In addition, we examined whether perceived risk was a predictor of the satisfaction of behavioural conditions. In doing these analyses, which are reported below, we tried to minimise the impact of optimistic bias as far as possible, by using a fairly long scale to assess perceived risk and by examining closely the distribution of responses to these items.

The subjects in the study comprised two major samples. One was a group of 71 male and 78 female undergraduate students, aged 17–21 years ($M = 18.0$). All these people reported that they had had intercourse and that they were exclusively heterosexual; about 40% were in regular sexual relationships, but none was married. The second sample was made up of 85 heterosexual women, 85 heterosexual men and 82 gay men, all volunteers from the general community and matched as closely as possible on age and socioeconomic status. The age range of these subjects was 17–66 years; mean ages were 26.7 for heterosexual women, 27.4 for heterosexual men and 31.2 for gay men. Between 80 and 85% of the heterosexuals and 45% of the gay men were in regular sexual relationships, but 75% of the heterosexuals and 95% of the gay men were unmarried.

As part of their participation in the project, these people completed structured measures of perceived risk to self and others (using 7-point scales where 4 represented average risk), intentions to practise safer sex, attitude and subjective norm towards safer sex, and perceived evaluations and likelihood beliefs about safer sex, as well as normative beliefs (all using 7-point bipolar scales). They also indicated the major sources of information from which they received information about HIV/AIDS, and how much they trusted each source (see above). Finally, they indicated the number of people they knew (acquaintances, friends, family members, sexual partners) who had HIV or AIDS or who had died of AIDS. The number of people in the student sample who had any personal contact with people with HIV was too small to use these data in the analyses, but they were included for the community sample.

For the student group, intention was operationalised as the intention to use a condom at the next sexual encounter. For the community group, it was operationalised as the intention to practise their preferred safer sex strategy on the next sexual encounter. Preferred strategy was elicited in another part of the questionnaire, and in the vast majority of cases involved either the use of condoms or sex in an exclusive relationship (see Gallois, Kashima, *et al.*, 1992, for more details). The student group also completed measures of satisfaction of behavioural conditions for using a condom: they indicated whether they had a condom available for use and whether they had made an agreement with their sexual partner to use one (see Kashima *et al.*, in press, for more details). Students received a score of 3 if they had satisfied both behavioural conditions, 2 if they had a condom available but no agreement with the partner to use one, and 1 if they had not satisfied either condition.

### Perceived Personal Risk and the Theories of Reasoned Action and Planned Behaviour

We conducted a series of analyses in order to examine the relationships between perceived personal risk and variables in TRA and TPB.

#### Factors in the Belief-Based Measure of Attitude

First, we conducted principal axis factor analyses, followed by varimax rotation, of 13 costs and benefits of the preferred safer sex strategy for heterosexuals and gay men in the community sample. A similar factor analysis was conducted for costs and benefits of condom use for the men and women in the student sample. Variables in this analysis were the products of evaluations and likelihood beliefs for each cost or benefit. Results of all analyses showed that the costs and benefits could be divided into three similar factors. One factor included having or causing physical pain, discomfort, emotional problems and doing something the partner may not like; this factor, which explained 23.7–29.5% of the variance in each analysis, was labelled 'pain.' A second factor, explaining 7.8–11.9% of the variance, included having sexual arousal, having orgasm and being intimate with the partner, and was labelled 'pleasure/intimacy.' The third factor, explaining 6.9–10.3% of the variance, included catching HIV and catching STDs, and was labelled 'risk.' Factor scale scores were calculated by summing the cross-products for variables loading highly on each factor. The scale score for the risk factor was significantly correlated for all groups except the female students with the perceived personal risk item rated elsewhere in the questionnaire.

#### Perceived Personal Risk as a Predictor of Attitude

Hierarchical multiple regression analyses were carried out separately for each group in the study, to examine the strength of perceived risk of HIV and STDs in predicting attitude. In the first step of each analysis, attitude was predicted from the scale score on the risk factor. In the second step, the other two scale scores (for the pain and pleasure/intimacy factors) were added to the equation. The results were fairly similar for all groups, although there were a few interesting differences. In all analyses, the three scale scores together significantly predicted attitude ($R^2$ ranged from .28 to .39, $p < .001$ for all analyses).

For heterosexual and gay men in the community sample, risk scores did not predict attitude significantly, but when the other factors in the belief-based measure of attitude were added to the equation, there was a significant increment in explained variance and the full model was significant. The pleasure/intimacy score proved to be the only significant predictor of attitude for gay men in the sample. For the two female groups and the student male group, however, risk was a significant predictor of attitude in the first step of the equation. The addition of the other scale scores involved a significant increment in explained variance and subsumed the influence of risk for these groups. Pleasure/intimacy was the only significant predictor of attitude in this step; thus, pleasure/intimacy mediated the relationship between perceived risk and attitude for these groups.

Overall, pleasure/intimacy was a significant predictor of attitude, as TRA would propose (betas for this factor for the five subject groups ranged from .40 to .51, $p < .001$). It appears that for the older men in the sample, risk was not particularly salient in their attitude to safer sex. On the other hand, for the women and younger men, risk was taken into account, even though it was mediated by intimacy with their partner and sexual pleasure in influencing attitude toward condom use or other safer sexual behaviours.

*Perceived Personal Risk as a Predictor of Subjective Norm*

Analyses similar to those described above were conducted to examine the power of the risk score in predicting subjective norm. In this case, the risk factor scale score from the belief-based measure of attitude was entered in the first step of the hierarchical multiple regression analysis, and the pain and pleasure/intimacy scores were entered on the next step. This time, risk was a significant predictor of subjective norm only for the gay men in the community sample ($R^2 = .17$, $p < .001$), although it approached significance for both heterosexual men and women in the community sample ($p < .06$). Risk did not predict subjective norm for either men or women in the student sample. Pain and pleasure/intimacy scores did not predict subjective norm significantly for any group. This time, pleasure/intimacy did not mediate the relationship between risk and subjective norm.

These two sets of results taken together suggest that risk may function differently for women and men, as well as for younger and older people. For the students, risk predicted attitude (although it was mediated by intimacy) but not subjective norm. For the older men, risk predicted subjective norm but not attitude; this result was strongest for gay men. For the older women, there was a weak relationship between risk and both subjective norm and attitude.

Members of all five groups said that the sexual partner was the most important normative influence on their decisions about sex (followed by friends). Thus, a brief examination of the association between the risk factor score and partner normative belief seemed worthwhile. Correlations between risk and partner normative belief revealed significant associations for all three groups in the community sample ($r$ s ranged from .26 to .35, $p < .05$ in all cases). For these subjects, the perception of risk of STDs and HIV infection as a high cost of unsafe sex was related to a stronger partner norm in favour of safer sex. For the student sample, the correlation was not significant for either males ($r = .15$) or females ($r = -.06$). These results may reflect to some extent the fact that the older participants were more likely than the younger ones to be in regular sexual relationships. It seems that the presence of a current sexual partner whose norms were known was important for the community sample, while it had little impact for the younger students.

The clear results for gay men may also reflect the different normative climate in their community. Our recruiting methods were such that the men in the sample were fairly strongly identified with the gay community in Brisbane. This community had received a good deal of targeted information about HIV/AIDS, much of it emphasising the important role of peers in safe sex. They had responded to the messages. About 98% of the gay men either had non-penetrative sex, used a condom, or had sex in an exclusive relationship (self-defined and including only one sexual partner in the past year or longer), as against 70% of the heterosexuals in the community sample. The gay men rated their risk as higher than did the heterosexuals, and risk influenced their norms, but not their attitude to safer sexual behaviour.

Another normative influence, but not one dealt with directly by TRA, involves contact with people with HIV or AIDS. To examine the impact of contact on perceived risk, we conducted an analysis of variance for the subjects in the community sample, with sex/sexual orientation (heterosexual women, heterosexual men, gay men) and contact with people with HIV (no contact or some contact) as between-subjects independent variables, and perceived personal risk as the dependent variable. Results indicated that heterosexual men in the sample who had no contact with HIV rated their risk as significantly lower (mean personal risk = 2.1) than those who had some contact (mean risk = 3.4). In fact, these two scores represented the lowest and the highest means for perceived personal risk in the sample. The difference in perceived personal risk as a function of contact with HIV was not significant for heterosexual women or gay men, although in both cases, those subjects who had contact with people with HIV/AIDS rated their personal risk as higher. Overall, gay men rated their risk as higher than did heterosexuals in the sample. These results taken together give further support to the link between perceived risk and subjective norm for gay men.

*Risk as a Predictor of Intention and Satisfaction of Behavioural Conditions*

The risk factor scores did not correlate significantly with intention for any group. The perceived personal risk item showed a significant correlation for only one group, men in the student sample ($r = .27$, $p < .05$), but the addition of attitude and subjective norm to the regression equation subsumed this influence. Thus, as TRA predicts, risk did not predict intention to use a condom or engage in other safer sex beyond the influence of attitude and subjective norm.

Finally, we examined the association between perceived personal risk and the satisfaction of conditions important for condom use; namely, having a condom available and making an agreement with the partner to use one. Correlations between perceived personal risk and the score on satisfaction of these conditions were calculated for the student sample, for whom the target behaviour was condom use. The correlation (.09) did not approach significance.

*Summary*

Table 1 summarises the results of the regression analyses. As can be seen, the impact of risk in this study accords with the predictions of TRA, and supports the suggestion by Fishbein and Middlestadt (1989) that risk is likely to be related to subjective norm. Perceived risk was not related to intention, but did show some relationship to attitude (in the younger samples and for the women in the community sample) and to subjective norm (for the older men and women). Risk was related to partner norm in this study; partner norm has been shown to be related to subjective norm, attitude, intention and behaviour (see Kashima & Gallois, this volume).

While perceived risk as a cost of unsafe sex can be added to the belief-based measure of attitude, there is no obvious way to include it in the measures of normative beliefs. It may be advisable, therefore, to include measures of perceived personal risk in future studies of safer sex, to gain information that may be lost by relying on TRA variables alone. On the other hand, these results support the findings of other research, in that risk was not a direct predictor of intention, or of behaviours necessary for condom use. Thus, the prediction of TRA, that attitude and subjective norm are more important influences on intention than external variables, was borne out by these results.

**Conclusions and Implications**

These results support the view that risk in the case of safer sex operates at the social level more than at the strictly personal one. Like other

Table 9.1. *Summary of Results of Regression Analyses, Indicating Significant Support for Predictive Relationships*

| Predictive relationship | Student sample | | Community sample | | | |
|---|---|---|---|---|---|---|
| | Women | Men | Het Women | Het Men | Gay Men | Support for TRA |
| Risk predicts attitude (mediated by pleasure) | ✓ | ✓ | ✓ | X | X | ✓ |
| Risk predicts subjective norm | X | X | ✓ᵃ | ✓ᵃ | ✓ | ✓ |
| Risk predicts partner norm | X | X | ✓ | ✓ | ✓ | - |
| Risk predicts intention | X | X | X | X | X | ✓ |
| Risk predicts satisfaction of behavioural conditions | X | X | - | - | - | - |

[a]$p<.06$.

studies, we found little relationship between perceived personal risk and the practice by individuals of safer sex. We did find, however, that personal risk was related to perceived risk to friends, and especially to people with the same sexual practices. In addition, perceived risk was related to the perception that important other people would want the actor to engage in safer behaviour, which suggests a perception that others are aware of the risks of unprotected sex. Perhaps more importantly, risk was seen to be related to the sexual partner's norm about safer sex, for older people at least.

Changing perceptions of risk, thus, may be important in changing behaviour, through promoting a normative climate of safer sex (Fisher, 1988; Fisher & Fisher, 1992). Therefore, while researchers may be justified in dropping risk as a direct predictor of individual behaviour, AIDS educators would probably be seriously mistaken in doing so. The messages about risk do appear to be having an impact, especially when one considers the very high practice of safer sex by the gay men in this study. Messages about personal risk have eventually changed the normative climate in the case of other behaviours, such as smoking and wearing seat belts while driving. Sex is a private behaviour, however, and in this case, the role of the partner is pivotal.

As we noted earlier, there are problems with the conceptualisation and measurement of risk in the area of safer sex and HIV/AIDS. In this study, we attempted to deal with some of these problems, but we have only been partly successful in this. There is still a great need for the development of more sophisticated measures of risk. Such measures can take account of the relationship between perceived risk, perceived risk to others, and the normative climate. For example, we know very little about what constitutes an acceptable level of risk for different groups in the context of HIV/AIDS. The assumption that AIDS is so serious that any risk of HIV infection at all is too great, an assumption reflected frequently in the mass media, may be unwarranted for many people (e.g., see Gold, this volume).

In addition, it is important for researchers to examine the impact of the perceived prevalence of HIV and AIDS on perceived risk to self and others. Many studies have shown that heterosexuals in particular are inaccurate in their judgements of the prevalence of HIV, but few researchers have explored the relationship of perceived prevalence to other variables. Siegel and Gibson (1988), however, theorised a clear relationship between stereotypes about prevalence and denial of risk.

In recent unpublished work, Timmins found that the use of the availability heuristic (in this case, the perception that AIDS is the most important cause of death for Australian young people), was related to the judgement that a young person described in a vignette was likely to have AIDS, rather than another disease. In addition, the use of the representativeness heuristic (the perception that AIDS is associated mainly with gay men) was related to the judgement that a young man described as gay was likely to have AIDS, rather than another disease. Neither of these heuristics was related to perceived personal risk, however. These results lead to the hypothesis that perceived prevalence and stereotypes associated with HIV/AIDS may lead to a denial of risk for people like oneself. In turn, denial at the social level may lead to a normative climate promoting unsafe behaviour, and thence to unsafe behaviour at the personal level.

There is still a need for research into these and other questions concerning risk and safer sex. Such research is important for informing AIDS education programmes, where it is premature to drop risk from consideration. The theory of reasoned action provides a good framework for this research, in that it includes specific predictions about the influence of norms on individual behaviour. As other contributors to this book (see Kippax and Crawford, this volume) point out, however, it may not be enough—research on risk at the collective level may be crucial to understanding and changing the normative climate of groups potentially at risk of HIV.

# 10

# Application of the Theory of Reasoned Action to the Measurement of Condom Use among Gay Men

MARY-LOUISE MCLAWS

*University of New South Wales, Sydney, Australia*

BRIAN OLDENBURG

*University of Sydney, Sydney, Australia*

MICHAEL W. ROSS

*Albion AIDS Centre, Division of Medicine, Prince of Wales Hospital, Sydney, Australia.*

It is well known that the most important HIV-preventive behaviours are related to the use of condoms and safe injecting of drugs. These will remain critical behaviours, even after the introduction of an HIV-preventive vaccine (Fishbein & Middlestadt, 1989). Along with the proliferation of research on condom use and safe needle use in response to the AIDS epidemic, there has been a reliance on the use of a plethora of scales and questionnaires, which have neither been subjected to proper scale development based on qualitative research with appropriate target groups nor developed within the framework of appropriate theories of human behaviour. This chapter describes the development of a scale to measure intentions to use condoms, which is based on the components of the theory of reasoned action (TRA). Using the TRA as part of such an approach has the potential to increase our understanding of sexual behaviour and those determinants which are associated with an increased risk of HIV infection (Parker & Carballo, 1990).

Even in the 1990s, the illicit nature of injecting drug use and societal views of sexual behaviour can make it difficult to develop valid and reliable measures of these behaviours. A rigorous scientific approach to scale construction, along with theory-driven research into the identification of determinants of HIV-related behaviours, will assist the development of more effective intervention programs and campaigns (Fisher & Fisher, 1992). Research into the development of acceptable, accurate and economic measures of HIV-related behaviours can then be followed by research into the determinants of these behaviours, information which in turn can be used to develop appropriate and effective intervention strategies.

## General Issues in Scale Development

There are a number of well-established steps which are important in the development of any new scale, or conversely, to consider when reviewing the suitability and acceptability of an existing scale or measure. These steps are important regardless of the theory underpinning the scale. They include:

(1) identification of the purpose for which a scale is required and evaluation of any existing scales;

(2) review and field testing of items available from an existing scale;

(3) generation of an item pool where there is no existing appropriate scale;

(4) construction of the scale;

(5) piloting of the new or modified scale;

(6) refinement and psychometric testing of the new (or existing) scale to assess its reliability and validity;

(7) preparation of the final scale.

The order of these steps is only intended as a guide, and in some instances the order may vary. For example, there will inevitably be more pilot testing and refinement required for a new scale than for an existing scale, which may only require formal testing of some of its psychometric properties. The basic principles involved in questionnaire design and the psychometric testing which is required are discussed in a number of texts, including Hawe, Degeling and Hall (1990), Crocker and Algina (1986) and Carmines and Zeller (1979).

While the idea that measurement is crucial to any scientific endeavour such as the evaluation of an HIV prevention program would appear to be only a statement of the obvious, behavioural and social scientists frequently have not given it sufficient attention (Catania, Gibson, Chitwood & Coates, 1990). This lack of attention has resulted, at least in part, from a lack of consideration of the importance of validity and reliability, which after all, are the measuring sticks against which any scale should be judged. Developing reliable and valid measures is undoubtedly a very complex and time consuming endeavour, but while no measurement instrument will ever be perfectly reliable or valid, these are the keys to the development of good measures (McLaws, Oldenburg, Ross & Cooper, 1990).

## Critical Overview of Behavioural Measures in HIV/AIDS Research

As reviewed elsewhere (McLaws, Oldenburg, Irwig, & Ross, 1993), there have been many scales reported in the literature which purport to measure many different AIDS-related behaviours and their determinants. For example, measures of the determinants of condom use by homosexually active men have been reported or used by many different researchers, including Campbell, Burgess, Goller and Lucas (1988), Carr (1988a,b), Golombok, Sketchley, and Rust (1989), Hays, Kegeles, and Coates (1990), Kelly, St. Lawrence, Betts, *et al.* (1990), McKusick, Coates, Morin, Pollack, and Hoff (1990), McCusker, Stoddard, Zapka, Zorn, and Mayer (1989), Ross (1988a,b,c, 1990a), Ross, Freedman, and Brew (1989), Siegel, Mesagno, Chen & Christ (1989), and Valdiserri, Lyter, Leviton, Callahan, Kingsley, and Rinaldo (1988). Close scrutiny of these scales reveals a number of problems.

Firstly, the psychometric properties of the scales are often not reported, which makes an assessment of their reliability and validity impossible. If these properties are not reported, researchers, for example working with a different population, are not able to assess whether the scale is appropriate to use or not. Secondly, a measurement scale needs not only to sample adequately the full range of behaviours, but also to sample in such a way as to reflect the behaviours, attitudes and beliefs of different cultural and social groups (Ross & McLaws, 1992).

Thirdly, Parker and Carballo (1990) note that the study of sexual behaviour, particularly the explosive growth of this research in response to the HIV epidemic, has relied mainly on quantitative research for scale development and for the development of intervention strategies. Scales purporting to examine HIV-related behaviours have rarely been developed from qualitative research (Gold, Skinner, Grant, & Plummer, 1991; Golombok, Sketchley, & Rust, 1989; Silvestre, Lyter, Valdiserri, Huggins, & Rinaldo, 1989). Instead, scales are often based on anecdotal evidence or on researchers' knowledge of the subject, rather than being a product of systematic qualitative research which should normally be used as an aid to developing a pool of items for a new scale. As Terry *et al.* (this volume) point out, TRA describes qualitative pilot procedures to specify behaviour, the costs and benefits associated with it and the relevant people for subjective norms items.

Qualitative research, however, can do much more than this. Indeed, such research can ultimately greatly enhance the validity of an instrument. If done properly, it can ensure adequate sampling of items from the target group, and it can broaden the range of important issues pertaining to the behaviour of interest (Leninger, 1985). Additionally, it can enhance the style of language and appropriate wording of individual items. Whether an existing scale is to be used or a new scale is being developed, qualitative research should always be used to develop an item pool that reflects the study population. Qualitative research, when linked with a model such as the TRA, has the potential to generate scales with excellent psychometric properties. It also avoids the testing only of hypotheses generated by researchers from their own expectations, and thus often missing the generation and testing of hypotheses which may not have occurred to the researcher, yet are central to the understanding of the phenomenon under investigation.

The remainder of this chapter describes the development of a questionnaire designed to measure the determinants of condom use in homosexually active men (the questionnaire is described in more detail in McLaws *et al.*, 1993). The scales, which together form the Intention to Use a Condom (IUC) Questionnaire, were based on the theory of reasoned action. As originally conceived, the scales were developed to measure the major components of Fishbein and Ajzen's (1975) model; that is, intention to use condoms, attitudes towards condom use and subjective norms (measured as normative beliefs and motivation to comply) about condom use.

However, in addition to the two main predictor variables included in most tests of TRA, there are a range of other variables, such as personality, social role, intelligence, age and gender, which may also have an impact on behaviour. These may also need to be incorporated into a TRA-based measure, particularly if the questionnaire is to be used for modelling purposes. According to the theory, many of these variables are 'external' factors; that is, they do not have any direct relationship with the major determinants of behavioural intention. Nevertheless, they were included in the present research design.

It has also been suggested that, when measuring behaviours involving a moral obligation or decision, the theory of reasoned action may require a personal norm component (Schwartz, 1973; see also Kashima & Gallois, this volume). When moral norms were combined with Schwartz's model, there was no increase in the predictive power of the basic TRA model. The inclusion of moral norm in the earlier Fishbein (1967) model, however, enabled blood donation to be predicted (Zuckerman & Reis, 1978). Therefore, moral norm was initially included as a variable.

The present authors were also interested in considering the utility of another component, behavioural norms, as a determinant of condom use. Behavioural norms refer to one's perception of the behaviour of significant others. For example, observing the smoking behaviour of peers has been shown to have a greater influence on a person's behaviour, compared with subjective norms (Grube, Morgan & McGree, 1986). Thus, it would be reasonable to expect that the condom use of peers might have a similar effect. This may be especially so for HIV-related behaviours, such as injecting drug and condom use, which occur in the presence of other people.

**Development of the Intention to Use a Condom (IUC) Questionnaire**

*Purpose of the IUC Questionnaire*

Originally, McLaws *et al.* (1993) were keen to develop a measure which would have multiple functions, including the following: to test the various components of TRA, to predict behaviour and inform intervention strategies, and to measure the effect of HIV-prevention programs or campaigns. The primary target group for the IUC Questionnaire was gay men in Sydney, the main centre of the AIDS epidemic in Australia, who practised anal sex regularly. It goes without saying that if a theory such as the TRA is to underpin the conceptualisation of a questionnaire, then it should of necessity guide the development, framing and wording of each item. On the other hand, researchers should also be open to the possibility of additional variables, often situation- or context-specific, which may explain variance additional to the TRA model.

For example, an important aspect of measurement using the theory of reasoned action involves the specificity of the behavioural criteria (Fishbein & Middlestadt, 1989). Fishbein and Middlestadt make a distinction between behaviour, behavioural categories, goals and outcomes. They suggest that it is important to distinguish between overt, observable actions and an inference based on one or more acts. They also make the point that there are often a number of different HIV-related behavioural or non-behavioural paths to the same goal or outcome. Therefore, the target behaviours of interest need to be precisely specified. For example, buying condoms, they argue, is different from using condoms, and the determinants of the two behaviours may also differ. Finally, factors that lead to the initiation of a behaviour may be very different from factors which maintain, increase, decrease, or delay the same activity. Thus, Fishbein and Middlestadt stress, very specific selection of the target behaviours must be made if the theory of reasoned action model is to be useful. In order to do this for the IUC Questionnaire, McLaws *et al.* undertook a large qualitative study, which is described briefly below.

*Using Qualitative Research to Generate an Item Pool*

Crocker and Algina (1986) make the point that the process by which constructs have been translated into a specific set of questionnaire items has often been atheoretical and has remained private, informal and largely undocumented. As already discussed in this chapter, such an approach is likely to result in the omission of important areas of behaviour, or in inclusion of areas that are relevant only in the mind of an individual researcher. Crocker and Algina (1986) suggest a number of strategies which can be used to broaden, refine, or verify the construct being measured, including content analysis of open-ended questions with potential subjects, review of research, direct observation of behaviour and consultation of the views of experts.

Given the criticisms of many existing AIDS-related scales, the present authors used qualitative research methods, including content analysis, to develop the item pool for the scales of the IUC Questionnaire. One way to obtain such data involves focus discussion groups, which have been used by behavioural and social scientists for many years (Bogardus, 1926). Focus groups have become increasingly common in health-related fields in recent years. The technique has been described extensively (Basch, 1987; Bellinger, Bernhardt & Goldstucker, 1976; Folch-Lyon & Trost, 1981; Higginbotham & Cox, 1979; Krueger, 1986).

Typically, focus groups explore a defined topic. Nevertheless, their structure is quite open and flexible, thus allowing for detailed discussion of emotions, attitudes and behaviours, which is simply not possible using more quantitative methods. There are a number of advantages associated with the use of focus groups as a means of gathering data to assist in the development of a questionnaire, particularly one which is ultimately to be used for testing a model. Participants can respond naturally because as part of a group, they do not have to feel pressured into answering every question (Basch, 1987). Another advantage of this method is that a wider range of issues may be examined more easily than during a more formalised and structured data collection procedure (Atkins, 1979). Sensitive issues can be openly discussed in the group setting, because the other participants are unacquainted with each other, which provides a sense of anonymity (Folch-Lyon & Trost, 1981). The major disadvantage of the focus discussion group method for generating qualitative data is that it does not represent a probability sample, so that the generalisability of the data is limited (Bellinger, Bernhardt & Goldstucker, 1976). In addition, the contribution of persons who are ill or physically impaired, or who cannot verbalise their opinions, can also be less than optimal (Basch, 1987); this is a salient issue for any research on HIV.

To generate discussion about behaviour, including HIV-related behaviour, a group of six to 12 participants is required (Folch-Lyon & Trost, 1981). Any fewer participants, and it may be difficult to generate discussion about sensitive issues; however, any more participants and it may be difficult to control the group dynamics. The constituency of the group is also important. It is usually advisable to separate groups, so that, for example, injecting drug users can discuss their sexual practices and views free from a pejorative reaction from non-injecting drug users.

In some instances a focus discussion group cannot be formed easily, and other means of collecting qualitative data need to be explored. This is often the case in HIV-related research, particularly that concerning at-risk populations. In the research described here, McLaws *et al.* conducted interviews with individual homosexually active men over the telephone, as well as in a predesignated area in bars for gay men, and on the streets outside venues for gay men. In this way, the researchers were able to contact men who were not accessible to the focus group procedure, thus increasing the representativeness of the sample. Even so, while the content validity of a scale developed using such strategies may be very high for the population from whom the items were generated, it should be remembered that generalisability to other populations may still be quite poor.

In the qualitative research phase of the development of the IUC Questionnaire, each focus group or discussion with an individual was introduced with a brief introductory explanation, delivered in a way so as not to bias participants towards or against the subject matter. They were then told that their thoughts, likes and dislikes about condom use and non-condom use were sought. The researchers sampled a reasonably diverse group of gay men, almost 200 in all. A similar number of participants were interviewed via focus groups, telephone interviews, street interviews and at gay clubs and social venues. Participants were recruited by one of two main methods: advertisements and active recruitment. Free supper and movie tickets were offered as incentives for participation.

Basch (1987) proposes a number of extremely practical guidelines for the conduct of focus group discussions, which we adapted for the various groups and individuals we interviewed. Examples of the questions that were used to explore items relevant to TRA included:

(1) What do your friends think about anal sex without a condom?

(2) What do you think about anal sex without a condom?

(3) Could you tell us about any situations or partners where you've forgotten or chosen not to use a condom?

(4) Do you think your partners do or don't really want to use condoms?

(5) How important is it for you to please your partner if he doesn't want to use a condom?

(6) What sort of experiences have your friends had using condoms?

(7) Who made you change to using condoms?

(8) Where have you got information about the need to use condoms?

There are a number of standard direct probing techniques which were also used to elicit extra information from participants who give incomplete responses, including pausing, repeating the question, asking the participant to 'tell me more about what you're thinking on that issue?', asking 'are there any other reasons for why you feel/think/believe that?' and asking 'what do you mean?'.

## Construction of the Subscales and Piloting of the Questionnaire

### Identification of Critical Issues

Interviews, whether from groups or individuals, were tape recorded and then transcribed verbatim onto a computer file. There are a number of steps involved in analysing qualitative data and in using this information to develop questionnaire items. Generally, grounded theory (Strauss & Corbin, 1990) and content analysis are used when the decision-making process or a detailed description of behaviour of interest is the objective. In these instances, computer packages such as Ethnograph and the Non-numeric Unstructured Data Indexing Searching and Theorising (NUDIST: Qualitative Solutions and Research Pty. Ltd, 1993) computer programs, have been designed to categorise qualitative findings and are available to help the researcher to analyse large amounts of data. For this research, NUDIST was used to categorise the data and extract themes and examples for questionnaire items (see below). In the development of the IUC Questionnaire, given that TRA was being used to guide the development of the subscales, the authors were concerned with using the qualitative data to identify the local jargon, as well as to identify behaviours and commonly expressed beliefs and cultural attitudes which were related and relevant to condom use in the target group. A print-out of all the transcripts was examined for critical phrases and sentences concerning condom use. The phrases and sentences were then extracted and grouped by issue or theme. Following the guidelines proposed by Knafl and Webster (1988), codes were assigned to sentences or phrases pertaining to specific issues, so as to facilitate quick identification of all the different items. Codes can be assigned manually while reading the print-out or with the use of qualitative software packages. Some computer software packages can also assist in coding by searching for particular phrases and then coding them.

### Enhancing the Generalisability of the Scale

If a questionnaire is ultimately to be used with a wide age range of participants, as was intended with the IUC Questionnaire, items common to chosen age groups need to be identified and, where necessary, expanded. For example, in our qualitative research, the retrieved codes for behaviours revealed that younger gay men tended to talk about prospective permanent partners, and said that they wanted these partners to have an HIV antibody test before having insertive anal intercourse. The older men interviewed, however, did not dwell on this issue. Hence, we ensured that we interviewed a similar number of gay men representing youth (17–24 years of age), mid-life (25–40 years of age) and middle age (40 years and over).

*Identification of Major Issues to be Covered by Items*

The qualitative research identified 14 major issues related to condom use:

(1) use of excessive drugs and alcohol intake;

(2) availability of condoms and the withdrawal method as an alternative;

(3) uncontrolled sexual desire;

(4) no condom because of the need to become emotionally involved;

(5) HIV antibody results;

(6) knowing a partner's lifestyle;

(7) evaluation of partner's risk based on discussion;

(8) the length of a relationship;

(9) the belief that the insertive partner was at less risk of HIV infection compared with the receptive partner;

(10) protection given by condoms;

(11) negative implications of asking a partner to have an HIV antibody test;

(12) condom use with a lover while having anal sex outside that relationship;

(13) implications that a new partner is a one-night stand if a condom is used;

(14) implication of distrust in a relationship if a condom is used.

The following key peer groups were also identified as being important: lovers, friends, the gay community as a whole, and casual sexual partners.

Once the range of issues and potential items for the various scales of the IUC Questionnaire were identified, the wording of each item for the component scales was guided by the Ajzen and Fishbein (1980) version of TRA (see Terry *et al.,* this volume). The precise wording of each item and the jargon used is critical to the adequacy of the items. For example, coded behaviours showed that 'insertive' anal intercourse was an acceptable term for 'penetrative' anal intercourse in the gay community.

### Development of the Questionnaire

With the important issues and potential scale items identified, the initial versions of the items themselves were developed. Some examples of transcript quotes, and the way in which they were translated into behavioural intention, attitude, normative belief and behavioural norm items, are presented below:

*Example 1.* Unprotected anal intercourse happens when participants have consumed alcohol and drugs.

*Transcript :*' (I) choose not to (use a condom) ... when I am drunk, out of it, because of drugs.'

*Behavioural norm item* : Your casual partners don't use a condom for anal sex when they've had too much drugs and alcohol.

*Example 2.* The problems of availability of condoms and the use of the withdrawal method as an alternative to condoms.

*Transcript* : '...I'd just go along with that (partner not using a condom), as long as the withdrawal method was used.'

*Behavioural intention item* : The next time a condom is unavailable for anal sex you will use the withdrawal method.

*Subjective norm item* : Most of your gay friends who are important to you think you should use the withdrawal method if you don't use a condom for anal sex.

*Example 3.* The decision to use a condom during heightened sexual desire.

*Transcript* : 'When you're feeling really lusty and buzzed up and going for it you don't use a condom.'

*Attitude item* : When you feel really lusty and buzzed up and going for it you don't use a condom for anal sex.

*Example 4.* The problem of condom use when the participant was emotionally involved with his sexual partner.

*Transcript* : (one of many quotes) 'It's (using a condom) not much of a problem ... it's more the emotional situation.'

*Subjective norm items* : Your casual partner (or lover or gay community or friends) think you should use love as a basis to decide not to use a condom.

*Attitude item* : When you're in love you decide not to use a condom for anal sex.

*Behavioural norm item* : Most of your casual partners (etc.) use a condom with a new partner that they think will become a permanent partner.

*Example 5.* The decision to have unprotected anal intercourse with a concordant HIV antibody partner.

*Transcript* : 'Again, if I were in a permanent relationship, it would depend on the antibody status of the other person.'

*Behavioural intention item* : You and your lover will have an AIDS antibody test before you decide to have anal sex without a condom.

*Subjective norm items* : Your lover (or gay community or friends) think that both you and your partner should have an AIDS antibody test before you decide not to use a condom for anal sex.

*Attitude item* : Anal sex without a condom happens because both partners have had an AIDS antibody test.

*Example 6.* The belief about condom protection.

*Transcript* : 'Lets face it, nobody wants AIDS' '(I get) no benefits at all really.'

*Attitude item* : You will stop the spread of AIDS by using a condom for anal sex.

*Example 7.* The decision to use a condom with a lover only while having anal sexual intercourse outside that relationship.

*Transcript* : 'It's something you use when you're having sex outside your relationship.'

*Attitude item* : In an open relationship you use a condom for anal sex with your lover.

*Subjective norm items* : Your casual partner (or lover or gay community or friends) think you should use a condom for anal sex with your lover if you're in an open relationship.

As already mentioned, there were four peer groups which were frequently referred to during the interviews:

(1) Male homosexual friends

*Transcript* : 'A lot of my friends won't wear condoms.'

(2) Male homosexual community

*Transcript* : 'I guess the general consensus is that it's (unsafe sex) not something you do.'

(3) Male homosexual lover

*Transcript* : 'My lover has no hesitation (in using condoms).'

(4) Male homosexual casual sexual partner

*Transcript* : 'There's a lot of unsafe sex going on, but if pressured ... people don't really hesitate to put one on.'

As we noted above, and as can be seen from the transcript examples, the major issues identified from the qualitative work were beliefs related to uncontrolled sexual desire, emotional involvement, their partner's lifestyle, the value of discussion, the risk for the insertive partner, the benefits of the HIV antibody test, condom use and one-night stands and the belief that condoms prevent HIV. All these issues were represented in each part of the questionnaire. The pilot version of the Behavioural Intention (BI) scale consisted of nine items concerning future condom use in relation to HIV antibody testing and alternative methods of safe sex. Items in the Subjective Norms (SN) scale measured each of the identified issues in relation to the four important peer groups. Each item was included four times in the SN scale, so that the influence of the four identified key peer groups could be measured separately; each SN item had a corresponding item to measure motivation. Thus, there were 32 pairs of items in this scale. Items in the scale measuring attitudinal beliefs (ATT) were developed to measure beliefs and evaluation of those beliefs. Thus, each belief item had a corresponding statement to measure evaluation of the behavioural belief; that is, a total of 19 pairs. The Behavioural Norms

(BN) scale included items which pertained to the perceived use of condoms by the four key peer groups. There were 15 items in the pilot scale.

There are many other tasks which are necessary at this stage of scale development, in addition to the wording and formatting of the individual scale items. Crucial to the development of individual items and appropriate response choices or options is the use of a scaling method that will permit assessment of the extent to which the numbers used to identify positions on a continuum have the properties of both order and equal units (Crocker & Algina, 1986). This is a far from trivial issue which has been the source of much vigorous debate among psychologists over the past 50 years. The way we undertook this task is described in the next section.

*Scaling and Scoring of Items*

Each item from the four scales was scaled on a 7-point scale for the sake of consistency, ease of scoring and to aid good response rates. The response choices for the subjective norms, attitudinal and behavioural norm questions were scaled from 1, 'extremely unlikely,' to 7, 'extremely likely'. The paired items measuring motivation to comply with normative beliefs were scaled from 7, 'a lot/extremely motivated' to 1, 'a little motivated.' Each paired item evaluating an attitudinal belief was scaled from 7, 'extremely good' to 1, 'extremely bad.' Safer sex questions in the four scales were scored so that 'extremely unlikely' score 1 and 'extremely likely' scored 7. Scoring for unsafe sex questions was reversed.

As Ajzen and Fishbein (1980) proposed that the items in a behavioural intention scale have an additive relationship, the BI items to be summed were placed consecutively in the BI scale. Given that each normative belief and motivation pair of items have a multiplicative relationship, they were placed together in the SN scale, and then the products were summed. The same was done for the attitudinal beliefs and evaluation items in the ATT scale. BN items were placed consecutively to allow for summation. As the IUC Questionnaire and the subscales were reviewed by other experts and ongoing piloting continued, adjustments were made to the items and the layout of the questionnaire in order to improve item accuracy and wording, ensure appropriateness or relevance of the items according to the original test specifications and improve the level of readability (Crocker & Algina, 1986).

*Psychometric Testing of the Questionnaire*

Following the development of the full pilot version of the IUC Questionnaire and the four scales, a further study was conducted to begin an examination of some of the psychometric properties of the instrument, and at the same time, refine the various subscales. In particular, at this stage we were interested in reliability of the scales and in face validity and internal construct validity. It was important to examine characteristics such as the distribution of scores from each of the scales, which also have a bearing on reliability and validity. The additional piloting also provided a further opportunity to ascertain from respondents any difficulties they had in completing the questionnaire and to ascertain how long it took to complete (if a questionnaire is found to be unacceptably time consuming, reliability is likely to be compromised; Abramson, 1984; Bailey, 1991).

As has already been indicated earlier in this chapter, there are no definitive rules concerning the establishment of the psychometric properties of a new scale, and in any case, it is often simply not practical or feasible to do the variety of substudies which are required to carry out this task comprehensively. In this research, it was decided to use Cronbach's alpha (Cronbach, 1951) for each component scale as the primary means for deleting individual items. Although principal component or factor analyses would have identified items to be excluded from the IUC Questionnaire, there was no prior knowledge that any of the scales were multi-dimensional. In any case, TRA generally uses single scales for outcomes and predictors.

As a check on the face validity of the items, a further sample of gay men was recruited from the same venues as were used in the original qualitative study. Field workers sat across from the participants and read aloud every question, to ensure the participant understood each question. The participant was asked to interpret each question. In addition, participants were asked to comment on the language used in the questionnaire, and the lay-out of the questionnaire.

Using the responses of a new sample of gay men who completed the IUC Questionnaire, the internal consistency of each of the three scales was calculated in order to ascertain the extent to which each of the scales was homogeneous. Table 1 presents the items from the final version of the scale. Cronbach's alpha for the Behavioural Intention Scale with nine items was .61, but this was increased to .76 following the deletion of two items, reducing the final scale to 7 items. For the Attitude scale, the highest internal consistency of .79 was achieved following the deletion of seven pairs of items from the original 19. The remaining 12-item scale describes attitudes towards anal sex without a condom as a result of different influences including the perceived efficacy of condoms. The items referred to drugs and alcohol, passion, love, discussions with a lover and the length of the relationship. This scale also includes attitudinal beliefs concerning the potential for condoms to prevent the spread of HIV and using condoms with lovers while in an open relationship.

For the Subjective Norm scale, following the deletion of five of the original 32 paired items, alpha was increased to .87. In its final form, this 27-item scale describes the influence of perceived peer expectations

Table 10.1. *Items in the Intention to Use a Condom Questionnaire*[*]

| Behavioural intention | Behavioural norms |
|---|---|
| The next time you have anal sex with a new partner (lover)† you'll use a condom for anal sex. | Most of your gay friends who are important to you (casual partners; lover; gay community) use a condom for anal sex. |
| You'll use a condom for anal sex with every man you fall in love with. | Your casual partners (gay community) use a condom for anal sex with their lovers while they're in an open relationship. |
| If a condom isn't available you will still have anal sex. | Most of your gay friends who are important to you (casual partners; lover; gay community) use a condom for anal sex with a new partner that they think will become a permanent partner. |
| You will CHOOSE not to use a condom for anal sex. | **Attitude** |
| If your casual partner (lover) doesn't want a condom you will still have anal sex. | When you have too many drugs or too much alcohol you have anal sex without a condom. |
| | When you feel really lusty and buzzed up and going for it you don't use a condom for anal sex. |
| **Subjective norms** | |
| | When you're in love you decide not to use a condom for anal sex. |
| Most of your gay friends who are important to you (casual partners; lover; gay community) think you should use a condom for anal sex. | You will help stop the spread of AIDS by using condoms for anal sex. |
| Most of your gay friends who are important to you (casual partners; lover; gay community) think you should use a condom for anal sex with a new partner who you would like to become a permanent partner. | You're protected from HIV infection when you use a condom for anal sex. |
| Most of your gay friends who are important to you (casual partners; gay community) think you should use love as a basis to decide not to use a condom. | Your casual partner (lover; gay community) is protected from HIV infection when you use a condom for anal sex. |
| Most of your gay friends who are important to you (lover; casual partners; gay community) think you should use the withdrawal method if you don't use a condom for anal sex. | Knowing your partner's lifestyle means he doesn't have to have an AIDS antibody test before you decide not to use a condom. |
| Most of your gay friends who are important to you (lover; casual partners; gay community) think you should use a condom for anal sex with your lover if you are in an open relationship. | Having a discussion with your partner rather than having an AIDS antibody test is the only basis you need to decide not to use a condom for anal sex with him. |
| Most of your gay friends who are important to you (lover; gay community; casual partners) think that the length of a relationship with a lover is a basis you should use to decide not to use a condom. | The length of a relationship with a lover is a basis you use to decide you trust him enough not to use a condom. |
| Your gay friends who are important to you (lover; casual partners; gay community) think that you should have trust in a relationship with a lover which means that a condom for anal sex shouldn't be needed. | In an open relationship you use a condom for anal sex with your lover. |

[*] See text for scales used with each type of item.
† Words in brackets indicate additonal referents for an item; the item is repeated for each referent.

about condom use within different types of sexual relationships. The items describe condom use in general, use of condoms with a new partner, the use of love as a basis for not using a condom, use of the withdrawal method, using a condom with a lover while in an open relationship, using the length of a relationship as a basis for not using a condom, and having trust in a relationship and therefore having no need to use a condom. For the Behavioural Norm scale, following the deletion of four items, alpha was increased to its highest value of .85. The 11-item BN scale in its final form describes perceived general condom use and condom use in open relationships and with new partners, by the four key peer groups.

Correlations between each pair of the scales were calculated to examine the degree of overlap between the constructs being measured by each of the scales. The correlation coefficients between each pair of the three predictor scales were low to medium in size. The correlation coefficient between ATT and SN was .26, ATT and BN, .45, and SN and BN, .45. Internal construct validity was thus considered adequate to continue with testing of the scale. Other technical information on the subscales of the IUC Questionnaire, including the frequency distribution of scores on each of the scales, is detailed elsewhere (McLaws *et al.*, 1993).

This questionnaire has now also been used to determine the extent to which each of the three predictor scales: BN, SN and ATT, can predict behavioural intention, and whether age and HIV antibody status can add to this prediction (McLaws, 1992). These analyses showed that both the Attitude scale and the new scale which was added to the model, the Behavioural Norm scale, were significant predictors of behavioural intention. The Subjective Norm scale, however, was not an independent predictor of intention in this analysis. Both HIV antibody positivity and age were found to directly influence intention to use a condom. Testing of the scale and its use with gay men to test predictions based on TRA and its extension to include behavioural norm, will continue in our research. Analyses like these, which are based on valid and reliable measures, have the capacity not only to increase our understanding of the determinants of condom use and the utility of the theory of reasoned action, but also to provide more evidence concerning the construct validity of the IUC Questionnaire.

## Summary and Conclusions

The IUC Questionnaire includes many items in common with previous scales, but some items have not been tested previously. For example, although other scales have included items about the effects of alcohol and drugs on an actor's behaviour, our qualitative research indicated the likely importance of these on the behaviour of peers as well. As have other workers in the field, we also identified HIV antibody status and the partner's attitude as being important and likely to distinguish between condom users and non-users. There are some additional elements to these issues, however, which we believe require measurement. The belief that non-use of condoms is an indicator of commitment to a relationship, the use of condoms only in open relationships and the length of a relationship are such variables. Moreover, the IUC Questionnaire differs from others in that it includes items which measure intention to use a condom with different types of partners, and within different types of relationships. To date, the four subscales of the IUC Questionnaire have been found to be stable, internally consistent and to have acceptable construct validity.

In the end, research like this must have an application in interventions to promote HIV-preventive behaviour. Effective programs targeting those individuals most at risk of HIV infection can only be developed and implemented if we can identify the determinants associated with high risk behaviours. Increasing our understanding of these is dependent on having reliable and valid measures. Given the limitations of existing measures, especially those for use with high risk groups, any new questionnaire should be developed from qualitative research. The steps we used, which are outlined in this chapter, can be used to develop questionnaires for the modelling of any HIV-related behaviour. Scales based on the theory of reasoned action to model HIV-related behaviours will help us understand and identify predictors which can be subsequently used to develop health education programs.

# 11

# A Theory-Based Intervention: The Theory of Reasoned Action in Action

MALCOLM MCCAMISH, PERRI TIMMINS, DEBORAH TERRY AND CYN-
THIA GALLOIS

*The University of Queensland, Brisbane, Australia*

The first, and indisputably the most important, objective of the World Health Organisation's Global Program on AIDS is to prevent infection with HIV (WHO, 1992). This objective is increasingly important for, though the HIV epidemic has entered its second decade, promises of vaccine and cure remain unfulfilled. Even were a successful vaccine or therapy to appear, this would not eliminate the need for preventive education. Already some countries in the developing world have indicated that current treatments such as AZT will not be made available. Moreover, no prophylactic nor therapeutic strategies which successfully grapple with the dual difficulties of availability and affordability have been promulgated, especially in the developing world where the brunt of the epidemic is being borne. Consequently it would be unwise for the world to become too dependent on a biological arsenal, even were it stocked with still fictional preventive and curative weaponry.

The concession that the social and behavioural sciences should be pivotal in the design and implementation of prevention was not easily won. Public health authorities were more familiar with models derived from the containment of tuberculosis or syphilis. Brandt (1985) has argued that this directed the early U.S. approach to AIDS prevention. Certainly the development and availability of the various HIV-antibody tests in 1985 led to a glut of studies attempting to assess (or endorse) the benefits of testing on the change in the frequency of behaviours known to transmit HIV. At the VI International Conference on AIDS, the Centers of Disease Control reviewed the results of forty-five studies of the impact of testing on behaviour (Higgins, Galavotti, Johnson, O'Reilly, & Rugg, 1990). While the majority of studies revealed that homosexual seropositives reduced their sexual risk taking, the results of those investigating the sexual behaviour of injecting drug users and heterosexuals were less sanguine.

For example, Landis, Earp, and Koch (1992) compared the impact of testing and counselling at an anonymous testing site on subsequent sexual behavior. Interviews and follow-up 12 months later revealed no significant changes in high risk sexual behaviour. Furthermore, as current understanding suggests that the period prior to seroconversion (and hence prior to detection by any antibody test) is one of highest viral concentration and potential transmission, even if the discovery of seropositivity resulted in the total cessation of all risk behaviour, it would be too late for even the most efficient testing programs to eliminate HIV transmission. As Coates (1990) pointed out, "Testing for antibodies to HIV can only be a part, *and not the centrepiece* (his emphasis), of a comprehensive AIDS prevention program."

Early in the epidemic, community groups which developed as a direct response to the epidemic initiated a series of preventive strategies, as varied as they were ingenious. These occurred almost exclusively within well organised gay communities and took advantage of local conditions. Governments were slower to respond, but the World Health Organisation was able to present a global strategy to the United Nations General Assembly in October, 1987, and to a World Summit of Ministers of Health on Programs for AIDS Prevention, in London in January, 1988. Some countries had already developed strategies and initiated campaigns by this time. Switzerland had begun its national campaign in 1986. Australia's National Strategy was published in 1989 and is currently being evaluated. An evaluation of national strategies of thirteen European countries has been published by Wellings (1991).

National campaigns, by their very nature, comprise a number of different interventions. Some, such as mass media messages, are designed for an undifferentiated population, others, such as those being co-ordinated by gay community groups, injecting drug users and the like, are highly targeted. While the design of these interventions may draw on the theoretical frameworks which exist in the social and behavioural sciences, all too often these have been ignored.

Likewise, as has been pointed out by Fisher and Fisher (1992) and Lewis and Kashima (this volume), individual interventions, with few exceptions, have been developed without the benefits of any theoretical underpinning. One consequence of this has been that interventions, have typically not been evaluated. As Wellings (1991) has stated:

> What has passed for outcome evaluation to date is more properly described as monitoring. In many cases what have been measured have been the *effects* of campaigns (whether they achieved any results at all) rather than their *effectiveness* (whether an intervention achieved its objectives) or *efficacy*, (whether it achieved its objectives more effectively than an al-

ternative course of action or none at all)—the question which
is seen by many as being at the heart of the evaluative process.

The result is that little is known about the successes, and even less
about the failures of these programs (see for example Committee on AIDS
research and the Behavioral, Social, and Statistical Sciences, 1989). In addition, too often have policies and programs been developed which lack
a sufficient research base or which overlook or ignore the results of research. Leviton (1989) has summarised the need for and value of theoretically based interventions. The centrality of preventive research and the
need for rapid dissemination of the results are central to Australia's National HIV/AIDS Strategy (Commonwealth of Australia, 1989). Despite
this recognition of the importance of research and the need for educational
interventions to be driven by the results of that research, this custom too is
found 'more honoured in the breach than the observance.' Dowsett (1988)
signalled the concern: "More disappointing to the researcher is the sight
of educational campaigns either uninformed by research findings, or developing in a direction contradicted by research evidence." Yet the links
which for example connect biomedical research with clinical practice are,
for social and behavioural research and HIV education, yet to be forged.

In a recent article, Hochbaum, Sorenson and Lorig (1992) have attempted to characterise the differences between theory- and practice-
oriented projects and to shrink the gap between health education 'aca-
demicians' and 'practitioners'. A similar attempt to remove the barriers
to the use of theory and to enumerate the benefits of theory to practice
have been made by van Ryn and Heaney (1992). Yet if the barriers they
identify are difficult to surmount by professionally trained public health
officers dealing with 'normal' issues, how much more problematic are
those associated with the HIV/AIDS epidemic.

Initially, interventions in the AIDS epidemic were communal, not professional: there was neither interest nor response from public health authorities. Fortunately, in U.S. cities such as San Francisco and New York,
where the gay community included health educators and allied professionals, appropriate research based and sophisticated prevention programs
were rapidly introduced. The San Francisco AIDS Foundation developed
the 'STOP AIDS Project' using the Morin Model (see below) while in
New York, the Gay Men's Health Crisis, as a result of research described
as the '800 Men Project', developed a workshop called 'Eroticising Safe
Sex' (Palacios-Jimenez & Shernoff, 1986). Elsewhere, however, the formation of AIDS Councils and the development of preventive strategies
were less structured. Professional health educators avoided the epidemic.
Early appointments were of staff, often unpaid, who lacked any formal
training in health promotion and who had never heard of health promotion
theories, but were concerned for their communities, were prepared to be

public, and were willing to fight an at best apathetic but more often hostile government. While the minatory advice of Fishbein and Middlestadt (1989) that "the AIDS epidemic is too serious to allow interventions to be based on some communicator's untested and all too often incorrect intuitions" cannot be gainsaid, it must be recognised that in the earlier days of the epidemic there were few alternatives!

## Interventions Based on the Health Belief Model

Early models of HIV-infection prevention that had a theoretical foundation were based on versions of the health belief model (HBM) (Becker, 1974; Janz & Becker, 1984; Rosenstock, 1974a), which proposes that people's decisions to engage in a particular health-related behaviour will be influenced by their perceived susceptibility of contracting the disease, their perceptions of the severity of the disease, the perceived benefits of engaging in the behaviour, and the extent to which barriers are perceived to limit the likelihood that the behaviour will be performed (see Warwick *et al.,* this volume).

### *Morin Model*

The health belief model was the foundation of perhaps the most celebrated model, the Morin model (Morin & Batchelor, 1984) developed specifically to address AIDS by the San Francisco AIDS Foundation (Puckett & Bye, 1987). The Morin model differed from the HBM in a number of significant ways. Specifically, it used market research techniques and focus groups to elicit what were identifiable barriers to and costs of adopting a safer sex response to the epidemic; also it emphasised the importance of the norms of the peer group, and the role of self efficacy (Bandura, 1977, 1989). According to the Morin model, the following beliefs are necessary for the adoption of safer behaviour: (i) the belief that AIDS is a personal threat; (ii) the belief that AIDS is preventable; (iii) the belief that sex, modified to avoid or minimise HIV transmission, is still satisfying; (iv) that the change to this modified sex is manageable; and (v) that there is widespread peer support to make the change. Equally importantly, though often overlooked, is the fact that the Morin model was developed by the gay community in San Francisco for the gay community and facilitated by the gay community. Concepts of community support were strengthened by using members of the gay community to recruit participants and organise meetings which were held in the homes of gay men who acted as hosts for the Stop AIDS meetings. As such this approach differed from traditional didactic models, "restricted almost entirely to the communication of health education messages regarding the risks of certain behaviors" (Stall, Coates & Hoff, 1988) delivered by 'experts.'

The San Francisco STOP AIDS Project, incorporating the Morin tenets, was a single meeting workshop billed as a 'community experiment in communication,' which ran virtually every day for two and a half years until mid-1987, often simultaneously at multiple sites (Puckett & Bye, 1987). Programs based on the Morin model have been implemented in other communities in the U.S.A. Evaluations of these (for example Miller, Booream, Flowers, & Iverson, 1990; Flowers *et al.*, 1991) have shown that the programs are effective in eliciting intentions to change behaviour, though no studies have measured actual behaviour changes.

Although the Morin model has been a useful basis for interventions, it has shortcomings which limit its generalisability to groups outside U.S. gay communities in major cities. It is interesting to note that early attempts to import HIV-prevention interventions into Australia did not succeed. In fact, the early development in Australia of HIV-prevention education strategies which extended beyond information dissemination (for a partial overview of which, see Dowsett, 1989) was characterised by the slow shedding of the Morin model.

Attempts to run Stop AIDS workshops in Brisbane by the Queensland AIDS Council ceased after about six months of relative failure. A number of forces may have contributed to this, including the fact that homosexual acts were still illegal in Queensland. Whatever the causes, recruitment was exceedingly slow, and only a handful of meetings were held. Similar experiences have been recorded by the AIDS Council of New South Wales. Davis (cited in Galbraith, 1992) has stated that it was [erroneously] assumed that gay men would fit the patterns found by Morin in San Francisco and that "gay men in Sydney are not used to going to groups of 15 and talking about their innermost sexual desires and practices with a group of men they don't like, and then making lifestyle decisions on that basis." These experiences suggest that the nature of gay communities in Australia is very different from that in the U.S.A. where the programs had been successful.

*Role of Personal Susceptibility*

The beliefs contained in the health belief model and the Morin model are, in their own right, all complex variables which do not necessarily operate in the same way for everyone. The perception of personal susceptibility, for example, which could hardly be ignored in an epidemic epicentre such as San Francisco, has less influence in regions of low seroprevalence, where people without any close personal contact with the infected might be less aware of biomedical progress and display unrealistic optimism regarding the imminence of a vaccine or cure (McCamish, Cox, Frazer, & North, 1988). Perceived susceptibility has also been shown to have little influence on the young who, influenced by the norms of adolescence, are likely to have perceptions of invulnerability (Irwin & Millstein, 1986; Weinstein, 1989; Moore,*et al.* , this volume). Moreover, perceived susceptibility may be influenced by ethnicity (Vazquez-Nuttal, Avila-Vivas, & Morales-Barreto, 1984; Rigby, this volume), for many heterosexuals, by homophobia (Siegel & Gibson, 1988), and by knowing someone infected with HIV (Valdiserri *et al.*, 1988; Frazer, McCamish, Hayes, & North, 1988; McCamish, Timmins, Gallois, Terry, & Kashima, 1991).

### Individual Bias

An additional restriction of the health belief model is that it is directed towards the individual and, when applied to safer sexual behaviour, does not take into consideration the sexual partner. It is self-focussed and motivations to change behaviour, directed as they are by perceptions of susceptibility and severity, are selfish and self-centred. While this focus on 'what is best for me' may be appropriate for health care behaviours such as weight loss and the cessation of smoking, it is an inadequate motivation when considering HIV-preventive strategies. Considerations of adopting safer sex have to wrestle with two distinct forms of risk: not only the risk of my becoming infected as a result of unsafe sex with an infected partner but also the risk that, if I am infected, I might infect an uninfected partner. Successful HIV-preventive strategies must not only provide resources for those who do not wish to become infected: they cannot ignore the need to generate altruistic motivation for those already infected so they will not infect others.

### Role of Peer Support

A novel aspect of the Morin model was its acknowledgment of the influence of peers, and the fact that the program was implemented by peers. Many preventive education programs designed for gay identified men (with, for example, recruitment in gay venues) have adopted a peer education format. The predicted success of the interventions was predicated on the assumption of widespread peer support for safer sex (e.g., Gallois & McCamish, 1989; Kelly, St Lawrence, & Brasfield, 1991) leading to the concept of a safe sex community (Pucket & Bye, 1987). However, while such a supportive community might be available in, for example, San Francisco (Research and Decisions Corporation, 1984), it is much less likely to exist in environments where discrimination and/or legislation militate against it (Kelly, St Lawrence, Brasfield, Stevenson, *et al.,* 1990c).

The faith placed in the importance of peer support has been vindicated. In a survey of New York adolescents which compared constructs of the health belief model with self-efficacy and behavioural norms and values (Walter *et al.,* 1992),, it was found that only beliefs derived from norms (i.e., beliefs about friends and class members) and values (i.e., beliefs that persons of their age should be involved in these behaviours) and self efficacy were associated with higher risk behaviours. Leviton *et al.* (1990) showed that peer support resulted in more sustained positive attitudes to safe sex and Valdiserri *et al.* (1988) found, in a comparison of those who always or never used condoms, that those who never used condoms had peers who 'were less convinced of condom efficacy'. Peer support has also been related to the adoption of monogamy and the avoidance of anonymous sexual partners, though not to the modification or avoidance of receptive anal sex (Joseph *et al.,* 1987). Not only has peer support been shown to play an important role in the change to safer behaviours, it also is significant in their maintenance. In the Chicago MACS study, less peer support significantly predicted relapse to less safe practices (Adib, Joseph, Ostrow, & James, 1991). Readoption of unsafe sexual practices has also been linked significantly to involvement with peer groups which had not established risk reduction norms (Kelly St. Lawrence, Brasfield, Stevenson, *et al.,* 1990).

The absence of peer support has also been linked with unsafe sexual behaviour. Perceptions that their friends were having unsafe sex predicted unsafe sex among young gay men in San Francisco (McKusick, Coates, Morin, Pollack, & Hoff, 1990), while Doll *et al.* (1991) found significantly higher levels of unprotected anal sex and lower perceptions of peer support for condom use among the non-white men.

Evidence linking peer support to HIV-preventive behaviour suggests that peer-based interventions should be successful. The concepts of 'peer support' and even of 'peers' are complex, however. Leaving aside the question whether support embraces acceptance or requires reassurance and encouragement, it is not easy to define who constitute peers, and none of the studies cited above has attempted it. The complexity of this concept is demonstrated by research conducted in gay communities. All studies on the role of peer support among gay men, however, have seemed to assume that not only homosexuality but also gay identity would be a *sine qua non* of the definition of peer support. The implicit equation has been that 'peers' equals 'other members of the gay community'. Whether this concept of peers, distinguished through sexual and community identity, could translate into successful interventions beyond the specialised target groups exemplified above is uncertain.

Even with this construction, difficulties arise. As a gay community evolves, it may develop rigid norms which may discriminate, for example, against certain sexual practices, places where sexual partners are met, non 'gay identity', specific dress codes and so forth (Longo, 1992; Power, 1992; Sandford, 1992). The existence of such tensions is likely to reduce the effectiveness of interventions which are purely 'peer' based, as Davis (in Galbraith, 1992), giving his reasons for the failure of the Morin model in Sydney, implied. These constructs also beg the question what is a *gay community*? Difficulties in answering the question are exacerbated once other, non-Western, cultural influences are considered. Concepts of sexuality developed by Western medical discourse are not necessarily relevant to societies outside the western world. Horton (1992) also has asserted that the western concept of 'gay identity' does not work elsewhere, especially in cultures where marriage is universal.

Peer-based programs may also be less effective for heterosexuals, as heterosexuality, though it is assumed, is unlikely to be regarded as an identifying characteristic of a peer group. For bisexual men whose sexuality may be a closely guarded secret, and for non-gay-identified homosexual men who are categorised by exclusion from a peer group, such targeted programs are, by definition, unlikely to be effective.

Individuals may also be subjected to, at the same or at different times, a clash of loyalties to competing peer groups, such as male injecting drug users who have sex with men, male prostitutes and gay members with differing ethnic allegiances. It has been well documented that, among injecting drug users (IDUs), changes towards safer injecting behaviour are not paralleled by equivalent changes in sexual practices. Female sex workers who professionally insist that clients use condoms (with significant peer support) may be less demanding with steady partners (for example, see Dorfman, Derish & Cohen, 1992). while male sex workers may fail to identify with the gay community because of discrimination and stigmatisation (McMillan & Hunter, 1992), which may reduce access to otherwise effective HIV interventions. Similarly, a study of Doll *et al.* (1991) comparing white and non-white populations showed that ethnic identity was significantly more important than gay identity in influencing behaviour. Where ethnic norms are highly prejudicial to, for example, homosexual behaviour (Rigby, Anagnostou, Brown, Rosser, & Ross, 1988; Rigby *et al.*, this volume), the conflict and choice of loyalties will have a negative effect on HIV prevention.

Concentration on peers may also mean that we ignore the possibility that 'non-peers' may also contribute, perhaps even more significantly than peers, to our decision making. For adolescents in a school setting, peer facilitated vs. teacher led programs were shown to have no difference in impact in six out of seven measures used (Zimmerman, Langer, Starr, & Enzler, 1991). Moreover, being a peer does not automatically endow a person with other, perhaps more necessary attributes, as an assessment of peer educators in San Francisco high schools (Melesed'Hospital & Strauss, 1992) revealed. In that study, peer educators were found, despite their training, to be more interested in the formation of relationships (both emotional and sexual) with friends and partners than in HIV/AIDS education.

Cultural (for example, the 'machismo' expectations of some ethnic groups), religious (for example, the opposition of the Roman Catholic Church to condoms), family values and other non-peer influences, as well as peer norms, may all be involved in the shaping of our decisions. Fisher (1988) reviewed social processes which have significant normative influence on behaviours. He also pointed out that because group norms tend to be conservative, they initially oppose behaviour change from unsafe to safer sex. Attempts to change these social norms are more likely to succeed if the impetus comes from leaders, a feature that was successfully exploited by the 'popular people' interventions reported by Kelly, St Lawrence and co-workers (Kelly, St. Lawrence, Diaz *et al.*, 1991; Kelly, St. Lawrence, Stevenson *et al.*, 1991; Kelly *et al.*, 1992). We know little about what constitutes an (influential) peer group and who counts as significant peers. The assumptions of many models are that peers are the (gay) community, but such a construction is unlikely to be independent of age, sexual orientation, ethnicity and visibility. In addition, the assumption that peers always support change may be misguided.

Some researchers have widened the concept of peers (though the term is seldom precisely defined) and chosen to measure 'social' support and perceived 'social' norms, both of which have been identified as predictors of preventive practices in both cross sectional (Emmons *et al.*, 1986) and longitudinal (Joseph *et al.*, 1987) studies of gay men. Relevant social supports may differ depending on the target group and the preferred safer sex strategy. For gay men, whose 'coming out' may have involved clashes with family and parents, these may not play as important a role in shaping norms as for others. The need to conform to family norms are likely to be greater for adolescents and those still living at home.

Just as some persons or groups might be less influential than one intuitively thought, so others can assume a greater significance. In the early market research which preceded the formulation of the Morin model, it was found among gay men in San Francisco that the fear of rejection by a potential sex partner was greater than the fear of AIDS (Pucket & Bye, 1987). Fisher (1988) has also drawn attention to the significance of the sexual partner for heterosexuals, which may be greater than peer or social pressure. The primacy of norms and the importance of the sexual partner in influencing condom use among injecting drug users has been reported (Magura, Shapiro, Siddiqi, & Lipton, 1989). Wilson and Lavelle (1992) in a study of Zimbabwean adolescents found that social and specifically sexual partner support was the most significant influence on intended condom use for females, while for males not using condoms 'if I thought insisting on condoms would upset my sexual partner' was a significant barrier for intended condom use. This was further illustrated in a study of gay men associated with anonymous testing and counselling. When asked (separately) why they practised insertive (or receptive) anal sex, more than 90% answered both questions in terms of their partners' likes, which was the most frequently cited reason for having receptive anal sex (McCamish, Dunne, Hamilton, & Orth, 1992). Thus, males might be more willing to use condoms if it were indicated to them that their sexual partners (of either sex) were positively disposed towards them (St Lawrence *et al.*, 1992). This supposition has been supported by a study of young heterosexuals by Fisher (1990), in which he found that while the desire to use condoms was expressed by both sexes, many did not use them because they feared partner opposition.

In a direct demonstration of the primacy of the partner, Gallois, Kashima *et al.*, (1992) showed that for homosexual men and heterosexual men and women, the sexual partner was the most important person influencing safe sexual behaviour, though friends and peers were also influential. In other studies, (Kashima, Gallois & McCamish, in press; Nucifora *et al.*, this volume) partner norms have been shown to be one of the major influences in condom use.

In summary, although the inclusion of peer support in interventions (including those based on the Morin model) is useful, the role of peers in promoting HIV-preventive behaviour is complex. It is not always easy to identify the relevant peer group. Moreover, people may have competing loyalties to different peer groups and they may pay more attention to some peers than others. In this respect there is considerable support for the central role of the sexual partner.

## Concepts of Safer Sex

Like peer support, the concept that safer sex is satisfying is central to the Morin model. Again, however, safer sex does not mean the same to everyone. We cannot assume that the experience of the often ingenious programs which were developed in epicentres of the epidemic and which were tailored to take advantage of unique features of the gay communities there, and the rapidity with which those gay men have modified their sexual behaviour, will be repeated for homosexual men in other social circumstances or cultural environments, or for other groups, including heterosexuals. Unlike gay men, who regard a repertoire of practices as sex (Frazer *et al.*, 1988; Gallois & McCamish, 1989), which may not even include orgasm as a goal (Hunt & Davies, 1991), heterosexuals identify sex almost exclusively as vaginal intercourse (Gallois, Kashima *et al.*, 1992). Even self-identified homosexuals who have female partners report less anal sex with their male partners than vaginal intercourse (Weatherburn, Davies, Hunt, Coxon, & McManus, 1990). Though non-penetrative forms of sexual expression may be an option for young heterosexuals (Gallois, Kashima *et al.*, 1992), in general, other practices performed by heterosexuals do not seem to be identified as sex (Wellings *et al.*, 1990). By and large, HIV prevention for heterosexuals has meant reducing the number of sexual (i.e., penetrative) partners or using condoms, rather than changing to non-penetrative forms of sexual expression. Thus, concepts of eroticising safer sex for gay men (e.g., Palacios-Jimenez & Shernoff, 1986) which, while also eroticising condoms, include an emphasis on non-penetrative practices, have no equivalent in HIV-preventive education for heterosexuals, nor indeed may they be successful unless heterosexuals can learn to accommodate a wider range of behaviours under the umbrella of sex.

## Other HIV-Prevention Programmes

In addition to those based on the Morin or the 'Eroticising Safe Sex' models, a variety of other intervention programmes have been designed. As recognised earlier in this chapter, the prevailing social climate at the beginning of the HIV epidemic did not attract a professional public health response. Some community responses had the benefit of professional input; most did not. Circumstances have, at least in the Western world, changed somewhat. HIV-behavioural and educational research can now access funding, and academic and public health interests are attracted to the problem. Despite this, as Fisher and Fisher (1992) and Kashima and Lewis (this volume) have both emphasised, most HIV-prevention interventions so far reported have been atheoretical or at best quasi-theoretical.

Many of the interventions tested in schools and colleges are directed towards measuring attitude changes rather than changes in behaviour. This may reflect in part the sensitivity surrounding the asking of questions relating to sexual behaviours of a young audience. Likewise, the interventions are often passive with little participation by the target audience, such as attending a lecture or viewing films, videos, posters and the like. For example, Rhodes and Wolitski (1989) showed a series of AIDS-information videos to different groups of college students. Compared with a control group, the four test groups showed gains in knowledge but revealed no significant differences in attitudes regarding perceived severity of the epidemic, perceived personal vulnerability, or desire for additional information, when surveyed post test and at a follow up, 4–6 weeks later. Only in measures of perceived effectiveness of AIDS prevention were significant increases recorded. A similar study by Gilliam and Seltzer (1989), which measured the effectiveness of an AIDS movie, reported that 'the differences between the two (control and experimental) groups on the knowledge and attitudes measures was slight. In particular, there was little effect on social attitudes.' Other interventions have used drama to promote HIV prevention. As an example, McEwan, Bhopal, and Patton (1991) used *Body Talk* , a play and workshop about HIV and AIDS. Pre- and post-intervention surveys revealed some changes in attitudes, but no changes were recorded in measures of *intention* to keep to one sexual partner, to avoid casual sex, or to have sex in the future.

Similar results were obtained from a study on the effects of an 'AIDS awareness week', a knowledge-based intervention which 'saturated' a campus with information, hosted a series of presentations including symposia and discussions by people with AIDS, and distributed free condoms (Dommeyer, Marquard, Gibson, & Taylor, 1989). Evaluation showed no effect on the AIDS-related attitudes of staff and faculty, and only minor effects on some of the AIDS-related attitudes of students.

A common feature of all these interventions is that they lack skills-training components. Yet as Elizabeth Taylor, in an address at the VIII International Conference on AIDS, eloquently pointed out, "Providing people with condoms without giving them the skills to use them is like giving a typewriter to somebody who cannot spell." When skills training is included in an intervention, more beneficial results are obtained. For example, a ten session intervention was tested on three groups of adolescents: gay males, runaway males and runaway females, who were predominantly Black or Hispanic (the Triple A, or Adolescent AIDS Awareness Project; Rotheram-Borus, Koopman, Haignere, Hunter & Ehrhardt, 1990). Components of the program included knowledge, attitudes towards preventing AIDS, coping skills and developing access to comprehensive health services. Contrasted with controls, runaways but not gay males, reduced their high risk pattern of sexual behaviour, but it must be noted that this was defined as 'unprotected sexual intercourse with more than two partners and/or frequent occasions of unprotected sexual intercourse.'

It seems that interventions do not need to be lengthy or multi-sessional to achieve results, specifically, if the target group seems to be highly focussed and share common norms. Corby, Barchi, Wolitski, Smith and Martin (1990) have measured the relative efficacy of testing and counselling, skills training (which comprised a 15–30 minute session that included condom skills and negotiation skills) and a combination of both, on condom use by female sex workers for vaginal intercourse. MANOVAs comparing changes in self reported condom use showed that there were significant increases only in the group that had received both counselling and testing and the condom skills training. A brief intervention with condom knowledge and skills components was devised by Cohen, Dent and

MacKinnon (1991) and delivered to patients attending an STD clinic. By examining the medical records for reinfection data one year after the presentation, they found that those who attended the intervention were only half as likely to return to the clinic. Similarly, a study by Valdiserri *et al.*, (1989) contrasted the efficacy of two peer led interventions, one comprising an information lecture on safer sex given by a gay health educator and lasting $1-1\frac{1}{2}$ hours, the other the same lecture with an added skills training component of about 1 hour conducted by a psychotherapist. Follow up one year later showed that self reported condom use increased by 44% in the skills group, but only 11% in the group in which skills training was absent.

Other interventions have contained greater theoretical basis and have sought to modify those components which are acknowledged to influence behaviour. Galavotti, Schnell and O'Reilly (1990) tested an intervention which contained HIV counselling and testing, risk reduction information and skills training, and specific attempts to influence the perceived social norms (specifically behavioural norms, see Kashima & Gallois, this volume) of the participants regarding risk reduction. The program was administered in four U.S. cities. Analysis of follow up data collected six months later showed significant increases in self efficacy in all four cities, significant increases in self-reported safe sex skills in three cities, and a significant increase in perceived behavioural norms in two of the cities. This is one of few interventions that have attempted to address the predictors of behaviour change rather than the change itself.

Another intervention which sought to modify risk behaviour through its predictors, was Project ARIES (Kelly *et al.*, 1989; Kelly & St Lawrence, 1990), a twelve session workshop designed (i) to provide knowledge about HIV and risk reduction messages; (ii) to develop self-management, assertiveness and other skills necessary top reduce risk; and (iii) to establish the social norms and supports that encourage low risk and discourage high risk behaviour. The evaluation, measuring self-reported frequency of unprotected anal sex and the percentage of intercourse occasions when condoms were used, was carried out a number of times over a period of 24 months and showed a high level of maintained safer sex behaviour.

This same team developed a 'popular people' intervention based on a diffusion of innovations/peer education model (Kelly, St. Lawrence, Betts *et al.*, 1991; Kelly, St. Lawrence, Stevenson *et al.*, 1991; Kelly *et al.*, 1992). The project was run in a series of small cities where gay men who were well known, liked and natural opinion leaders, were trained and asked to talk to a number of other gay men, serving as risk reducing trend setters. Follow up evaluation showed reductions of 20–25% in risk behavior compared with control cities where education materials were distributed widely in the gay clubs. As well as the success of the project, it is interesting to note that the authors report that little change occurred in the comparison cities over the time of the studies, suggesting that the distribution of posters etc., by itself, has little impact on sexual behaviour.

## A TRA based intervention

### Background and Aims

This by no means exhaustive summary of intervention programmes reveals the variety of different interventions that have been designed and implemented in an endeavour to encourage people to engage in HIV-preventive behaviour. There are a number of features that have characterised the successful interventions. These include the incorporation of skills training, the necessity of modifying group norms to be supportive of safer sex, and the need to change people's beliefs and evaluations about safer sex as Morin did in the San Francisco 'Stop AIDS Project'. These components are all incorporated in the theories of reasoned action (and its extension, the theory of planned behaviour); thus this model may be a useful theoretical basis for the development of an HIV-prevention programme.

Other researchers have identified the role that the theory of reasoned action (and the theory of planned behaviour) may play in this respect. Fisher and Fisher (1992) in their overall model of HIV/AIDS prevention used the theory of reasoned action to represent the motivational component of the model (the model also comprises knowledge and skills components) (see Lewis & Kashima, this volume; Terry *et al.,* this volume). A similar model has been described by Schaalma, Kok and Peters (1993), who analysed the determinants of condom use among Dutch adolescents in terms of the constructs of the theory of reasoned action and self-efficacy theory. While both these models agree that the theory of reasoned action is a useful theoretical framework for the study of HIV-preventive behaviour (a claim which is supported by empirical results, such as those presented in this book), the central tenets of the theory have not been translated into a design for an HIV-prevention program.

In this section, we will describe an intervention designed on the basis of the theories of reasoned action/planned behaviour. This intervention aims to encourage people to engage in HIV-preventive behaviour. It is designed not only to encourage behaviour change, but also to engender change in the key antecedents of behaviour identified by the theory of reasoned action, namely, norms, attitudes, and intentions. The antecedents of behavioural choice are targeted in an endeavour to bring about sustained behaviour change. Even if behaviour change does occur, this is unlikely to be enduring if a person's underlying beliefs are not supportive of the change. We also sought to increase people's control over performing safer sex (as suggested by Ajzen's (1988, 1991) theory of planned behaviour) by providing them with an adequate knowledge base, equipping them with the necessary behavioural skills and fostering feelings of self-efficacy. This conceptual framework, combined with a structure used in the previously successful ARIES project developed by Kelly and St. Lawrence (1990), formed the basis for the intervention project.

Although the program was multifaceted, it was based on the premise that normative change is the key component of a successful HIV-intervention program. This premise was supported by findings of numerous studies that have demonstrated the powerful influence of norms (particularly from the sexual partner) on sexual behaviour (e.g., Kashima & Gallois, this volume; Nucifora *et al.*, this volume; Rigby *et al.*, this volume). To target norms successfully, the workshop is designed for use with people from the same social network. By definition, norms are social (see Kippax *et al.*, this volume). An individual by himself or herself is likely to have considerable difficulty in changing the norms of a group. However, if sufficient members of a social network change their beliefs about what are accepted attitudes and behaviours (see Brown, 1988, for a discussion on norms), then normative change in the wider social network is possible. To maximise the chance of normative change, we employed peer facilitators, with whom the participants could identify. We also encouraged the participants to become peer educators themselves. In doing this, we hoped to further increase the likelihood that normative change would occur in the wider social group.

When targeting the norms of the group, we went beyond the normative influences incorporated into the theory of reasoned action by focusing not only on what the person thinks others would want them to do (subjective norm), but also by considering what people think others do and believe (behavioural norms and group attitude), and by emphasising the persuasive role that the sexual partner may have as a source of normative pressure.

An additional feature of the workshop is that it acknowledges the characteristics of the local population. In our test of the intervention, we analysed the questionnaire responses of the larger social group so that the salient norms and attitudes of the social group could be determined and fed back to the participating sub-group (in other instances, this procedure could be based only on the responses of the workshop participants). Thus, the intervention is able to elicit and then emphasise the local characteristics of the participating group, and target the specific factors that identify and distinguish risk for that group. For example, groups (and often individuals within groups) will differ in their level of sophistication of knowledge about HIV/AIDS, their attitudes towards homosexuality, or the riskiness of their behaviour. Therefore, our approach allows for common goals to be reached from different directions for each group.

*General Overview of Intervention*

Specifically, the intervention has a number of specific goals. These include: (a) to recognise the need for change; (b) to know which behaviour(s) are safe and which are not; (c) to learn skills for performing and maintaining the behaviour; and (d) to develop or enhance social and peer support for maintaining the desirability of behaviour change.

The first two of these goals (which may be summarised as defining the problem and deciding what has to be done) lie within the constructs of the theory of reasoned action. That is, the costs and benefits of a behaviour are considered and an intention is undertaken to carry out the behaviour. The third and fourth goals (knowing how to achieve the behaviour and how to keep doing it) address the control and support issues involved in translating an intention into a behaviour. These goals target concepts from the theory of planned behaviour.

The workshops, therefore, aim to correct perceptions of personal vulnerability to HIV infection and to reduce the riskiness of sexual behaviour by identifying and making the norms of each group more explicit to its members; reducing their use of risk-denial and confrontational strategies as a means of anxiety reduction; identifying the individual preferred safe sexual behaviours and making them as safe as possible and, where necessary, by changing norms in the direction of advocating safer sexual behaviour; and by enhancing their ability to talk about sex and HIV/AIDS and enhancing norms advocating talking to others about it.

In designing the content of the workshop we were conscious of the need to impose realistic time limits and to seek the best compromise between the demands of the goals of the workshop and the expectation that many persons, especially heterosexuals, do not identify with risk for HIV infection and therefore do not place HIV-prevention interventions high on their personal agendas. A program which lasted too long could make effective recruitment too difficult and might render sustained attendance unlikely. Fisher and Fisher (1992) have commented on the unusually high motivational levels (influenced both by the levels of HIV infection and the well knit nature of the community) observed in, say, San Francisco which provided an undoubted incentive to participate in HIV-preventive interventions. Previous experience has shown it would be naive to anticipate these same motivational levels in centres of relatively low HIV prevalence, even among gay men, let alone heterosexual men or women. We were also conscious of the success of the relatively short-term interventions referred to above, but most of all to the evaluation of an abridged Project ARIES (Kelly, St Lawrence, Betts *et al.*, 1990), which showed no significant differences in results between their original twelve session (approximately 18 hour) workshop and abridged one.

The intervention comprises four sessions each lasting about $2\frac{1}{2}$ hours and occurring at weekly intervals. The first session defines the problem addressed by the workshop and the goals of the workshop; the second session identifies appropriate safe sex strategies; the third session provides skills for implementing preferred safe sex strategies; and the fourth session addresses issues in the maintenance of the safe sex strategies. A brief synopsis of the components of each session and their theoretical underpinning are discussed below. A full description can be found in the manual (McCamish, Timmins, Gallois, & Terry, 1993)

Altogether, 16 groups have participated in the workshops to date. They comprised (separately) homosexual men, heterosexual men, and heterosexual women, who may or may not have been sexually active at the time of recruitment. Groups were contacted by a number of gay and heterosexual recruiters, some of whom facilitated the subsequent workshops for their groups. The only recruitment requirement for participation was that there existed some cohesive identity within the group—whether the members were friends or more formally associated as part of a sporting, social, or other group or society. As many members of the group as possible completed the initial questionnaires, and a sub-section of the group participated in the workshops. In the present chapter, we provide some initial qualitative data to describe the responses of the groups who have participated in the workshop to date.

## *Session 1*

In the first session, past and present sexual behaviour and attitudes towards sexuality, homosexuality, and sex roles are raised and discussed. Also discussed are norms regarding HIV/AIDS and safe sex, such as how much members of the group talk about HIV/AIDS with friends, talk about safe(r) sex with friends, believe friends think safe(r) sex is sensible and believe friends practise safe sex.

The agenda for the remainder of the session is set according to where the group sits on the issues raised. For example, if a group is not knowledgeable on HIV/AIDS, this will be the first issue addressed in detail, whereas if the group's collective attitude towards homosexuality is negative (in a way that blames homosexuals for HIV/AIDS), this will be given greater emphasis.

The first session, therefore, sets the scene for the workshop by bringing to surface the norms, attitudes and practices of the group. The remainder of the workshop re-confirms these norms and addresses the very important, and often ignored, issue of the skills and control required to convert a safe sex intention into maintainable safe sex behaviour. Keeping in line with the emphasis on norms in the framework of the workshop, an underlying goal of 'peer' education, that is the need to support and encourage one's peers to engage in safer sex, is constantly stressed. For those groups that are already practising safer sex, this will be the major goal pursued.

For participants, the most positive aspect of this session was being able to talk freely about various HIV/AIDS and sex-related issues. Other positive aspects included learning about HIV/AIDS and safer sex, and hearing the opinions and practices of others. This suggests that people not only want to learn more about HIV/AIDS, they also want to learn about what their friends know and think about HIV/AIDS and HIV/AIDS-related issues. For some, talking about sexual issues was difficult. However, this illustrates and emphasises the value of the flexibility of the workshop which can incorporate different agendas for different groups or individuals within the group.

### *Session 2*

The norms and attitudes associated with, and the intention to practise one's preferred safe sex strategy (be it condoms, exclusivity, nonpenetrative sex, or even abstinence) comprise the major part of this session. The first task is to establish that the norms and attitudes of the group are in line with the preferred safe sex strategies of the group members. For instance, if a member prefers abstinence as a safe sex strategy but the group has a strong negative attitude towards abstinence and asserts a strong normative influence on its members not to abstain from sex, then this member may have difficulty in remaining true to this intention. It is also not unusual for some people to be reluctant to use condoms if there are group norms and attitudes against the use of condoms. Some groups have even been split between condoms and exclusivity as preferred strategies. In such situations, it is important for the group norms to support both positions. For instance, for those in continuing relationships, exclusivity may be the accepted group norm, whereas for those not in relationships the group norms may favour condom use (McCamish *et al.*, 1992).

The next task is to examine factors which might prevent the safe sex intention becoming a stable behaviour. Different groups, by nature of their affiliation, emphasise different factors which may lead to risky behaviours. Hence, the session needs to focus on the factors relevant to the group and, if necessary, sub-groups and individuals within the group.

The essence of this session is intention, and control over intention. First the intentions and their antecedent norms and attitudes are identified. Then the threats to control over the intentions are examined. Intentioninterfering factors raised in this session ranged from individual vulnerability, to alcohol use (and its potentially detrimental effects on safer sex), to peer norms regarding sexual activity.

Being able to talk freely, learning about safe sex, and hearing the opinions of others were nominated as the most positive aspects of the session. Learning skills was also nominated as a positive aspect. Again, this suggests that the members of the groups enjoyed talking about their behaviours and attitudes and hearing those of others, as well as learning about safe sex and specific skills, such as condom acquisition and use. Some people, however, were uncomfortable with the practical condom exercise, while others, particularly gay men, did not see the relevance of some of the antecedents to risky behaviour.

## Session 3

This session concentrates on achieving safer sex by teaching assertiveness and communication skills. The need for these skills derive from the notion that the factor which is perhaps most likely to interfere in the control of the safer sex intention becoming a behaviour is the reluctance of the partner (or potential partner) to adopt the same safer sex strategy.

With respect to safer sex, assertiveness means retaining your right to practice safer sex while at the same time appreciating the wishes and feelings of your partner. The goal is to carry out the safer sex intention, and not to allow the partner norms to interfere with this intention, rather than to demand a specific behaviour. Maintaining your original intention to have safer sex but adopting another safer sex strategy represents a successful outcome of negotiation; failure in this process would include having unsafe sex, or not having sex due to the breakdown in negotiation.

Not surprisingly, the practical exercises involved in this session (viz. role playing) were nominated as the most positive aspect of the session by some participants, and the most negative aspect by others. Also nominated as a negative aspect was the embarrassment involved in the role plays. Nevertheless, for most participants, the session provided practical tuition in how to communicate one's safer sex wishes to a potential sexual partner, and as such addressed perhaps the major issue of control over one's safer sex intentions.

## Session 4

The first part of this session reviews the participants' attitudes and their evaluation (perceived costs and benefits) of their preferred safer sex strategies. With these reconfirmed, the issue of maintenance of safer sex behaviour by support from others is addressed. Particularly important are the moral and practical supports from friends and, for some, parents. But also important is the support from the community, in terms of educational information about HIV/AIDS, and of course, the support from the partner is crucial. The whole point of the workshop series is summed up in this session in that knowledge and skills are important, but in order to accept and then maintain safer sex, one needs to either have in place social, partner, and (perhaps) parental support. To help establish these supports, the session emphasises the need for participants to assume the role of peer educators and to disperse the knowledge and skills gained in the workshops among friends so that their attitudes and norms change to reinforce a safer sex culture.

In line with the format of this final session, the most overwhelmingly positive aspect nominated was the ability to talk freely. Some participants still, at this late stage, decided that some of the workshop's content was irrelevant to them. The majority of participants, however, had by this stage expressed greater confidence, not to mention desire, to practise safer sex, and had already commenced communicating their knowledge and skills to friends and peers.

### Overview and Conclusions

From the brief summaries given at the end of each session it is clear that participants found the discovery of group norms and the development of specific skills to be important. Some identified the role playing as especially difficult. This was not unexpected but, as has been stated above, we are aware that for many when placed in a subsequent situation needing sexual negotiations, these role plays became identified as the most important part of workshops. Of further benefit was the fact that most participants found the workshop beneficial and had started spreading their newly-gained skills to their own social networks so that they would engender a set of social norms which would support their intentions to adopt safer behaviours and provide asocial environment in which they could be successfully maintained. Because insufficient time has elapsed since the completion of the majority of the workshops for sensible measures of subsequent behaviour to be made, we are unable to report fully on the behavioural outcomes at this stage; a full analysis based on the constructs of TRA will be made. Thus, we can determine, at a practical level, what influences changed attitudes and subjective and other norms have in modifying the intentions of participants to practise safer sex, and on their actual behaviour. In the meantime, examination of the comments made by participants in questionnaires at the end of each session suggests several things. First, the opinions of others in the group were important to individual participants, and the greater expression of desire to practise safer sex at the end of the workshops, compared to the begining, imply greater subjective, behavioural and personal normative support for those intentions. Similarly, participants reported that they were talking positively to friends about safer sex, which can be seen as helping to establish a wider normative environment within which their own safer intentiones can be nurtured into safer behaviours.

The intervention described in this section has taken the theory of reasoned action not merely as a model for predicting behaviour, but as a model for changing (or when safer sex is already practised, reinforcing) behaviour. This has been achieved:

—by targeting and recruitment of a pre-existing social group and, through elicitation, identifying the components of TRA, attitudes, norms, intentions and behaviour;

—through determining where participants stand, starting with and from the specific characteristics of the individual groups;

—in the context of already formed social networks, that is of self selected peers, by changing attitudes and norms to influence behavioural intentions;

—in the same context, by changing intention to change behaviour; and

—by identifying threats to control over the intention–behaviour link and developing skills to eliminate or minimise those threats.

There has been a past need for a theory-based as opposed merely to need-based intervention and TRA has had the potential to satisfy that need. These workshops constitute one answer to that need and a realisation of that potential.

# 12

# The Theory of Reasoned Action and Problem-Focused Research

YOSHIHISA KASHIMA

*La Trobe University, Melbourne, Australia*

CYNTHIA GALLOIS

*The University of Queensland, Brisbane, Australia*

The theory of reasoned action (TRA) has been successfully used for both applied and basic research into the determinants of many social behaviours. With its elegant theoretical formulation and methodology, TRA has been especially popular for problem-oriented research designed to produce policy recommendations and interventions. In research on HIV-preventive behaviour, which this book is about, there is a burgeoning literature using the framework of TRA. Nevertheless, TRA has its critics. In this chapter, we will review some recent criticisms of TRA, and we will suggest how they may best be dealt with by researchers interested in safer sex. This chapter is written from within the framework of psychological theories of decision-making and attitude–behaviour relations, and we will not consider criticisms of TRA from outside this framework (see Kippax & Crawford, this volume, for criticism based on a social-constructionist perspective).

First, we will examine the *theoretical structure* of TRA. In this part of the chapter, we will not question the assumptions of the theory. Rather, we will examine the variables in TRA in the light of current literature on attitudes and social cognition. In the second part of the chapter, we will turn briefly to the *metatheoretical underpinning* of the theory of reasoned action. Here, our attention will be directed towards the explicit and implicit assumptions made by TRA and whether they are warranted.

In considering TRA, it is important to find a balance between the adequacy of prediction and explanation on the one hand, and parsimony and simplicity on the other. The literature reveals a number of new variables and new relationships among variables that are proposed to improve the predictive power of TRA. The metatheoretical criticisms are also focused on widening the range of prediction and explanation of TRA. The theory of planned behaviour has already extended the range of prediction of TRA, and we must now ask whether new variables and relationships add sufficiently to have practical value. For the case of safer sex, this question can be answered in part by looking at the kind of activity safer sex is, and the particular factors that are important in safer sexual behaviours.

## Theoretical Issues

The theory of reasoned action includes the concepts of beliefs, attitudes, subjective norms, intentions, and behaviour as its major components. Fishbein and Ajzen (1975; Ajzen & Fishbein, 1980) argued that these variables were necessary and sufficient to predict behaviours under the volitional control of actors. Despite the intuitive appeal of the theory, the past decade or so has seen a number of questions raised. These have included the adequacy of the conceptualisation of attitude, the measurement of the belief-based determinants of attitude and their relation to the direct measure, and the best way to determine which beliefs are salient to behaviour. In addition, the capacity of subjective norm to capture all the important normative influences on intention has been challenged, and additional normative variables have been proposed. Interactions between attitude and norm in predicting intention have also been posited. Finally, intention, its predictors, and its relation to behaviour have been questioned. We will examine each of these concepts in the context of research on safer sex and HIV-preventive behaviour.

### *Attitude*

The theory of reasoned action adopts an expectancy-value (EV) model of attitude. The EV model claims that attitude is determined by expectations about the object, which are evaluated as positive or negative. The attitude, then, is some function of the expectations and their associated values (e.g., see Bagozzi, 1984, 1985; Feather, 1982). In TRA, this formulation can be seen in the belief-based measure of attitude, where behavioural beliefs (e.g., the perceived likelihood of various outcomes of using condoms for sexual intercourse) are multiplied by the evaluation of each outcome (see Terry *et al.*, this volume). The direct measure of attitude is a straightforward rating of the behaviour (using condoms for sex over a specified time period) on the evaluative dimension (good–bad, pleasant–unpleasant) of the semantic differential.

A number of authors have questioned this conceptualisation of attitude. The first issue involves the extent to which the evaluation of a behaviour needs to be distinguished from feelings about it.

*Evaluation and Affect*

TRA assumes that attitude *is* affect, and the direct measure of attitude makes no distinction between *feelings* about a behaviour and *evaluations* of it. Other researchers (e.g., Breckler & Wiggins, 1989a; Triandis, 1977), however, have argued for a distinction between evaluation and affect. It should be noted that evaluation in this context is different from the cognitive component of attitude as traditionally conceptualised; this component is captured by the notion of beliefs in TRA. Clearly, TRA distinguishes between whether one judges an object as good or bad and whether one endorses positive or negative beliefs about the object. Rather, the criticism is that there is a difference between whether one says an object is good or bad (evaluation) and whether the object makes one feel good or bad (affect).

While the research evidence is not strong at this stage, it is worth some consideration. For the case of safer sex, the distinction between evaluation and affect allows for the possibility that a person may evaluate a safer sex practice (say, consistent condom use) positively; that is, the person may rate condom use as good, pleasant, valuable, and so forth. Nevertheless, the person may feel negative about condoms (i.e., feel anxious, depressed, unhappy, or angry at the thought of using condoms). If evaluations and feelings are different in the way they are related to intention (in this case, the intention to use condoms), it is practically as well as theoretically important to assess which is the better predictor.

Drawing on current theories of affect, Breckler and Wiggins (1989a) have suggested that the affective component of attitude may be both propositionally and motorically represented. In Breckler and Wiggins' view, propositionally represented attitudes are called evaluations, while motorically represented attitudes are called affect (their term, and perhaps not altogether a happy choice of words). Thus, evaluation takes the form that 'Object O is good (or bad) by degree X'; affect constitutes a rather undifferentiated memory of motor movements and vascular sensations associated with the object. Consistent with this, Breckler and Wiggins (1989b) showed that measures designed to tap affect ('Object O makes me feel ...') and semantic differential measures of evaluations ('Object O is ...') could be discriminated empirically. More importantly, they also reported that affect associated with blood donation correlated better with past blood donation and with current mood than did evaluations of blood donation. Ajzen (1991) also reports the results of studies on several leisure activities where affect and evaluation were independent influences on the direct measure of attitude in TRA. These results all appear to support a distinction between evaluation and affect.

As we noted earlier, if the distinction between affect and evaluation is sufficiently large, it may be especially relevant to research on safer sex.

Many researchers have suggested that young adults and adolescents evaluate condom use as a good idea, but feel negative about it. The suggestion, usually untested, is that feelings will have the strongest influence on condom use or non-use. A dissociation of thinking and feeling ("I think this is a good thing to do, but I don't like it") may occur for a great many behaviours in the sexual context, and may be one reason why sexual behaviour is often thought of as irrational. In reality, feelings may be better predictors of intentions about sex than are evaluations. Some HIV educators seem to believe this, as a number of mass-media campaigns for safer sex are aimed at promoting more positive feelings about condoms, by associating them with fun (laughter, rock music) and pleasure.

Nucifora *et al.,* (this volume) included affect items like those of Breckler and Wiggins. They found that positive and negative feelings about anticipated condom use predicted the direct measure of attitude independently of the belief-based measure (the product of evaluations and behavioural beliefs about condoms), but affect did not contribute significantly to intention once attitude and subjective norm were controlled for. Of course, this may be due to the way attitude was measured in their study. In addition, feelings may be a greater influence on intention and behaviour when people are sexually aroused (see Gold, this volume). In any case, understanding people's feelings about a safer sexual practice may help to explain their attitudes. On balance, the distinction between affect and evaluation seems to be worth further investigation in the area of safer sex.

*Measurement of Beliefs and Evaluations*

A second criticism of the conceptualisation of attitude is of a very different type from that raised above, and involves the way in which the belief-based measure of attitude is obtained. TRA proposes that beliefs and evaluations should be measured as bipolar constructs; that is, beliefs are represented as likely to unlikely (i.e., positive through zero to negative), and evaluations are also measured from negative to positive (see Terry *et al.,* this volume). The bipolar conception of evaluations is fairly well accepted (e.g., Fazio, Powell, & Herr, 1983; cf. Pratkanis, 1989), but the bipolar conception of beliefs is more contentious.

Hewstone and Young (1988) coded beliefs as both unipolar or bipolar, and found that expectancy-value attitudes predicted the direct measure of attitude better when they were based on unipolar than on bipolar beliefs. Several studies, however, have failed to replicate this finding (Kashima, Gallois, & McCamish, 1992; Nucifora, 1990; Sparks, Hedderley, & Shepherd, 1991). From a practical point of view, the most important thing is to obtain a belief-based measure that optimally predicts the direct measure of attitude. Ajzen (1991) provides a neat method of doing this, in which the direct measure of attitude is regressed onto evaluations and beliefs scaled both ways, and optimal scaling coefficients are determined. If methods such as summation (Hewstone & Young, 1988; see also Bagozzi, 1985) and testing for interaction effects between beliefs and evaluations (Evans, 1991), are used, such coding makes little difference.

Finally, it is important to examine the relationship of each belief with overall attitude and other variables in TRA. This is the only way by which researchers can ascertain which beliefs contribute to decisions about HIV-preventive behaviour, and thus which beliefs they should target in interventions. In the case of condom use, a wide range of costs and benefits usually emerges from pilot research, including different reasons for using condoms (preventing HIV, preventing pregnancy, etc.), assessments of personal issues (condoms reduce my pleasure, condoms delay orgasm, etc.), and assessments of the partner's reactions (condoms reduce intimacy, partner may not like condoms, etc.). As an example, Timmins *et al.* (this volume) found three factors of costs and benefits in their belief-based measure of attitude to safer sexual practices. One factor, intimacy, significantly predicted attitude, but another factor, risk of HIV and other STDs, predicted subjective norm for some subject groups (see also Bagozzi, 1981). Galligan and Terry (in press) also found that their belief-based measure was multidimensional, and that the two factors (risk reduction and destruction of romance and intimacy) had a different relation to intention and actual condom use. It may be that intimacy-related beliefs should be targeted to influence condom use in populations like these.

The questions raised in the preceding paragraphs imply that it is not a good idea to gather only belief-based measures of attitude and to use these to predict intention, as some researchers in the area of safer sex have tended to do. On the other hand, use of only the direct measure of attitude without the belief-based measure, as other researchers have done, means that a study will lose much of the richness and applicability to a local population that are a strength of TRA (see Fishbein & Middlestadt, 1989). Much information can be gained from examining the costs and benefits associated by a particular group of people with a particular sexual practice (see Terry *et al.*, this volume). On balance, the questions raised in this section point to the importance of taking both direct and belief-based measures of attitude, as TRA suggests.

## Determination of Salient Beliefs

The theory of reasoned action suggests that the beliefs which form attitudes should be salient. Salient, or cognitively accessible, beliefs about a behaviour form the basis of attitudes. The idea that salient cognitions contribute to judgments and behaviours is well established and leaves little room for dispute (Sedikides & Skowronski, 1991). The best way to represent and to measure the salience of beliefs is still contentious, however. Eiser, van der Pligt, and their colleagues (Eiser & van der Pligt, 1979; Spears, van der Pligt, & Eiser, 1986), as well as Budd (1986), have compared the *personal* salience of beliefs with *modal* salience (beliefs that are salient for many people in a given population). While some of the results are fairly weak, this research generally suggests that personally salient beliefs predict attitudes better than modal salient beliefs. In trying to assess the personal salience of beliefs, researchers have typically used subjects' importance ratings of various belief statements. It may not be appropriate to equate cognitive accessibility with importance, however. Jaccard and Sheng (1984) compared six methods of measuring the salience of beliefs, including importance ratings and cued recall. They found relatively low correlations among all the measures investigated.

A pilot study in which salient beliefs are elicited from a group in the target population gives information about modal salient beliefs. Finding salient beliefs is best done in a context as close as possible to that of the behaviour under investigation. Thus, in the case of sexual behaviours, salient beliefs may best be elicited when subjects are sexually aroused (see Gold, this volume), which is not always easy to do. Whatever method is chosen to gather modal salient beliefs, collecting information about the personal importance of salient beliefs may provide valuable information regarding variation in belief salience within the target population. Given the diversity of sexual practices in relation to HIV/AIDS, this knowledge is very worthwhile indeed.

## Norms

The theory of reasoned action is one of the very few theories of social decision making that explicitly acknowledge the effects of social norms (see also Dulany, 1968; Triandis, 1977). TRA and TPB include the concept of *subjective norm* , or perceived expectations held by significant persons in the actor's life about what the actor should do, as their main index of perceived normative pressure to perform a behaviour. Subjective norm is predicted by perceived normative beliefs (the expectation of each significant person) multiplied by the motivation to comply with each person.

Ajzen and Fishbein (1980) argue that subjective norm should be adequate to represent all of the normative influences on the intention to perform a behaviour. In this way, TRA remains parsimonious, with only two proximal predictors of intention (attitude and subjective norm) in the model. Several researchers have suggested, however, that other perceived social influences must also be taken into account. Two major normative variables have been put forward: personal norm and behavioural norm. The concept of *personal norm* is an attempt to take account of the actor's own values, which are likely to be especially salient for sexual behaviour. *Behavioural norms*, on the other hand, represent the influence of models (mainly friends and peers) in the actor's social environment. As we shall see, if one accepts the importance of these norms, some reconceptualisation of the normative influences in TRA is desirable.

## *Personal Norm*

Personal norm is the actor's sense of personal normative pressure (I think I should perform a behaviour), rather than the perception of significant others' opinions. A number of researchers (e.g., Budd & Spencer, 1985, 1986; Kashima & Kashima, 1988; Kilty, 1978; Pagel & Davidson, 1984; Schwartz & Tessler, 1972) have argued that this variable should be distinguished from subjective norm for some behaviours, including condom use (Boyd & Wandersman, 1991). Budd and Spencer (1985) suggested that personal norm is best thought of as an ideal behavioural intention; that is, what the actor would do in ideal circumstances. In their view, attitudes, subjective norms and past behaviour should be predictors of personal norms reconceptualised as ideal intentions.

Ajzen and Fishbein (1973) suggested dropping personal norm from Fishbein's original theory (1967), because they thought personal norm was empirically indistinguishable from intention. Some researchers, however, have been able to distinguish them. For instance, Kashima and Kashima (1988) showed that factors other than personal norms have significant independent influences on behavioural intention, and that the impact of personal norm on intention varied with the level of subjects' authoritarianism. These results suggest that behavioural intention and personal norm are not identical.

In the case of sexual behaviour, the few results available to date about personal norm are mixed. For example, Kashima *et al.* (1992) found that subjective norm and past behaviour predicted personal norm about condom use for a sample of heterosexual students. In addition, subjective norm interacted with personal norm to predict intention. Nucifora *et al.* (this volume), however, found that measures of personal norm about condom use and intention were largely redundant for their subjects. It may turn out that personal norm does not help much in the prediction of sexual behaviour. On the other hand, the intuitive appeal of this variable in a value-laden context like sex is undeniable. Whether this intuition is borne out in actual sexual behaviour is a question for future research.

*Behavioural Norm*

Over the years, many researchers (e.g., Chassin, Presson, Bensenberg, Corty, & Sherman, 1981; Chassin, Presson, Sherman, Corty, & Olshavsky, 1984; Jessor, 1976; Kandel, 1980; McAllister, Krosnick, & Milburn, 1984; Murray, Swan, Johnson, & Bewley, 1983) have found that young people's decisions to take up and keep smoking cigarettes or taking other drugs are strongly influenced by whether their friends and peers are perceived to do the same thing. On the basis of such research, Grube, Morgan and McGree (1986) suggested that behavioural norms should also be included in the TRA model for the prediction of intention. These norms constitute actors' perceptions about whether significant others perform the behaviour.

Behavioural norms are conceptually different from subjective norms, in that behavioural norms have to do with what significant others are perceived to *do* , whereas subjective norm is concerned with what they are perceived to *think the actor should do*. Adding them to the TRA model broadens considerably the conceptualisation of social influence in TRA/TPB. One must therefore ask whether behavioural norms have sufficient impact to justify this additional complexity.

Despite a long tradition of research showing the importance of behavioural norms on behaviours such as smoking and drinking, especially among young people, the empirical literature gives mixed results on the impact of behavioural norms on sexual intentions and behaviour. Most studies on condom use which have included behavioural norms have found that they are significant independent predictors of intention, and sometimes of behaviour (e.g., Gardner, 1992; Ross & McLaws, 1992; see Nucifora *et al.*, this volume). On the other hand, they tend to explain rather small amounts of additional variance, once subjective norm and attitude have been controlled for (see Ross & McLaws, this volume).

One might be tempted to argue, with Ross and McLaws (1992), that behavioural norms are weak predictors, and that the original variables in TRA are sufficient. It may be possible, however, to conceptualise social norms in a way which allows us to evaluate the relative contribution of various normative variables more easily. In the next section, we suggest a way of doing this which also allows researchers to take more account of past behaviour, another problem variable for TRA.

*Conceptualising the Variety of Social Norms*

Burnkrant and Page (1988) were able to link subjective norm empirically to the reward value of significant others. They noted that subjective norm is thus similar to Kelman's (1958) concept of compliance as a social influence process, in that it captures the decision maker's acceptance of influence from other people or groups in order to obtain rewards or avoid punishments. Kashima and Kashima (1988) suggested that personal norm may reflect the incorporation of normative demands into the self-concept, thereby internalising them (Kelman, 1958). Finally, behavioural norms are the decision maker's perceptions of significant others' behaviours (e.g., Jessor, 1976). To the extent that others' behaviours are modelled, this modelling process can be characterised as identification, in Kelman's terms.

Based on these considerations, Kashima *et al.* (1992) proposed a two-facet classification of norms as influences on the intention to perform a behaviour. One facet is the *perceived source* of the social norm. For personal norm, the source of normative pressure is the self, whereas the source of subjective and behavioural norms is significant others. The second facet involves whether the norm pertains to *thinking or doing.* Subjective and personal norms have to do with what the source thinks the actor should do, whereas behavioural norm involves what the source actually does. Thus, subjective norm has to do with others' thinking, personal norm, with the actor's thinking, and behavioural norm, with others' doing. Kashima *et al.* (1992) found that these three norms were significant independent predictors of the intention to use condoms.

There is one cell left in this two-way classification: the actor's doing. The actor's own past behaviour appears to fit well into this cell. Past behaviour is generally recognised as a good predictor of future behaviour; indeed, it is often the strongest predictor. Fishbein and Ajzen (1975), however, argued that past behaviour is not worth including in a model of action like TRA because it carries little explanatory power; there is no role for attitudes, social influence, or decisions if we simply agree that people will do in the future what they have done in the past. Thinking of past behaviour as a normative influence gives it more explanatory power, however. Past behaviour is not typically considered to function as a norm, but it may well carry normative force, because actors are expected to behave consistently across situations in Western and to some extent non-Western cultures (Kashima, Siegal, Tanaka, & Kashima, 1992).

This classification expands the normative term in TRA to four variables: subjective and personal norms, behavioural norms and past behaviour. The relative importance of each of them, the extent to which they interact in predicting intention, and the extent to which they predict each other is likely to vary for different behaviours and different subject groups. The impact of behavioural norm in particular has been shown to be different for people of different ages and different social classes. In our own research (Gallois, Terry, Timmins, McCamish, & Kashima, in press), past behaviour emerged as by far the most important influence on the safer sex intentions of gay men.

Sexual practice, as we have already noted, is a highly normatively-controlled area of social life. Therefore, in the area of safer sex, examination of the variety of norms is a pressing research issue. Social norms—

subjective, personal and behavioural norms, as well as past behaviour—are likely to influence HIV-preventive behaviours in many ways. Because safer sex generally requires the cooperation of two people, the normative climate largely determines the probability that they will agree on a particular safer sexual behaviour. For instance, if using a condom is perceived to be a general social norm (i.e., if an actor's behavioural norm suggests that significant people use condoms), it is easier to raise the issue of condom use in a sexual encounter, to persuade a sexual partner to use one and to terminate the encounter if persuasion is not successful (these are all important skills in Fisher and Fisher's, 1992, model of AIDS-preventive behaviour).

## *Intention*

### *Predictors of Intention*

TRA assumes that attitude and norm additively affect intention. The relative importance of attitude and subjective norm is typically assessed by comparing the relative magnitude of the two standardised regression coefficients when intention is regressed on them, but TRA does not specify the conditions under which attitudes are more important than norms, or vice versa. Indeed, few studies have examined this issue. In the studies that have done so, the influence of sex (Ajzen & Fishbein, 1980), culture (Rigby *et al.*, this volume), and personality (Miller & Grush, 1986; Kashima & Kashima, 1988) on relative importance of attitude and subjective norm has been examined. In the case of safer sex, Middlestadt and Fishbein (1990) found that for sexually inexperienced women, attitude was a more important influence on the intention to ask the sexual partner to use a condom for intercourse, while for sexually experienced women, subjective norm was more important (Gardner, 1992, did not replicate this result). Beyond these few findings, little is known about situational influences on the relative importance of norm and attitude on decision making in any context, including that of sexual practice and other HIV-preventive behaviours.

The assumption that attitude and norm combine additively to influence intention has also been questioned in the literature. The theory of reasoned action does not allow for interactions between attitudinal and normative factors in predicting intention. Researchers including Andrews and Kandel (1979), Grube *et al.* (1986), and Liska (1984), however, have suggested that people's intentions to perform a behaviour are stronger when their attitude is positive toward the behaviour and when social norms also support the performance of the behaviour. In short, attitudes and social norms can have an interactive effect on intentions. Overall, however, there has not been a great deal of support for this interaction. It is left for future research to examine the potential interactive effects of the variety of norms and attitude, but at this stage, the main effects model in TRA appears to hold up well.

### Relation Between Intention and Behaviour

The relation between intention and behaviour is not entirely straightforward, particularly for sexual behaviours. The theory of planned behaviour, indeed, was proposed to handle some of the reasons for people not following their intentions (see below). Sometimes, however, methodological problems, rather than the participants in research, weaken the association between these two variables. Two methodological issues that have great importance for sexual behaviour are often ignored by researchers.

First, self-report measures of behaviour may have large errors, thus reducing their reliability and validity. Many question the accuracy of self-reports of condom use or other safer sex behaviours, because of the influence of social desirability, failure of memory, and so forth. In another context, Fredericks and Dossett (1983) criticised Bentler and Speckart's (1979) use of self-report measures of alcohol, marijuana and hard drug use in their tests of TRA. Fredericks and Dossett noted that self-reports of illegal or socially disapproved behaviour should be checked by more objective measures. This same criticism could be applied to many other studies using TRA.

This criticism is not without its own complications, however. For example, Hessing, Elffers and Weigel (1988) found that actual tax evasion was predicted neither by attitude to tax evasion nor by subjective norm about it, but that attitudes and norms predicted self-reports of tax evasion. These researchers also pointed to the problems of self-reports for illegal behaviour. The use of externally-gathered behavioural data also contains errors, however; actual tax evasion can only be determined for those people caught evading tax, who may be the most inept tax evaders. Given the difficulty of assessing behaviour other than by self-report, researchers studying safer sex have similar problems. Not much can be done about this other than to be very cautious in the interpretation of results.

A second methodological issue concerns the use of within-subject vs across-subject analyses of the relation between intention and behaviour. In across-subject analyses, one dependent variable (e.g., condom use) is chosen and assessed according to TRA. This is a reasonable strategy when the action-goal unit (Ajzen, 1985) involves conjunctive behaviours. For example, in order to lose weight, one can diet, exercise, eat more low-calorie foods, or engage in all these behaviours; they combine to enhance weight loss. A researcher who chooses any of these behaviours as the dependent variable is thus likely to find a reasonable correspondence between intention and behaviour.

In the case of safer sex, however, the various possibilities (using a condom, having only non-penetrative sex, having sex in an exclusive relationship, etc.) are disjunctive and tend to be mutually exclusive; choosing one of them means that others will not be chosen. This means that different safer sex intentions and, particularly, different behaviours are likely to be negatively correlated with each other, even though all of them lead to the goal of safer sex. The situation is even more complicated because people sometimes change alternatives with changing situations. A gay man, for example, may have non-penetrative sex with one partner and use a condom for anal sex with another (or on another occasion); these are both good choices in terms of safer sex, but the choice of one eliminates the other on that occasion. Thus, the question for a researcher must be one of predicting choice intention and relating it to behaviour, rather than predicting the strength of intention to perform any HIV-preventive behaviour.

In the framework of TRA, Jaccard (1981) and Pagel and Davidson (1984) raised this issue; Nickerson and McClelland (1989) have recently provided a more general discussion. Briefly, a person may have a strong intention to perform a behaviour, but he or she may have an even stronger intention to perform an alternative behaviour. For example, a gay man may have a strong intention to use condoms for sex, but he may have an even stronger intention to have only non-penetrative sex with any new partner, so that he does not need a condom to avoid HIV transmission. In this case, he may not use a condom, despite his strong intention to do so, as long as he can negotiate to have non-penetrative sex with his partner. Thus, within a single person, intentions for several alternatives must be compared, in order to predict behaviour (within-subject comparison). Typically, however, researchers compare intentions for a single behaviour with actual behaviour across people (across-subjects comparison).

As Nickerson and McClelland (1989) suggest, under some circumstances the across-subject method gives a good approximation to the within-subject analysis. Nevertheless, it is likely that TRA, along with most other theories of decision making, is best tested by using the within-subject method. For example, Gallois, Kashima et al. (1992) went some way toward conducting within-subject analyses by determining the preferred safer sex strategy (non-penetrative sex, condom use, exclusive relationship, or the last two in combination) for each of their subjects. They then compared subjects' attitudes and norms as a function of their preferred strategy, as well as predicting intention to perform the preferred strategy and actual behaviour. This approach was essential because the participants in the study were gay men and heterosexual men and women, some of whom were in regular sexual relationships and some of whom were not, so that no single dependent variable would have represented the preferences of most people in the study. Gallois and her colleagues found strong relationships between intentions and behaviour for each preferred strategy. To conduct a complete within-subject analysis, they would have needed to gather information from each subject on a number of safer sex behaviours, and then compared these for each person. Such a research approach gives a clearer picture than does across-subject comparisons on a single behaviour.

## Metatheoretical issues

All the issues discussed so far involve the measurement and conceptualisation of the variables proposed in the original version of TRA (Fishbein & Ajzen, 1975): attitude, subjective norm, intention and behaviour. A number of authors have made criticisms of TRA that go beyond this, and challenge the assumptions underlying the theory. We will briefly discuss some of these criticisms here. In doing this, we will nevertheless remain within the general framework of psychological theories of decision-making and the attitude–behaviour relationship, and we will leave broader attacks on this type of theory for others.

Four major metatheoretical issues have been raised in the literature. These issues can be summarised in four normative sentences. The first is that a social psychological theory should be able to account for behaviours that are not under complete volitional control; TRA is too limited in scope because it covers only volitional behaviours. The second is that social psychological theories should not aim only at predicting specific behaviours, but should be able to account for more global behaviours also; TRA is too limited in scope because it is designed to deal with very specific behaviours. The third sentence says that social psychological theories should describe or explain the psychological processes by which behaviours are performed; TRA is inadequate because it aims only to predict behaviour parsimoniously. The fourth sentence says that social psychological theories should not be overly individualistic, but should account for influences in the social context; TRA is inadequate because it focuses on the individual.

### Volitional Control of Behaviour

The first metatheoretical issue, that TRA is too limited because it accounts only for volitional behaviour, has been well-canvassed in the literature (e.g., Bentler & Speckart, 1979). As Lewis and Kashima (this volume) noted, it is debatable whether this is a crucial limitation of the theory. Nevertheless, the theory of planned behaviour (Ajzen, 1985, 1988,

1991) was designed specifically to expand the scope of TRA to the prediction of non-volitional behaviours (see Terry *et al.*, this volume, for a brief review of TPB, and other chapters for tests of TPB). Ajzen treats most social behaviours as action–goal units: various actions that are under volitional control are performed to attain goals. This reconceptualisation of behaviours as goal-directed activities raises the following question: when does intention predict non-volitional behaviour? Ajzen's solution was behavioural control. Intention predicts behaviour when the actor has behavioural control over the behaviour; it does not when behavioural control is low. This predicts an interaction effect on behaviour of intention and behavioural control. As Ajzen (1991) has conceded, however, this interaction effect has often proved to be elusive. Whether this lack of support is due to faulty measures or to conceptual problems remains to be seen.

Some researchers have argued that Ajzen's conceptualisation of behavioural control confounds two independent concepts (see Kashima *et al.*, in press; Nucifora *et al.*, this volume). The first concept is what Kashima *et al.*, called behavioural conditions, or conditions that are necessary for a behaviour to be carried out. For example, availability of a condom and an agreement with the partner to use it are two of the behavioural conditions necessary for condom use. the second concept is what may be termed intervening events between behaviours and goal attainment. Condom use is a behaviour used to attain the goal of reducing the risk of HIV transmission. If a condom breaks or leaks, however, the goal may not be attained. The intervening events—rupture or leakage—must be favourable to the actor before the goal—HIV risk reduction—can be attained. The distinction between behavioural conditions and intervening events is important, because they are likely to have different predictors. While behavioural conditions can be met by performing other volitional behaviours, intervening events may not be controlled by volitional behaviours. A more careful examination of the notion of behavioural control seems necessary.

Terry (this volume) has raised another conceptual and methodological issue. Ajzen and his colleagues have often used perceived behavioural control as a surrogate for behavioural control, noting the difficulty of measuring actual behavioural control. Measures of perceived behavioural control appear to confound pure control with self-efficacy, however. Terry developed a measure of perceived behavioural control containing two factors: self-efficacy (I believe I can perform this behaviour) and pure control (I believe I have control over this behaviour). When self-efficacy was removed, the contribution of perceived behavioural control to predicting the intention to use a condom and actual condom use was reduced to nonsignificance. These are only two of the conceptual and methodological issues surrounding the theory of planned behaviour. We have certainly not heard the final word about the prediction of non-volitional behaviour.

In the meantime, researchers interested in HIV-related behaviour would do well to include measures of self-efficacy and behavioural conditions necessary for performing specific safer sexual behaviours.

### Prediction of Specific Behaviours

The second metatheoretical issue is whether a social psychological theory should attempt prediction only of specific behaviours. The theory of reasoned action was originally developed to deal with the problem of the relationship between attitude and behaviour. Many researchers have noted that global attitudes do not predict specific behaviours very well (e.g., Wicker, 1969); Ajzen and Fishbein (1977) pointed out that the correspondence in the level of specificity of measures of attitudes and behaviour was one of the major factors that determine the strength of attitude–behaviour relationship. TRA was a direct result of this insight.

Nevertheless, some theorists have criticised this move. For instance, Abelson (1982) argued that TRA, by focusing on very specific relationships, ignores some of the most important parts of the attitude–behaviour dynamic; others (e.g., Rokeach, 1980) have echoed this criticism. This metatheoretical critique is based on the assumption that the theory of reasoned action intends to provide an answer to the attitude–behaviour question. Considered in this frame, TRA misses many issues of theoretical importance. On the other hand, if TRA is taken to be a theory of social decision making and behaviour change, it deals with the single most important question of human decision making in socially relevant settings.

As is often the case, this metatheoretical criticism comes down to differences in conceptual frame of reference and value judgments. We believe that it should be understood in the context of researchers' and theorists' purposes. The theory of reasoned action and its extensions cannot be the final word about the attitude–behaviour relationship. On the other hand, if a researcher wishes to change a specific behaviour, then this specific behaviour must be targeted, and a theory that allows this to be done accurately is the most helpful. In addition, if we conceptualise social processes as processes in which specific behaviours are produced by actors and interpreted by others, prediction and understanding of the performance of specific behaviours is important.

In the end, researchers must choose whether to try to predict specific behaviours or global patterns of behaviours. In some cases, TRA can be used to predict behaviour from more global attitudes, as long as a multi-act criterion is used; the disjunctive nature of safer sex behaviours makes this sort of procedure impossible, however. If those studying safer sex aim to change specific behaviours, prediction of specific behaviours is the only way to go. Given the disjunctive nature of safer sexual behaviours, studying global attitudes and norms toward HIV prevention is not an adequate vehicle for intervention.

## Explanation of Psychological Processes

The third metatheoretical critique of TRA involves its status as a theory of psychological processes. The theory of reasoned action describes relations between variables in terms of algebraic functions. For instance, attitude and subjective norm are additively combined to predict intention. Some researchers have, however, raised questions about the adequacy of this formulation. People probably do not add up numbers in their minds to form their intentions. The problem is even more acute with regard to the expectancy-value model of attitude. People are supposed to deal with not only two, but numerous beliefs. Do they really multiply beliefs and evaluations?

Fazio (1990) appears to think that this type of manipulation of beliefs and evaluations, and attitudes and subjective norms, might take place under some circumstances. He argues that when actors are motivated to consider behavioural choices carefully, and have opportunities to do so, they may use elaborate decision strategies such as TRA to form their intentions. Consistent with this formulation, Sanbonmatsu and Fazio (1990) manipulated motivation and opportunity, and reported that people formed specific intentions based on detailed consideration of information only when they had both motivation and opportunity. Gold (this volume) argues that this type of reasoning is unlikely in the context of high sexual arousal.

In any case, interpretation of algebraic models is not straightforward. According to Marr (1982), three levels of information processing theories can be differentiated. At the lowest *implementation* level, theories describe what brains (or organisms) do in terms of biochemical processes. At the *algorithmic* level, theories describe what people do in terms of psychological processes. For example, when computing '1+2', people can use fingers, draw circles, or count marbles; these are all different processes. At the *computational* level, theories describe what people produce as a result of their psychological processes. So, the answer '3' may be computed on the basis of some numerical theory, but this theory does not describe the psychological processes by which the answer was produced.

Algebraic theories such as the theory of reasoned action should be seen as computational rather than algorithmic theories. If this view is correct, the criticism that TRA does not describe psychological processes may be dismissed as irrelevant, as the algebraic relations postulated by TRA describe at a computational level relations between important psychological variables. TRA can be complemented by algorithmic theories; Bagozzi's (1992) self-regulation formulation, for example, may be seen as an attempt to provide an algorithmic-level description of psychological processes which are captured computationally by TRA and its extensions.

Whatever position one takes in the argument that TRA is a computational and not an algorithmic theory, it is important to examine whether the causal structure it describes actually holds up in a given behavioural domain. Whatever the process behind the formation of intention and enactment of behaviour, if some psychological variables measured by beliefs indeed cause certain intentions and corresponding behaviours, in the end this is what matters most to research and especially to intervention. The question about underlying psychological processes is useful to the extent that understanding these processes may inform intervention programmes.

Finally, it is a truism in psychology that correlational methods cannot answer questions about causality. In the literature on attitudes and behaviour, however, causal questions are often delegated to the theory of reasoned action, because of its theoretical and intuitive appeal. We believe that the causal structure postulated by TRA often does hold true, as demonstrated by causal designs testing TRA with longitudinal data sets and using structural equation modelling or path analysis (e.g., Bentler & Speckart, 1979; Fredericks & Dossett, 1983). Even so, people also justify their intentions and behaviours in some cases by modifying their attitudes and beliefs. In other words, the correlational structure between the components of TRA may be consistent with the theory because causality can run both ways, from beliefs to intentions *and* from intentions to beliefs. The former is TRA's causal structure; the latter is justification and rationalisation. For instance, people may reason that they are unlikely to contract HIV even if they do not use condoms, because they are in exclusive relationships with faithful partners (belief leads to intention). On the other hand, it is quite possible that people justify their decision not to use a condom by telling themselves that their partners are faithful (intention leads to belief).

One pressing question is whether TRA's causal structure is accurate for a given behaviour; this issue must be examined empirically before policy recommendations can be made. For this purpose, it may be a good general practice to combine correlational and experimental studies using the theory of reasoned action. First, TRA may be used to identify the major predictors of a behaviour. Then, an experimental study can be designed, in which these predictors are manipulated and their effects on behaviours observed (see Brubaker & Fowler, 1990; Fishbein, Ajzen, & McArdle, 1980; McCarty, 1981). Unfortunately, the experimental method is not an option for most safer sex behaviours, for obvious reasons. Even so, interventions designed to change norms and attitudes can be evaluated in terms of their impact on intention and behaviour, and quasi-experimental designs can be employed. Kelly, St. Lawrence, Diaz *et al.*, (1991) did something like this when they used opinion leaders in a number of selected gay communities as agents to change norms and attitudes about condom use. Their measure of behaviour, the number of condoms distributed, showed dramatic increases after each intervention. This type of quasi-experiment is costly and difficult to conduct, but it is very convincing.

### Individualism and the Theory of Reasoned Action

The fourth and final metatheoretical issue involves the question of whether social psychological theories should deal only with behaviour at an individual level. The theory of reasoned action conceptualises social behaviour as the result of an individual's decision making. The focus of its analysis is a reasonable, if not rational, individual, who makes reasoned decisions. All other factors are set aside as external. As Liska (1984) has pointed out, however, social behaviours are often constrained by other people. Even if large-scale cultural and social factors can be accommodated through the belief structures postulated by TRA, there may be times when one individual's behaviour cannot be explained without considering at least one other person.

One example of this problem in the area of HIV-preventive behaviour is the role of the sexual partner. Safer sex requires cooperation between sexual partners. This fact often pushes HIV-preventive behaviour outside TRA's scope, because it is not under individual control, although behaviours where partners cooperate for goal attainment can be theorised within the conceptual framework of goal-directed activity (TPB). In this case, the agreement of the partner can be seen as an important condition that must be satisfied before attaining the goal of safer sex. Kashima *et al.* (in press) examined the extent to which the partner's agreement was necessary for a condom to be used. When actors had access to condoms, nearly three quarters of those who had their partners' agreement to use condoms did in fact use them. By contrast, only about a quarter of those who did not have an explicit agreement about condom use actually used them.

In addition, the partner in a co-operative behaviour potentially plays three roles in the formation of intention. First, the sexual partner is one of the important people in the actor's social environment and can provide many rewards and punishments, so that he or she influences subjective norm (through compliance; see the earlier section on norms), as TRA proposes. Secondly, the partner's cooperation is a necessary condition for the performance of a cooperative behaviour, and the actor's perception of what the partner thinks can be conceptualised as a mental representation of the social constraints on the behaviour. Such beliefs about social constraints are likely to have a direct effect on intentions, unmediated by attitudes and norms, because social constraints hinder performance of the behaviour and force the actor to change intentions (Fishbein & Ajzen, 1975; Ajzen, 1985). This line of reasoning is consistent with the theory of planned behaviour; the partner's agreement may contribute to perceived behavioural control. Finally, if a person expects that the behaviour will cause some unpleasantness to the relationship, or that the partner may not like it, the person's attitude is likely to be more negative. Thus, the partner can influence intentions through attitudes, which is not in accord with TRA.

Consistent with these considerations, Kashima et al. (in press) showed that the perceived wish of the partner (partner norm) predicted subjective norm, intention and attitude. Similarly, Smetana and Adler (1980) reported that expectancy-value subjective norm predicted attitude toward having an abortion. Because abortion is typically based on both parents' agreement, attitude toward having an abortion may have been influenced directly by that part of expectancy-value subjective norm which involved judgements about the subject's partner as a significant other.

These findings suggest that the theory of reasoned action and its extensions may have a metatheoretical limitation in dealing with cooperative social behaviour. Underlying this problem is their orientation, in which the individual actor is taken to be the unit of analysis. In predicting HIV-preventive behaviours in the sexual context, which require cooperation, it is important to examine the social context and the interpersonal dynamics of the target behaviours. In particular, the communication process between partners in the sexual encounter is a question that needs further examination.

## Conclusions

Despite these theoretical and metatheoretical issues, the theory of reasoned action and its extensions have many strengths in providing a theoretical and methodological package for problem-oriented research. Their theoretical framework is general; with appropriate modifications, it is likely to be able to accommodate an ever-increasing number of social behaviours. This is a great advantage over behaviour-specific theories, in that new theories do not have to be invented every time new social issues emerge. In addition, TRA gives a methodological framework in which to design problem-oriented and policy-relevant research, like research on safer sex. The major aims of such research are to identify key variables that account for large proportions of variance in problematic behaviours (e.g., unsafe sexual behaviours), and to make policy recommendations about interventions. TRA and its extensions can attain both these aims. Finally, TRA incorporates as a central tenet that behaviour and intentions are influenced by attitudes, norms and beliefs specific to particular groups of people and contexts (see Fishbein & Middlestadt, 1989, for a discussion of this issue in the context of HIV prevention). The methodology includes ways of gathering and using relevant local information. Again, this aspect of TRA is very important in applied research.

We believe that the future of the theory of reasoned action lies in this line of problem-oriented research. Theoretical efforts may be fruitfully directed to refining TRA's concepts and the causal relations among them. A useful theoretical project may be to spell out the boundary conditions under which TRA's causal structure is likely to hold (e.g., Fazio, 1990). In the meantime, we have attempted to describe some issues that those doing research on HIV-preventive behaviour should keep in mind, and a set of ideas for the application of the theory of reasoned action. The theory of reasoned action (or any theory for that matter) only provides general concepts. It is up to individual researchers to make the most of this theory in designing research and intervention strategies for HIV prevention.

# 13

# On the Need to Mind the Gap: On-Line versus Off-Line Cognitions Underlying Sexual Risk-Taking

RON S. GOLD

*Deakin University, Gealong, Australia*

Over the last few years, I and my colleagues have carried out a series of studies on behavioural aspects of AIDS (Gold, Karmiloff-Smith, Skinner, & Morton, 1992; Gold & Skinner, 1992; Gold, Skinner, Grant, & Plummer, 1991; Gold, Skinner, & Ross, 1992). The studies targeted different populations—three employed samples of gay men, and one a sample of heterosexual students[1]—but each had the same aim: to investigate factors that may contribute to decisions to have anal/vaginal intercourse without using a condom (I will refer to this as 'unprotected' intercourse).

Within this framework, there were two main goals. The first had to do with the thought processes that are associated with a decision to have unprotected intercourse; our aim was to identify the types of justification (if any) that people give themselves at the time they make this decision. The second aim was to identify the types of occasion on which individuals are most at risk of ending up having unprotected intercourse. The term 'types of occasion' here refers to factors in the life of an individual which can vary over a relatively short period of time: type of sexual partner, mood, state of intoxication, physical location, etc.

In the first section of this paper, I will provide the background for our interest in these questions, and describe the research design and methodology employed in our studies. In the second part I will present some of the findings we obtained. Finally, I will turn to the unifying theme of this book and discuss the application of the theory of reasoned action to HIV/AIDS prevention work. In fact, the approach we have used in our studies owes little or nothing to this theory, and I will use the last section of the paper to explain why I do not consider that it provides a very useful framework within which to study AIDS-related behaviours.

## Background and Methodology

Our studies derived primarily from a concern to improve HIV/AIDS education and, in particular—since this group is still at greatest risk in Western countries—the HIV/AIDS education directed at gay men. To date, the main education strategies which have been used for gay men have involved providing information about the threat from AIDS and the types of behaviours that are high-risk for HIV transmission, as well as exhortations to have safe sex.

These strategies achieved considerable success in the early years of the epidemic: many gay men made very great changes in their sexual behaviour (e.g., Connell *et al.*, 1988; Ekstrand & Coates, 1990; McCusker *et al.*, 1988). However, there is evidence that for many men these changes are difficult to sustain, so that there is an appreciable incidence of relapse into unprotected intercourse (e.g., Adib, Joseph, Ostrow, Tal, & Schwartz, 1991; Kelly, St. Lawrence & Brasfield, 1991). Further, among young gay men—those who reached sexual maturity during the epidemic and who therefore never experienced the sexual freedom which characterised the pre-AIDS era—the incidence of unprotected intercourse is nevertheless disturbingly high (Hays, Kegeles & Coates, 1990; Stall *et al.*, 1992).

It may be that, a decade into the epidemic, gay men have become somewhat habituated to living with the threat from AIDS. Possibly connected with this, the education strategies which were effective in the first phase of the epidemic may no longer be having as much impact as they did initially. Accordingly, it is important to develop new approaches to AIDS education.

### *Our Focus on Self-Justifications for Unprotected Intercourse*

The fact that unprotected intercourse is a major vector for the transmission of HIV has been very widely publicised. We therefore began our studies with the hypothesis that the great majority of people who decide to have unprotected intercourse probably do so despite knowing of the potential danger. Further, we reasoned that people who deliberately decide to behave in a way they know to be dangerous may need to find ways of 'giving themselves permission' to do so, i.e., they may need to find ways of justifying their decision to themselves at the time they make it. Underlying the self-justifications used would be cognitions—beliefs, thoughts, attitudes, judgments, inferences, values, etc.—relating to the behaviour and the risk involved. The self-justifications, and their constituent cognitions, would help to cause the behaviour, at least in the sense of enabling it to occur. It follows that, if one could appropriately modify or extinguish these self-justifications/cognitions, the behaviour too should be modified or cease.

This model recalls that which sociologists have proposed to account for the behaviour of juvenile delinquents (Sykes & Matza, 1957). Within psychology, it is similar to the model employed in much cognitive therapy (e.g., Beck, 1976; Ellis, 1962; Meichenbaum, 1977). Cognitive therapists assume that thoughts and/or the cognitions that underlie them contribute causally to symptomatic behaviours and, accordingly, that cognitive change is a particularly effective therapeutic intervention. The extent to which this is in fact the case remains arguable (e.g., Brewin, 1989; Coyne & Gotlib, 1983; Haaga, Dyck & Ernst, 1991) and it is unclear how generally the thesis that cognitions are instrumental in causing symptoms will prove to be true. It should be noted, however, that our proposal is much more limited in scope than that of cognitive therapists: the only 'symptom' it addresses is people's deliberate decisions to engage in behaviours they know are potentially very dangerous.

*Limitations of Studying Only 'Off-Line' Cognitions*

AIDS-related beliefs, attitudes and judgments, etc. have been investigated in many studies. Almost without exception, however, the researchers concerned have studied only those cognitions that are present in respondents' minds at the time they are answering the researcher's questions (that is, 'in the cold light of day'), rather than those that are present during actual sexual encounters. Adapting terminology used in other fields (e.g., Hastie & Park, 1986; Sanford & Garrod, 1981), I will refer to the AIDS-related cognitions that are present during sexual encounters—i.e., at times when people are actively pursuing the goal of having sex—as 'on-line' cognitions, and to those that are present at other times as 'off-line' cognitions.[2] (I prefer this terminology to the related distinction, drawn by Kuhl (1985), between 'action orientation' and 'state orientation' because Kuhl seems to conceive of these primarily as traits, characteristic of a given individual.)

There are good reasons for hypothesising that there may in fact be considerable differences between on-line and off-line AIDS-related cognitions. I will mention just some (partially overlapping) reasons.

First, and most obviously, in actual sexual encounters (both when the individual is searching for a partner to have sex and, even more so, when a desirable partner is present) strong arousal is present; on-line cognitions are thus 'hot' cognitions (Zajonc, 1980). This is likely to affect the values attached to different possible outcomes. On-line, an urgent desire that demands immediate fulfilment—the desire to have unprotected intercourse—is set against negative consequences that are much more remote; the former is thus likely to loom relatively large and be accorded considerable value (e.g., Ainslie, 1975). The presence of a desired partner would compound this, since the person would partially adapt to the notion of satisfying his/her desire and begin to feel that to abstain would be to suffer actual deprivation (Hoch & Loewenstein, 1991). Off-line, by contrast, where cognition is relatively 'cold,' the long-term consequences would be more salient and greater importance would be attached to them.

Indeed, the value attached to immediate gratification in an actual sexual encounter may be so great that 'motivated reasoning' (Kunda, 1990) may occur: on-line, the individual may—whether consciously or not—distort AIDS-related cognitions, or even manufacture new cognitions, specifically in order to enable unprotected intercourse to take place. Thus, for instance, individuals who want unprotected intercourse may tailor their cognitions to enable them to conclude that their partner is uninfected, or that they have a natural resistance to HIV, or that a cure will be found soon so that they are unlikely to die even if they do become infected.

The presence of a desirable partner brings with it perceptual cues relating to the partner's looks, behaviour and physical location. Off-line, such cues are absent, or present in a less concrete fashion (e.g., they may be present in the imagination). As well as contributing to sexual arousal, these cues may trigger the activation of AIDS-related cognitions having to do with them. On-line, for example, a partner's good looks (or speaking style, or wedding ring) may activate a belief that a partner who is good-looking (or well-spoken, or married) is unlikely to be infected; these beliefs may not be accessed, or perhaps not even exist, off-line.

Given that, on-line, time and attention are so fully taken up with the goal of having sex, there would be relatively little information-processing capacity free and available for other purposes. An individual who is under cognitive pressure in this way is more likely to use cognitive 'short-cuts', the abbreviated processing strategies that lead to biases (Freund, Kruglanski & Shpitzajzen, 1985; Kruglanski, & Freund, 1983). Accordingly, there may be a greater use of such short-cuts on-line than off-line. For example, on-line there may be a greater reliance on stereotypes, such as stereotypes about the type of person who is likely to be infected.

A final point concerns mood. Given that sex is generally pleasurable, individuals might be in a better mood, in general, during a sexual encounter than outside this context. But a good mood may itself affect their AIDS-related cognitions: they might, for instance, start to feel over-confident about the risk of becoming infected, or deliberately refuse to think about the potential danger, in order not to spoil their mood (e.g., Clark & Isen, 1982; Johnson & Tversky, 1983); or employ cognitive short-cuts because a good mood imposes additional processing demands (Mackie & Worth, 1991). Further, the topic of AIDS is by its nature a sombre one, and one would expect that, at the times individuals were exposed to AIDS education in the past, they would, by that very fact, have been somewhat depressed. But research on state-dependent learning (e.g., Bower, 1981) suggests that one can access learned material more easily when one is in the same mood as when it was learned than when one is in a different mood. It follows that there may be less access to information about the danger of infection on-line than off-line.

For all these reasons, the AIDS-related cognitions which are present on-line may differ in important ways from those which are present off-line. Of course, this is not to deny that off-line cognitions are significant determinants of behaviour. Given the gap which may exist between them and on-line cognitions, however, it seems important to try to study the latter as well as the former.

How may this be done? Clearly, the problem of reactivity of measures precludes the use, during sexual encounters, of 'think-aloud' techniques (Genest & Turk, 1981): an individual cannot simultaneously have sex and record observations. (I will not even suggest the use of direct observation methods!) In the studies we have carried out to date, we sought to address the problem using retrospective recall: we asked respondents to reconstruct in their minds an occasion when they had engaged in unprotected intercourse and to recall any self-justifications they had used at the time of making the decision to do this. I will describe in more detail the methodology we used after providing some background to the second major concern of our studies.

## Our Focus on the Types of Occasion Which Pose Special Danger for Having Unsafe Sex

Our concern to establish the types of occasion on which people are particularly likely to end up having unprotected intercourse was informed by three main considerations. First, as just noted, on-line cues such as physical location, or mood, or the partner's looks or behaviour, may trigger AIDS-related cognitions which then enable unprotected intercourse to occur. It is therefore important to find out which cues act in this way.

A second reason had to do with the possibility that situational cues can sometimes trigger unprotected intercourse directly, without the mediation of AIDS-related cognitions. Our 'self-justifications' hypothesis concerns people who, knowing of the potential danger, nevertheless deliberately decide to have unprotected intercourse. It is also conceivable, however, that people who know of the potential danger may sometimes engage in unprotected intercourse—and do so voluntarily—without making anything that could be called a deliberate decision on the matter. After considerable experience in a given type of situation, behaviour in that situation can become so highly automatic that it is directly evoked by situational cues. No thinking occurs; the behaviour occurs 'mindlessly'

(Langer, Blank & Chanowitz, 1978; see also Fazio, 1990). In a sexual encounter, unprotected intercourse could thus sometimes occur in a purely reactive manner, unaccompanied by AIDS-related cognitions.

A third consideration was educational utility. An AIDS education program emphasising that certain types of occasions pose special danger for 'slip-ups' into unsafe sex would put the focus on factors that are relatively controllable—one can avoid or take special care in particular situations more easily than one can, say, change one's personality or level of education. A variety of research findings suggest that attributing negative experiences to controllable factors is associated with more positive long-term outcomes. Thus, for example, Janoff-Bulman (1979) distinguished between two types of self-blame, focusing, respectively, on one's behaviour and on one's character. It was found that depressed female students exhibited more characterological self-blame than non-depressed female students, while the two groups were equally likely to use behavioural self-blame. Marlatt and Gordon (1985) made a distinction between an initial slip or lapse into a health-threatening behaviour and subsequent relapse into regular engagement in the behaviour. They argued that a lapse is more likely to escalate into a relapse to the extent that it is attributed to internal, relatively stable factors that are perceived to be uncontrollable. Curry, Marlatt and Gordon (1987) reported evidence consistent with this hypothesis. The fact that more desirable long-term outcomes seem to be associated with attributions to controllable factors suggests that it may be useful, in AIDS education programs, to highlight the danger posed by certain types of situations.

*Limitations of Correlational Studies of Situational Factors*

In addressing the role of situational factors, most authors other than ourselves have collected only correlational data. Such an approach unnecessarily limits the conclusions which can be drawn. Thus, for example, several authors have found that respondents who had sex with casual partners were less likely to have unprotected intercourse than those having sex with regular partners (Chapman, Stoker, Ward, Porritt, & Fahey, 1990; Connell & Kippax, 1990; Fitzpatrick, Boulton, Hart, Dawson, & McLean, 1989; Moore & Rosenthal, 1991a). While these results may indicate that type of partner affects the likelihood of unsafe sex, it is also possible, for instance, that different personality types tend to have sex with different types of partner and, quite independently, are differentially likely to have safe sex; personality type would then be a third factor accounting for the observed correlation. A similar point applies to studies finding that alcohol consumption or drug use is associated with the occurrence of unsafe sex (Bagnall, Plant & Warwick, 1990; Kelly *et al.*, 1991;

McKirnan & Peterson, 1989; Robertson & Plant, 1988; Siegel, Mesagno, Chen, & Christ, 1989; Stall, McKusik, Wiley, Coates & Ostrow, 1986); again, the association may actually be due to a variable such as personality type acting as a *tertium quid*.

In order to overcome this problem, in all our studies we used a within-subjects design to investigate this issue. Respondents were asked to recall both an encounter in which they had ended up engaging in unprotected intercourse (for convenience, this is referred to as the 'unsafe' encounter) and one in which they had been very tempted to have unprotected intercourse, but made a deliberate decision not to do so (the 'safe' encounter). These two types of encounter were then compared; using respondents as their own controls in this way enabled us to exclude the effects of variables such as age, level of education, social class and personality.

## Samples and Procedure

The populations sampled in our studies were: young—up to 21 years old—gay men in Melbourne (Gold & Skinner, 1992); older gay men in Melbourne (Gold *et al.,* 1991); older gay men in Sydney (Gold, Skinner, Ross, 1992); and heterosexual students in London (Gold, Karmiloff-Smith, Skinner & Morton, 1992). In each case, the only criterion for inclusion in the sample was that the individual should have had a recent unsafe encounter. In the Sydney study only, we found that an appreciable minority of the sample had known themselves to be HIV-infected at the time of the unsafe encounter; accordingly, we presented results separately for these men (the 'infected' group) and the rest of the sample (the 'uninfected' group[3]). Sample sizes, and the percentage able to recall a safe encounter in addition to the unsafe encounter, were: young gay men in Melbourne, $n = 219$, 53%; older gay men in Melbourne, $n = 219$, 83%; infected gay men in Sydney, $n = 88$, 86%; uninfected gay men in Sydney, $n = 207$, 82%; heterosexual students in London, $n = 284$, 61%.

Data were collected by means of interviews in the study of young gay men and self-administered questionnaires in the other studies. Respondents were asked to try to reconstruct each encounter as vividly as possible; they were told to try to 'relive' the encounter. To assist them in this, the encounter was divided into four temporal stages—at the start of the 'evening' (it was made clear that it did not have to be literally an evening), at the time the respondent met the person with whom he/she later had sex, at the start of sex and during sex—and the questions asked dealt with each of these stages in turn. There were a few variations in the questions used in the different studies, but the following questions were typical.

For each encounter, respondents were asked: how recently it had taken place; whether they had known at the time that unprotected intercourse is considered a high-risk activity for the transmission of HIV; who their sexual partner had been; where they had met the partner that evening; where the sex had taken place; whether intercourse (in the case of the safe encounter) or ejaculation into the rectum/vagina (in the case of the unsafe encounter) had occurred; whether, at any point in the evening, they had looked at or read any pornographic material showing or describing unprotected intercourse; and whether they had known their antibody status and that of their partner.

For one or more stages of the encounter, respondents were asked to indicate: the extent to which various desires—some sexual in nature (e.g., to have exciting sex), others not sexual (e.g., to have a drink or get mildly 'stoned')—had been in their mind; how intoxicated (from alcohol) and 'stoned' (from any drugs) they had been; what their mood had been like (descriptors such as 'happy,' 'relaxed,' 'depressed,' 'under stress,' 'mentally tired' and 'lonely' were used); and how sexually attracted to the partner and sexually aroused they had been. They were also asked whether they had communicated to their partner their wishes—and whether the partner had communicated his/her wishes—regarding use/non-use of a condom; and, if this had occurred, what mode of communication (e.g., direct verbal communication, indirect verbal communication, body language) had been employed. Other questions asked whether either they or their partner had used any 'dirty talk' during sex, and if so, whether it could have been interpreted as an invitation to have unprotected intercourse. Respondents also indicated whether they had known about the availability or otherwise of a condom at the time they were having sex.

These questions were asked about both types of encounter. Additional questions were asked about only the unsafe encounter. One question presented a series of statements describing ways in which respondents might have engaged in unprotected intercourse without really wanting to; they might, for example, have been physically forced, been emotionally blackmailed, or been too intoxicated or tired to prevent it from happening. Respondents were asked to rate the truth of each statement. Another question presented a long list of possible self-justifications for having intercourse without a condom. These had been generated in discussion with AIDS counsellors and pilot studies, and each was preceded by the words 'I thought to myself something like'[4]. For each self-justification, respondents indicated how strongly it had been in their mind at the time they had decided to have unprotected intercourse. Respondents were also asked how big a risk of contracting HIV they had thought they were taking at the moment of deciding to have unprotected intercourse.

### *The Question of Validity: Some Caveats*

Before presenting some of our findings, I will briefly comment on the question of the (internal) validity of the data we have collected. Bias or inaccuracy could have been introduced into our studies by respondents being insufficiently motivated to care very much how they responded, by any tendency on their part to select atypical sexual encounters to report, and by any distortions in their reconstruction of the encounters.

It seems extremely unlikely that participants in our studies were insufficiently motivated to care very much how they responded. Although the questionnaires used were very long, it is clear that they were filled out with great care. Instructions were followed accurately and many respondents wrote in extra comments to qualify their responses. While almost invariably these comments did not cover new ground, the fact that respondents made the effort to write them suggests that they took the exercise seriously. Further, in every study exhaustive checks revealed that, where effects should have been present almost by definition, they were indeed found. At every point our data appear sensible, suggesting that respondents gave considered answers.

The possibility of bias in respondents' selection of sexual encounters to describe is always present where respondents are asked to recall unspecified individual encounters (or, indeed, where they are asked to report what 'usually' happens in their sexual encounters). It would be useful to compare the findings from our studies with those obtained where the selection of encounters to report is constrained in some way—where respondents are asked to describe their most recent safe and unsafe encounters, for example.

As to the possibility that distortion occurred in respondents' reconstruction of the encounters, in the case of most of the questions asked in our studies—those dealing with mental states or processes—there does not seem to be any direct means of establishing the validity of the responses that were given. How could one establish empirically, for example, that the self-justifications reported by respondents had really been present at the time of their decision to engage in unprotected intercourse (let alone that the self-justifications had in fact played a causal role in permitting this decision to be taken)? An alternative possibility is that the reported self-justifications were simply rationalisations, devised or invoked either during the unsafe encounter but after unprotected intercourse had already commenced, or after the encounter had ended. It may be that the only evidence on the point would come from an intervention study. If it can be shown that an intervention which extinguishes self-justifications also succeeds in decreasing the incidence of unprotected intercourse, then—provided that appropriate control groups have been employed—it seems that the self-justifications must have been present at the time of, and played

Table 13.1. *Types of Partner in the Unsafe Encounter*

| Group | $\underline{N}$ | Percentage of sample whose partner was a/an | | |
| | | Lover | Casual but not anonymous partner | Anonymous partner |
|---|---|---|---|---|
| Young gay men in Melbourne | 219 | 31 | 41 | 24 |
| Older gay men in Melbourne | 219 | 37 | 30 | 26 |
| Uninfected gay men in Sydney | 207 | 37 | 36 | 23 |
| Infected gay men in Sydney | 88 | 28 | 28 | 35 |
| Heterosexual students in London | 284 | 68 | 24 | 3 |

a causal role in, the decision to have unprotected intercourse.

## Overview of Results

In this section, it is not my aim to present our results exhaustively, but to convey their flavour and draw attention to some that I consider particularly interesting or important. After briefly reporting the type of partner with whom unprotected intercourse had occurred in the unsafe encounter, I will present findings relating to the self-justifications employed in this encounter; finally, I will report findings relating to the comparison of the unsafe and safe encounters.

### Type of Partner in the Unsafe Encounter

Partners were categorised into three broad types: lover/significant other (hereafter referred to as just 'lover'), regular sex partner other than a lover and casual sex partner. Fewer than 10% of partners fell into the second category in any sample; I will therefore not report results relating to this category. Within the third category, one subgroup—that of anonymous partner—was particularly common in the gay samples. Table 1 presents the proportion of partners in each sample who were lovers, casual but not anonymous partners and anonymous partners.

## Self-Justifications Used in the Unsafe Encounter

### Use of Self-Justifications

In the older gay samples and the heterosexual sample, almost all respondents (over 95% in each case) had known at the time of the unsafe encounter that unprotected intercourse is considered a high-risk activity for the transmission of HIV. While fewer of the young gay men had possessed this information, even in this sample the great majority (84%) had known of the potential risk.

Given that most respondents had decided to have unprotected intercourse despite knowing of the potential danger, it would follow from our hypothesis that most should have sought to justify their decision to themselves at the time they made it. The evidence was consistent with this proposal: the great majority in each sample (proportions ranged from 85% to 97%) reported that at least one of the self-justifications listed in the questionnaire/interview had been in their mind strongly or moderately.

### Resolution to Withdraw

In all the gay samples, a particularly common self-justification had been the thought that unprotected intercourse would occur, but that the insertive partner would withdraw before ejaculating. Exactly one-third of the older gay men in Melbourne and the uninfected gay men in Sydney, 40% of the infected gay men in Sydney and 21% of the young gay men reported that this self-justification had been in their mind strongly or moderately at the time they had decided to have unprotected intercourse. It was the single most common self-justification reported by the older gay men in Melbourne and the uninfected gay men in Sydney.

The reasoning involved in the resolution to withdraw without ejaculating is dangerous. First, as one would expect, such a resolution is difficult to keep: in about a quarter of cases in which it was used, ejaculation into the rectum occurred anyway. Second, it is known that HIV particles can be present in the rectal mucosa and can be transferred even where no semen exchange occurs. It may be that many gay men are still unaware that HIV can be transmitted even when no semen exchange occurs; AIDS educators might use an analogy with diseases such as gonorrhea and syphilis to convey this information. Alternatively, gay men may plan to withdraw, not out of ignorance, but because they feel that by doing so they will reduce the risk to a level they consider acceptable.

Table 13.2. *Young Gay Men: Self-Justifications with the Highest Loadings on Factor 2.*

| Self-justification | % of respondents reporting that this self-justification had been strongly or moderately in their mind | Factor loading |
|---|---|---|
| (1) "This guy looks so healthy, he can't possibly be infected." | 29 | 0.55 |
| (2) "I'm sure this guy isn't infected. I can just tell." | 26 | 0.59 |
| (3) "This guy seems so clean; he doesn't look at all grotty or dirty. So he can't possibly be infected." | 19 | 0.53 |
| (4) "This guy is so beautiful, he can't possibly be infected." | 18 | 0.61 |
| (5) "This guy seems intelligent/well-educated, so I'm sure he's been careful. So he can't possibly be infected." | 16 | 0.70 |
| (6) "This guy seems such a nice person-he's got a lovely personality - so he can't possibly be infected." | 11 | 0.74 |

## Inferences from Perceptible Cues

In each study we carried out a principal factor analysis with varimax rotation on the self-justification data. One factor that emerged prominently in all samples except for the infected gay men had to do with inferring from perceptible characteristics—from the way a partner looks, speaks or behaves—that he/she is unlikely to be HIV-infected. Self-justifications of this type were particularly common in the sample of young gay men, where the relevant factor was the second to emerge from the factor analysis. Table 2 presents the details. In this group Cronbach's alpha for the self-justifications in the table was 0.85. Slightly over two-fifths of respondents reported that at least one of these self-justifications had been in their mind strongly or moderately at the time they decided to have unprotected intercourse. Self-justification 1 in the table was the one reported most commonly by the young gay men. There was a low but significant correlation between the factor scores on this factor and respondents' age, with younger men in the sample reporting greater use of the self-justifications.

These self-justifications ignore the fact that, because HIV has a very long incubation period, one cannot deduce just from appearances who is and who is not infected. I do not think it likely, however, that individuals who use these self-justifications are unaware of this fact. On the contrary, I suspect that most of them do indeed have this information and can access it readily, *when they are off-line*. It is a different matter on-line, however. I suspect that the inferences that underlie these self-justifications are present primarily (though perhaps not uniquely) during actual sexual encounters.

It may be that such inferences are 'motivated cognitions', used merely to enable a desire for unprotected intercourse to be fulfilled, and therefore present only when that desire is most immediate. But it is at least as likely, I think, that they derive from the use of cognitive 'shortcuts' that are employed on-line because the goal of having sex leaves little information-processing capacity free for other purposes. Such shortcuts might take the form of a reliance on stereotypes about who is most likely to be infected; the inference underlying self-justification 3 in Table 2 may be an example in this regard. Cognitive pressure could also lead to unthinking use of the 'availability heuristic' (Kahneman, Slovic, & Tversky, 1982), involving over-reliance on instances which come most readily to mind. The inference underlying self-justification 1 may come about in this way: most common diseases generally have relatively short incubation periods, so that for these diseases it is in fact true that people who look healthy are generally not infected. The error lies in generalising this reasoning to the case of HIV.

*'Bargaining'*

In each sample, respondents reported the use of self-justifications that seemed to involve 'bargaining' or special pleading. These self-justifications emphasised how much the respondent had given up since the start of the epidemic, or how good he/she usually was or would be in future. Presumably, the implication was that the respondent therefore deserved to be protected from danger—to be allowed 'time out' from the need to take care—on this particular occasion. Such self-justifications were reported to varying degrees by the different samples. In some cases they formed a distinct factor; in others they were attached to other factors. Table 3 gives examples of 'bargaining' self-justifications reported by the uninfected gay men in Sydney.

Underlying these self-justifications is the notion that one's effort and sacrifice in trying to stick to safer sex will be rewarded. The view of the world as a just place is, of course, deep-seated within our culture; it underpins most moral and religious teaching. It is at least conceivable, therefore, that individuals believe just as much off-line as they do on-line that their usual good behaviour will be 'taken into account' if they 'slip up.' Again, however, I think it much more likely that this notion is limited to actual sexual encounters, that it is present primarily on-line.

Table 13.3. *Uninfected Gay Men in Sydney: "Bargaining" Self-Justifications*

| Self-justification | % of respondents reporting that this self-justification had been strongly or moderately in their mind |
|---|---|
| (1) "Most of the time I'm careful, but I can't be perfect - it's only human to break out occasionally." | 20 |
| (2) "There are so many things I've given up since AIDS. e.g., I've reduced the number of guys I have sex with/changed what I do when I have sex/have sex much less often than I did, etc. I feel I really have been very good. So I <u>deserve</u> to be allowed to fuck without a condom today, as a reward." | 16 |
| (3) "I'll have one last fling and do only safe sex from then on. I'll be good starting tomorrow - I won't fuck without a condom after this last time." | 13 |

## The Infected Sample

The results from the Sydney study suggest that the infected group had a greater orientation than the uninfected group towards exciting, 'adventurous' sex. Thus, for example, in the unsafe encounter, the desires to have unprotected intercourse, to have anonymous sex, to be pursued sexually, to have exciting sex, to have sadomasochistic sex and to find excitement in any way possible, had all been greater in the infected than the uninfected men; the reverse was true of the desire for a cuddle.

It seems very possible that the infected men had been sexually adventurous even before they became infected—and that this, indeed, was how their infection had come about. The self-justification data pointed to another possibility as well, however: that these men's 'fast-lane' approach to sex was to some extent the result, rather than the cause, of their becoming infected. It has been suggested that the stress of being diagnosed HIV-positive can produce lack of concern both about one's own welfare and that of others (Ross, 1990c). The data provided evidence of both forms of unconcern. The most common self-justification reported by the infected group was that they had nothing more to lose since they were already infected; 43% reported that this thought had been in their minds strongly or moderately at the time they had decided to have unprotected intercourse. This reasoning contrasts with the 'official' view that it is in an infected man's own interest to refrain from unprotected intercourse, first because he may contract other sexually transmitted diseases whose effect could be serious given his compromised immune system, and secondly (and more controversially, e.g., Meyer-Bahlburg *et al.*, 1991) because he may increase his risk of progressing to full AIDS. As regards lack of concern about the welfare of others, 31% of the infected group reported having had strongly or moderately in their mind the thought '...if this guy is willing to fuck without a condom that's his affair. I'm not responsible for him.'

## Comparison of the Unsafe and Safe Encounters

### Type of Partner

Among the older gay men in Melbourne and the uninfected gay men in Sydney, type of partner distinguished between the unsafe and safe encounters: the partner was more likely to have been a lover in the unsafe encounter than in the safe encounter, and more likely to have been a casual sex partner in the safe encounter than in the unsafe encounter. In the heterosexual sample, the former of these effects was also present, though in much attenuated form (it appeared as a non-significant trend only), while the latter effect was not obtained.

One possible explanation for respondents' going further sexually with a lover than a casual partner is encapsulated in the adage 'Love is blind'. Love and affection may serve to put all other considerations, including any concern about AIDS, into the shade. Another possibility is more pragmatic: one generally knows more about a lover, so that one is more likely to know, or be in a better position to guess, whether or not he/she is HIV-infected. The self-justification data suggest that the second of these possibilities applied more often than the first. Self-justifications having to do with knowledge that the partner was not promiscuous, or knowledge of his/her antibody status, were generally reported more commonly than those relating to romance taking precedence over other concerns.

In the sample of young gay men, type of partner did not distinguish between the unsafe and safe encounters. The proposal that the reasoning behind the partner effect has more to do with knowing the partner than with being in love is consistent with this result. Lovers had generally had that status for a much shorter period of time in the young than in the older gay samples. (Indeed, in the young sample, two-fifths of the relationships with lovers had been in progress for less than three months at the time of the unsafe encounter.) In a relationship that is still relatively new, one may know less about the partner and his history, so the rationale for the partner effect would lose some of its force. The fact that the young gay men's relationships were so new may thus have partially undermined the reasoning responsible for the partner effect.

Effects of type of partner were also not found among the infected gay men in Sydney. In this case, no explanation in terms of the relationships with lovers being very new can be proposed. But if the infected men did not use the strategy of deciding whether to have unprotected intercourse according to whether they were with a lover or a casual partner, they do seem to have used a related strategy. The pattern of results suggests that, for a given type of partner—whether lover or casual—they had been better acquainted with him in the unsafe than in the safe encounter. They were thus more willing to have unprotected intercourse with a partner the closer were their ties to him.

I add a brief warning. It is tempting to conclude from the findings on the partner effect that, for example, the older gay men in Melbourne and the uninfected gay men in Sydney were being extremely discerning when deciding with whom to have and with whom not to have unprotected intercourse. One must not exaggerate the point, however. It is important to remember that, as shown in Table 1, about a quarter of the unsafe encounters in each of these samples had been with a completely anonymous partner.

*Drug and Alcohol Use*

In each sample, the extent to which respondents had been 'stoned' at any stage of the evening, and the quantity of nitrites they had used during sex, did not distinguish between the unsafe and safe encounters. The degree to which respondents had been intoxicated from alcohol failed to distinguish between the encounters in the two Melbourne samples or among the Sydney infected men. Among the Sydney uninfected men and the heterosexual sample, however, intoxication had been greater in the unsafe than in the safe encounter.

In principle, the association between intoxication and the occurrence of unprotected intercourse in these last two samples can be explained in three ways. First, it is possible that alcohol consumption had been used as a deliberate strategy to enable unprotected intercourse to occur. Individuals who wanted unprotected intercourse may have consumed alcohol to give themselves the courage to suggest it to a partner, or in order to provide an excuse—to themselves or others—for their behaviour. Alternatively, alcohol consumption may have helped to produce a desire for unprotected intercourse, either by impairing the ability to think clearly or by increasing sexual arousal. A third possibility is that there was no causal relationship between intoxication and the occurrence of unprotected intercourse, with both being independently caused by a third variable.

Although our data cannot definitively rule out any of these possibilities, the pattern of results suggests that the first explanation is implausible in the case of both samples and that the last explanation is implausible in the case of the heterosexual sample. If respondents deliberately consumed alcohol in order to facilitate unprotected intercourse, one would expect to see evidence of a greater desire for alcohol in the unsafe encounter than the safe encounter. No such effect was found, however: in both samples, neither the desire to have a drink nor the desire to get drunk had been greater in the unsafe encounter. Further, in the Sydney uninfected sample, level of intoxication had been greater in the unsafe encounter even in subsamples of men who had desired unprotected intercourse to exactly the *same* extent in both encounters. At least for these men, their greater intoxication in the unsafe encounter could not have been produced by a greater desire for unprotected intercourse. As regards the 'third variable' explanation, it is hard, in the case of the heterosexual sample, to see what variable could have played this role; while one can propose a number of candidate variables, none distinguished between the unsafe and safe encounters in the way that would be expected if it had, in fact, functioned as a *tertium quid*.

Why might intoxication have been associated with unprotected intercourse among gay men in Sydney but not among gay men in Melbourne? The difference in findings can possibly be attributed to the existence in Sydney, but not in Melbourne, of a gay 'ghetto'. In Sydney, the majority of gay venues are concentrated in one part of a single street and large numbers of gay men live close by; a gay man wanting to go out drinking at a venue can thus simply walk there. In Melbourne, by contrast, a gay man who wants to go drinking at a venue generally has to travel by car, the distances being too great to walk. Because the police are very active in prosecuting drink–drivers, he must either arrange for a friend to act as his driver for the night, or be prepared to hire taxis (which are expensive). Either way, when he wishes to go drinking he needs to plan ahead and take care in a way that his Sydney counterpart does not; he has less freedom to be spontaneous. It is possible that this, in turn, also constrains his sexual behaviour on such occasions, with the result that in Melbourne 'slip-ups' into unsafe sex are less often associated with drinking. It may be added that, in the case of the sample of heterosexual students—among whom intoxication was also associated with unprotected intercourse— conditions like those for the Sydney gay men obtained: the students lived in colleges that were very close to the pubs they frequented.

*Mood*

In all the gay samples, respondents' mood at the start of the evening distinguished between the encounters. However, it did so in opposite ways in the young and the older samples. While the older gay men in Melbourne and the infected and uninfected gay men in Sydney had been in a *better* mood in the unsafe than in the safe encounter, the young gay men had been in a *worse* mood in the unsafe encounter.

In principle, the result for older gay men can be explained in three ways. First, it is possible that being in a good mood contributes causally to the occurrence of unprotected intercourse. It may be that a good mood produces greater confidence about approaching a partner for unsafe sex, over-confidence about the risk involved, a refusal to spoil one's mood by thinking about unpleasant things like AIDS, or greater use of cognitive 'short-cuts.' It is also possible, however, that a good mood is the result, rather than the cause of (anticipated) unprotected intercourse. A man who wants to have unprotected intercourse and expects that this desire will be met later that evening may be put in a good mood by that very expectation. Finally, it is possible that there is in fact no causal relationship between being in a good mood and the occurrence of unprotected intercourse, with the association between them deriving from the fact that both are independently caused by a third variable. Unfortunately, our data do not enable us to choose among these possible explanations.

As regards the result obtained in the case of the young gay men, the first factor that emerged in the factor analysis of their self-justifications had to do with risk-taking in response to a negative mood state. The self-justifications making up this factor suggested that respondents had reacted to the negative mood state by, for example, 'switching off' from the topic of AIDS (or, indeed, from thinking altogether), by telling themselves that the risk of infection was no worse than other risks encountered in the normal course of events, or by deciding to have unprotected intercourse specifically in order to improve their mood. It seems that AIDS educators must view as one of their most important tasks the inculcation in young gay men of non-destructive ways of dealing with emotional problems and negative mood states. Usual mass education techniques—posters, pamphlets and media campaigns—seem unlikely to be very helpful in achieving this aim; the establishment of peer support groups and networks, while necessarily reaching much smaller numbers, may nevertheless prove more useful.

*Communication of Desires Regarding Use/Non-Use of a Condom*

In all the gay samples, desires regarding use/non-use of a condom had more often been communicated verbally in the safe than in the unsafe encounter. It may be that, in a sexual encounter, even mention of a condom helps to make the occurrence of safe sex more likely, by serving as a reminder of the threat from AIDS and thereby promoting a more reflective approach. Alternatively, verbal communication about desires regarding use of a condom may simply be a consequence of, rather than actually change, the pattern of desires: it may just be socially more acceptable for a gay man to tell his partner that he wants to have safe sex than that he does not. To the extent that the first explanation holds, AIDS educators need to encourage explicit communication about desires regarding use of a condom.

## Use of 'Dirty Talk'

The question about the use of 'dirty talk' during sex was not asked in the study of older gay men in Melbourne or the study of heterosexual students. Among the young gay men, and the infected and uninfected Sydney gay men, 'dirty talk' that could have been or was interpreted as an invitation to have unprotected intercourse had occurred more often in the unsafe than the safe encounter. There are a number of ways in which 'dirty talk' could facilitate the occurrence of unprotected intercourse: by heightening sexual arousal; by providing an indirect, socially acceptable means of communicating that one wants to have unprotected intercourse, and thus of finding out whether the partner is also willing; or by raising doubts in the mind of one of the partners about what the other really wants to do, doubts that could lead him to go further than he otherwise would. It is also possible, however, that the use of 'dirty talk' is not related causally to the occurrence of unprotected intercourse, with the association between them arising because both variables independently derive from a third. The desire to be 'raunchy' or 'sleazy'—to flout conventional restraints—might be such a third variable.

## Desire for Excitement

Among the older gay men in Melbourne and the infected gay men in Sydney, the desire for excitement—including, specifically, sexual excitement—had been greater in the unsafe than the safe encounter. It therefore seems important to try to make gay men see safe sex as exciting. Just how this might be achieved, however, is hard to say. Among the heterosexual students, desire for excitement also distinguished between the encounters, but in the *opposite* direction: it had been greater in the safe than the unsafe encounter. It seems that in heterosexual students the desire for excitement operates within very well-defined constraints, being associated with safe rather than unsafe sex.

## Use of Pornography

We included a question on the use of pornographic material that showed or described unprotected intercourse in order to test for the possibility of a modelling effect: such material might conceivably suggest unprotected intercourse to individuals, and lead them to follow suit in their own sexual encounters. In fact, use of pornographic material did not distinguish between the unsafe and safe encounters in any of the samples.

## The Theory of Reasoned Action and AIDS Prevention

In this section I will make some comments regarding the application of the theory of reasoned action to the field of AIDS prevention. More specifically, I will discuss the theory of planned behaviour, Ajzen's (1985) extension of the theory of reasoned action. In the original theory, the occurrence or non-occurrence of a behaviour was predicted from prior intention to perform that behaviour. Ajzen noted that for various reasons such an intention may not in fact be realised. Thus, for example, intentions can change over time, so that a prior intention may no longer hold when the time comes to carry out the behaviour, or the person may not have the time, opportunity, skills, or necessary co-operation from others to perform the behaviour. Ajzen sought to improve the theory's predictive ability by introducing the variable 'perceived behavioural control', a person's estimate of how easy or difficult it would be for him/her actually to perform the behaviour.

Given my interest in how on-line cognitions may differ from off-line cognitions, I am very sympathetic to any theory that even considers possible differences between on-line and off-line intentions to perform a behaviour. Nevertheless, I am dissatisfied with what the theory of planned behaviour actually contributes in this regard.

First, the theory does not put much emphasis on the *processes* whereby intentions change over time. Ajzen does list some of the factors that might cause on-line intentions to differ from off-line intentions; he mentions, for example, the effects of strong emotions, and how the relative salience of the advantages and disadvantages of performing the behaviour may vary as the time to perform it approaches. But the theory does not direct researchers' attention to these factors as worthy of study and analysis in their own right. From Ajzen's perspective, they seem to be important merely as pointers to the insufficiency of the original theory. In effect, their role is simply to justify introducing the construct of perceived behavioural control, the variable that is to be the real focus of attention.

This construct does not seem to me very profound from an explanatory point of view. I readily accept that confidence in one's ability to perform a behaviour should help to *predict* whether one does in fact perform the behaviour. But to what extent can it be said, in any interesting sense, to *explain* whether one performs the behaviour? Confidence in one's ability to perform a behaviour presumably derives, in substantial measure, from one's own past experience with the behaviour (or other, related behaviours): one scrutinises one's past record in performing the behaviour.

That, in turn, however, simply shifts the problem a step, for the question immediately arises of how to explain that past record. It remains unclear how this regress may be escaped. Accordingly, it seems to me that there is more than a touch of tautology in using perceived behavioural control (or, indeed, the related construct of self-efficacy, e.g., Bandura, 1977) as an explanatory construct.

I think, then, that the theory of planned behaviour in fact does very little to explain how intentions can change when the time comes to carry out a behaviour. Ultimately, any gap between on-line and off-line intentions is left with the status just of measurement error; in Ajzen's words, it presents "largely a technical problem" (1985, p.18). The 'meaty' part of the theory remains its explication of off-line intentions.

This defect is likely to be particularly important in the field of AIDS-related behaviour. In our studies we have examined, for each stage of the unsafe encounter, the proportion of respondents who, at that stage, had a desire *specifically for unprotected intercourse* (i.e., the proportion of respondents who wanted unprotected intercourse more than they wanted either intercourse using a condom or non-penetrative sex). Figure 1 presents the relevant data relating to the start of the evening, for respondents in each sample having sex with the types of partner that were listed in Table 1.

It is seen that, in all samples, desire specifically for unprotected intercourse had been appreciably less common among respondents having sex with a casual but not anonymous partner than among those having sex with a lover. In all samples except one (the young gay men), this desire had been either somewhat less common again, or about as common, among those having sex with an anonymous partner. Of course, since this was the unsafe encounter, all these respondents had in fact ended up having unprotected intercourse. If we take 'desire specifically for unprotected intercourse' as a measure of 'intention to have unprotected intercourse' (Fishbein & Stasson, 1990), the data therefore suggest that the temporal relationship between the intention to have unprotected intercourse and the occurrence of unprotected intercourse varies with the type of partner involved: roughly speaking, the closer an individual's partner is to being a lover, the more likely it is that engagement in unprotected intercourse is preceded by an off-line intention to do so.

Is this so only because the closer the partner is to being a lover, the more confident the individual can be, at the start of the evening, that the partner will be *available* for sex later on? (It is very plausible, for example, that an individual is more likely to know that his/her lover will be present later that evening and that sex will occur, than an individual is to know that he/she will meet a suitable casual partner and that sex will occur.) The data in Figure 2 suggest that the effect cannot be explained in this way. The figure presents the same information as Figure 1, but for a point

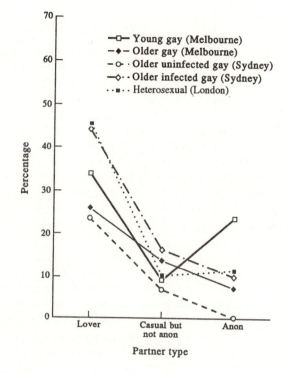

FIG. 1. Percentage specifically desiring unprotected intercourse at the start of the evening in the unsafe encounter, by type of partner.

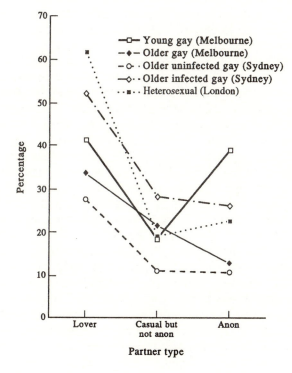

FIG. 2. Percentage specifically desiring unprotected intercourse at the start of sex in the unsafe encounter, by type of partner.

later in time—at the start of sex. It is seen that the pattern of results is not radically different from that in Figure 1. That is, even when sex with the partner has already begun, there is still an effect of type of partner: even at this point, the intention to engage in unprotected intercourse is present much more often when the partner is a lover than when he/she is not.[5]

So an off-line intention to have unprotected intercourse is more likely to precede unprotected intercourse the closer the partner is to being a lover. But, compared to heterosexuals, gay men take a more casual, 'recreational' view of sex: as has already been seen in Table 1, a gay man's partner in unprotected intercourse is far less likely to be a lover and far more likely to be an anonymous partner. It follows that an off-line intention to have unprotected intercourse would precede unprotected intercourse much less often in the population of gay men than in the heterosexual population. That is, in the very population which is by far at greatest risk of contracting HIV—in part, precisely because they take a more casual view of sex—focusing only on off-line intentions is especially unrevealing; it would leave us with a particularly incomplete picture. The same factors (or some of them, at least) which account for the pattern of the epidemic render a theory which fails to explain the gap between on-line and off-line intentions particularly ill-suited to the field.

The theory of planned behaviour's focus on off-line processes, at the expense of what happens on-line, also limits its approach to studying the types of occasion on which people are most likely to end up having unsafe sex. When Fishbein and Middlestadt (1989) recommend the use of 'elicitation surveys' to determine the salient beliefs a population holds about a given behaviour, they emphasise that these surveys need to be extremely specific and detailed. Investigators, they argue, need to survey beliefs held by *particular populations* about *particular behaviours* carried out in *particular contexts*. This point is well taken; indeed, it accords well with the approach adopted in our studies. At the same time, it is clear that the surveys Fishbein and Middlestadt have in mind would assess off-line cognitions only. Situational variables that affect solely on-line cognitions would not be revealed using this methodology. And situational variables that affect behaviour directly, without the mediation of cognitions at all, would also go undetected. Certainly, it is possible that people have off-line awareness of how some situational factors affect them on-line. Type of partner may be one such factor: I think it highly probable that people are generally aware off-line that they would think differently about unprotected intercourse if they were with a lover than if they were with a casual partner. In the case of other variables, by contrast, off-line awareness seems much less likely to be present. For example, it does not seem very probable that older gay men are aware off-line that being in a good mood at the start of a sexual encounter may influence them to have unprotected intercourse. (Indeed, I suspect that they are probably not even aware of this on-line, c.f., Nisbett & Wilson, 1977).

Finally, I am dissatisfied with the direction that the theory of planned behaviour imparts to AIDS education. Its focus on off-line cognitions means that the theory in effect promotes the view that it is these which should be the target of educational intervention—that the aim of AIDS educators should be to modify off-line cognitions. On this model, the prescription for ensuring generalisation to the on-line situation is simply to induce deeper learning—indeed, overlearning—off-line (c.f., Kirschenbaum & Tomarken, 1982). It is conceivable, however, that on-line cognitions are activated via qualitatively different paths to off-line cognitions, so that the 'entry points' for the two are different (see, for example, the 'headed records' model of Morton, Hammersley, & Bekerian, 1985). To the extent that this is so, there may be important limitations to what can be achieved on-line by means of overlearning off-line.

How might AIDS education attempt to overcome this problem? One approach might involve trying to make AIDS education materials evoke real sexual encounters as closely as possible (c.f. Brewin, 1989). Obviously, only certain features of real encounters could be evoked in this way; it would not be possible, for example, to simulate the lack of free information-processing capacity that is hypothesised to characterise real encounters. One could, however, seek to make the education materials sexually very arousing, in order to maximise the chance that they will elicit 'hot' cognitions. In fact, to a considerable degree, AIDS educators have already taken this path. The posters, pamphlets and videos that are employed in AIDS education (particularly AIDS education for gay men) often feature images that are designed to be erotically arousing, so much so, indeed, that it is hard to see what more could be done in this regard.

An alternative strategy, which has so far not been tried in AIDS education, would involve leading individuals to reflect on and evaluate, off-line, the thinking that they employ on-line. In effect, they would be asked to focus on any differences between their on-line and off-line cognitions. To the extent that such differences exist and are recognised, the resulting conflict may be sufficient to forge a link between the two varieties of cognition, so that later, if a particular thought occurs on-line, the fact that it is inadequate (from an off-line perspective) will also be accessed on-line. This may be sufficient to counter or modify its use on-line.

We are currently investigating whether a brief intervention of this type is possible and useful. Our sample consists of gay men who have recently broken their safer sex rules by having unprotected intercourse. The study is taking place over several months, with the men using sexual diaries to record their sexual behaviour throughout. In the intervention phase, the men in the experimental group are asked to think of an unsafe encounter they have had, and to recall and evaluate any self-justifications they employed at the time; their subsequent behaviour is then compared with that of appropriate control groups. At this point it is too early to report any results.

Of course, the proposal that there are important differences between off-line and on-line AIDS-related cognitions remains, at the moment, no more than a plausible hypothesis. To date, there is no direct empirical evidence on the matter. Nevertheless, it seems to me that researchers and educators need to be very much aware that there may indeed be an important gap between off-line and on-line mental processes. (Perhaps it would even be helpful if we started thinking of each individual as actually composed of two distinct individuals: one off-line and one on-line.) In the London Underground, trains often pull up a few inches away from the platform and one constantly hears a recorded warning: 'Mind the gap!' The same advice seems useful in this field.

## Notes

[1]The groups of interest are more accurately described as 'men who have sex with men' and 'those who have sex with the opposite sex,' but I prefer the terms 'gay' and 'heterosexual' as being less clumsy.

[2]Dare I suggest that in the context of AIDS research the distinction might perhaps be better rendered as 'on-loin' vs. 'off-loin'?

[3]Again, we use this term for convenience only; a more accurate description would be 'not knowingly infected.'

[4]We included this introductory phrase in an attempt to make each self-justification listed stand for a range of possible self-justifications with roughly similar meaning. Thus, for example, one self-justification was couched in terms of the notion that, since the partner was very good-looking he/she was unlikely to be infected. We intended this to cover also the related notion that an ugly person is most likely to be infected, and the partner was not ugly. Further, we used the introductory phrase to try to let each self-justification stand also for self-justifications which had been present at the time of the unsafe encounter, but not in the declarative, propositional form employed in the questionnaire/interview (they may, for example, have been present in the form of perceptual images rather than propositions).

[5]It is clear that in Figures 1 and 2, the pattern of results is broken by the sample of young gay men. In this sample, the desire specifically for unprotected intercourse had been present almost as often among those having sex with an anonymous partner as among those having sex with a lover. This is an important—and worrying—finding, but it is not the point I want to emphasise here.

# 14

# Flaws in the Theory of Reasoned Action

SUSAN KIPPAX and JUNE CRAWFORD

*Macquaries University, Sydney, Australia*

This chapter addresses the failure of the theory of reasoned action to give an adequate account of behaviour change, with particular reference to HIV-related behaviour. Our critique of the theory of reasoned action derives from a social constructionist standpoint and, thus, our analysis of the theory's limitations derives from a position *outside* the theory. Our argument is that the theory is bound to fail because it ignores the essentially social nature of human action, in this case, sexual conduct.

The summary statement of Fishbein and Middlestadt (1989) sets the stage for our discussion of the weaknesses in the theory of reasoned action.

> The theory of reasoned action is based on the assumption that humans are reasonable animals who, in deciding what action to take, systematically process and utilise the information available to them. Thus, in the final analysis, changing behaviour is viewed primarily as a matter of changing the cognitive structure underlying the behaviour in question.

The authors go on to stress that "most behaviours can be understood in terms of the same small set of theoretical constructs and psychological processes," which are deemed to be cognitive. These cognitive structures and processes set the stage for an asocial analysis. In the early formulations of the theory, the constructs were beliefs, attitudes and behaviours (Fishbein, 1967a,b). Later, intentions, subjective norms and normative beliefs were added (Ajzen & Fishbein, 1980; Fishbein, 1980; Fishbein & Ajzen, 1975; see Terry *et al.*, this volume). The psychological processes are more difficult to specify but are couched in cognitive terms; that is, they are processes which occur *within* individual minds. The model of the theory of reasoned action indicates that beliefs about salient outcomes of particular behaviours influence attitudes and that beliefs about what salient individuals or groups think influence subjective norms. Intention to act is determined by the relative importance of such beliefs, attitudes

253

and normative considerations, and intention, in turn, determines behaviour unless some external variable, such as lack of control, intervenes.

Similar theories, such as the health belief model (Becker, 1974), have also been applied to AIDS prevention. Variables such as perceived self-efficacy (Bandura, 1977, 1989b), perception of severity of outcome, perception of risk or personal susceptibility (Weinstein, 1984), as well as perceptions of the benefits of behaviour change or risk-reduction have been explored in attempts to improve the predictive power of the theory of reasoned action and other similar cognitive models.

Each of the theories has something to recommend it (especially the theory of reasoned action, because of its inclusion of concepts such as norms, action and reason), but none has been consistently successful in application. Although this chapter does not attempt to review the applications of the models referred to above, we note that a number of authors have commented on their deficiencies in predicting HIV-related behavioural outcomes. Brown, DiClemente and Reynolds (1991) in reviewing the utility of the health belief model, as applied to predicting HIV-related behaviours in samples in the United States, conclude that the model is inadequate. Results such as the almost total lack of relationship between beliefs and any change relating to receptive anal practices among homosexually active men, noted by Kirscht and Joseph (1989), are common. Montgomery *et al.,* (1989), with reference to the same study population, noted that perceived severity of the illness and socio-economic advantage had the most consistently beneficial effect on various measures of behaviour, while little or no beneficial effect was observed for other components of the model.

Salt, Boyle and Ives (1990), in reviewing recent studies investigating the impact of AIDS government campaigns in the United Kingdom, concluded that although there is evidence of increasing public knowledge of HIV and AIDS, there is little if any corresponding change in sexual behaviour. In Australia, Turtle *et al.* (1989) found no relationship between knowledge of HIV transmission and sexual behaviour in a sample of university students. Although these studies are not, in the strict sense, tests of health belief or reasoned action models, they have found little relationship between important predictor variables in these models and behaviour change (see also Warwick *et al.,* this volume).

A number of chapters in this book address these problems and others from *within* the framework of the theory of reasoned action: Chapters 3 and 4 address the problems faced by the theory of reasoned action in its application to HIV-related behaviour, while Chapters 8 and 12 examine extensions to the model. In this chapter we address the question of the theory's adequacy in explaining sexual behaviour change in the context of HIV/AIDS from a position *outside* the model.

## Identifying the Flaws

The major problem for the theory of reasoned action, we believe, is related to a reliance on 'cognitive structure' to explain behaviour change. Our basic argument is that such a reliance means that the theory ignores the connections between individuals, both the interpersonal and social relations in which they act, and the broader social structures which govern social practice. Social relations and structures are important, for without them individual behaviours have no meaning. Action is constituted with reference to *shared* meanings.

Although the theory of reasoned action recognises the importance of social norms and 'significant others,' strategies for including these constructs at the measurement level are limited to a consideration of individual perceptions of these social phenomena. The model then seeks to relate these perceptions to behavioural outcomes; that is, to predict what an individual will do on the basis of individual perceptions, beliefs and so on.

To put the argument rather baldly, we reject the model whereby an individual (or many individuals), on receipt of certain information which is processed in terms of each individual's set of beliefs, evaluations, subjective norms, etc., reaches some decision or intention to act, which, other things being equal, is then acted on. Rather, we maintain that an individual (or many individuals), on receipt of certain information, processes and makes sense of that information in interaction with other individuals. A *common* sense is reached. The model we advocate contends that a person's beliefs, attitudes and understandings are constituted in that person's talk with others and in their joint and coordinated activity. It is in terms of these shared understandings that the person will act. The actions may be intended, that is more or less reasoned and deliberate, or they may be non-deliberate and automatic. Thought (or cognitive activity) may not occur until *after* the behaviour in question has been enacted.

Beliefs, intentions, behaviours, and so on, are thus not solely the product of individual processes. Similarly, change is not necessarily or purely an individual process. We argue that explanation for social change is not to be sought through examining changes in an individual 'piece' of behaviour by an individual person, and then aggregating these pieces across a number of individuals. This approach insufficiently reflects the essentially social nature of human action. Social change may occur through a large number of people individually changing their behaviour in ways similar to each other. But to conceptualise such change as the product of each person's individual cognitive processing of the same or similar information is limited. Such an explanation may be partially successful, but if we are correct in our argument then a social process model which emphasises shared understandings and collective action is a more parsimonious and robust one.

Further, social change may occur in other ways. Social change may be generational; rather than merely being the sum of individual *change* , it may be the taking up of new and different practices by succeeding generations. Or it may result from behaviour change amongst only a small number of persons, provided that such persons are influential in relevant ways. What is needed is a theory or model which will capture both the social processes of change and the social nature of the change itself: a model in which people collectively appropriate and construct new meanings and practices.

In the remainder of this chapter, we use a number of examples from empirical work to illustrate the points in our argument. The empirical work to which we refer has been guided by a social theory of change, and in our discussion we indicate what such a social theory can offer.

## A Social Constructionist Theory of Sexual Practice

It is not an accident that in the dominant discourse of HIV/AIDS research, the social-science contribution is translated as 'behavioural' research. The philosophical individualism that underpins much of mainstream medicine and psychology makes 'the individual' or the piece of 'behaviour' the basic unit of analysis. Combined with abstracted research methods, this produces an elision of history and social process. In policy discourse, the process of elision results in categories such as 'behaviour change as an outcome of intervention programs,' which effectively deny the agency, and especially the collective agency, of groups who are responding to the epidemic among them. In popular discourses, such as media talk about AIDS, the elided history is liable to be replaced by simplistic moral categories, such as the 'innocent victim' and the 'gay plague.'

There have been significant alternatives to individualistic models which have asserted the social character of human sexuality (e.g., Gagnon & Simon, 1973). But the long-term trend to assimilate the study of human sexuality to natural science and medicine, and to treat sexuality as a bundle of discrete 'behaviours' has had a powerful influence on AIDS research in the social sciences. For example, it has been common in survey studies for sexuality to be measured by one, or at best a few, discrete items reporting particular behaviours, with little consideration of the interpersonal and cultural meanings of these actions, their character as social transactions, or their larger social contexts.

We argue that a rational HIV-prevention policy *cannot* only be concerned with the specific practices in which HIV transmission occurs. For human sexuality does not consist of separate, isolated items of behaviour. In real life, a person's sexuality involves a complex of actions, emotions and relationships. Particular practices (such as unprotected anal intercourse) *always* occur in a wider repertoire of sexual and social activities. To change a particular practice requires a reshaping of the wider pattern of sexuality.

The rise of a social constructionist view of sexuality in the last two decades has been important in offering an alternative to positivist sexology. Our approach derives from social constructionism (Bhaskar, 1979; Harré, 1979, 1983; Haug *et al.*, 1987; Shotter, 1984) and, in the context of HIV research, focuses on the way of life in populations and groups where HIV has spread, on the cultural contexts which shape people's understandings of sexuality and their sexual practice, as well as their understandings of HIV, and the interpersonal interactions in which sexual practice is constructed and enacted.

The focus is on practice or collective action, rather than individual action, but the person is not forgotten. Social constructionism is not a structuralist theory which views structure as determining behaviour or practice. Rather, although social constructionism argues that all human action is constituted within the framework of social structures, which both prescribe and proscribe behaviours, it acknowledges that the social structures are not unitary and cohesive but contain contradictions; rules and norms may be and are contested and the social structures may be and are transformed. Agency is central to social constructionism, for without it social structures could not be transformed. It is the intended and unintended consequences of collective human action that reproduce and transform social structures.

Social life is plural and divisive, as well as cohesive. And although individuals' actions are coordinated and meanings are shared, they are also fragmented and contested. Meanings are contested in action and interaction with others, and they are modified and transformed in reflection on past events. People do things in ways which they and others find intelligible, for which they can account, and which make sense, *common* sense. In their appraisal of the situations in which they find themselves (such as an AIDS epidemic), people appropriate new information and question the taken-for-granted. Appropriation is not always passive. It often involves the active negotiation of contradictory messages (only gay men are at risk of HIV, heterosexuals should use condoms for sex), and attempts to resolve the conflict (use condoms only with sexual partners whose sexual history is unknown). As Connell and Dowsett (1992) have argued, we must see sexual activity as inherently social practice, a kind of practice through which living bodies are incorporated into social relations.

In making this analysis we wish to emphasise the variety of possible types of sexuality. Cross-cultural research has documented the range of human sexualities, as in the notable work on homosexuality in Melanesia by Herdt (1981) and in the United Kingdom by Weeks (1977). Most pertinent here are: (a) the sexuality of heterosexuals, both male and female, whose relations are shaped by the powerful 'male sex drive' and 'have/hold' discourses (Hollway, 1984; Kippax, Crawford, Waldby & Benton, 1990); and (b) the sexuality of the Western gay man, whose sexuality is constructed in pleasure and promiscuity as well as deviance (Altman, 1979, 1982; Weeks, 1977, 1987). HIV-prevention information has to be appropriated and safe sexual practice constructed within these prevailing discourses and within the interpersonal relations in which people work and play. Social context and social process are central.

To put all this in a formula, the level of *the social* needs to be reinserted into HIV/AIDS research in a constitutive way. Thus, for instance, 'gay community'[1] *as such* becomes a focus of research, reflection and analysis, not just the 'homosexual individual' or aggregate of homosexual individuals. Similarly, the networks of injecting drug users (one is less willing to speak of a 'community' here), and the underground industry that supports them, appear as a key object of knowledge. We need to research folkways, communication networks, sexual negotiation, etc., to grasp the capacities for sustainable change in specific milieux.

e use the term 'gay community' in preference to 'the gay community' both because we recognise that there are many gay communities and because we use the term in its broader more abstract conceptualisation.

## Flaws in the Theory of Reasoned Action

Our discussion of the weaknesses in the theory of reasoned action is guided by the social constructionist theory outlined above. We shall make reference to much of our own work on the social aspects of the prevention of AIDS (Crawford, Kippax & Tulloch, 1992); in particular to findings from two projects, the social aspects of the prevention of AIDS (SAPA) project, which explored the changing sexual practices of homosexually active men in the context of the AIDS epidemic (described in Kippax, Connell, Dowsett & Crawford, in press), and the heterosexuality and AIDS project (outlined in Waldby, Kippax, & Crawford, 1990).

It is not the case that studies using surveys are necessarily limited to a consideration of individualistic models, even though the data are collected from individuals. Both the SAPA and the heterosexuality and AIDS studies used questionnaire surveys as a method of inquiry. In the SAPA study, for example, we found that we were able to use a survey to great effect. This was because the questionnaire and the data analysis were designed in accordance with the social theory outlined above, and although the theory is quite general, it is one which is specifically social. What this meant in practice was that the questions which were included and the ways in which the analysis proceeded reflected the emphasis on sexual practice rather than on behaviour.

Sexual practice, which was the major focus in our empirical work (referred to above), is socially constructed, relational, situational and culturally specific (Caplan, 1987; Gagnon & Simon, 1973). The major focus of the questionnaire, therefore, was on what people actually did: whole patterns of action rather than isolated behaviours. For example, questions relating to a variety of sexual activities were contextualised with reference to the relationship in which they took place. In addition, instead of asking whether a respondent saw himself as gay community-identified, we measured gay community attachment via sixty questions which addressed practices, such as membership of gay organisations, frequency of outings with gay friends and so on. We asked about patterns of social interaction, about media use, about the social and interpersonal contexts of sexual practice. In the light of what we now know, one particularly important distinction we made was between 'regular' and 'casual' sexual partners.

We included some questions in the questionnaire which were at an individualistic level, inasmuch as they provided measures of attitudes, judgments of the safety of sexual practices and knowledge. In the analysis, however, these 'cognitive' measures were interpreted with reference to the social structures, such as ease of access to information and the degree and nature of attachment to gay communities, and they were related to measures of social practice and change. On the whole, our analysis confirmed that sexual practice, both safe and unsafe, could be best understood in terms of social and cultural variables, such as different kinds of attachment to the gay community. The type or nature of sexual relationship between the two (or more) people involved was also of prime importance.

In the heterosexuality and AIDS project, our questionnaire and the analysis were more traditional, although we maintained the distinction between regular and casual partners. In this and the SAPA projects, we supplemented the questionnaire data with in-depth interviews and group discussions, which were designed to enable a focus on social processes.

We consider that there are a number of weaknesses in the theory of reasoned action that are inter-related, but we shall discuss them initially as though they were independent of each other. The first problem concerns the individualistic bias of the model. Secondly, we discuss the linearity of the model particularly in relation to the assumed direction of causality. We then take issue with the implicit 'rationality' of the model, and what, in the theory of reasoned action, appears to be a confounding of rationality with choice and a confounding of agency with deliberation. As well as using our own work to illustrate our discussion of weaknesses in the theory of reasoned action, we also refer to the work of authors who have mounted criticisms of the theory. In particular, we refer to the work of Ingham and his colleagues (Ingham, 1991; Ingham & Memon, 1990; Ingham,

Woodcock & Stenner, 1992). The work of Gagnon (1988), Prieur (1990) and Rugg, O'Reilly and Galavotti (1990) provides further evidence of problems presented by the theoretical constructs of or related to 'reasoned action.'

## Individualistic Bias

The individualism of the theory of reasoned action is apparent in the way in which the constructs 'belief,' 'subjective norm' and 'action' are conceptualised and measured.

### Beliefs

In applications of the theory of reasoned action, beliefs about HIV and AIDS are treated as though they were acquired without reference to other beliefs already held by oneself or by others and as though they were separate from behaviour (which it is assumed beliefs determine, at least in part). They are often measured as discrete bits of information unrelated to context, either cultural, social or interpersonal, instead of being conceptualised as grounded in social and cultural representations, and in action.

What these models appear to ignore is that information is not simply acquired in a passive way, but the meanings are contested and debated; the information may be modified, transformed and used selectively, to make it fit with previous shared understandings. We illustrate this with an example from the SAPA project (Kippax, Crawford, Bond et al., 1990; Kippax et al., 1992).

Homosexually active men interviewed in 1986 and 1987 had a reasonably accurate knowledge of safe and unsafe sexual practices with reference to HIV transmission. To our initial surprise, the items which measured accuracy of that knowledge or 'beliefs about HIV infection' formed not one but two distinct sets: one which measured the accuracy of information with regard to safe sexual practice, and another which measured the accuracy of knowledge with regard to unsafe sexual practice. The two scales were negatively correlated ($r = -0.51$); there were a large number of men who, at one and the same time, were both reasonably well informed about unsafe practices and not very well informed about safe practices or vice versa.

An examination of the data revealed that social factors such as place of residence, attachment to gay communities, identification with at-risk populations, and sexual practice itself mediated the ways in which the HIV-prevention information was received and appropriated. The men's immediate social relations, which framed their social and sexual practice, were extremely important in the building of their beliefs about HIV transmission, a point made also by Prieur (1990) in regard to her work with Norwegian gay men. In the SAPA study, men with a strong attachment to the Sydney gay community, as measured by their involvement in it (assessed in terms of sexual, social, cultural and political practices), and who lived in inner Sydney knew what they could practise safely, while men unattached to the gay community and who lived in extra-metropolitan areas had a more accurate knowledge of unsafe practice. The men's judgments were grounded in the understandings and expectations which they shared with men like themselves. Men who had regular partners as well as casual relationships were more likely than men in monogamous relationships to have an accurate knowledge of safe sexual practice. Their judgments were constituted in their talk and interactions with others. The process is a social one; it is not purely cognitive.

## Subjective Norms

The theory of reasoned action does include a normative component which, according to the theory, influences action. But norms in the theory are reduced to cognitions, subjective norms, and in applications of the theory, become reduced to another type of belief. Their connection with the social is lost, and the same criticisms discussed above still apply.

Further, there appears to be little recognition in the theory that normative beliefs are part of the taken-for-granted reality of cultural values and ideologies. The theory of reasoned action includes an evaluative component in its model, but the link between individual attitudes and cultural values and discourses is at best weak. We illustrate the conceptual and methodological importance of linking normative beliefs to cultural values, using the practice of condom use as an example.

Norms governing condom use are related to broader social and cultural values such as those of fidelity and romance, and honesty and concern for others. Messages about the importance of condom use will be appropriated differently by young gay men living in inner Sydney close to the AIDS epicentre, who have had many casual sexual partners, and by young heterosexual men living in a country town, who have been in one steady relationship for six months, particularly if the relationship is their first. For the gay men, condoms may signify a concern for self and others; for the heterosexual, infidelity. Condom use is intelligible only with reference to broader social and cultural values. Within a regular relationship, the introduction of a condom is likely to signify heterosexual men's infidelity or their lack of trust in their partner's fidelity, *because* of the underlying 'have/hold' discourse of 'coupledom.' Within a casual gay encounter, a condom is likely to signify care for self and others, *because* condom use is understood within the context of an HIV-prevention strategy.

The actions are different, even though the behaviour 'condom use' is the same. The practice of condom use is governed by cultural values. Further, to speak of 'condom use' as though it were merely an individual action is misleading. Meanings are shared and derive from cultural values and norms governing sexual practices, such as condom use, which are situated within discourses of sexuality. Normative rules are not fixed; they differ across sub-cultural groups and are modified by collective action. Again, the social process cannot be captured by a model such as the theory of reasoned action, which encourages measures of subjective, that is, individual cognitive processes.

### Action/Behaviour

The issue here is similar to the ones discussed above. Although the theory of reasoned action recognises the importance of action as opposed to behaviour, action is conceptualised at the individual level. Condom use, for example, is a collective practice, that is intelligible only with reference to prevailing normative structures as discussed above, which in turn cannot be understood without reference to the discourses governing sexuality in relation to contraception and HIV/AIDS. Actions are not the outcome of individual reflection, but are constituted in the shared meanings negotiated in interactions with others; that is, they exemplify a collective practice.

Again we illustrate this point with reference to the SAPA project and the heterosexuality and AIDS project (Crawford, Turtle & Kippax, 1990; Kippax, 1992; Kippax, Crawford, Davis, Rodden & Dowsett, 1993). First we describe four HIV-related strategies adopted by homosexually active men and by heterosexuals, as follows:

(A) Changes to sexual practice: Condom use, avoidance of anal penetrative sex and the adoption of safer forms of sexual expression.

(B) Changes to nature/type of sexual relationships: Reduction in the number of casual partners, reliance on 'regular' partner/s or monogamy.

(C) Negotiated safety: Reliance on partner's sexual and drug use history, reliance on concordance of negative HIV-antibody status.

(D) Avoidance: Avoidance of certain sorts of partners, selection of 'clean' partners.

Some of the above strategies have been advocated in national and targeted educational campaigns; others have been contained in newspaper and other media presentations and reports; and still others have been created by men and women over time in response to their own experience. What we have documented in our research is *part* of a distinctive, diverse and changing response to HIV. In their attempts to make sense out of what was happening to themselves, to their acquaintances, friends, lovers, to their social groups and communities, men and women modified and transformed their sexual practice.

Strategies B and A (in that order) were the ones most strongly endorsed by the heterosexuals we studied. Heterosexual men, particularly those young men who were relatively sexually inexperienced, were also likely to endorse strategy D. In general, we found that sexually inexperienced men and women were more likely to turn to strategy B than A, a finding confirmed by Rosenthal, Moore and Brumen (1990) in Australia, Maticka-Tyndale (1991) in the United States and Abrams, Abraham, Spears and Marks (1990) in the United Kingdom. Heterosexuals, to a very large degree, rely on the safety and trustworthiness of their regular partner. The responses of adolescents indicate that, although they believe sex is risky and that their peers are sexually active, they seem convinced that none of their friends or potential partners could be HIV seropositive. The 'have/hold' discourse of coupledom makes it extremely difficult, although not impossible, to do otherwise. Some heterosexuals, however, have adopted strategy A, in particular condom use, notably those 18-years-old and under. There is an indication that norms governing condom use may be changing, at least for some young heterosexuals.

Homosexually active men choose amongst the first three strategies. The social relations in which the men live govern, to a large degree, the choices that are open to them. The contexts of their relationships, too, play an important role. A 'safe sex' culture has developed; gay men with some attachment to and involvement with gay communities have to explain why there are *no* condoms if they are having anal intercourse, not why they use condoms. They may choose to negotiate unprotected anal intercourse within a concordant serostatus relationship, but in their casual sexual encounters these men will either refrain from anal intercourse or use a condom. Men not attached to gay communities, on the other hand, are more likely to rely on the safety of their regular partner, avoid anal intercourse or rely on strategy D. The social relations in which they engage in homosexual practice are very different from those men attached to gay communities. The context, both interpersonal and social, of sexual activity is central to an understanding of sexual practice and its change. It is in these contexts that the meanings that constitute safe sex are negotiated, debated and appropriated (Gold, this volume).

So although the theory of reasoned action would probably predict that gay community attached men, for example, would have different beliefs, evaluations, norms, intentions (we take up the issue of intention later in the chapter) and would act differently from either non gay community attached men or heterosexual men, it cannot give an adequate account of why. The theory of reasoned action ignores social processes by reducing them to cognitive processes. This may account for the failure of applications of the theory. The social is hidden, and if the social is not explicitly built into any application, it will undermine it.

## *The Linearity of the Model*

It should be clear from the above, that we argue that norms and beliefs do not necessarily precede nor determine behaviour or action, such as condom use. The shaping of the beliefs, the arriving at new understandings and new meanings, is likely to proceed at the same time as the condom use behaviour. Meanings which modify normative beliefs are produced intersubjectively, in the talk and actions that take place between people, and within the discourses which govern social relations.

The dynamic nature of belief and norm formation and the intimate connection between belief and norm, on the one hand, and practice on the other, are not adequately captured by the theory of reasoned action. Norms are shared expectations which signal the appropriate forms of behaviour for members of a group; they proscribe and prescribe behaviour. They have two functions: the sharing of joint frames of reference by group members; and the enabling of action.

Again we refer to the SAPA project, which documented the very close correspondence between judgments of safety with reference to a number of practices and the enactment of that same practice (Kippax, Crawford, Bond *et al.,* 1990). There was a general tendency amongst the men to judge practices in which one engages as safe and those not practised as unsafe. This may be a function of knowledge leading to practice, but the accumulated findings of our research suggest that the relationship works in both directions. Changing cognitive structures does not necessarily lead to changes in behaviour, the equation often works in the opposite direction.

This interconnectedness between belief and action is recognised by extension to the theory of reasoned action in terms of the impact of past behaviour on present behaviour (see Kashima & Gallois, this volume). Past behaviour has been found to be a better predictor of present sexual behaviour than knowledge, attitudes, social norms or in some cases intentions, as Gallois, Kashima *et al.,* (1992) among others have noted. But when does behaviour become 'past' or 'present'? If, for example, unprotected penetrative sex is widely practised and 'taken-for-granted,' it makes no sense to treat it as though it were some discrete past behaviour of an individual.

A final problem which is associated with the assumption of linearity concerns the nature of change. Linearity denies contradiction and conflict. In terms of the theory of reasoned action, change is not problematic. There is a dynamic interplay between practice, beliefs and normative structures that the theory of reasoned action avoids. People act in ways which conform to the normative structures, and these same structures imbue their actions with meaning. Many actions are not deliberate and are not reflected on—they are enacted as part of the taken-for-granted reality. Some actions, however, are deliberate and are reflected on, particularly in the context of something new, unfamiliar or problematic. New information, about HIV for example, has to be accommodated and the meanings negotiated and re-negotiated through talk, action and interaction, until common meanings are arrived at which render changes intelligible. This process is not necessarily achieved without conflict and contradiction. For some it will make no sense to change their sexual practice, for others a new practice, safe sex, will emerge as beliefs and norms are modified and restructured. Any measure of change which does not and can not recognise and acknowledge the dynamic nature of information appropriation will fail to account for the differing and varied responses of people.

The links between beliefs, norms and behaviour or action are *not* direct, but complex and multi-layered. Nor are the links between beliefs, norms and action rational, in the sense used in the theory of reasoned action.

### Rationality and Choice

There are three issues here. The first concerns the *asocial* account of rationality; the second the confounding of rationality and choice; while the third addresses the question of conscious deliberation with reference to agency. In the theory of reasoned action there is a confusion between rationality, choice, agency and deliberation.

### Abstracted Logic

As Ingham *et al.* (1992) point out, the assumption that any links among belief, norms and behaviour should be rational is not a sensible one, particularly with respect to sexual behaviour. That is not to say that sexual behaviour is necessarily irrational, but rather to claim that rationality is not something that can be abstracted from culture. Ingham *et al.* (1992) refer to seven impediments which "intervene between what many young people 'know' and their willingness and/or ability to act on such knowledge." Siegel and Gibson (1988) mount a similar argument with respect to barriers to the modification of sexual practice. In other words, what may be construed by an HIV/AIDS educator as irrational behaviour may not appear as such to an adolescent trying to make sense out of the conflicting demands on him/her.

The seven impediments that Ingham *et al.* (1992) list are perceived invulnerability, range of understandings of terminologies, positive reasons for 'non-rationality,' external and internal pressures, ideologies and power, the mystique of sexual behaviour, and negotiation and joint decision-making. There is some attempt in the theory of reasoned action model to deal with some of these, for example invulnerability (or susceptibility) in terms of the 'role of external variables' (see Fishbein & Middlestadt,

1989). The theory also deals with external events which prevent the person from doing what s/he intends by distinguishing action from intention (see below). Nevertheless the theory cannot deal with the main point that rationality itself is culture-bound. It may be rational, from the point of view of the young man we introduced in an example earlier, not to use a condom when having sex with his regular partner. His understandings of the context of their sexual activity, his reputation, his considerations with respect her reputation, are all important. As Ingham *et al.* (1992) conclude: "... people can *choose* on what basis they will make decisions— always subject to (often powerful) constraints." The bases of the choice are the social relations in which the young people's sexuality is enacted and in which they may be asked to give an account of, or explanation for, their sexual behaviour. The social contexts in which such accounting or warranting takes place, as well as the nature of what is accounted for, govern the extent to which 'rationality' is an acceptable justification.

Although the theory of reasoned action acknowledges that 'reasoned' means 'rational' from the person's own point of view, no account can be given of the processes by which the person arrives at his/her reasons for action, except in cognitive terms. There is no recognition that the reasoning is fundamentally a social process.

## *Choice*

There is a sense in the theory of reasoned action that rationality has been confused with choice. In the above discussion, there are reasons for action (and it is this that constitutes agency), and the choices made are based on the reasoning. It is, however, possible for agents to act in opposition to their reasoning, that is, to choose to act irrationally (as defined in their own terms). Taylor (1977) refers to this as the strong sense of agency. There is choice but no rationality, something that is not atypical in sexual encounters.

## *Deliberation and reflection*

Finally, many sexual episodes take place without forethought and decision-making, at least at the conscious level. In other words, as has been noted above, action may precede thought and intention. There may be no conscious deliberation, no intention to act in a certain way. Such actions, and they are actions, may be reflected on afterwards and accounted for, but not consciously planned. The theory of reasoned action appears to assume that cognitions determine behaviour and that actions are dependent on intentions; many actions are habitual and are not the result of deliberate reflection and reasoning, and many are spontaneous.

The details of one's own sexual activity are seldom the subject of discussion. Phrases such as 'swept off my feet' and 'I don't know how it happened' are common. The very rationality of the theory of reasoned action is at odds with cultural meanings of sexuality as something mysterious and impulsive.

## *Constraints on Action*

The above discussion of the weaknesses of the theory of reasoned action has not addressed the fact that sex, in most of its forms, takes place between two people. There is joint decision-making, something that increases complexity and threatens the predictive power of the model. The inclusion of 'intention' as a construct in the theory of reasoned action allows for the effect of external variables, such as lack of freedom, to intervene between intention to act and behaviour. In this sense, the model allows for constraints on action, but again in a simplistic fashion. In general, the theory is unable to deal with the social context, at either the interpersonal or collective levels.

## Conclusions

The theory of reasoned action, on the basis of the above arguments, is not an appropriate one in the context of sexual practice—nor, we believe, in other contexts. Our major point is that the theory is essentially *asocial* , and it is this aspect of the theory that makes it unfit. This is not a trivial argument in the sense that we have simply shifted the grounds of the debate from cognitive to social psychology; rather we have argued that the behaviour in question, sexual behaviour, cannot be adequately understood from a cognitive point of view. We believe that the theory has fundamental flaws which will severely restrict its application.

It is true that the theory of reasoned action, unlike some others to which it bears a number of similarities, includes norms in its model. It does not, however, adequately account for the normative constitution of practice, nor the way in which actions reproduce those same normative structures (see Bhaskar, 1979). Norms are not cognitions and cannot be reduced to some sort of internalised beliefs. They are not to be found in human minds but rather in their talk, in their accounting for and warranting of their actions and in their (usually very accurate) interpretations of the accounting and warranting of others. Nor is it enough to gesture towards the social as something outside the person, a context, in which the 'cognising' individual behaves or acts. The resolution of this dilemma does not lie in placing the norms inside the person's head, so to speak, nor in conceptualising the norms as a 'social frame,' lying outside the person and independent of practice. Rather the solution rests in recognising the dynamic interplay between them; an account of social process is necessary.

In the theory of reasoned action, we find 'information' that is rather mysteriously absorbed or acquired via the operation of cognitive processes; the constructs—belief, norm, attitude and intention—playing a crucial role. The introduction of a notion of action and the recognition of agency, decision-making and choice is to be applauded, but notions of agency and choice become confused with rationality. People act within and make choices from amongst the socially produced possibilities open to them and in terms of what makes sense to them and to others. So, although we agree that agency is central to an understanding of behaviour and its modification and change, action is best understood in the context of collective practice.

The individualist perspective of the theory of reasoned action leaves one in a very uncomfortable position. In attempts to improve the predictive power of the model, more and more variables, exceptions and qualifiers are added. In one sense this move is inevitable. If human action is conceived of as individual and explicable in terms of cognitive structures and processes then, in order to predict it, a detailed history is required. This is because action, by definition, is meaningful. As meaning is constituted in the intersubjective realm in interaction, any application of a theory that relies on a cognitive explanation must capture and detail all individual appropriations of meaning. For example, an explanation of the action 'condom use' will require a description of all the thoughts (cognitions) deriving from past behaviour, interactions, talk and so on, which led to its use on each occasion. Such a detailed account-gathering may be possible (although it is extremely doubtful that agents can always give a complete account of their actions) but it is time consuming and, we believe, impossible to capture adequately using a survey methodology.

A theoretical framework which treats actions as the outcome of individual processes is constrained to seek explanation in either individual minds or bodily responses. An action such as condom use may be *partly* explained by reference to beliefs and judgments and subjective norms, and this may account for the partial success of the theory of reasoned action. But the processes which form and modify these beliefs, etc., are not cognitive. As we have argued above, such beliefs are formed and judgments made in talk and coordinated activity. The processes which underpin behaviour change lie outside the individual; to be more correct between persons. If social process and collective practice are acknowledged, then a small set of theoretical constructs and psychological and social processes might succeed where the theory of reasoned action has failed.

## *Application*

The significance of such a social conceptualisation of behaviour change or changing practice in the context of public health lies in the political and educational implications inherent in it. Attention is focused on the community, on practice, and *not* on the individual or aggregates of individuals and their individual actions. The field of AIDS/HIV research was colonised from the start by medical discourse—a discourse of 'cause' and 'cure', of 'prevention' and 'treatment', of 'intervention', 'monitoring', 'risk groups', 'risk categories' and so on. Had the question of *social action* been dominant from the start, we might have had a discourse derived from sociology, adult education and community activism instead of or, at least as well as, education derived from cognitive psychology. We might be talking about 'needs analysis', 'curriculum', 'empowerment', 'networking', 'mobilisation', 'reflexivity.' Perhaps we should make an effort now to change the vocabulary of AIDS-talk, or at least to set this discourse alongside the medical or psychological language.

There is a need to continue to direct attention away from traditional public health models which focus on individuals, and to strengthen the focus on public health models which stress collective responsibility. In the non-traditional public health models there is a focus on the promotion of health through the re-structuring of social norms in ways which are relevant to the members of the communities and groups. A collective response enables safe sexual practice by turning such practice into what is taken-for-granted. It is then that it becomes intelligible and sensible.

# Epilogue

CYNTHIA GALLOIS, MALCOLM MCCAMISH, and DEBORAH TERRY

*The University of Queensland, Brisbane, Australia*

The preceding chapters present a plethora of results, although most results give support to the theory of reasoned action. In addition, they include a number of competing explanations and theoretical viewpoints, in their focus on the status of the theory of reasoned action in the area of safer sex. Three issues which have appeared to us as repeating themes across the chapters are the importance of normative influences on sexual behaviour, the need to measure attitudes, norms, intentions, and behaviour appropriately in the area of safer sex, and the relative merit of the social as compared to the psychological level of explanation. We will not repeat the arguments made earlier, but we will draw some general conclusions about each of these issues in turn.

## The Importance of Norms in Predicting Sexual Behaviour

When the research presented in this book is taken as a whole, probably the most striking result is the strong and pervasive influence of norms on safer sexual behaviour. The large majority of studies reported and reviewed have revealed norms as significant predictors of intention, and intention as the major (often the only) predictor of behaviour. Indeed, those authors in the book who have criticised the theory of reasoned action most forcefully have in general asked for more emphasis to be placed on the social, or normative, aspects of HIV/AIDS and safer sex. Certainly, they have justification for this, given the importance of norms and normative pressure in predicting intention. In addition, their concerns are shared by those authors who have extended the theories of reasoned action and planned behaviour, in that most extensions have involved the addition of new normative components: behavioural norm, partner norm, and the like.

Even when subjective norm and attitude toward a behaviour are considered as the only proximal predictors of intention, it is important for the theory of reasoned action to make predictions about the relative impact of these variables on intention, for different types of intended behaviour. Fishbein and Middlestadt (1989) allude to this need when they suggest that attitude is likely to be a more important predictor of intention for some behaviours and some groups, while norms are more salient for others. Middlestadt and Fishbein (1990), in fact, found that the relative importance of attitude and subjective norm about condom use varied as a function of sexual experience. Ajzen (1991) has made the same point about behavioural control; namely, that control is likely to be an important predictor of intention and behaviour for some but not all behaviours. Neither Fishbein and Middlestadt nor Ajzen, however, has made a thorough systematic effort to specify theoretically the behaviours or contexts where one variable or another is likely to be more important. As a result, when the relative importance of attitudes and subjective norms is left to be determined empirically, the theories are open to the criticism that they are not falsifiable (see Rigby *et al.*, this volume; thanks to Ken Rigby for his comments on this point).

If we think about the cooperative nature of sexual behaviour, it is easy to see this behaviour as under normative more than attitudinal influence. Unlike behaviours such as losing weight or even taking the contraceptive pill, changing the behaviour that takes place during a sexual encounter requires at least the tacit agreement of another person. In addition, an actor cannot use a condom or engage in only non-penetrative sex without the knowledge of at least one other person. Indeed, the partner as a normative influence appears to be central to sexual behaviour. Many studies have shown that pleasing the partner and intimacy with the partner are important benefits of sex, and that doing something the partner does not like is an important cost. It is quite likely that pleasing the partner is more important to sexual practice for many people than even individual pleasure. It is also not surprising that partner norm emerged as a very important predictor of the intention to use a condom in a number of studies reviewed in this book. Research on the impact of partner norm is still in its early stages, but it seems to be a very fruitful area of investigation for the prediction of safer sexual behaviour.

In addition to the partner, friends and peers are very salient to the intention to practice safer or unsafe sex. Peers are an important source of influence about sex for young people. Peer support has also proved central to the change to safer sex among gay men, to the extent that the knowledge base, attitudes, norms, intentions and practices of homosexual men are often differentiated on the basis of the men's identification with a gay community. Peer education has been successful in promoting safer sex among many groups of gay men, and the concept has more recently been extended to young heterosexuals. These results suggest that normative pressure from peers may be more influential than individual attitudes on sexual practice. Whether this normative pressure is best conceptualised in terms of behavioural norms, as some researchers have suggested, or whether it is entirely mediated through the subjective norm, as Fishbein and his colleagues have maintained, is still an open question.

All this may lead to the conclusion that only norms are influential in the prediction of sexual behaviour, yet clearly this is not the case. Attitudes were significant predictors of intentions in most of the studies in this book (as well as in other research on sexual behaviour); in some cases, they were more powerful predictors than subjective norms. One way of understanding this situation is to invoke once more the impact of partner norm. As Kashima and Gallois (this volume) point out, partner norm is a predictor of attitude; sometimes, it is a better predictor of attitude than even the belief-based measure of attitude. The partner's views may well determine to a large extent what is seen as pleasant and unpleasant in a sexual encounter; in fact, as the research presented here shows, the partner is inextricably tied up in the costs and benefits of sex, safe or unsafe. Again, the impact of partner norm shows how important it is to explore in detail the role of the partner in determining attitudes, norms, and intentions about sexual behaviour, and not simply to theorise this person as just another, albeit a very important, significant other.

## Measuring Behaviour and its Predictors Appropriately

A second issue to emerge from the chapters in this book involves the measurement of attitude, norm, intention, and behaviour. As we noted in Chapter 1, the theory of reasoned action claims that attitudes and norms about a particular behaviour are the major predictors of the intention to perform that behaviour, which in turn is the most important predictor of actual performance. Thus, it is essential that all measures refer to a specific behaviour, and that the behaviour is the same throughout; there must be compatibility across measures (see McLaws *et al.*, this volume, for an example). If compatibility and specificity are not present, the level of prediction is much lower.

Unfortunately, it is very easy in research on safer sex to lose sight of the behaviour under study. Researchers are usually motivated to examine condom use, for example, for purposes of prevention of HIV or other STDs. For subjects, on the other hand, prevention may not be the most important reason, or even an important reason, for condom use; the need for contraception, or the partner involved (e.g., regular or casual), may be much more salient. If the reason for condom use is to be examined, it must be measured at all levels: attitude, subjective norm, intention, and indeed behaviour. On the other hand, if condom use (reason unspecified) is the behaviour in question for some measures, it should be the behaviour for all measures. Similarly, type of partner, time, and so forth, must be specified throughout or not at all. Some of the contradictory findings reported in different chapters in this book may well have resulted from differences in specificity of measures, compatibility, or both (e.g., compare Nucifora *et al.*, this volume; Moore *et al.*, this volume).

Although they may present problems, the principles of specificity and compatibility also open up possibilities for research. For example, it may be possible to test subtly different behaviours in the area of safer sex, and to determine the most salient influences on each one. To continue the example in the previous paragraph, condom use for HIV prevention may have different predictors, especially at the level of belief-based measures of attitude and subjective norm, than condom use for contraception (see Ross & McLaws, this volume). In addition, the extent of perceived control over the behaviour may vary with the reason for it; a young woman, for example, may find it much easier to insist on condoms for contraception than for prevention of STDs. These possibilities are already acknowledged tacitly in current safer sex education programmes, which stress the value of condom use for all three of the reasons above. Such programmes can only be enhanced by research which systematically tests these predictions.

One important behaviour that receives surprisingly little consideration is the *change* to safer sex. None of the studies reported in this book examined this behaviour. One likely reason is that it is difficult to gain access to sexual intentions and behaviour at all, much less to distinguish between those who change to safer behaviour, those who maintain it, and those who do not practice it (there has been some research on relapse, or the change from safer to unsafe sex, but this research has not tended to use TRA). Nevertheless, the conceptual structure of the theories of reasoned action and planned behaviour provide a basis for the examination of behaviour change, and change has been studied for other behaviours. To do this, however, researchers must come to grips with the status of past sexual behaviour and its impact on present and future beliefs and behaviour (see Kippax & Crawford, this volume).

### Consideration of the Population under Study

One aspect of appropriate measurement involves consideration of the special features of different social groups with respect to sexual behaviour. Nearly every author in this book has commented on the differences between groups, whether they are men and women, heterosexuals and homosexuals, members of different ethnic groups or social classes, adolescents and adults, or others, in sexual practices, attitudes, norms, risk evaluations, and even language and jargon. Thus, a questionnaire or a dependent variable that is very appropriate to one group may be irrelevant or inappropriate to another.

A strength of the theory of reasoned action is its recognition of differences across groups and its capacity to incorporate these differences into a predictive model. To achieve this objective, however, researchers must be prepared to do pilot work on the targeted group. Many chapters in this book show the benefits of pilot work of this kind. Too often, however, pilot work is not done, and researchers simply rely on previously-developed questionnaires or their own intuitions. Not surprisingly, the results of such research tend to be uninformative.

In the context of safer sex, there is still much room for research based on TRA/TPB that takes up the specific characteristics of a target group. For example, there have been few studies of the intention to have non-penetrative sex among gay men or among adolescent heterosexuals. There have also been few studies examining the intention to have unsafe sex and its implications for behaviour, even though this behaviour is acknowledged as an important issue for gay men (see Gold, this volume). Such research has educational implications, as well as providing further tests of TRA and TPB.

There may be a need to extend the variables in a predictive model based on TRA for a particular population. Variables such as behavioural norm and perceived susceptibility are usually consigned by the theory to the role of external variables, whose influence on intention and behaviour is mediated by attitudes or subjective norms. It is important to check this mediation hypothesis for the case of safer sex among particular groups of people. In addition, even if the influence of external variables is mediated by TRA variables, an understanding of this influence is still very important for HIV education programmes, which may benefit from addressing the things that influence attitudes and norms.

## Social versus Individual Level of Prediction

A final issue to emerge from the chapters in this book concerns a metatheoretical criticism: that TRA takes insufficient account of social forces and influences in its account of behaviour prediction. TRA and its extensions represent a theory of behaviour prediction at the individual, not the social level. Thus, by definition, the theory cannot provide an explanation of the ways in which meaning, attitudes, values and the like are determined at the collective level.

This is not to imply that explanation at the social level is not important for the development of both policy and education in the area of HIV/AIDS. Clearly, for policy to be adequate, an understanding of cultural meanings, values and priorities is essential. Educators, in addition, must be aware of the language and discourse, attitudes, and norms, that lead a group of people to be receptive to an appeal for social change (such as a change to safer sex) or to resist it. Without such understanding at the social level, the prediction of individual behaviour loses much of its interest.

As well as an understanding of culture, however, we must also understand the influences on individual behaviour, for it is individuals and couples who ultimately do or do not adopt safer sexual practices. Individual people interpret the norms and values around them, and their perceptions determine much of their own behaviour. The methodology appropriate for an understanding of culture, such as ethnography, is not as useful for understanding individual behaviour. Therefore, in addition to theory and methodology at the social level, it is important to develop theory at the individual level which is powerful in predicting behaviour and which is flexible enough to take account of cultural and social differences. TRA and TPB offer this capacity (see Kashima & Gallois, this volume).

## Conclusion

In this book, we hope to have given an account of the strengths of the theory of reasoned action, as well as some of the problems connected with it, in the prediction and understanding of safer sex. We hope also that we have represented the active research scene in Australian social psychology in the area of HIV prevention. The authors in this book differ in their assessment of TRA; this is a debate that will not be settled soon. It is worth repeating, however, that no theory can explain everything, and that TRA, like every theory, must be evaluated in terms of what it sets out to do.

As the research presented here attests, the performance of TRA and TPB in the prediction of safer sex behaviour is impressive. Intention is a strong predictor of behaviour in nearly every instance, and attitudes and norms are salient predictors of intention. Nonetheless, a number of extra variables have been suggested as important in predicting and explaining safer sexual behaviour. It is in the replication of research like this, not in the results of one or a few studies, that the importance of new variables, as well as the relative importance of attitudes, norms, and behavioural control, will ultimately be evaluated. The establishment of robust research results is also essential for educators in the development of programmes promoting safer sex. It is the appearance of such results that will establish the contribution of TRA as a theory for the prediction of safer sexual behaviour.

# References

Abbott, S. (1988). AIDS and young women. *The Bulletin of the National Clearinghouse for Youth Studies*, **7**, 38–41.

Abelson, R. P. (1972). Are attitudes necessary? In B. T. King and E. McGinnies (Eds.), *Attitudes, conflict, and social change*. N.Y.: Academic Press.

Abelson, R. P. (1982). Three modes of attitude–behavior consistency. In M. P. Zanna, E. T. Higgins, & C. P. Herman (Eds.), *Consistency in social behavior* (pp. 131–146). Hillsdale, NJ: Lawrence Erlbaum.

Abrams, D., Abraham, C., Spears, R., & Marks, D. (1990). AIDS invulnerability: Relationships, sexual behaviour and attitudes among 16- to 19-year-olds. In P. Aggleton, P. Davies, & G. Hart (Eds.), *AIDS: Individual, cultural and policy dimensions*. London: The Falmer Press.

Abramson, J. H. (1984). *Survey methods in community medicine: An introduction to epidemiological and evaluative studies*. Melbourne: Churchill Livingston.

Adib, S. M., Joseph, J. G., Ostrow, D. G., & James, S. A. (1991b). Predictors of relapse in sexual practices among homosexual men. *AIDS Education and Prevention*, **3**, 293–304.

Adib, S. M., Joseph, J. G., Ostrow, D. G., Tal, M., & Schwartz, S. A. (1991a). Relapse in sexual behavior among homosexual men: A 2-year follow-up from the Chicago MACS/CCS. *AIDS*, **5**, 757–760.

Adib, S.M., & Ostrow, D.G. (1991). Trends in HIV/AIDS behavioural research among homosexual and bisexual men in the United States: 1981–1991. *AIDS Care*, **3**, 281–287.

Ainslie, G. (1975). Specious reward: A behavioral theory of impulsiveness and impulse control. *Psychological Bulletin*, **82**, 463–496.

Ajzen, I. (1971). Attitudinal vs normative messages: An investigation of the differential effects of persuasive communication on behavior. *Sociometry*, **34**, 263–280.

Ajzen, I. (1985). From intentions to actions: A theory of planned behavior. In J. Kuhl & J. Beckman (Eds.), *Action control: From cognition to behavior* (pp. 11–39). Berlin: Springer-Verlag.

Ajzen, I. (1987). Attitudes, traits, and actions: Dispositional prediction of behavior in personality and social psychology. *Advances in Experimental Social Psychology,* **20,** 1–63.

Ajzen, I. (1988). *Attitudes, personality, and behavior.* Chicago: Dorsey Press.

Ajzen, I. (1991). The theory of planned behavior. *Organizational Behavior and Human Decision Processes,* **50,** 179–211.

Ajzen, I., & Fishbein, M. (1973). Attitudinal and normative variables as predictors of specific behaviors. *Journal of Personality and Social Psychology,* **27,** 41–57.

Ajzen, I., & Fishbein, M. (1977). Attitude–behaviour relations: A theoretical analysis and review of empirical research. *Psychological Bulletin,* **84,** 888–919.

Ajzen, I., & Fishbein, M. (1980). *Understanding attitudes and predicting social behavior.* Englewood Cliffs, NJ: Prentice Hall.

Ajzen, I., & Madden, T. (1986). Prediction of goal-directed behaviour: Attitudes, intentions, and perceived behavioral control. *Journal of Experimental Social Psychology,* **22,** 453–474.

Allegrante, J. P., Mortimer, R. G., & O'Rourke, T. W. (1980). Social psychological factors in motorcycle safety helmet use: Implications for public policy. *Journal of Safety Research,* **12,** 115—126.

Allender, J., Senf, J., Bauman, K., & Reid-Duffy, P. (1991) Effects of subject variables on attitude change and knowledge acquisition in an AIDS education program. *AIDS Education and Prevention,* **3,** 341–352.

Altman, D. (1979). *Coming out in the seventies.* Sydney: Wild & Woolley.

Altman, D. (1982). *The homosexualization of America, the Americanization of the homosexual.* New York: St. Martin's Press.

Andrews, K. H., & Kandel, D. B. (1979). Attitude and behavior: A specification of the contingent consistency hypothesis. *American Sociological Review,* **44,** 298–310.

Argyle, M. (1993). *The psychology of social class.* London: Routledge.

Atkins, C. (1979). Research evidence on mass mediated health communication campaigns. In D. Nimmo. (Ed.), *Communications yearbook No. 3.* (pp. 655–668). New Brunswick, New Jersey: Transaction Books.

Australian Institute of Family Studies (1981–82). *Australian family formation project. Study 1: A longitudinal survey of Australians aged 13 to 34 years.* Canberra: Australian University Social Science Data Archives.

Australian Market Research (1987). Unpublished report prepared by the National Advisory Committee on AIDS, Canberra.

Bagnall, G., Plant, M., & Warwick, W. (1990). Alcohol, drugs and AIDS-related risks: Results from a prospective study. *AIDS Care,* **2,** 309–317.

Bagozzi, R. P. (1984). Expectancy-value attitude models: An analysis of critical measurement issues. *International Journal of Research in Marketing,* **1,** 295–310.

Bagozzi, R. P. (1985). Expectancy-value attitude models: An analysis of critical theoretical issues. *International Journal of Research in Marketing,* **2,** 43–60.

Bagozzi, R. P. (1992). The self-regulation of attitudes, intentions, and behavior. *Social Psychology Quarterly,* **55,** 178–204.

Bagozzi, R. P., & Burnkrant, R. E. (1979). Attitude organisation and the attitude–behavior relationship. *Journal of Personality and Social Psychology,* **37,** 913–919.

Bagozzi, R. P., & Yi, Y. (1989). The degree of intention formation as a moderator of the attitude–behavior relationship. *Social Psychology Quarterly,* **52,** 266–279.

Bailey, D. M. (1991). *Research for the health professional: A practical guide.* Philadelphia: FA Davis Company.

Baldwin, J. D., & Baldwin, J. I. (1988). Factors affecting AIDS-related sexual risk-taking behavior among college students. *The Journal of Sex Research,* **25,** 181–196.

Bandura, A. (1977). Self-efficacy: Toward a unifying theory of behavioral change. *Psychological Review,* **84,** 191–215.

Bandura, A. (1982). Self-efficacy mechanisms in human agency. *American Psychologist, 37,* 122–147.

Bandura, A. (1986). *Social foundations of thought and action: A social cognitive theory.* Englewoods Cliffs, NJ: Prentice-Hall.

Bandura, A. (1989a). Perceived self-efficacy in the exercise of control over AIDS infection. In V. M. Mays, G. W. Albee, & S. F. Schneider (Eds.), *Primary prevention of AIDS: Psychological approaches* (pp. 128–141). Newbury Park: Sage.

Bandura, A. (1989b). Self-efficacy mechanisms in physiological activation and health-promoting behavior. In J. Madden IV, S. Matthysse, & J. Barchas (Eds.), *Adaptation, learning and affect.* New York: Raven.

Bandura, A., & Cervone, D. (1983). Self-evaluative and self-efficacy mechanisms governing the motivational effects of goal systems. *Journal of Personality and Social Psychology*, **45**, 1017–1028.

Bandura, A., & Cervone, D. (1986). Differential engagement of self-reactive influences in cognitive motivation. *Organizational Behavior and Human Decision Processes*, **38**, 92–113.

Barling, N. R., & Moore, S. M. (1990). Adolescents' attitudes towards AIDS precautions and intention to use a condom. *Psychological Reports*, **67**, 883–890.

Basch, C. E. (1987). Focus group interview: An under utilised research technique for improving theory and practice in health education. *Health Education Quarterly*, **14**, 411–448.

Basen-Engquist, K., & Parcel, G. S. (1992). Attitudes, norms and self-efficacy: A model of adolescents' HIV-related sexual risk behavior. *Health Education Quarterly*, **19**, 263–277.

Bauman, L. J., & Siegel, K. (1987). Misperception among gay men of the risk for AIDS associated with their sexual behavior. *Journal of Applied Social Psychology*, **17**, 329–350.

Beale, D. A., & Manstead, A. S. R. (1991). Predicting mothers' intentions to limit frequency of infants' sugar intake: Testing the theory of planned behavior. *Journal of Applied Social Psychology*, **21**, 409–431.

Beck, A. T. (1976). *Cognitive therapy and the emotional disorders*. Madison: International Universities Press.

Beck, K. H., & Lund, A. K. (1981). The effects of health threat seriousness and personal efficacy intentions and behavior. *Journal of Applied Social Psychology*, **11**, 401–415.

Becker, M. H., (1974). The health belief model and personal health behavior. *Health Education Monographs*, **2**, 324–508 (reprinted as Becker, M. (Ed.). (1974). *The health belief model and personal health behavior.* Thorofare, NJ: Charles B. Slack).

Becker, M. H., Haefner, D., Mainman, L., Kirscht, J., & Drachman, R. (1977). The health belief model and prediction of dietary compliance: A field experiment. *Journal of Health and Social Behavior*, **18**, 348–366.

Becker, M. H., & Joseph, J. G., (1988). AIDS and behavioral change to reduce risk: A review. *American Journal of Public Health*, **78**, 394–410.

Bellinger, D. N., Bernhardt, K. L., & Goldstucker, J. L. (1976). Qualitative research techniques: Focus group interviews. In *Qualitative Research in Marketing*. Chicago: American Marketing Association.

Bentler, P. M., & Speckart, G. (1979). Models of attitude–behavior relations. *Psychological Review*, **86**, 452–464.

Bernard, J., Hebert, Y., de Man, A. Farrar, D. (1989a). Attitudes of French-Canadian students towards the use of condoms: A structural analysis. *Psychological Reports*, **65,** 851–854.

Bernard, J., Herbert, Y., de Man, A., & Farrar, D. (1989b). Factors related to the use of condoms among French-Canadian university students. *Journal of Social Psychology*, **129,** 707–709.

Bertrand, J.T., Makani, B., Hassig, S.E., Niwembo, K.L., Djunghu, B., Muanda, M., & Chirhamolekwa, C. (1991). AIDS-related knowledge, sexual behavior, and condom use among men and women in Kinshasa, Zaire. *American Journal of Public Health*, **81,** 53–58.

Bhaskar, R. (1979). *The possibility of naturalism: A philosophical critique of the contemporary human sciences.* Brighton: Harvester Press.

Bogardus, E. S. (1926). The group interview. *Journal of Applied Sociology*, **10,** 372–382.

Boldero, J., Moore, S., & Rosenthal, D. (1992). Intentions, context and safe sex: Australian adolescents' responses to AIDS. *Journal of Applied Social Psychology*, **22**(17), 1375–1397.

Borland, R. M. (1992). Relationship between mood around slip-up and recovery of abstinence in smoking cessation attempts. *International Journal of Addictions*, **27,** 1079–1086.

Bower, G. H. (1981). Mood and memory. *American Psychologist*, **36,** 129–148.

Bowman, C. H., & Fishbein, M. (1978). Understanding public reactions to energy proposals: An application of the Fishbein model. *Journal of Applied Social Psychology*, **8,** 319–340.

Boyd, B., & Wandersman, A. (1991). Predicting undergraduate condom use with the Fishbein & Ajzen and the Triandis attitude–behavior models: Implications for public health interventions. *Journal of Applied Social Psychology*, **21,** 1810–1830.

Brandt, A. M. (1985). *No magic bullet: A social history of venereal disease in the United States since 1880.* New York: Oxford University Press.

Brattebo, G., Wisborg, T., & Sjursen, H. (1990). Health workers and the human immunodeficiency virus: Knowledge, ignorance and behaviour. *Public Health*, **104,** 123–130.

Breckler, S. J., & Wiggins, E. C. (1989a). Affect versus evaluation in the structure of attitudes. *Journal of Experimental Social Psychology*, **25,** 253–271.

Breckler, S. J., & Wiggins, E. C. (1989b). On defining attitude and attitude theory: Once more with feeling. In A. R. Pratkanis, S. J. Breckler, &

A. G. Greenwald (Eds.), *Attitude structure and function* (pp. 407–428). Hillsdale, NJ: Erlbaum.

Breckler, S. J., & Wiggins, E. C. (1991). Cognitive responses in persuasion: Affective and evaluative determinants. *Journal of Experimental Social Psychology*, **27**, 180–200.

Brewin, C. R. (1989). Cognitive change processes in psychotherapy. *Psychological Review*, **96**, 379–394.

Brinberg, D., & Durand, J. (1983). Eating at fast-food restaurants: An analysis using two behavioral intention models. *Journal of Applied Social Psychology*, **13**, 459–472.

Brown L. K., DiClemente, R. J., & Reynolds, L. A. (1991). HIV prevention for adolescents: Utility of the health belief model. *AIDS Education and Prevention*, **3**(1), 50–59.

Brown, I. S. (1984). Development of a scale to measure attitude toward the condom as a measure of birth control. *Journal of Sex Research*, **20**, 255–63.

Brown, R. (1988). *Group processes: Dynamics within and between groups.* Oxford: Basil Blackwell.

Brown, W. (1991). An AIDS prevention campaign: Effects of attitude, beliefs, and communication behavior. *American Behavioral Scientist*, **34**, 666–678.

Brubaker, R. G., & Fowler, C. (1990). Encouraging college males to perform testicular self-examination: Evaluation of a persuasive message based on the revised theory of reasoned action. *Journal of Applied Social Psychology*, **17**, 1411–1422.

Bruce, K. E., Shrum, J. C., Trefethen, C., & Slovik, L. F. (1990). Students' attitudes about AIDS and homosexuality, and condoms. *AIDS Education and Prevention*, **2**, 220–234.

Buckham, C., Najman, J., & McCamish, M. (1990). Depravity Kills: The foundation of medical students' attitudes towards AIDS. *New Doctor*, **54**, **7–10**.

Budd, R. J. (1986). Predicting cigarette use: The need to incorporate measures of salience in the theory of reasoned action. *Journal of Applied Social Psychology*, **16**, 663–685.

Budd, R. J., & Spencer, C. P. (1984). Predicting undergraduates' intentions to drink. *Journal of Studies on Alcohol*, **45**, 179–183.

Budd, R. J., & Spencer, C. P. (1985). Exploring the role of personal normative beliefs in the theory of reasoned action: The problem of discriminating between alternative path models. *European Journal of Social Psychology*, **15**, 299–313.

Budd, R. J., & Spencer, C. P. (1986). Lay theories of behavioural intention: A source of response bias in the theory of reasoned action? *British Journal of Social Psychology, 25,* 109–117.

Burnkrant, R. E., & Page, T. J., Jr (1988). The structure and antecedents of the normative and attitudinal components of Fishbein's theory of reasoned action. *Journal of Experimental Social Psychology,* **24,** 66–87.

Buzwell, S., Rosenthal, D., & Moore, S. (1992). Idealising the sexual experience. *Youth Studies Australia Resources,* **1,** 3–10.

Callan, V. J. (1985). *Choices about children.* Melbourne: Longman Cheshire.

Campbell, I. M., Burgess, P. M., Goller, I. E., & Lucas, R. (1988). *A prospective study of factors influencing HIV infection in homosexual and bisexual men: A report of findings: Stage I.* Melbourne: Department of Psychology, University of Melbourne.

Caplan, P. (1987). *The cultural construction of sexuality.* London: Tavistock.

Carmines, E. G., & Zeller, R. A. (1979). *Reliability and validity assessment.* Newbury Park: Sage.

Carr, A. (1988a). *Behavioural change in Australia in response to the threat of HIV infection, 1983–1988: A survey of current knowledge.* Canberra: Commonwealth Department of Community Services and Health.

Carr, A. (1988b). Drugs and alcohol: Reasons or excuses for unsafe sex? *National AIDS Bulletin,* **Feb.,** 14–20.

Carroll, L. (1988). Concern with AIDS and the sexual behaviour of college students. *Journal of Marriage and the Family,* **50,** 405–411.

Catania, J. A., Gibson, D. R., Chitwood, D. D., & Coates, T. J. (1990). Methodological problems in AIDS behavioral research: Influences on measurement error and participation bias in studies of sexual behaviour. *Psychological Bulletin,* **108,** 339–362.

Chan, D. K.-S, & Fishbein, M. (in press). Determinants of college women's intentions to tell their partners to use condoms. *Journal of Applied Social Psychology.*

Chapman, S., & Hodgson, J. (1988). Showers in raincoats: Attitudinal barriers to condom use in high-risk heterosexuals. *Community Health Studies,* **12,** 97–105.

Chapman, S., Stoker, L., Ward, M., Porritt, D., & Fahey, P. (1990). Discriminant attitudes and beliefs about condoms in young, multi-partner heterosexuals. *International Journal of STD and AIDS,* **1,** 422–428.

Chassin, L., Presson, C. C., Bensenberg, M., Corty, E., & Sherman, S. J. (1981). Predicting adolescents' intentions to smoke cigarettes. *Journal of Health and Social Behavior*, **22**, 445–455.

Chassin, L., Presson, C. C., Sherman, S. J., Corty, E., & Olshavsky, R. W. (1984). Predicting the onset of cigarette smoking in adolescents: A longitudinal study. *Journal of Applied Social Psychology*, **14**, 224–243.

Chown, P. (1986). *Non-English speaking AIDS and STD information campaign: A report on the findings of preliminary research.* Sydney: Ethnic Communications.

Clark, M. S., & Isen, A. M. (1982). Toward understanding the relationship between feeling states and social behavior. In A. H. Hastorf & A. M. Isen (Eds.), *Cognitive social psychology* (pp. 73–108). New York: Elsevier/North-Holland.

Coates, T.J. (1990). *Testing in a comprehensive AIDS prevention strategy.* Presented at VI International Conference on AIDS, San Francisco, June.

Coburn, D., & Pope, C. R. (1974). Socioeconomic status and preventive health behavior. *Journal of Health and Social Behavior*, **15**, 67–78.

Cohen, D., Dent, C., & McKinnon, D. (1991). Condom skills education and sexually transmitted disease reinfection. *Journal of Sex Research*, **28**, 139ndash;144.

Committee on AIDS research and the Behavioural, Social, and Statistical Sciences (1989). Evaluating the effects of AIDS interventions. In C. F. Turner, H. G. Miller, & L. E. Moses (Eds.), *AIDS Sexual Behavior and Intravenous Drug Use.* Washington DC: National Academic Press.

Commonwealth of Australia (1989). *A national HIV/AIDS strategy: A policy information paper.* Canberra: AGPS.

Connell, R. W., Crawford, J., Bond, G., Sinnott, V., Baxter, D., Berg, R., Dowsett, G. W., Kippax, S., & Watson, L. (1988). *Social aspects of the prevention of AIDS: Facing the epidemic.* (Study A Report No. 3). Sydney: Macquarie University.

Connell, R. W. & Dowsett, G. W. (1992). (Eds.), *Rethinking sex: Social theory and sexuality research.* Melbourne: Melbourne University Press.

Connell, R. W., & Kippax, S. (1990). Sexuality in the AIDS crisis: Patterns of sexual practice and pleasure in a sample of Australian gay and bisexual men. *Journal of Sex Research*, **27**, 167–196.

Corby, N., Barchi, P., Wolitski, R. J., Smith, P. K., & Martanz (1990). *Effects of condom-skills training and HIV testing on AIDS-prevention behaviours of female sex workers.* Presented at VI International Conference on AIDS, San Francisco, June.

Coyne, J. C., & Gotlib, I. H. (1983). The role of cognition in depression: A critical appraisal. *Psychological Bulletin*, **94**, 472–505.

Crawford, J., Kippax, S. & Tulloch, J. (1992). *Appraisal of the National AIDS Education Campaign.* Canberra: Department of Health Housing and Community Services.

Crawford, J., Turtle, A., & Kippax, S. (1990). Student-favoured strategies for AIDS avoidance. *Australian Journal of Psychology*, **42**, 123–137.

Crocker, L., & Algina, J. (1986). *Introduction to classical and modern test theory.* Sydney: Holt, Rinehart and Winston.

Crofts, N. (1992). The global pandemic of HIV infection. *Today's Life Science*, *4*, 10–18.

Cronbach, L. J. (1951). Coefficient alpha and the internal structure of tests. *Psychometrica*, **16**, 297–334.

Cummings, K. M., Jette, A. M., & Rosenstock, I. M. (1978). Construct validation of the health belief model. *Health Education Monographs*, **6**, 394–405.

Curjel, H. E. (1964). An analysis of the human reasons underlying the failure to use a condom in 723 cases of venereal disease. *Journal of the Royal Navy Medical Service*, **50**, 203.

Curry, S., Marlatt, G. A., & Gordon, J. R. (1987). Abstinence violation effect: Validation of an attributional construct with smoking cessation. *Journal of Consulting and Clinical Psychology*, **55**, 145–149.

Darrow, W. W. (1974). Attitudes toward condom use and the acceptance of venereal disease prophylactics. In M. H. Radford, G. W. Duncan, & D. J. Prager (Eds.), *The condom: Increasing utilization in the United States.* San Francisco Press, San Francisco.

Davidson, A. R., & Jaccard, J. J. (1975). Population psychology: A new look at an old problem. *Journal of Personality and Social Psychology*, **31**, 1073–1082.

Davidson, A. R., & Jaccard, J. J. (1979). Variables that modify the attitude-behavior relation: Results of a longitudinal study. *Journal of Personality and Social Psychology*, **8**, 1364– 1376.

de Vries, H., Dijkstra, M., & Kuhlman, P. (1988). Self-efficacy: The third factor besides attitude and subjective norm as a predictor of behavioral intentions. *Health Education Research*, **3**, 273–282.

Detels, R., English, P., Visscher, B. R., *et al.* (1989). Seroconversion, sexual activity, and condom use among 2915 HIV seronegative men followed for up to 2 years. *Journal of Acquired Immune Deficiency Syndrome*, **2**, 77–83.

DiClemente, R. J., Forrest, K. A., Mickler, S., & Principal Site Investigators (1990). College students' knowledge and attitudes about AIDS and changes in HIV-preventive behaviors. *AIDS Education and Prevention*, **2**, 201–212.

DiClemente, R. J., Zorn, J., & Temoshok, L. (1986). Adolescents and AIDS: A survey of knowledge, attitudes and beliefs about AIDS in San Francisco. *American Journal of Public Health*, **76**, 1443–1445.

Doll, L., Harrison, J., Douglas, J., Bartholomew, B., Bolan, G., Joy, D., Moss, P., & Delgado, W. (1991). *Perceptions of normative behavior, support for condom use, and high risk sex: White vs nonwhite homosexual men.* Presented at VII International Conference on AIDS, Florence, June.

Dommeyer, C. J., Marquand, J. L., Gibson, J. E., & Taylor, R. L. (1989). The effectiveness of an AIDS education campaign on a college campus. *Journal of American College Health*, **38**, 131–135.

Dorfman, L. E., Derish, P. A., & Cohen, J. B. (1992). Hey girlfriend: An evaluation of AIDS prevention among women in the sex industry. *Health Education Quarterly*, **19**, 25–40.

Dowsett, G. W. (1988). The place of research in AIDS education: A critical review of survey research among gay and bisexual men. *In report of the III National Conference on AIDS. Hobart.* (pp. 159–164). Canberra, Australia: AGPS.

Dowsett, G.W. (1989). *"You'll never forget the feeling of safe sex": AIDS prevention strategies for gay and bisexual men in Sydney, Australia.* Report prepared for the World Health Organisation workshop: AIDS Health Promotion Activities directed towards gay and bisexual men. Geneva: WHO.

Dulany, D. E. (1968). Awareness, rules, and propositional control: A confrontation with S–R behavior theory. In D. Horton & T. Dixon (Eds.), *Verbal behavior and S–R behavior theory* (pp. 340–387). Englewood Cliffs, NJ: Prentice-Hall.

Dusenbury, L., Botvin, G. J., Baker, E., & Laurence, J. (1991). AIDS risk knowledge, attitudes, and behavioral intentions among multi-ethnic adolescents. *AIDS Education and Prevention*, **3**, 367–375.

Edgar, T., Freimuth, V.S., & Hammond, S.L. (1988). Communicating the AIDS risk to college students: The problem of motivating change. *Health Education Research*, **3**, 59–65.

Eiser, J. R., & van der Pligt, J., (1979). Beliefs and values in the nuclear debate. *Journal of Applied Social Psychology*, **9**, 524–536.

Ekstrand, M. L., & Coates, T. J. (1990). Maintenance of safer sexual behaviors and predictors of risky sex: The San Francisco men's health study. *American Journal of Public Health*, **80**, 973–977.

Elkind, D. (1967). Egocentrism in adolescence. *Child Development*, **38**, 1025–1034.

Elkind, D. (1985). Egocentrism redux. *Developmental Review*, **5**, 218–226.

Ellis, A. (1962). *Reason and emotion in psychotherapy.* New York: Lyle Stuart.

Emmons, C. A., Joseph, J. G., Kessler, R. C., Wortman, C. B., Montgomery, S. B., & Ostrow, D. G. (1986). Psychosocial predictors of reported behaviour change in homosexual men at risk for AIDS. *Health Education Quarterly*, **13**, 331–345.

Evans, M. G. (1991). The problem of analyzing multiplicative composites. *American Psychologist*, **46**, 6–15.

Farrell, C. (1978). *My mother said: The way young people learned about sex and birth control.* London: Routledge & Kegan Paul.

Fazio, R. H. (1990). Multiple processes by which attitudes guide behavior: The MODE model as an integrative framework. *Advances in Experimental Social Psychology*, **23**, 75–109.

Fazio, R. H., Powell, M. C., & Herr, P. M. (1983). Toward a process model of the attitude–behavior relation: Accessing one's attitude upon mere observation of the attitude object. *Journal of Personality and Social Psychology*, **44**, 723–735.

Feather, N. T. (1982). *Expectations and actions: Expectancy-value models in psychology.* Hillsdale, NJ: Lawrence Erlbaum.

Felman, Y. M., & Santora, F. J. (1981). The use of condoms by VD clinic patients. *Cutis*, **27**, 330–336.

Festinger, L. (1957). *A theory of cognitive dissonance.* Evanston, IL: Row, Peterson.

Fishbein, M. (1963). An investigation of the relationships between beliefs about an object and the attitude toward that object. *Human Relations*, **16**, 233–240.

Fishbein, M. (1966). Sexual behavior and propositional control. Paper presented at the annual meeting of the Psychonomic Society. Reported in Fishbein & Ajzen (1975).

Fishbein, M. (1967a). Attitudes and the prediction of behavior. In M. Fishbein (Ed.), *Readings in attitude theory and measurement* (pp. 477–492). New York: Wiley.

Fishbein, M. (1967b). A consideration of belief, and their role in attitude measurement. In M. Fishbein (Ed.), *Readings in attitude theory and measurement* (pp. 275–266). NY: John Wiley & Sons.

Fishbein, M. (1967c). A behavior theory approach to the relations between beliefs about an object and the attitude toward the object. In M. Fishbein (Ed.), *Readings in attitude theory and measurement* (pp. 389–400). NY: John Wiley & Sons.

Fishbein, M. (1980). A theory of reasoned action: Some applications and implications. In H. E. Howe & M. M. Page (Eds.), *Nebraska Symposium on Motivation, 1979.* Lincoln: University of Nebraska Press.

Fishbein, M. (1990). AIDS and behavior change: An analysis based on the theory of reasoned action. *Interamerican Journal of Psychology,* **24**(1), 37–56.

Fishbein, M., & Ajzen, I. (1975). *Belief, attitude, intention, and behavior: An introduction to theory and research.* Reading, MA: Addison-Wesley.

Fishbein, M., Ajzen, I., & McArdle, J. (1980). Changing the behavior of alcoholics: Effects of persuasive communication. In Ajzen, I., & Fishbein, M. (Eds.), *Understanding attitudes and predicting social behavior* (pp. 217–242). Englewood Cliffs, NJ: Prentice Hall.

Fishbein, M., Albarracin, D., & Ajzen, I. (in preparation). *Twenty-five years of reasoned action: An annotated bibliography.*

Fishbein, M., Bandura, A., Triandis, H. C., Kanfer, F. H., Becker, M. H., & Middlestadt, S. E. (1992). *Factors influencing behavior and behavior change.* Final Report, Theorist's Workshop. Bethesda, MD.: NIMH.

Fishbein, M., Chan, D. K-S, O'Reilly, K., Schnell, D., Wood, R., Beeker, C., & Cohn, D. (1992). Attitudinal and normative factors as determinants of gay men's intentions to perform AIDS-related sexual behaviors: A multisite analysis. *Journal of Applied Social Psychology,* **22,** 991–1011.

Fishbein, M., & Jaccard, J. J. (1973). Theoretical and methodological considerations in the prediction of family planning intentions and behavior. *Representative Research in Social Psychology,* **4,** 37–57.

Fishbein, M., & Middlestadt, S. E. (1989). Using the theory of reasoned action as a framework for understanding and changing AIDS-related behaviors. In V. M. Mays, G. W. Albee, & S. F. Schneider (Eds.), *Primary prevention of AIDS: Psychological approaches* (pp. 93–110). Newbury Park: Sage.

Fishbein, M., Middlestadt, S. E., & Hitchcock, P. J. (1991). Using information to change sexually transmitted disease-related behaviors: An analysis based on the theory of reasoned action. In J. N. Wasserheit, S. O. Aral, & K. K. Holmes (Eds.), *Research issues in human behavior and sexually transmitted diseases in the AIDS era* (pp. 243–257). Washington, D.C.: American Society for Microbiology.

Fishbein, M., & Raven, B. H. (1961). The AB scales: An operational definition of belief and attitude. *Human Relations,* **15,** 35–44.

Fishbein, M., & Stasson, M. (1990). The role of desires, self-predictions, and perceived control in the prediction of training session attendance. *Journal of Applied Social Psychology, 20,* 173–198.

Fisher, J. D. (1988). Possible effects of reference group-based social influence on AIDS-risk behavior and AIDS prevention. *American Psychologist,* **43,** 914–920.

Fisher, J. D., & Fisher, W. A. (1992). Changing AIDS-risk behavior. *Psychological Bulletin,* **111,** 455–474.

Fisher, W. A. (1984). Predicting contraceptive behaviour among university men: The role of emotions and behavioural intentions. *Journal of Applied Social Psychology,* **14,** 104–123.

Fisher, W. A. (1990). Understanding and preventing teenage pregnancy and sexually transmitted disease/AIDS. In J. Edwards *et al.* (Eds), *Social influence processes and prevention* (pp. 71–101). New York: Plenum.

Fitzpatrick, R., Boulton, M., Hart, G., Dawson, J., & McLean, J. (1989). High risk sexual behaviour and condom use in a sample of homosexual and bisexual men. *Health Trends, 21,* 76–79.

Flowers, J. V., Booraem, C., Miller, T. E., Iverson, A. E., Copeland, J., & Furtado, K. (1991). Comparison of the results of a standardized AIDS prevention program in three geographic locations. *AIDS Education and Prevention, 3,* 189–196.

Folch-Lyon, E., & Trost, J. (1981). Conducting focus group sessions. *Studies in Family Planning,* **12,** 443–449.

Ford, K., & Norris, A. (1991). Urban African-American and Hispanic adolescents and young adults: Who do they talk to about AIDS and condoms? What are they learning? *AIDS Education and Prevention, 3,* 197–206.

Ford, N., & Morgan, K. (1989). Heterosexual lifestyles of young people in an English city. *Journal of Population and Social Studies, 1,* 167–185.

Franzini, L. R., Sideman, L. M., Dexter, K. E., & Elder, J. P. (1990). Promoting AIDS risk reduction via behavioral training. *AIDS Education and Prevention,* **2,** 313–321.

Frazer, I. H., McCamish, M., Hayes, I., & North, P. J. (1988). Influence of HIV testing on sexual behaviour in a "high risk" population from a "low risk' area. *Medical Journal of Australia,* **149,** 365–368.

Fredericks, A., & Dossett, K. (1983). Attitude–behavior relations: A comparison of the Fishbein–Ajzen and the Bentler–Speckart models. *Journal of Personality and Social Psychology, 45,* 501–512.

Freund, T., Kruglanski, A. W., & Shpitzajzen, A. (1985). The freezing and unfreezing of impressional primacy: Effects of the need for structure and the fear of invalidity. *Personality and Social Psychology Bulletin, 11,* 479–487.

Gagnon, J. (1988). Sex research and sexual conduct in the era of AIDS. *Journal of Acquired Immune Deficiency Disease, 1,* 593–601.

Gagnon, J. & Simon, W. (1973). *Sexual conduct: The social sources of human sexuality.* Chicago: Aldine.

Galavotti, C., Schnell, D., & O'Reilly, K. R. (1990). *Impact of four HIV/AIDS prevention programs on psychosocial factors thought to facilitate risk behavior change.* Presented at VI International Conference on AIDS, San Francisco, June.

Galbraith, L. (1992). *HIV/AIDS and education models.* Background Paper No. 7 for the National HIV/AIDS Evaluation.

Galligan, R. F., & Terry, D. J. (in press). Romantic ideals, fear of negative implications, and practice of safe sex. *Journal of Applied Social Psychology.*

Gallois, C., Kashima, Y., Terry, D., McCamish, M., Timmins, P., & Chauvin, A. (1992a). Safe and unsafe sexual intentions and behavior: The effects of norms and attitudes. *Journal of Applied Social Psychology, 22,* 1521–1545.

Gallois, C., & McCamish, M. (1989). *Assessment of AFAO national peer education programme.* Australian Federation of AIDS Organisations, Canberra.

Gallois, C., Terry, D., Timmins, P., McCamish, M., & Kashima, Y. (in press). Safe sex intentions and behaviour among heterosexuals and homosexual men. *Psychology and Health.*

Gallois, C., Statham, D., & Smith, S. (1992b). *Women and HIV/AIDS education in Australia.*, Canberra: Commonwealth Department of Health, Housing and Community Services.

Gallop, R. M., Lancee, W. J., Taerk, G., Coates, R. A, Fanning, M., & Keatings, M. (1991). The knowledge, attitudes and concerns of hopital staff about AIDS. *Canadian Journal of Public Health, 82,* 409–412.

Gardner, J. (1992). *Prediction of AIDS risk behaviours: The influence of norms and past behaviour.* Unpublished Honours thesis, The University of Queensland, Brisbane, Australia.

Genest, M., & Turk, D. C. (1981). Think-aloud approaches to cognitive assessment. In T. V. Merluzzi, C. R. Glass, & M. Genest (Eds.) *Cognitive assessment* (pp. 233–269). New York: Guilford Press.

Gilliam, A., & Seltzer, R. (1989). The efficacy of educational movies on AIDS knowledge and attitudes among college students. *Journal of American College Health, 37,* 261–265.

Godin, G., Valois, P., Shephard, R. J., & Desharnais, R. (1987). Prediction of leisure-time exercise behavior: A path analysis (LISREL V) model. *Journal of Behavioral Medicine, 10,* 145–158.

Goggin, M. (1989). *Intimacy, sexuality, and sexual behavior among young Australian adults.* Unpublished Honours thesis, University of Melbourne, Australia.

Gold, R. S., Karmiloff-Smith, A., Skinner, M. J., & Morton, J. (1992). Situational factors and thought processes associated with unprotected intercourse in heterosexual students. *AIDS Care, 4,* 305–323.

Gold, R. S., & Skinner, M. J. (1992). Situational factors and thought processes associated with unprotected intercourse in young gay men. *AIDS, 6,* 1021–1030.

Gold, R. S., Skinner, M. J., Grant, P. J., & Plummer, D. C. (1991). Situational factors and thought processes associated with unprotected intercourse in gay men. *Psychology and Health, 5,* 259–278.

Gold, R. S., Skinner, M. J., & Ross, M. W. (1992). *Unprotected intercourse in HIV-infected and non-HIV-infected gay men.* Manuscript submitted for publication.

Goldman, R. J., & Goldman, J. D. G. (1988). *Show me yours: Understanding children's sexuality.* Ringwood: Penguin.

Golombok, S., Sketchley, J., & Rust, J. (1989). Condom use among homosexual men. *AIDS Care, 1,* 27–33.

Gottlieb, N. H., & Green, L. W. (1988). Ethnicity and lifestyle health risk: Some possible mechanisms. *American Journal of Health Promotion, 2,* 37–45, 51.

Grube, J. W., Morgan, M., & McGree, S. T. (1986). Attitudes and normative beliefs as predictors of smoking intentions and behaviours: A test of three models. *British Journal of Social Psychology, 25,* 81–93.

Haaga, D. A. F., Dyck, M. J., & Ernst, D. (1991). Empirical status of cognitive theory of depression. *Psychological Bulletin, 110,* 215–236.

Hallal, J. (1982). The relationship of health beliefs, health locus of control, and self concept to the practice of breast self examination in adult women. *Nursing Research, 31,* 137–142.

Harré, R. (1979). *Social Being.* Oxford: Basil Blackwell.

Harré, R. (1983). *Personal Being.* Oxford: Basil Blackwell.

Harrison, J. A., Mullen, P. D., & Green, L. W. (1992). A meta-analysis of studies of the health belief model with adults. *Health Education Research: Theory and Practice*, **7**, 107–116.

Hart, G. (1974). Factors influencing venereal disease in a war environment. *British Journal of Venereal Disease*, **50**, 68–72.

Hastie, R., & Park, B. (1986). The relationship between memory and judgment depends on whether the judgment task is memory-based or on-line. *Psychological Review*, **93**, 258– 268.

Haug, F. *et al.* (1987). *Female sexualization: A collective work of memory.* E. Carter (Trans.). London: Verso.

Hawe, P., Degeling, D., & Hall, J. (1990). *Evaluating health promotion: A health worker's guide.* Sydney: MacLennan and Petty.

Hayes, J. A. (1991). Psychosocial barriers to behavior change in preventing human immunodeficiency virus (HIV) infection. *The Counseling Psychologist*, **19**, 585–602.

Hays, R. B., Kegeles, S. M., & Coates, T. J. (1990). High HIV risk-taking among young gay men. *AIDS*, **4**, 901–907.

Heaven, P., Connors, J., & Kellehear, A. (1992). Health locus of control beliefs and attitudes toward people with AIDS. *Australian Psychologist*, **27**, 172–175.

Heider, F. (1958). *The psychology of interpersonal relations.* N.Y.: Wiley.

Hein, K. (1989a). AIDS in adolescence: A rationale for concern. *New York State Journal of Medicine*, **87**, 290–295.

Hein, K. (1989b). Commentary on adolescent Acquired Immunodeficiency Syndrome: The next wave of the Human Immunodeficiency Virus epidemic? *Journal of Pediatrics*, **114**, 144–149.

Herdt, G. H. (1981). *Guardians of the flute: Images of Masculinity.* New York: McGraw Hill.

Herek, G. M., & Glunt, E. K. (1988). An epidemic of stigma: Public reactions to AIDS. *American Psychologist*, **43**, 886–891.

Hessing, D. J., Elffers, H., & Weigel, R. H. (1988). Exploring the limits of self-reports and reasoned action: An investigation of the psychology of tax evasion behavior. *Journal of Personality and Social Psychology*, **54**, 405–413.

Heusser, R., Tschopp, A., Beutter, H. J., & Gutzwiller, F. (1992). *Determinants of condom use—results from the Swiss HIV cohort study (Part B = HIV prevention study: HIPS).* Presented at the VIII International Conference on AIDS, Amsterdam, July.

Hewstone, M., & Young, L. (1988). Expectancy value models of attitude: Measurement and combination of values and beliefs. *Journal of Applied Social Psychology*, **18,** 958–971.

Higginbotham, J. B., & Cox, K. K. (1979). *Focus group interviews.* Chicago: American Marketing Association.

Higgins, D. L. Galavotti, C., Johnson, R., O'Reilly, K. R., & Rugg, D. L. (1990). *The effect of HIV antibody counselling and testing on risk behaviors.* Presented at VI International Conference on AIDS, San Francisco, June.

Hill, D., Gardner, G., & Rassaby, J. (1985). Factors predisposing women to take precautions against breast and cervix cancer. *Journal of Applied Social Psychology*, **15,** 59–79.

Hoch, S. J., & Loewenstein, G. F. (1991). Time-inconsistent preferences and consumer self-control. *Journal of Consumer Research*, **17,** 492–507.

Hochbaum, G. M., Sorenson, J. R., & Lorig, K. (1992). Theory in health education practice. *Health Education Quarterly*, **19,** 295–313.

Hofferth, S. L., & Hayes, C. D. (Eds.) (1987). *Risking the future: Adolescent sexuality, pregnancy and child bearing* (Vol. 2). Washington, DC: National Academy of Sciences.

Holland, J., Ramazanoglu, C., Scott, S., Sharpe, S., & Thomson, R. (1991). *Pressure, resistance, empowerment: Young women and the negotiation of safer sex.* The women's risk AIDS project paper (No. 6). London: Tufnell Press.

Hollway, W. (1984). Gender difference and the production of subjectivity. In J. Henriques, W. Hollway, C. Urwin, C. Venn, & V. Walkerdine (Eds.), *Changing the subject: Psychology, social relations and subjectivity.* London: Methuen.

Horton, M. (1992). *Patterns and structures of male homosexuality.* Presented at the VIII International Conference on AIDS, Amsterdam. July.

Hunt, A., & Davies, P. (1991). What is a sexual encounter? In P. Aggleton, G. Hart, & P. Davies (Eds.), *AIDS: Responses, interventions and care.* London: Falmer.

Ingham, R. (1991). *Some speculations on the use of the concept of 'rationality'.* Paper presented at the Small Group Meeting of the European Association of Experimental Social Psychology 'Social Psychology Models in Health and Safety Research', University of Kent, Canterbury, September.

Ingham, R., & Memon, A. (1990). *Methodological issues in the study of sexual behaviour in the context of HIV-infection: An overview.* Southampton: Department of Psychology, University of Southampton.

Ingham, R., Woodcock, A., & Stenner, K. (1992). The limitations of rational decision-making models as applied to young people's sexual behaviour. In P. Aggleton, P. Davies, & G. Hart (Eds.), *AIDS: Rights, risk and reason.* London: The Falmer Press.

Intergovernmental Committee on AIDS (1992). *A report on HIV/AIDS activities in Australia, 1990–1991.* Canberra Commonwealth Department of Health, Housing and Community Service.

Irwin, C. E., & Millstein, S. G. (1986). Biopsychosocial correlates of risk-taking behaviours during adolescence. *Journal of Adolescent Health Care,* **7**, 582–596.

Jaccard, J. (1981). Attitudes and behavior: Implication of attitudes toward behavioral alternatives. *Journal of Experimental Social Psychology,* **17**, 286–307.

Jaccard, J., & Davidson, A. R. (1972). Toward an understanding of family planning behaviors: An initial investigation. *Journal of Applied Social Psychology,* **2**, 228–235.

Jaccard, J., & Sheng, D. (1984). A comparison of six methods for assessing the importance of perceived consequences in behavioral decisions: Applications from attitude research. *Journal of Experimental Social Psychology,* **20**, 1–28.

Janis, I. L., & Mann, L. (1977). *Decision making: A psychological analysis of conflict, choice and commitment.* New York: Free Press.

Janoff-Bulman, R. (1979). Characterological versus behavioral self-blame: Inquiries into depression and rape. *Journal of Personality and Social Psychology,* **37**, 1798–1809.

Janz, N., & Becker, M. (1984). The health belief model: A decade later. *Health Education Quarterly,* **11**, 1–47.

Jessor, R. (1976). Predicting time of onset of marijuana use: A development study of high school youth. *Journal of Consulting and Clinical Psychology,* **44**, 125–134.

Jette, A., Cummings, K., Brock, B., Phelps, M., & Naessens, J. (1981). The structure and reliability of health belief indices. *Health Services Research,* **16**, 81–98.

Johnson, E. J., & Tversky, A. (1983). Affect, generalization, and the perception of risk. *Journal of Personality and Social Psychology,* **45**, 20–31.

Joseph, J., Montgomery, S. B., Emmons, C.-A., Kessler, R. C., Ostrow, D. G., Wordman, C. B., O'Brien, K., Eller, M., & Eshleman, S. (1987). Magnitude and determinants of behavioral risk reduction: Longitudinal analysis of a cohort at risk for AIDS. *Psychology and health,* **1**, 73–96.

Kahneman, D., Slovic, P., & Tversky, A. (Eds.) (1982). *Judgment under uncertainty: Heuristics and biases.* Cambridge, Cambridge University Press.

Kamenga, M., Ryder, R. W., Jingu, M., Mbuyi, N., Mbu, L., Behets, F., Brown, C., & Heyward, W. L. (1991). Evidence of marked sexual behavior change associated with low HIV-1 seroconversion in 149 married couples with discordant HIV-1 serostatus: Experience at an HIV counselling center in Zaire. *AIDS,* **5,** 61–67.

Kandel, D. B. (1980). Drug and drinking behavior among youth. *Annual Review of Sociology,* **6,** 235–285.

Kashima, Y., Gallois, C., & McCamish, M. (1992a). Predicting the use of condoms: Past behavior, norms, and the sexual partner. In T. Edgar, M. A. Fitzpatrick, & V. S. Freimuth, (Eds.), *AIDS: A communication perspective* (pp. 21–46). Hillsdale, NJ: Lawrence Erlbaum.

Kashima, Y., Gallois, C., & McCamish, M. (in press). The theory of reasoned action and cooperative behaviour: It takes two to use a condom. *British Journal of Social Psychology.*

Kashima, Y., & Kashima, E. (1988). Individual differences in the predictions of behavioural intentions. *The Journal of Social Psychology,* **128,** 711–720.

Kashima, Y., Siegal, M., Tanaka, K., & Kashima, E. S. (1992b). Do people believe behaviours are consistent with attitudes? Towards a cultural psychology of attribution processes. *British Journal of Social Psychology,* **31,** 111–124.

Kegeles, S. M., Adler, N. E., & Irwin, C. E. (1988). Sexually active adolescents and condoms: Changes over one year in knowledge, attitudes and use. *American Journal of Public Health,* **78,** 460–461.

Keith, L., Keith, D., Bussell, R., & Wells, J. (1975). Attitudes of men toward contraception. *Archiv für Gynäkologie,* **220,** 89–97.

Keller, S. E., Schleifer, S. J., Bartlett, J. A., & Johnson, R. L. (1988). The sexual behavior of adolescents and risk of AIDS. *Journal of the American Medical Association,* **260,** 3856.

Kelly, J. A., Sikkema, K. J., Winett, R. A., Solomon, L. J., Roffman, R. E., Kalichman, S. C., Stevenson, L. Y., *et al.* (1992). *Outcomes of a 16 city randomised field trial of a community level HIV risk reduction intervention.* Presented at VIII International Conference on AIDS, Amsterdam, July.

Kelly, J. A., & St Lawrence, J. S. (1988). *The AIDS health crisis: Psychological and social interventions.* New York: Plenum.

Kelly, J. A., & St Lawrence, J. S. (1990). *Behavioural group intervention to teach AIDS risk reduction skills.* University of Mississippi Medical Center, Jackson MS.

Kelly, J. A., St Lawrence, J. S., Betts, R., Brasfield, T. L., & Hood, H. V. (1990). A skills-training group intervention model to assist persons in reducing risk behaviors for HIV infection. *AIDS Education and Prevention,* **2,** 24–35.

Kelly, J. A., St Lawrence, J. S., & Brasfield, T. L. (1991). Predictors of vulnerability to AIDS risk behavior relapse. *Journal of Consulting and Clinical Psychology,* **59,** 163–166.

Kelly, J. A., St Lawrence, J. S., Brasfield, T. L., Lemke, A., Amidei, T., Roffman, R. E., Hood, H. V., Smith, J. E., Kilgore, H., & McNeill, C., Jr (1990). Psychological factors that predict AIDS high-risk versus AIDS precautionary behaviour. *Journal of Consulting and Clinical Psychology,* **58,** 117–120.

Kelly, J. A., St Lawrence, J. S., Brasfield, T. L., Stevenson, L. Y., Diaz, Y. E., & Hauth, A. C. (1990). AIDS risk behaviour patterns among gay men in small southern cities. *American Journal of Public Health,* **80,** 416–418.

Kelly, J. A., St Lawrence, J. S., Diaz, Y. E., Stevenson, L. Y., Haugh, A. C., Brasfield, T. L., *et al.* (1991). HIV risk reduction following intervention with key opinion leaders of population: An experimental analysis. *American Journal of Public Health,* **81,** 168–171

Kelly, J. A., St Lawrence, J. S., Hood, H. V., & Brasfield, T. L. (1989). Behavioral intervention to reduce AIDS risk activities. *Journal of Consulting and Clinical Psychology,* 57, 60–67.

Kelly, J. A., St. Lawrence, J. S., Stevenson, L. Y., Brasfield, T. L., Haugh, A. C., Murphy, D. A., Morgan, M. G., Kalishman, S. C., & Diaz, Y. E. (1991). *Producing population wide reductions in HIV risk reduction behaviour among small city gay men: Results of an experimental field trial in three cities.* Presented at VII International Conference on AIDS, Florence, June.

Kelly, P. (1979). Breast self-examinations: Who does them and why. *Journal of Behavioural Medicine,* **2,** 31–38.

Kelman, H. C. (1958). Compliance, identification, and internalization: Three processes of attitude change. *Journal of Conflict Resolution,* **2,** 51–60.

Kilty, K. M. (1978). Attitudinal and normative variables as predictors of drinking behavior. *Journal of Studies of Alcohol,* **39,** 1178–1194.

King, G. W. (1975). An analysis of attitudinal and normative variables as predictors of intentions and behaviors. *Speech Monongraphs,* **42,** 237–244,

King, G. W. (1975). An analysis of attitudinal and normative variables as predictors of intentions and behaviors. Speech Monongraphs, 42, 237-244.

Kippax, S. (1992). *HIV prevention: Personal strategies, collective responses.* Plenary paper presented at the 5th National AIDS Conference, Sydney, November.

Kippax, S., Crawford, J., Connell, R. W., Dowsett, G. W., Watson, L., Rodden, P., Baxter, D., & Berg, R. (1992). The importance of gay community in the prevention of HIV transmission: A study of Australian men who have sex with men. In P. Aggleton, P. Davies, & G. Hart (Eds.), *AIDS: Rights, Risk and Reason.* London: The Falmer Press.

Kippax, S., Crawford, J., Davis, M., Rodden, P., & Dowsett, G. W. (1993). Sustaining safe sex: A longitudinal study of a sample of homosexual men. *AIDS.*

Kippax, S., Crawford, J., Bond, G., Sinnott, V., Baxter, D., Berg, R., Connell, R. W. Dowsett, G. W., & Watson, L. (1990). Information about AIDS: The accuracy of knowledge possessed by gay and bisexual men. *Australian Journal of Social Issues,* **25,** 199–219.

Kippax, S., Crawford, J., Waldby, C. and Benton, P. (1990). Women negotiating heterosex: Implications for AIDS prevention. *Women's Studies International Forum,* **13,** 133–146.

Kippax, S., Connell, R. W., Dowsett, G. W., & Crawford, J. (in press). *Sustaining safe sex: Gay communities respond to AIDS.* London: The Falmer Press.

Kirschenbaum, D. S., & Tomarken, A. J. (1982). On facing the generalization problem: The study of self-regulatory failure. In P. C. Kendall (Ed.), *Advances in cognitive–behavioral research and therapy* (Vol. 1, pp. 119–200). New York: Academic press.

Kirscht, J. P. (1983). Preventive health behavior: A review of research and issues. *Health Psychology,* **2,** 277–301.

Kirscht, J. P., & Joseph, J. G. (1989). The health belief model: Some implications for behavior change, with reference to homosexual males. In V. M. Mays, G. W. Albee, & S. F. Schneider (Eds.), *Primary prevention of AIDS: Psychological approaches.* Newbury Park: Sage.

Klitsch, M. (1990). Teenagers' condom use affected by peer factors, not health concerns. *Family Planning Perspectives,* **22,** 95.

Knafl, K. A., & Webster, D. C. (1988). Managing and analysing qualitative data: A description of tasks, techniques, and materials. *Western Journal Nursing Research,* **10,** 195–218.

Krueger, R. A. (1986). *Focus group interviews as an evaluation tool.* Adapted from a presentation at the 1984 Joint Meeting of the Evaluation Research Society and the Evaluation Network. Minnesota: University of Minnesota.

Kruglanski, A. W., & Freund, T. (1983). The freezing and unfreezing of lay–inferences: Effects on impressional primacy, ethnic stereotyping, and numerical anchoring. *Journal of Experimental Social Psychology*, **19**, 448–468.

Kruglanski, A. W., & Klar, Y. (1985). Knowing what to do: On the epistemology of actions. In J. Kuhl & J. Beckmann (Eds.), *Action control: From cognition to behavior* (pp. 41–60). Berlin: Springer-Verlag.

Kuhl, J. (1985). Volitional mediators of cognition-behaviour consistency: Self-regulator processes and action versus state orientation. In J. Kuhl & J. Beckman (Eds.), *Action-control: From cognition to behaviour* (pp. 101-128). Berlin: Springer-Verlag.

Kuhl, J. (1985). Volitional mediators of cognition-behavior consistency; Self-regulatory processes and action versus state orientation. In J. Kuhl & J Beckman (Eds.), *Action-control: From cognition to behavior* (pp. 101–128). Berlin: Springer-Verlag.

Kunda, Z. (1990). The case for motivated reasoning. *Psychological Bulletin*, **108**, 480–498.

Landis, S. E., Earp, J. L., & Koch, G. G. (1992). Impact of HIV testing and counselling on subsequent sexual behavior. *AIDS Education and Prevention.* **4**, 61–70.

Langer, E., Blank, A., & Chanowitz, B. (1978). The mindlessness of ostensibly thoughtful action. *Journal of Personality and Social Psychology*, **36**, 635–642.

Lau, R. R. (1988). Beliefs about control and health behavior. In D. S. Gochman (Ed.), *Health behavior: Emerging research perspectives* (pp. 43–64). New York: Plenum Press.

Lehmann, P., Hausser, D., Somaini, B., & Gutzwiller, F. (1987). Campaign against AIDS in Switzerland: Evaluation of a nationwide educational programme. *British Medical Journal*, **295**, 1118–1120.

Leninger, M. M. (1985). Nature, rationale, and importance of qualitative research methods in nursing. In M.M. Leninger (Eds.), *Qualitative research methods in nursing* (pp. 1–25). New York: Grune and Stratton.

Leventhal, H., & Cleary, P.D. (1980). The smoking problen: A review of research and theory in behavioral risk modification. *Psychological Bulletin*, **88**, 370–405.

Leviton, L. C. (1989). Theoretical foundations of AIDS-prevention programs. In R. O. Valdiserri (Ed.), *Preventing AIDS.* New Brunswick: Rutgers University Press.

Leviton, L. C., Valdiserri, R. O., Lyter, D. W., Callahan, C. M., Kingsley, L. A., Huggins, J., & Rinaldo, C. R. (1990). Preventing HIV infection in gay and bisexual men: Experimental evaluation of attitude change from two risk reduction interventions. *AIDS Education and Prevention*, **2,** 95–108.

Lierman, L., Young, H., Kasprzyk, D., & Benoliel, J. (1990). Predicting breast self-examination using the theory of reasoned action. *Nursing Research*, **39,** 97–101.

Lipson, J. M., & Brown, L. T. (1990). Do videotapes improve knowledge and attitudes about AIDS? *Journal of American College Health*, **39,** 235–243.

Liska, A. (1984). A critical examination of the causal structure of the Fishbein and Ajzen attitude–behaviour model. *Social Psychology Quarterly*, **47**(1), 61–74.

Longo, P. (1992). *Impact of homophobia and denial on HIV services.* Presented at the VIII International Conference on AIDS, Amsterdam, July.

Lule, G. S., & Gruer, L. D. (1991). Sexual behavior and the use of the condom among Ugandan students. *AIDS Care*, **3,** 11–19.

Lundy, J. R. (1972). Some personality correlates of contraceptive use among unmarried female college students. *Journal of Psychology*, **80,** 9–14.

Macey, L. P., & Boldero, J. M. (1992). *Attitudes, intentions and context: The prediction of condom use by adult males and females.* Paper presented at the 21st Annual Meeting of Social Psychologists, Auckland, New Zealand, April.

Mackie, D. M., & Worth, L. T. (1991). Feeling good, but not thinking straight: The impact of positive mood on persuasion. In J. P. Forgas (Ed.), *Emotion and social judgments* (pp. 201–219). Oxford: Pergamon Press.

Madden, T. J., Ellen, P. S., & Ajzen, I. (1992). A comparison of the theory of planned behavior and the theory of reasoned action. *Personality and Social Psychology Bulletin*, **18,** 3–9.

Maddux, J. E., Norton, L. W., & Stoltenberg, C. D. (1986). Self-expectancy, outcome expectancy, and outcome value: Relative effects on behavioral intentions. *Journal of Personality and Social Psychology*, **51,** 783–789.

Magura, S., Shapiro, J., Siddiqi, Q., & Lipton, D. S. (1989). *Variables influencing condom use among intravenous drug users.* Presented at the V International Conference on AIDS, Montreal, June.

Mak, R.P., & Plum, J.R. (1991). Do prostitutes need more health education regarding sexually transmitted diseases and the HIV Infection? Experience in a Belgian city. *Social Science and Medicine,* **33,** 963–966.

Manstead, A. S., Proffitt, C., & Smart, J. (1983). Predicting and understanding mothers' infant feeding intentions and behavior: Testing the theory of reasoned action. *Journal of Personality and Social Psychology,* **44,** 657–671.

Marlatt, G. A., & Gordon, J. R. (Eds.). (1985). *Relapse prevention: Maintenance strategies in the treatment of addictive behaviors.* New York: Guilford Press.

Marr, D. (1982). *Vision.* San Francisco: Freeman.

Maticka-Tyndale, E. (1991) Sexual scripts and AIDS prevention: Variations in adherence to safer-sex guidelines by heterosexual adolescents. *Journal of Sex Research,* **28**(1)**,** 45–66.

Mays, V. M., & Jackson, J. S. (1991). AIDS research methodology with black Americans. *Social Science and Medicine,* **30,** 47–54.

McAllister, A. L., Krosnick, J. A., & Milburn, M. A. (1984). Causes of adolescent cigarette smoking: Tests of a structural equation model. *Social Psychology Quarterly,* **47,** 24–36.

McCamish, M., Cox, S. D., Frazer, I. H., & North, P. J. (1988). *Self reported changes in sexual practice among gay and bisexual men as a result of AIDS-awareness in a "low risk" city.* Paper presented at IV International Conference on AIDS, Stockholm, June.

McCamish, M., Dunne, M., Hamilton, K., & Orth, D. (1992). *Preferred safe sex strategies: Information from 123 gay men in Brisbane.* Presented at V National Conference on AIDS, Sydney, Australia, November.

McCamish, M., Timmins, P., Gallois, C., & Terry, D. (1993). *APES: A Norm-Based Workshop for HIV Prevention and Safer Sex.* Brisbane: The University of Queensland.

McCamish, M., Timmins, P., Gallois, C., Terry, D., & Kashima, Y. (1991). *Perceived personal risk, sources of information, contact with PLWA/HIV: Relation to safe sexual practice.* Paper presented at VII International Conference on AIDS, Florence, June.

McCarty, D. (1981). Changing contraceptive usage intentions: A test of the Fishbein model of intention. *Journal of Applied Social Psychology,* **11,** 192–211.

McCusker, J., Stoddard, A. M., Mayer, K. H., Zapka, J., Morrison, C., & Saltzman, S. P. (1988). Effects of HIV antibody test knowledge on subsequent sexual behaviors in a cohort of homosexually active men. *American Journal of Public Health*, **78**, 462–467.

McCusker, J., Stoddard, A. M., Zapka, J. G., Zorn, M., & Mayer K. H. (1989). Predictors of AIDS-preventive behaviour among homosexually active men: A logitudinal study. *AIDS*, **3**, 443–448.

McCaul, K. D., O'Neill, K., & Glasgow, R. E. (1988). Predicting the performance of dental hygiene behaviours: An examination of the Fishbein and Arzen model and self-efficacy expectancies. *Journal of Applied Social Psychology*, **18**, 114–128

McEwan, R. T., Bhopal, R., & Patton, W. (1991). Drama on HIV and AIDS: An evaluation of a theatre-in-education programme. *Health Education Journal*, **50**, 155–160.

McKirnan, D. J., & Peterson, P. L. (1989). AIDS–risk behavior among homosexual males: The role of attitudes and substance abuse. *Psychology and Health*, **3**, 161–171.

McKusick, L., Coates, T. J., Morin, S. F., Pollack, M. A., & Hoff, C. (1990). Longitudinal predictors of reductions in unprotected anal intercourse among gay men in San Francisco: The AIDS behavioral research project. *American Journal of Public Health*, **80**, 978–983.

McKusick, L., Coates, T., Wiley, J., Morin, S., & Stall, R. M. (1987). *Prevention of HIV infection among gay and bisexual men: Two longitudinal studies*. Third International Conference on AIDS, Washington, DC, June.

McLaws, M. L. (1992). *Measurement and determinants of condom use behaviour in homosexually active men at risk of AIDS*. Unpublished PhD thesis, University of Sydney, Australia.

McLaws, M., Oldenburg, B., Irwig, L., & Ross, M. W. (1993). *Development of a questionnaire to measure intention of homosexual men to use condoms*. Manuscript submitted for publication.

McLaws, M., Oldenburg, B., Ross, M. W., & Cooper, D. A. (1990). Sexual behaviour in AIDS- related research: Reliability and validity of recall and diary measures. *Journal of Sex Research*, **27**, 265–281.

McMillan, B., & Hunter, A. (1992). *Men at work: Male sex workers and HIV*. Presented at VIII International Conference on AIDS, Amsterdam, July.

Meichenbaum, D. (1977). *Cognitive-behavior modification: An integrative approach*. New York: Plenum Press.

Melese-d'Hospital, I., & Strauss, A. L. (1992). *Sexual decision making processes among HIV-"savvy" adolescents.* Presented at VIII International Conference on AIDS, Amsterdam, July.

Merson, M. H. (1992). Longitudinal trends in the epidemic. *National AIDS Bulletin, September,* 28–30.

Meyer-Bahlburg, H. F. L., Exner, T. M., Lorenz, G., Gruen, R. S., Gorman, J. M., & Ehrhardt, A. A. (1991). Sexual risk behavior, sexual functioning, and HIV-disease progression in gay men. *Journal of Sex Research,* **28,** 3–27.

Middlestadt, S.E., & Fishbein, M. (1990). Factors influencing experienced and inexperienced college women's intentions to tell their partners to use condoms. Paper presented at the VIth International Conference on AIDS, San Francisco, June.

Miller, L. E., & Grush, J. E. (1986). Individual differences in attitudinal versus normative determination of behavior. *Journal of Experimental Social Psychology,* **22,** 190–202.

Miller, T. E., Booream, C., Flowers, J. V., & Iverson, A. E. (1990). Changes in knowledge, attitudes, and behavior as a result of a community-based AIDS prevention program. *AIDS Education and Prevention,* **2,** 12–23.

Miniard, P., & Cohen, J. B. (1981). An examination of the Fishbein–Ajzen behavioral intentions model's concepts and measures. *Journal of Experimental Social Psychology,* **17,** 309–339.

Moates, D. R., & Schumacher, G. M. (1980). *An introduction to cognitive psychology.* Belmont, California: Wadsworth.

Montgomery, S., Joseph, J., Becker, M., Ostrow, D., Kessler, R., & Kirscht, J. (1989). The health belief model in understanding compliance with preventive recommendations for AIDS: How useful? *AIDS Education and Prevention,* **1,** 303–323.

Moodie, R. (1992). Sexual behaviour and AIDS in Uganda. *National AIDS Bulletin,* **April,** 38–40.

Moore, S., & Rosenthal, D. (1991a). Adolescent invulnerability and perceptions of AIDS risk. *Journal of Adolescent Research,* **6,** 164–180.

Moore, S., & Rosenthal, D. (1991b). Adolescents' perceptions of friends' and parents' attitudes to sex and sexual risk-taking. *Journal of Community and Applied Social Psychology,* **1,** 189–200.

Moore, S., & Rosenthal, D. (1991c). Condoms and coitus: Adolescent attitudes to AIDS and safe sex behaviour. *Journal of Adolescence,* **14,** 211–227.

Moore, S., & Rosenthal, D. (1992). The social context of adolescent sexuality: Safe sex implications. *Journal of Adolescence*, **15**, 1–21.

Moore, S., & Rosenthal, D. (1993). *Sexuality in adolescence*. London: Routledge.

Morin, S. (1988). AIDS: The challenge to psychology. *American Psychologist*, **43**, 838–842.

Morin, S. F., & Batchelor, W. (1984). Responding to the psychological crisis of AIDS. *Public Health Reports*, **99**, 4–9.

Morrison, D. (1985). Adolescent contraceptive behavior: A review. *Psychological Bulletin*, **98**, 538–568.

Morton, J., Hammersley, R. H., & Bekerian, D. A. (1985). Headed records: A model for memory and its failures. *Cognition*, **20**, 1–23.

Moscicki, B., Millstein, S. G., Broering, J., & Irwin, C. E. (1988). *Psychosocial and behavioral risk factors for AIDS in adolescence*. Interim report submitted to University of California Taskforce on AIDS, San Francisco.

Moses, S., Plummer, F. A., Ngugi, E. N., Nagelkerke, N. J. D., Anzala, A. O., & Ndinya-Achola, J. O. (1991). Controlling HIV in Africa: Effectiveness and cost of an intervention in a high-frequency STD transmitter core group. *AIDS*, **5**, 407–411.

Mullen, P., Hersey, J., & Iverson, D. (1987). Health behavior models compared. *Social Science and Medicine*, **24**, 973–981.

Murray, M., Swan, A. V., Johnson, M. R. D., & Bewley, B. R. (1983). Some factors associated with risk of smoking by children. *Journal of Child Psychology and Psychiatry*, **24**, 223–232.

Nathanson, C. A., Upchurch, D. M., Dashti, R., Weisman, C., Kim, Y. J., Hook, E. W. III. (1991). *Heterosexual behavior patterns of high risk black men*. Presented at VII International Conference on AIDS, Florence, June.

Netemeyer, R. G., & Burton, S. (1990). Examining the relationships between voting behavior, intention, perceived behavioral control, and expectation. *Journal of Applied Social Psychology*, **20**, 661–680.

Nickerson, C. A., & McClelland, G. H. (1989). Across-persons versus within-persons tests of expectancy-value models: A methodological note. *Journal of Behavioral Decision Making*, **2**, 261–270.

Nisbett, R. E., & Wilson, T. D. (1977). Telling more than we can know: Verbal reports on mental processes. *Psychological Review*, **84**, 231–259.

Norman, D. A. (1976). *Memory and attention* (2nd edn). New York: Wiley.

Nucifora, J. (1990). *Psychological factors influencing condom use among undergraduates.* Unpublished Honours thesis, The University of Queensland, Brisbane, Australia.

Nzila, N., Laga, M., Thiam, M. A., Mayimona, K., Edid, B., Van Dyck, E., Behets, F., Hassig, S., Nelson,A., Mokwa, K., Ashley, R. L., Piot, P., & Ryder, R. W. (1991). HIV and other sexually transmitted diseases among female prostitutes in Kinshasa. *AIDS*, **5**, 715–721.

O'Leary, A. (1985). Self-efficacy and health. *Behavior Research and Therapy*, **23**, 437–451.

Okware, S. (1988). AIDS control in Uganda. *World Health*, **9**, 20–21.

Osgood, C. E., Suci, G. J., & Tannenbaum, P. H. (1957). *The measurement of meaning.* Urbana, IL: University of Illinois Press.

Pagel, M. D., & Davidson, A. R. (1984). A comparison of three social–psychological models of attitude and behavioral plan: Prediction of contraceptive behavior. *Journal of Personality and Social Psychology*, **47**, 517–533.

Palacios-Jimenez, L., & Shernoff, M. (1986). *Eroticising safer sex: A psychoeducational workshop approach to safer sex education.* New York, NY: Gay Men's Health Crisis, Inc.

Parker, R. (1992). *Patterns and structures of male homosexuality.* Presented at the VIII International Conference on AIDS, Amsterdam, July.

Parker, R. G., & Carballo, M. (1990). Qualitative research on homosexual and bisexual behavior relevant to HIV/AIDS. *Journal of Sex Research*, **27**, 497–525.

Peterson, C. C., & Feeney, J. A. (1993). *Parent–adolescent conflict resolution strategies and the development of romantic relationships.* Paper presented at the Australian Family Research Conference, Manly.

Petosa, R., & Jackson, K. (1991). Using the health belief model to predict safer sex intentions among adolescents. *Health Education Quarterly*, **18**, 463–476.

Pleck, J. H., Sonenstein, F. L., & Ku, L. C. (1990). Contraceptive attitudes and intention to use condoms in sexually experienced and inexperienced adolescent males. *Journal of Family Issues*, **11**, 294–312.

Porter, J., & Bonilla, L. (1991). *The health belief model as predictor of HIV-testing behavior among latinos in the USA.* Presented at the VII International Conference on AIDS, Florence, June.

Porter, J., & Bonilla, L. (1992). The health belief model as predictor of HIV-testing behavior in the USA. *Presented at the VIII International Conference on AIDS*, Amsterdam. July.

Power, L. (1992). *Impact of homophobia and denial on HIV services.* Presented at the VIII International Conference on AIDS, Amsterdam, July.

Pratkanis, A. (1989). The cognitive representation of attitudes. In A. R. Pratkanis, S. J. Breckler, & A. G. Greenwald (Eds. ), *Attitude structure and function* (pp. 71–98). Hillsdale, NJ: Erlbaum.

Prieur, A. (1990). Norwegian gay men: Reasons for continued practice of unsafe sex. *AIDS Education and Prevention,* 2(2), 109–115.

Puckett, S. B., & Bye, L. L. (1987). *The Stop AIDS project: An interpersonal AIDS prevention program.* San Francisco, CA: The Stop AIDS Project, Inc.

Qualitative Solutions and Research, Pty. Ltd. (1993). *NUDIST: MacIntoch Version 3.0.* Melbourne: La Trobe University.

Raven, B. H. (1965). Social influence and power. In I.D. Steiner & M. Fishbein (Eds.), *Current studies in social psychology.* N.Y.: Holt, Rinehart & Winston.

Reid, L., & Christensen, D. (1988). A psychological perspective in the explanation of patient's drug taking behavior. *Social Science and Medicine,* **27,** 277–285.

Reiss, I. L. (1967). *The social context of premarital sexual permissiveness.* New York: Holt, Rinehart & Winston.

Research and Decisions Corporation, (1984). *Designing an effective AIDS-prevention campaign strategy for San francisco: Results from the first probability sample of an urban gay male community.* San Francisco, CA: Research and Decisions Corporation.

Rhodes, F., & Wolitski, R. (1989). Effect of instructional videotapes on AIDS knowledge and attitudes. *Journal of American College Health,* **37,** 266–271.

Richard, R., & Van der Pligt, J. (1991). Factors affecting condom use among adolescents. *Journal of Community and Applied Social Psychology,* **1,** 105–116.

Rigby, K., Anagnostou, P., Brown, M., Rosser, B. R. S., & Ross, M. W. (1988). A preliminary survey of attitudes, beliefs and practices relevant to AIDS among selected ethnic groups in Adelaide. In *Living with AIDS—Towards the Year 2000* (pp. 279–285). Department of Community Services and Health, Canberra: Australian Government Publishing Service.

Rigby, K., Brown, M., Anagnostou, P., Ross, M. W., & Rosser, B. R. S. (1989). Shock tactics to counter AIDS: The Australian experience. *Psychology and Health,* **3,** 145–159.

## 306    References

Rigby, K., & Dietz, B. (1991). *The impact of the 1989 National Campaign against AIDS for people of non-English speaking background in Adelaide, South Australia.* Report for the South Australian Health Commission, May.

Rigby, K., & Rosenthal, D. (1990). *An evaluation of the National Campaign against AIDS for people of non-English speaking background.* Report for the Australian Commonwealth Department of Community Services and Health.

Robertson, J. A., & Plant, M. A. (1988). Alcohol, sex and risks of HIV infection. *Drug and Alcohol Dependence,* **22,** 75–78.

Rodin, J., & Salovey, P. (1989). Health Psychology. *Annual Review of Psychology,* **40,** 533–579.

Rogers, R. W. (1975). A protection motivation theory of fear appeals and attitudes change. *Journal of Psychology,* **91,** 93–114.

Rogers, R. W. (1983). Cognitive and physiological processes in attitude change: A revised theory of protection motivation. In J. Cacioppo & R. Petty (Eds.), *Social Psychophysiology* (pp. 153–176). New York: Guilford Press. 153–176.

Rokeach, M. (1980). Some unresolved issues in theories of beliefs, attitudes, and values. In M. M. Page (Ed.), *Nebraska symposium on motivation* (Vol. 27, pp. 261–304). Lincoln, NE: University of Nebraska Press.

Rollins, B. (1989). *Sexual attitudes and behaviours: A review of the literature.* Australian Institute of Family Studies, Melbourne.

Rosenstock, I. M. (1974a). Historical origins of the health belief model. *Health Education Monographs,* **2,** 328–335.

Rosenstock I. M. (1974b). The health belief model and preventative health behavior. *Health Education Monographs,* **2,** 354–386.

Rosenstock, I. M., Strecher, V. J., & Becker, M. H. (1988). Social learning theory and the health belief model. *Health Education Quarterly,* **15,** 175–183.

Rosenthal, D., Hall, C., & Moore, S. (1992). AIDS, adolescents and sexual risk-taking: A test of the health beliefs model. *Australian Psychologist,* **27,** 166–171.

Rosenthal, D., & Moore, S. (1991). Risky business: Adolescents and HIV/AIDS. *Bulletin for the National Clearing House of Youth Studies,* **10,** 20–25.

Rosenthal, D.A., Moore, S.M., & Brumen, I. (1990). Ethnic group differences in adolescents' responses to AIDS. *Australian Journal of Social Issues,* **25,** 220–239.

Rosenthal, D., Moore, S., & Flynn, I. (1991). Adolescent self-efficacy, self-esteem and sexual risk-taking. *Journal of Community and Applied Social Psychology*, **1**, 77–88.

Ross, M. W. (1988a). Attitudes toward condoms as AIDS prophylaxis in homosexual men: Dimensions and measurement. *Psychology and Health*, **2**, 291–299.

Ross, M. W. (1988b). Personality factors that differentiate homosexual men with positive and negative attitudes toward condom use. *New York State Journal of Medicine*, **88**, 626–628.

Ross, M. W. (1988c). Personality factors that differentiate homosexual men with positive and negative attitudes toward condom use. *New York State Journal of Medicine*, **88**, 626–628

Ross, M. W. (1988d). The relationship of combinations of AIDS counselling and testing to safer sex and condom use in homosexual men. *Community Health Studies*, **12**, 322–327.

Ross, M. W. (1990a). Psychological determinants of increased condom use and safer sex in homosexual men: A longitudinal study. *International Journal of STDs and AIDS*, **1**, 98–101.

Ross, M. W. (1990b). Psychovenereology: Psychological aspects of AIDS and other sexually transmissible diseases. In D. G. Ostrow (Ed.), *Behavioral aspects of AIDS* (pp. 19–40). New York: Plenum Medical Book Company.

Ross, M. W. (1990c). Reasons for non-use of condoms by homosexually active men during anal intercourse. *International Journal of STD and AIDS*, **1**, 432–434.

Ross, M. W., Freedman, B., & Brew, R. (1989). Changes in sexual behaviour between 1986 and 1988 in matched samples of homosexually active men. *Community Health Studies*, **13**, 276–280.

Ross, M. W., & McLaws, M. L. (1992). Subjective norms about condoms are better predictors of use than attitudes. *Health Education Research*, **7**, 335–339.

Rotheram-Borus, M. J., & Koopman, C. (1991a). Sexual risk behavior, AIDS knowledge, and beliefs about AIDS among predominantly minority gay and bisexual male adolescents. *AIDS Education and Prevention*, **3**, 305–312.

Rotheram-Borus, M. J., & Koopman, C. (1991b). Sexual risk behaviors, AIDS knowledge, and beliefs about AIDS among runaways. *American Journal of Public Health*, **81**, 208–211.

Rotheram-Borus, M. J., Koopman, C., Haignere, C., Hunter, J., & Ehrhardt, A. A. (1990). *An effective program for changing sexual risk behaviors of gay male and runaway adolescents.* Presented at VI International Conference on AIDS, San Francisco, June.

Rotter, J. B. (1966). Generalized expectancies for internal versus external control of reinforcement. *Psychological Monographs*, **80**.

Rugg, D. L., O'Reilly, K. R., & Galavotti, C. (1990). AIDS prevention evaluation: Conceptual and methodological issues. *Evaluation and Program Planning*, **13**, 79–89.

Sacco, W. P., Levine, B., Reed, D. L., & Thompson, K. (1991). Attitudes about condom use as an AIDS-relevant behavior: Their factor structure and relation to condom use. *Psychological Assessment: A Journal of Consulting and Clinical Psychology*, **3**, 265–272.

Sallis, J. F., & Nader, P. R. (1988). Family determinants of health behaviors. In D. S. Gochman (Ed.), *Health behavior: Emerging research perspectives* (pp. 107–124). New York: Plenum Press.

Salt, H., Boyle, M., & Ives, J. (1990). HIV prevention: Current health promoting behaviour models for understanding psychological determinants of condom use. *AIDS Care*, **2**(1), 69–75.

Sanbonmatsu, D. M., & Fazio, R. H. (1990). The role of attitudes in memory-based decision making. *Journal of Personality and Social Psychology*, **59**, 614–622.

Sandford, T. (1992). *Impact of homophobia & denial on HIV services.* Presented at the VIII International Conference on AIDS, Amsterdam, July.

Sanford, A. J., & Garrod, S. C. (1981). *Understanding written language: Explorations of comprehension beyond the sentence.* Chichester: John Wiley.

Sarver, V. T. Jr (1983). Ajzen and Fishbein's 'theory of reasoned action': A critical assessment. *Journal for the Theory of Social Behavior*, **13**, 155–163.

Schaalma, H., Kok, G., & Peters, L. (in press). Determinants of consistent condom use by adolescents: The impact of experience with sexual intercourse. *Health Education Research*, **8**(1).

Schlegel, R.P., Crawford, C.A., & Sanborn, M.D. (1977). Corresponence and mediational properties of the Fishbein model: An application to adolescent alcohol use. *Journal of Experimental Social Psychology*, **13**, 421–430.

Schifter, D. B., & Ajzen, I. (1985). Intention, perceived control, and weight loss: An application of the theory of planned behavior. *Journal of Personality and Social Psychology*, **49**, 843–851.

Schofield, M. (1968). *The sexual behaviour of young people.* Harmondsworth: Penguin.

Schwartz, S. (1973). Normative explanations of helping behaviour: A critique, proposal, and empirical test. *Journal of Experimental and Social Psychology*, **9**, 349–364.

Schwartz, S., & Tessler, R. C. (1972). A test of a model for reducing measured attitude–behaviour discrepancies. *Journal of Personality and Social Psychology*, **24**, 225–236.

Sedikides, C., & Skowronski, J. J. (1991). The law of cognitive structure activation. *Psychological Inquiry*, **2**, 169–184.

Sheeran, P., Abraham, S. C. S., Abrams, D., Spears, R., & Marks, D. (1990). The post-AIDS structure of students' attitudes to condoms: Age, sex and experience of use. *Psychological Reports*, **66**, 614.

Sheppard, B. H., Hartwick, J., & Warshaw, P. R. (1988). A theory of reasoned action: A meta-analysis of past research with recommendations for modifications and future research. *Journal of Consumer Research*, **15**, 325–343.

Shernoff, M., & Bloom, D. J. (1991). Designing effective AIDS prevention workshops for gay and bisexual men. *AIDS Education and Prevention*, **3**, 31–46.

Shotter, J. (1984). *Social accountability and selfhood*. Oxford: Basil Blackwell.

Shulkin, J. J., Mayer, J. A., Wessel, L. G., de Moor, C., Elder, J. P., & Franzini, L. R. (1991). Effects of a peer-led AIDS intervention with university students. *Journal of American College Health*, **40**, 75–79.

Siegel, K., & Gibson, W. (1988). Barriers to the modification of sexual behavior among heterosexuals at risk for acquired immunodeficiency syndrome. *New York State Journal of Medicine*, **8**, 66–70.

Siegel, K., Mesagno, F. P., Chen, J.-Y., & Christ, G. (1989). Factors distinguishing homosexual males practicing risky and safer sex. *Social Science Medicine*, **28**, 561–569.

Silvestre, A. J., Lyter, D. W., Valdisseri, R. O., Huggins, J., & Rinaldo, C. R. (1989). Factors related to seroconversion among homo- and bisexual men after attending a risk-reduction education session. *AIDS*, **3**, 647–650.

Siraprapasiri, T., Thanprasertsuk, S., Rodklay, A., Srivanichakorn, S., Sawanpanyalert, P., & Temtanarak, J. (1991). Risk factors for HIV among prostitutes in Chaingmai, Thailand. *AIDS*, **5**, 579–582.

Skurnick, J. H., Johnson, R. L., Quinones, M. A., Foster, J. D., & Louria, D. B. (1991). New Jersey high school students' knowledge, attitudes, and behavior regarding AIDS. *AIDS Education and Prevention*, **3**, 21–30.

Slovic, P., Fischhoff, B., & Lichtenstein, S. (1979). Rating the risks. *Environment*, **21**, 14–20.

Smetana, J. G., & Adler, N. E. (1980). Fishbein's value × expectancy model: An examination of some assumptions. *Personality and Social Psychology Bulletin*, **6**, 89–96.

Sorenson, R. E. (1973). *Adolescent sexuality in contemporary America.* New York: World Publishers.

Sparks, P., Hedderley, D., & Shepherd, R. (1991). Expectancy-value models of attitudes: A note on the relationship between theory and methodology. *European Journal of Social Psychology*, **21**, 261–271.

Spears, R., van der Pligt, J., & Eiser, G. R. (1986). Generalizing the illusory correlation effect. *Journal of Personality and Social Psychology*, **51**, 1127–1134.

St. Lawrence, J. S., Davis, J., Brasfield, T., Alleyne, E., Jefferson, K., Banks, P., Jones, M., Simms, S., Shirley, A., & Moore. D. (1992). *Gender differences relevant to AIDS prevention with African-American adolescents.* Presented at the VIII International Conference on AIDS, Amsterdam, July.

Stall, R. D., Barrett, D., Bye, L., Catania, J., Frutchey, C., Henne, J., Lemp, G., & Paul, J. (1992). A comparison of younger and older gay men's HIV risk-taking behaviors: The communication technologies 1989 cross-sectional survey. *Journal of Acquired Immune Deficiency Syndromes*, **5**, 682–687.

Stall, R. D., Coates, T. J., & Hoff, C. (1988). Behavioral risk reduction for HIV infection among gay and bisexual men. *American Psychologist*, **43**, 878–885.

Stall, R. D., McKusick, L., Wiley, J., Coates, T. J., & Ostrow, D. G. (1986). Alcohol and drug use during sexual activity and compliance with safe sex guidelines for AIDS: The AIDS behavioral research project. *Health Education Quarterly*, **13**, 359–371.

Stasson, M., & Fishbein, M. (1990). The relation between perceived risk and preventive action: A within-subject analysis of perceived driving risk and intentions to wear seat-belts. *Journal of Applied Social Psychology*, **20**, 1541–1557.

Sternberg, R. J. (1986). A triangular theory of love. *Psychological Review*, **93**, 119–135.

Strauss, A., & Corbin, J. (1990). *Basics of Qualitative research: Grounded theory procedures and techniques.* Newbury Park: Sage.

Strecher, V. J., deVellis, B. M., Becker, M. H., & Rosenstock, I. M. (1986). The role of self- efficacy in achieving health behavior change. *Health Education Quarterly*, **13**, 73–92.

Strunin, L., & Hingson, R. (1992). Alcohol, drugs, and adolescent sexual behavior. Special issue: Key issues in epidemiology and control policies. *International Journal of the Addictions, 7*(2), 129–146.

Sutton, S. (1989). Smoking attitudes and behavior: Applications of Fishbein and Ajzen's theory of reasoned action to predicting and understanding smoking decisions. In T. Ney and A. Gale (Eds.), *Smoking and Human Behavior*, (pp. 289–336). Great Britain: Wiley.

Sykes, G. M., & Matza, D. (1957). Techniques of neutralization: A theory of delinquency. *American Sociological Review, 22,* 664–670.

Taylor, C. (1977). What is human agency? In T. Mischel (Ed.), *The self: Psychological and philosophical issues.* Oxford: Basil Blackwell.

Taylor, S. E. (1991). *Health Psychology.* New York: McGraw-Hill.

Terry, D. J. (in press). Coping resources/styles, nature of the situation, and appraisal variables as predictors of coping behavior. Journal of Personality and Social Psychology.

Terry, D. J., Galligan, R. F., & Conway, V. J. (in press). The prediction of safe sex behaviour: The role of intentions, attitudes, norms, and control beliefs. *Psychology and Health,* **??**.

Terry, D. J., & O'Leary, J. (1993). The theory of planned behaviour: The effects of perceived behavioural control and self-efficacy. Manuscript submitted for publication.

Tesser, A., & Shaffer, D. R. (1990). Attitudes and attitude change. *Annual Review of Psychology, 41,* 479–523.

Timmins, P., Gallois, C., McCamish, C., & Terry, D. (1992). *Sournes of information about HIV/AIDS and perceived personal risk of HIV infection.* Manuscript submitted for publication.

Timmins, P., Gallois, C., McCamish, C., & Terry, D. (1993). *The influence oif sexual orientation and contact with HIV/AIDS on perceived risk and its relation to safe sex intentions.* Manuscript submitted for publication.

Treffke, H., Tiggemann, M., & Ross, M. W. (1992). The relationship between attitude, assertiveness and condom use. *Psychology and Health,* **6,** 45–52.

Triandis, H. C. (1964). Exploratory factor analyses of the behavioral component of social attitudes. *Journal of Abnormal and Social Psychology,* **68,** 420–430.

Triandis, H. C. (1977). *Interpersonal behavior.* Monterey, CA: Brooks Cole.

Triandis, H. (1980). Values, attitudes, and interpersonal behavior. In H. E. Howe & M. M. Page (Eds.), *Nebraska Symposium on Motivation 1979* (pp. 195–259). Lincoln, Nebraska: University of Nebraska Press.

Turtle, A. M., Ford, B., Habgood, R., Grant, M., Bekiaris, J., Constantinou, C., Mecek, M., & Polyziodis, H. (1989). AIDS-related beliefs and behaviours of Australian university students. *The Medical Journal of Australia*, **150**, 371–376.

Valdiserri, R. O. (1989). *Preventing AIDS: The design of effective programs*. New Brunswick, NJ: Rutgers University Press.

Valdiserri, R. O., Lyter, D., Leviton, L. C., Callahan, C. M., Kingsley, L. A., & Rinaldo, C. R. (1988). Variables influencing condom use in a cohort of gay and bisexual men. *American Journal of Public Health*, **78**, 801–805.

Valdiserri R. O., Lyter, D. W., Leviton, L. C., Callahan, C. M., Kingsley, L. A., & Rinaldo, C. R. (1989). AIDS prevention in gay and bisexual men: Results of a randomised trial evaluating two risk reduction interventions. *AIDS*, **3**, 21–26.

Valle, S. L. (1988). Sexually transmitted diseases and the use of condoms in a cohort of homosexual men followed since 1983 in Finland. *Scandinavian Journal of Infectious Diseases*, **20**, 153–161.

van der Velde, F. W., & van der Pligt, J. (1991). AIDS-related health behavior: Coping, protection motivation, and previous behavior. *Journal of Behavioral Medicine*, **14**, 429–451.

van Ryn, M., & Heaney, C. A. (1992). What's the use of theory? *Health Education Quarterly.* **19**, 315–330.

Vazquez-Nuttal, E., Avila-Vivas, Z., & Morales-Barreto, G. (1984). Working with Latin American families. *Family Therapy Collections*, **9**, 74–90.

Waldby, C., Kippax, S., & Crawford, J. (1990). Theory in the bedroom: A report from the Macquarie University AIDS and heterosexuality project. *Australian Journal of Social Issues*, **25**, 177–185.

Waldron, I. (1988). Gender and health-related behavior. In D. S. Gochman (Ed.), *Health behavior: Emerging research perspectives* (pp. 193–208). New York: Plenum Press.

Wallston, B. S., & Wallston, K. A. (1984). Social psychological models of health behavior: An examination and integration. In A. Baum, S. E. Taylor, & J. E. Singer (Eds.), *Handbook of psychology and health* (pp. 23–52). Hillsdale, N. J: Erlbaum.

Walter, H. J., Vaughan, R. D., Gladis, M. M., Ragin, D. F., Kasen, S., & Cohall, A. T. (1992). Factors associated with AIDS risk behaviours among high school students in an AIDS epicentre. *American Journal of Public Health*, **82**, 528–532.

Watson, D., & Tellegen, A. (1985). Toward a consensual structure of mood. *Psychological Bulletin*, **98**, 219–235.

Weatherburn, P., Hunt, A. J., Davies, P. M., Coxon, A. P. M., & McManus, T. J. (1991). Condom use in a large cohort of homosexually active men in England and Wales. *AIDS Care*, **3**, 31–41.

Weeks, J. (1977). *Coming out: Homosexual politics in Britain, from the nineteenth century to the present.* London: Quartet.

Weeks, J. (1987). Questions of identity. In P. Caplan (Ed.), *The cultural construction of sexuality.* London: Tavistock Publications.

Weinstein, N. D. (1980). Unrealistic optimism about future life events. *Journal of Personality and Social Psychology*, **39**, 806–820.

Weinstein, N. D. (1982). Unrealistic optimism about susceptibility to health problems. *Journal of Behavioral Medicine*, **5**, 441–460.

Weinstein, N. D. (1984). Why it won't happen to me: Perceptions of risk factors and illness susceptibility. *Health Psychology*, **3**, 431–457.

Weinstein, N. D. (1989). Perceptions of personal susceptibility to harm. In V. M. Mays, G. W. Albee, & S. F. Schneider (Eds.), *Primary prevention of AIDS: Psychological approaches.* Newbury Park, CA: Sage.

Weisenberg, M., Kegeles, S. S., & Lund, A. F. (1980). Children's health beliefs and acceptance of a dental preventive activity. *Journal of Health and Social Behavior*, **21**, 59–74.

Wellings, K. (1991). *Assessing AIDS/HIV preventive strategies in the general population.* Final Report. Lausanne, Institut universitaire de médecine sociale et préventive.

Wellings, K., Field, J., Wadsworth, J., Johnson, A. M., Anderson, R. M., & Bradshaw, S. A. (1990). Sexual lifestyles under scrutiny. *Nature*, **348**, 276–278.

White, K., Terry, D. J., & Hogg, M. A. (1993) Safer sex behaviour: The role of attitudes norm, and control factors. Manuscript submitted for publication.

Wicker, A. W. (1969). Attitudes vs. actions: The relationship of verbal and overt behavioral responses to attitude objects. *Journal of Social Issues*, **25**, 41–78.

Williams, A. F. (1972). Factors associated with seat belt use in families. *Journal of Safety Research*, **4**, 133–138.

Wilson, D., & Lavelle, S. (1992). Psychosocial predictors of intended condom use among Zimbabwean adolescents. *Health Education Research*, **7**, 55–68.

Wilson, D., Lavelle, S., Greenspan, R., & Wilson, C. (1991). Psychological predictors of HIV-preventive behavior among Zimbabwean students. *The Journal of Social Psychology*, **131**, 293–295.

Wilson, D. J., Lavelle, S., & Hood, R. (1990). Health knowledge and beliefs as predictors of intended condom use among Zimbabwean adolescents in probation/remand homes. *AIDS Care*, **2**, 267–274.

Wittkower, E. D., & Cowan, J. (1944). Some psychological aspects of sexual promiscuity. *Psychosomatic Medicine*, **6**, 287.

World Health Organization (1991). *Global programme on AIDS. Current and future dimensions of the HIV/AIDS pandemic: A capsule summary.* Geneva: WHO.

World Health Organisation. (1992). *Global Strategy for the prevention and control of AIDS: 1992 Update.* Geneva: WHO.

Worth, D. (1989). Sexual decision making and AIDS: Why condom promotion among vulnerable women is likely to fail. *Studies in Family Planning*, **20**, 297–307.

Wright, B. (1990). *Students' knowledge and beliefs about AIDS as predictors of sexual behaviour.* Unpublished Master's thesis, The University of Queensland, Brisbane, Australia.

Wurtel, S. (1988). Increasing women's calcium intake: The role of health beliefs, intentions, and health value. *Journal of Applied Social Psychology*, **18**, 627–639.

Yacenda, J. A. (1974). Knowledge and attitudes of college students about venereal disease and its prevention. *Health Services Reports*, **89**, 170–176.

Yarber, W. L., & Williams, C. E. (1975). Venereal disease prevention in a selected group of college students. *Journal of the American Venereal Disease Association*, **2**, 17–24.

Zajonc, R. B. (1980). Feeling and thinking: Preferences need no inferences. *American Psychologist*, **35**, 151–175.

Zelnick, M., Kantner, J., & Ford, K. (1981). *Sex and pregnancy in adolescence.* Beverley Hills CA: Sage.

Zimmerman, R. S., Langer, L. M., Starr, R., & Enzler, N. (1991). *Evaluation of a theory based high school AIDS prevention unit: The impact of teacher vs. peer education, lecture vs. discussion, and an HIV/AIDS awareness campaign on knowledge, attitudes and behaviors.* Presented at VII International Conference on AIDS, Florence, June.

Zuckerman, M., & Reis, H. T. (1978). Comparison of three models for predicting altruistic behaviour. *Journal of Personality and Social Psychology*, **36**, 498–510.

# Author Index

Abbott, S., 69
Abelson, R.P., 217
Abraham, C., 68, 100, 157, 259
Abrams, D., 68, 100, 157, 259
Abramson, J.H., 181
Adib, S.M., 44, 189, 228
Adler, N.E., 14, 68, 69, 85, 220
Ainslie, G., 229
Ajzen, I., 6, 10-17, 20-22, 25-36, 39, 41, 42,
   47-50, 55, 56, 60, 62-63, 70-71, 77, 79, 81,
   87, 89, 97, 98, 124, 128, 129, 131, 137,
   139-141, 144, 146, 149, 151, 160, 172, 177,
   180, 194, 208, 209-211, 213-217, 219, 239,
   241, 253, 271, 272
Algina, J., 171, 173, 174, 180
Allender, J., 37
Altman, D., 256
Anagnostou, P., 94, 95, 190
Anderson, R.M., 192
Andrews, K.H., 214
Anzala, A.O., 35
Argyle, M., 5
Atkins, C., 174
Avila-Vivas, Z., 188
Bagnall, G., 231
Bagozzi, R.P., 22, 46, 47, 51, 62, 123, 128, 146,
   208, 209, 218
Bailey, D.M., 181
Baldwin, J.I., 154
Bandura, A., 40, 41, 43, 49, 135-137, 146-148,
   187, 241, 254
Barchi, P., 192
Barling, N.R., 71, 76
Bartlett, J.A., 69
Basch, C.E., 174-175
Basen-Enguist, K., 90
Batchelor, W., 187
Bauman, K., 37
Bauman, L.J., 154, 158
Beale, D.A., 35, 150
Beck, A.T., 136
Beck, K.H., 228
Becker, M., 7, 38, 79, 118, 121, 136, 187, 254
Bekerian, D.A., 242
Bellinger, D.N., 174
Bensenberg, M., 211
Bentler, P.M., 17
Benton, P., 256

Bernard, J., 100
Bernhardt, K.L., 174
Bertrand, J.T., 35, 36
Betts, R., 195
Beutter, H.J., 120
Bewley, B.R., 211
Bhaskar, R., 255, 262
Bhopal, R., 192
Blank, A., 230
Bloom, D.J., 35
Bogardus, E.S., 174
Boldero, J.M., 1, 36, 39, 40, 65, 71, 72, 188
Bond, G., 257, 260
Bonilla, L., 119, 120
Booraem, C., 35, 187
Borland, R.M., 46
Boulton, M., 231
Bower, G.H., 229
Boyd, B., 33, 39, 40, 137, 138, 150, 211
Boyle, M., 254
Bradshaw, S.A., 275
Brandt, A.M., 33, 200
Brasfield, T.L., 171, 189, 193, 195, 228
Brattebo, G., 238
Breckler, S.J., 48, 208,
Brewin, C.R., 229, 242
Brock, B., 120
Broering, J., 67
Brown, I.S., 84, 85
Brown, L.K., 35
Brown, L.T., 38, 39
Brown, M., 95
Brown, R., 16
Brown, W., 190, 194, 254
Brubaker, R.G., 219
Bruce, K.E., 36
Brumen, I., 66, 155, 259
Buckham, C., 157
Budd, R.J., 48, 62, 210, 211
Burgess, P.M., 171
Burnkrant, R.E., 22, 47, 51, 62, 123, 128, 146,
   212
Burton, S., 35
Bussell, R., 84
Buzwell, S., 66, 79
Bye, L.L., 132, 154, 187, 189, 190
Callahan, C.M., 171, 188, 192
Campbell, I.M., 171

Caplan, P., 257
Carballo, M., 169, 172
Carmines, E.G., 171
Carr, A., 171
Carroll, L., 35, 47
Catania, J.A., 79, 171
Cervone, D., 147, 148
Chanowitz, B., 230
Chapman, S., 70, 71, 83, 85, 231
Chassin, L., 49, 63, 211
Chauvin, A., 24, 46, 52, 155, 191, 261
Chen, J.Y., 171, 231
Chitwood, D.D., 79, 171
Chown, P., 94
Christ, G., 171, 231
Clark, M.S., 229
Cleary, P.D., 5
Coates, T.J., 79, 136, 171, 186, 187, 189, 228, 231
Coburn, D., 4
Cohen, D., 48, 189
Cohen, J.B., 189, 192
Committee on AIDS research 187
Commonwealth of Australia 187
Connell, R.W., 2, 159, 228, 231, 256, 257
Connors, J., 35
Conway, V.J., 6, 40, 123
Cooper, D.A., 171
Copeland, J., 35
Corbin, J., 175
Corby, N.H., 192
Corty, E., 49, 211
Cowan, J., 82
Cox, K.K., 174
Cox, S.D., 188
Coxon, A.P.M., 191
Coyne, J.C., 229
Crawford, C.A., 11
Crawford, J., 1, 2, 45, 47, 79, 155, 158-159, 207, 253, 256, 257, 259, 260, 273
Crocker, L., 171, 173, 174, 180
Crofts, N., 33
Cronbach, L.J., 181, 234
Cummings, K.M., 7, 9, 120
Curjel, H.E., 82
Curry, S., 230
Darrow, W.W., 82, 83, 85
Davidson, A.R., 71, 76, 77, 211, 215
Davies, P., 191
Davis, P., 188, 189, 259
Dawson, J., 231
de Vries, H., 138, 147
Degeling, D., 171
Dent, C., 192
Derish, P.A., 189
Desharnais, R., 150
Detels, R., 86
Dexter, K.E., 35
Diaz, Y.E., 189
DiClemente, R.J., 35, 36, 68, 254

Dietz, B., 1, 96, 97
Dijkstra, M., 138
Doll, L., 189
Dommeyer, C.J., 192
Dorfman, L.E., 189
Dossett, K., 150
Dowsett, G.W., 2, 159, 187, 188, 256, 257, 259
Drachman, R., 7, 118
Dulany, D.E., 210
Dunne, M., 159, 191
Dusenbury, L., 35
Dyck, M.J., 229
Earp, J.L., 186
Edgar, T., 47
Ehrhardt, A.A., 192
Eiser, J.R., 210
Ekstrand, M.L., 228
Elder, J.P., 35
Elffers, H., 214
Elkind, D., 3
Ellen, P.S., 27
Ellis, A., 228
Emmons, C.A., 77, 154, 190
Enzler, N., 190
Ernst, D., 229
Evans, M.G., 209
Fahey, P., 70, 231
Farrar, D., 100
Farrell, C., 65
Fazio, R.H., 11, 137, 209, 217, 220, 230
Feather, N.T., 208
Felman, Y.M., 85
Field, J., 192, 235
Fischhoff, B., 157
Fishbein, M., 1, 2, 10-17, 20-22, 25-33, 35, 39, 42, 44, 45, 47, 48, 52, 55, 56, 60, 62, 63, 70-71, 77, 79, 81, 87, 97, 88, 121, 122-124, 128, 129, 131, 133, 140, 141, 145, 160, 167, 172, 173, 177, 180, 187, 208, 210, 211, 213, 214, 216
Fisher, J.D., 2, 34, 35, 36, 37, 42-44, 45, 60, 136, 148, 154, 155, 159, 170, 186, 190-192, 193, 213
Fisher, W.A., 2, 34, 35, 37, 42-44, 45, 60, 136, 148, 154, 155, 159, 170, 186, 190-192, 195, 213
Fitzpatrick, R., 231
Flowers, J.V., 35, 187, 188
Flynn, I., 37, 40, 77
Folch-Lyon, E., 174
Ford, K., 32, 35, 65
Ford, N., 66
Forrest, K.A., 36
Fowler, C., 219
Franzini, L.R., 35
Frazer, I.H., 188, 191
Fredericks, A., 150
Freimuth, V.S., 47
Freund, T., 229
Furtado, K., 35

Gagnon, J., 255, 257
Galavotti, C., 186, 192, 257
Galligan, R.F., 6, 40, 123, 209
Gallois, C., 1, 2, 4, 8, 12, 17, 21, 24, 25, 27, 38,
    44, 45, 46, 47, 48, 52, 60, 63, 71, 86, 90, 99,
    117, 121, 133, 151, 153, 154, 155, 159-163,
    167, 172, 185, 188, 189, 191, 192, 194, 196,
    207, 208, 213, 215, 216, 261, 338, 339, 342
Gallop, R.M., 36
Gardner, G., 121
Gardner, J., 63, 214
Garrod, S.C., 229
Genest, M., 229
Gibson, D.R., 79, 157, 261
Gibson, J.E., 121, 154, 169, 171, 192
Gibson, W., 188
Gilliam, A., 192
Glunt, E.K., 154, 156
Godin, G., 150
Goggin, M., 71, 79
Gold, R., 1, 11, 45, 77, 154, 155, 158, 159, 169,
    172, 208, 210, 217, 227, 260, 273
Goldman, R.J., 66
Goldstucker, J.L., 174
Goller, I.E., 171
Golombok, S., 86, 171
Gordon, J.R., 230
Gotlib, I.H., 229
Grant, P.J., 45, 172, 227
Green, L.W., 5, 8, 38
Greenspan, R., 39, 40
Grube, J.W., 5, 48, 63, 172, 211, 214
Grush, J.E., 214
Gutzwiller, F., 35, 120
Haaga, D.A.F., 229
Haefner, D., 118
Haignere, C., 192
Hall, C., 7, 39, 79
Hall, J., 171
Hallal, J., 118
Hamilton, K., 159, 191
Hammersley, R.H., 242
Hammond, S.L., 47
Harre, R., 255
Harrison, J.A., 8, 38, 39
Hart, G., 82, 85, 231
Hartwick, J., 14
Hastie, R., 229
Haug, F., 255
Haugh, A.C., 189
Hausser, D., 35
Hawe, P., 171
Hayes, C.D., 66
Hayes, I., 188
Hayes, J.A., 35, 43
Hays, R.B., 171, 228
Heaney, C.A., 187
Heaven, P., 37
Hedderley, D., 209
Hein, K., 67, 68

Herbert, Y., 100
Herdt, G.H., 256
Herek, G.M., 154, 156
Herr, P.M., 209
Hersey, J., 121
Hessing, D.J., 214
Heusser, R., 120, 130
Hewstone, M., 209
Higginbotham, J.B., 174
Higgins, D.L., 186
Hill, D., 121, 123, 124
Hingson, R., 68
Hoch, S.J., 229
Hochbaum, G.M., 187
Hodgson, J., 70, 83
Hoff, C., 171, 187, 189
Hofferth, S.L., 66
Holland, J., 70
Hollway, C., 256
Hood, H.V., 193, 195
Hood, R., 38
Horton, M., 189
Huggins, J., 172
Hunt, A.J., 191
Hunter, A., 189
Hunter, J., 192
Ingham, R., 257, 261
Irwig, L., 171
Irwin, C.E., 67, 68, 69, 85, 188
Isen, A.M., 229
Iverson, A.E., 35, 187
Iverson, D., 121
Ives, J., 254
Jaccard, J.J., 71, 7677 210 215
Jackson, J.S., 32
Jackson, K., 120
James, S.A., 189
Janis, I.L., 41
Janoff-Bulman, R., 230
Janz, N., 7, 38, 79, 118, 121, 187
Jessor, R., 49, 211
Jette, A.M., 7, 9, 120
Johnson, A.M., 192
Johnson, E.J., 211
Johnson, M.R.D., 229
Johnson, R.L., 69, 186
Joseph, J.G., 38, 39, 77, 121, 154, 189, 190, 228,
    254
Kahneman, D., 234
Kamenga, M., 35
Kandel, D.B., 211, 214
Kantner, J., 65
Karmiloff-Smith, A., 227, 231
Kashima, E.S., 48, 49
Kashima, Y., 1, 8, 12, 14, 17, 21, 24, 25, 29, 45,
    46, 55, 59, 63, 71-72, 76, 77, 906,99, 117,
    119, 133, 136, 151, 153, 154, 155, 159, 161,
    162, 163, 167, 172, 186, 188, 191, 207, 208,
    209, 211-214, 216, 217, 219, 220, 261, 272,
    274

Kasprzyk, D., 10, 118
Kegeles, S.M., 38, 68, 69, 85, 171, 228
Keith, D., 84
Keith, L., 84
Kellehear, A., 37
Keller, S.E., 69
Kelly, J.A., 35, 121, 154, 156, 171, 189, 190,
    193-195, 219, 228, 231
Kelly, P., 7
Kelman, H.C., 212
Kessler, R.C., 77, 154, 190, 254
Kilty, K.M., 211
Kingsley, L.A., 171, 188, 192
Kippax, S., 1, 2, 11, 45, 47, 79, 155, 159, 170,
    194, 207, 231, 253, 256, 257, 259, 260, 273
Kirschenbaum, D.S., 242
Kirscht, J.P., 4, 7, 38, 118, 254
Klitsch, M., 70
Knafl, K.A., 176
Koch, C.G., 186
Kok, G., 40, 136, 193
Koopman, C., 36, 192
Krosnick, J.A., 211
Krueger, R.A., 174
Kruglanski, A.W., 121, 229
Ku, L.C., 71
Kuhl, J., 229
Kuhlman, P., 138
Kunda, Z., 229
Landis, S.E., 186
Langer, E., 190
Langer, L.M., 230
Lau, R.R., 6
Lavelle, S., 38, 39, 40, 191
Lehmann, P., 35
Leninger, M.M., 172
Leventhal, H., 5
Levine, B., 37
Leviton, L.C., 171, 187, 188, 189, 192
Lichtenstein, C.F., 157
Lierman, L., 10, 118, 120
Lipson, J.M., 35
Lipton, D.S., 191
Liska, A., 17, 39, 47, 57, 62, 77, 214, 219
Loewenstein, C.F., 229
Longo, P., 189
Lorig, K., 187
Lucas, R., 171
Lule, G.S., 32, 35, 36
Lund, A.K., 38, 136
Lundy, J.R., 6
Lyter, D.W., 171, 172, 188, 192
Macey, L.P., 39
Mackie, D.M., 229
Madden, T.J., 16, 27, 33, 36, 41, 50, 71,
    79, 89, 137, 140, 144
Maddux, J.E., 136
Magura, S., 191
Mainman, L., 7, 118
Mak, R.P., 34, 36

Mann, L., 41
Manstead, A.S.R., 17, 35, 150
Marks, D., 68, 100, 157, 259
Marlatt, G.A., 230
Marr, D., 218
Maticka-Tyndale, E., 259
Matza, D., 228
Mayer, J.A., 35
Mayer, K.H., 171
Mays, V.M., 32
McAllister, A.L., 211
McArdle, J., 219
McCamish, M., 1-2, 17, 24, 25, 38, 46,
    47, 52, 71, 86, 151, 153,
    154, 155, 157, 159, 161,
    185, 188, 189, 191, 196,
    209, 261, 271
McCarty, D., 219
McClelland, G.H., 215
McCusker, J., 171, 228
McEwan, R.T., 192
McGalliard, J., 175
McGree, S.T., 5, 48, 171, 211
McKirnan, D.J., 231
McKusick, L., 71, 171, 189, 231
McLaws, M.L., 1, 12, 29, 36, 39, 40, 81,
    86, 87, 120, 154, 159,
    169, 171, 172, 174, 183,
    212, 272
McLean, J., 231
McManus, T.J., 191
McMillan, B., 189
Meichenbaum, D., 228
Memon, A., 257
Merson, M.H., 29, 32
Meyer-Bahlburg, H.F.L., 235
Mickler, S., 36
Middlestadt, S.E., 15, 39, 42, 44, 45, 52,
    62, 121, 122, 123, 133,
    145, 160, 167, 169, 173,
    187, 210, 214, 220, 242,
    253, 261, 271, 272
Milburn, M.A., 211
Miller, L.E., 214
Miller, T.E., 35, 187
Millstein, S.G., 67, 188
Miniard, P., 48
Moates, D.R., 77
Montgomery, S.B., 119, 120, 121, 130,
    154, 190, 254
Moodie, R., 35
Moore, S.M., 1, 36, 37, 39, 40, 60, 65-67,
    68, 70-71, 76, 77, 79,
    121, 123, 129, 130, 155,
    159, 188, 231, 259
Morales-Barreto, G., 188
Morgan, K., 5, 48, 66, 172, 211
Morin, S.F., 132, 136, 154, 171, 185,
    187-192, 193
Morton, J., 227, 242

Moscicki, B., 67
Moses, S., 35
Mullen, P.D., 8, 38, 121
Murray, M., 211
Nader, P.R., 5
Naessens, J., 120
Nagelkerke, N.J.D., 35
Najman, J., 157
Nathanson, C.A., 119
Ndinya-Achola, J.O., 35
Netemeyer, R.G., 35
Ngugi, E.N., 35
Nickerson, C.A., 215
Nisbett, R.E., 242
Norman, D.A., 77
Norris, A., 32, 35
North, P.J., 188
Norton, L.W., 136
Nucifora, J., 1, 12, 14, 21, 35, 47, 90, 129, 146, 151, 191, 194, 208, 209, 211, 212, 217, 272
Nzila, N., 34, 35, 36
O'Leary, A., 136
O'Reilly, K.R., 186, 192, 257
Okware, S., 35
Oldenburg, B., 29, 169, 171
Olshavsky, R.W., 49, 211
Orth, D., 159, 191
Osgood, C.E, 29
Ostrow, D.G., 33, 71, 154, 189, 190, 228, 231, 254
Page, T.J., 5, 212
Pagel, M.D., 211, 215
Palacios-Jimenez, L., 187, 192
Parcel, G.S., 90
Park, B., 229
Parker, R.G., 169, 172
Patton, W., 192
Peters, L., 40, 136, 193
Peterson, P.L., 5, 231
Petosa, R., 120
Phelps, M., 120
Plant, M., 231
Pleck, J.H., 71, 76, 77
Plum, J.R., 34, 36
Plummer, D.C., 35, 45, 172, 227
Pollack, M.A., 171, 189
Pope, C.R., 4
Porritt, A., 70, 231
Porter, J., 119, 120
Powell, M.C., 209
Power, L., 35, 36, 38, 39, 42, 43, 51, 58, 64, 79, 106, 107, 112, 128, 138, 145, 164, 172, 189, 207, 213, 254, 261, 262, 263
Pratkanis, A.R., 209
Presson, C.C., 49, 211
Prieur, A., 257

Proffitt, C., 17
Puckett, S.B., 132, 154, 187
Ramazanoglu, C., 70
Rassaby, J., 121
Reed, D.L., 37
Reid, L., 10, 37, 118
Reis, H.T., 172
Reiss, I.L., 67
Research and Decisions Corporation 189
Reynolds, L.A., 35, 254
Rhodes, F., 192
Richard, R., 40, 69, 70
Richards, L., 175
Richards, T., 175
Rigby, K., 95-97, 188, 190, 194, 214, 272
Rinaldo, C.R., 171, 172, 188, 192
Robertson, J.A., 231
Rodden, P., 259
Rodin, J., 2-5
Rogers, R.W., 41
Rokeach, M., 217
Rollins, B., 68
Rosenstock, I.M., 6, 8, 9, 38, 118, 136, 187
Rosenthal, D., 1, 7, 36, 37, 39, 40, 65-67, 68-71, 77, 79, 96, 121, 130, 155, 159, 188, 231, 259
Ross, M.W., 1, 2, 12, 29, 39, 40, 81, 84, 86-87, 89, 90, 95, 120, 154, 155, 159, 169, 171, 172, 190, 212, 227, 235, 272
Rosser, B.R.S., 95, 190
Rotheram-Borus, M.J., 36, 192
Rotter, J.B., 137
Rugg, D.L., 186, 257
Rust, J., 86, 171, 172
Sacco, W.P., 37
Sallis, J.F., 5
Salt, H., 254
Sanbonmatsu, D.M., 217
Sanford, A.J., 229
Santora, F.L., 85
Sarver, V.T., 141
Schaalma, H., 40, 136, 138, 193
Schifter, D.B., 35, 50, 151
Schleifer, S.T., 69
Schnell, D., 192
Schofield, M., 65
Schumacher, G.M., 77
Schwartz, S.A., 48, 172, 211, 228
Scott, S., 70
Sedikides, C., 210
Seltzer, R., 192
Senf, J., 37
Shaffer, D.R., 11
Shapiro, J., 191
Sharpe, S., 70

Sharrock, B., 175
Sheeran, P., 100
Sheng, D., 210
Shephard, R.J., 150
Shepherd, R., 209
Sheppard, B.H., 14, 16-17
Sherman, S.J., 49, 211
Shernoff, M., 35, 187, 192
Shotter, J., 255
Shpitzajzen, A., 229
Shulkin, J.J., 35
Sideman, L.M., 35
Siegal, M., 213
Siegel, K., 121,154, 157, 158, 169, 171, 188, 231, 261
Silvestre, A.J., 86, 172
Simon, W., 255, 257
Siraprapasiri, T., 34
Sjursen, H., 154
Sketchley, J., 86, 171, 172
Skinner, M.J., 45, 172, 227, 231
Skowronski, J.J., 210
Slovic, P., 157, 234
Smart, J., 17
Smetana, J.G., 14, 220
Smith, P.K., 192
Smith, S., 41, 44, 154
Somaini, B., 35
Sonenstein, F.L., 71
Sorenson, J.R., 187
Sorenson, R.E., 67
Sparks, P., 209
Spears, R., 68, 100, 157, 210, 259
Speckart, G., 17
Spencer, C.P., 48, 62, 211
St. Lawrence, J.S., 154, 156, 171, 194, 228
Stall, R.D., 32, 71, 136, 187, 228, 231
Starr, R., 190
Stasson, M., 22, 35, 241
Statham, D., 4, 44, 154
Stenner, K., 257
Sternberg, R.J., 12
Stevenson, L.Y., 189
Stoddard, A.M., 171
Stoker, L., 70, 231
Strauss, A.L., 175, 190
Strecher, V.J., 7, 136
Strunin, L., 68
Suci, G.J., 29
Sutton, S., 39
Swan, A.V., 211
Sykes, G.M., 228
Tal, M., 228
Tanaka, K., 213
Tannenbaum, P.H., 29
Taylor, C., 261
Taylor, R.L., 192
Taylor, S.E., 1, 2, 9, 136
Tellegen, A., 54

Temoshok, L., 68
Terry, D.J., 12, 14, 17, 24, 25, 38, 39-41, 44, 45, 46, 50, 52, 62, 70, 86, 90, 117, 118, 123, 135, 140, 153, 154, 155, 160, 172, 185, 188, 191, 193, 196, 208, 209, 212, 216, 217, 253, 271
Tesser, A., 11
Tessler, R.C., 48, 211
Thompson, K., 37, 70
Tiggemann, M., 89
Timmins, P., 2, 17, 24, 25, 46, 52, 77, 121, 130, 153, 155, 161, 188, 191, 196, 209, 261
Tomarken, A.J., 242
Treffke, H., 89
Triandis, H.C., 39, 48, 136, 150, 208, 210
Trost, J., 174
Tschopp, A., 120
Tulloch, J., 256
Turk, D.C., 229
Turtle, A.M., 47, 68, 69, 154, 159, 254
Tversky, A., 151, 229, 234
Valdiserri, R.O., 33, 35, 171, 172, 188, 189, 192
Valle, S.L., 86
Valois, P., 150
van der Pligt, J., 40, 41, 70
van Ryn, M., 187
Vazquez-Nuttal, E., 188
Wadsworth, J., 192
Waldby, C., 155, 256, 257
Waldron, I., 2, 4
Wallston, B.S., 9, 120, 131
Wallston, K.A., 9, 120, 131
Walter, H.J., 120, 189
Wandersman, A., 33, 39, 41, 137, 138, 150, 211
Warshaw, P.R., 14
Warwick, W. 1, 8, 12, 14, 25, 38, 62, 90, 117, 146, 154, 187, 231, 254
Watson, D., 54
Weatherburn, P., 36, 191
Webster, D.C., 176
Weeks, J., 256
Weigel, R.H., 214
Weinstein, N.D., 121, 157, 188, 254
Weisenberg, M., 38
Wellings, K., 186, 192
Wells, J., 84
Wessel, L.G., 35
White, K., 189
White, L.A., 79
Wicker, A.W., 217
Wiggins, E.C., 48, 208
Wiley, J., 71, 136, 231
Williams, A.F., 6
Williams, C.E., 83

Williams, P., 83
Wilson, C., 38, 39, 40
Wilson, D.J., 38, 39, 40, 191
Wilson, T.D., 242
Wittkower, E.D., 82
Wolitski, R.J., 192
Woodcock, A., 257
Worth, L.T., 208
Wortman, C.B., 154, 190
Wright, B., 121, 158, 159
Wurtel, S., 7, 118
Yacenda, T.A., 83

Yarber, W.L., 83
Yi, Y., 46
Young, H., 23, 118
Young, L., 238, 239
Zajonc, R.B., 229
Zapka, J.G., 171
Zeller, R.A., 171
Zimmerman, R.S., 190
Zorn, J., 68
Zorn, M., 171
Zuckerman, M., 172

# Subject Index

Subject IndexAbstinence 35, 196
Adolescent AIDS Awareness Project 192
Adolescent sexuality 65, 66, 67, 68, 79
Affect 38, 42, 47, 48, 51, 55, 60, 62, 63, 64, 65, 96, 124, 151, 208, 209, 214, 229, 242
AIDS (see HIV/AIDS)
Alcohol use 77, 197, 237
Algorithmic theories 218
Anal intercourse 2, 66, 67, 86, 87, 154, 159, 173, 175-179, 183, 189, 191, 192, 193, 215, 255, 260
ARIES project 193, 194, 196
Assertiveness 2, 8, 11, 35, 78, 90
Attachment 99, 106, 109, 112-115, 117, 257, 258, 260
Attitude
    conceptualisation of 21, 208, 209
    determinants of 14, 208
    effect on behaviour 13
    measurement of 16, 21, 22, 27, 51, 56-59, 62, 63, 64, 76, 101, 128, 129, 133, 146, 149, 150, 210, 272
    relation to subjective norm 13, 214, 271
    to condoms (see condom attitudes)
    to safer sex (see safer sex)
Attitude-behaviour model 39, 87, 137, 150, 207
Availability heuristic 170, 234

Behaviour
    measurement of 24, 159
Behaviour change
    barriers to 44
Behaviour change programmes (see intervention programmes)
Behavioural beliefs 9, 16, 23, 24, 39, 48, 56, 71, 87, 122, 125, 126, 128, 142, 208, 209
Behavioural conditions
    necessary 50, 51, 56, 62, 161, 162, 163, 167, 172, 217,
Behavioural control 25-27, 41, 45, 50, 51, 55-60, 62-65, 98, 137-145, 150-153, 217, 220, 241, 272, 275

Behavioural norm 49, 52, 55, 59, 60, 63, 64, 65, 178, 180, 183, 211, 212-214, 271, 273
Behavioural Norms Scale 91, 183
Behavioural skills 36, 42, 43, 45, 136, 194

Cognitive bargaining 235
Collective action 254, 256, 259
Communication skills 197
Compatibility principle 10, 20, 140, 272
Computational theories 218
Condom Assertiveness Scale 90
Condom attitudes
    and behaviour 81, 85, 86
    and myths 83
    dimensions of 86, 101, 113
    in adolescents 69
    studies of 83, 84
Condom use
    and assertiveness 90
    and social norms 91
    as contraceptive 84, 272
    as sexual strategy 163, 196
    communication about 76, 77, 78
    determinants of 55, 75, 81, 86, 89, 120, 171, 172, 183, 194
    embarrassment about 129
    in adolescents 68
    reasons for 272
    reasons for failure to use 82, 86
Condoms
    buying 10, 161
    dislike of 70, 86
Conflict theory 42
Content analysis 52, 174, 176
Contraceptive use 4, 71, 81
Control beliefs 4, 26, 27
Control factors 4, 11, 25, 26, 62, 137, 140, 143, 151
Cross-cultural research 256
Cultural beliefs 190

Discrimination (see HIV/AIDS victims, acceptance of)
Dread risk (see HIV/AIDS as a dread risk)

Drug use (see injected drug use)

Efficacy expectancies 135, 136, 137-141,
    145, 148, 150, 151
Elicitation study (see pilot study)
Emotions (see affect)
English language fluency 93, 96, 97, 99,
    106, 107, 112-115, 117
Eroticising Safer Sex workshop 35, 187,
    192
Ethnic groups
    AIDS-related beliefs 93, 95, 97, 110,
        114
    health care behaviour 2
Ethnic identity 190
Ethnic norms 190
Exclusivity 2, 4, 40, 93, 97, 98, 100, 101,
    103-110, 115, 159, 160, 163, 166, 196,
    215, 216
Expectancy-value model 14, 58, 208, 209,
    218, 220

Face validity 181, 183
Family modelling 4
Focus discussion groups 174

Gay community 1, 154, 158, 162, 166,
    177, 178, 179, 186, 187, 189, 256-258,
    266, 272, 321-324
Gay identity 189, 190, 257
Gender
    and condom intentions 113
    and theory of reasoned action 17, 40,
        91
    effect on health care behaviours 2
    effect on safer sex behaviour 2, 20, 106
Gender roles 93, 111
Grim Reaper campaign 154
Grounded theory 176
Group attitude 195

Health belief model
    and theory of reasoned action 124, 132
    description of 5, 120
    support for 6, 38, 39, 118, 119, 254
Health care 1-5, 29, 120, 121, 132, 189
Health care behaviour
    determinants of 1, 2, 4
Health locus of control 37
Heterosexuality and AIDS Project 257,
    259
HIV infection
    Australian patterns 1
    perceived risk of 130, 153, 161
    prevalence of 29
    worldwide patterns 29, 30
HIV status
    of partner 35, 98, 159

of self 183, 184, 186
HIV testing 186
HIV transmission routes
    knowledge of 68, 95, 155, 254
    types of 29-32, 33, 36, 69
HIV/AIDS
    as a dread risk 157
    concern about 75, 77, 95
    education 96, 154, 170, 190, 228, 229,
        230, 243
    fear of 39, 191
    knowledge 41, 47, 136, 257
    survey studies 36
    theory-based research 29, 37
HIV prevention campaigns (see
    information campaigns; intervention
    programmes)
HIV/AIDS victims
    acceptance of 95, 154
    contact with 163, 167, 188
HIV/AIDS-preventive behaviour 10, 20,
    119, 121-122, 124, 136, 184, 189, 191,
    193, 194, 207, 208, 209, 215, 221
HIV/AIDS-related behaviour
    discussion of 174
HIV/AIDS-related strategies (see sexual
    strategies)
Homosexuals
    acceptance of 95, 96, 114, 122, 188,
        196
    and HIV/AIDS 30, 32, 33, 158
    studies of 2, 17, 20, 85, 86-89, 91, 119,
        136, 159, 163-165, 171, 172, 183,
        186, 191, 254, 259, 272

IMB model 42, 43, 1136
Individualistic bias 253, 257
Information campaigns 35, 36, 94, 96, 97,
    154, 162, 186, 187, 208, 239, 259
Injected drug use 32, 169, 170, 237
Intention
    instability of 10, 46
    prediction of 12, 56
    relationship with behaviour 9-11, 13,
        14, 39-41, 47, 59, 77, 130, 199, 214,
        215
    to have exclusive relationship 100, 103,
        106 109
    to practise safer sex 78, 103, 197
    to use condoms 10, 40, 48, 54, 63, 64,
        71-74, 91-93, 986, 100, 103-112,
        125, 130, 163, 167, 169, 172, 173,
        183, 184, 217, 272
Intention to Use a Condom questionnaire
    169, 172-174, 176, 177, 181-184
Intercourse (see sexual activity)
Internal consistency 84, 95, 183
Internal construct validity 181, 183

Internal health beliefs 4
Internal validity 233
Intervention programmes
  cognitive-based 243
  for adolescents 35
  health belief model-based 154, 185,
    187
  peer-led 192
  skills training in 153, 192
  theory of reasoned action-based 185,
    193
Interviews 52, 79, 87, 95, 100, 106, 112,
  174, 175, 179, 186, 231, 257

Modelling
  of health care behaviour 1
Morin model 154, 185, 187, 191
Motivated reasoning 229
Motivation to comply 9, 14, 16, 24, 39,
  47, 55, 71, 79, 91, 102, 126, 128, 143,
  172, 180, 211

Non-penetrative sex (see sexual activity)
Normative beliefs 9, 14, 17, 23, 39, 45,
  47, 48, 55, 56, 71, 87, 102, 125, 126,
  128, 142, 143, 163, 172, 180, 208,
  211, 253, 258, 261
Normative change 194, 195
Normative influence
  classification of 212, 213
  on condom use 110
  on health care behaviour 1

Off-line cognitions 227, 229, 234, 235,
  240-244
On-line cognitions 227, 229-230, 235,
  240-244
Outcome evaluations 9, 16, 23, 126, 128,
  143
Overtraining 77, 148

Partner (see sexual partner)
Partner norm 48, 49, 52, 55, 59-62, 64,
  65, 166, 172, 220, 271, 272
Past behaviour 26, 39-42, 46, 89, 135,
  140, 144, 150, 155, 211-213, 261, 263
Peer groups 177, 179, 180, 183, 189, 191
Peer support 86, 185, 187, 189, 191, 195,
  239, 272
Peers
  as educators 190, 195, 198
  as facilitators 194
  influence of 4, 272
Perceived barriers 5, 6, 118, 119, 123,
  124, 130, 131, 137
Perceived behavioural control 25-27, 39,
  41, 45, 49-51, 55-59, 62, 64, 65, 98,
  102, 105, 106, 109, 112-114, 117,

137-145, 150-153, 161, 217, 220, 241,
  272
Perceived benefits 5, 6, 22, 71, 76, 77,
  118, 119, 120, 124, 131, 137, 187
Perceived invulnerability 2, 157, 188, 261
Perceived risk
  and attitude 164
  and perceived control 161
  and prediction of sexual behaviour 154,
    155
  and sexual partner 159
  and subjective norm 165
  assessment of 159
  of others 162, 163, 169, 170
  optimistic bias 153, 156-158, 162
Perceived severity 5, 6, 39, 42, 118-120,
  121, 124, 125, 130, 157, 182, 254
Perceived situational constraints 42
Perceived susceptibility 5, 6, 119, 120,
  121-122, 124, 127, 130, 154, 185, 187,
  254, 273
Personal norm 48, 49, 52, 55, 59, 63, 172,
  211-213
Personality 5, 17, 172, 214, 230, 231, 246
Pilot study 17, 20, 22, 27, 36, 38, 43, 45,
  47, 52, 55, 87, 117, 125, 131, 135,
  141, 160, 170, 172, 179-181, 199, 209,
  210, 232, 242, 273
Pornography 232, 241
Positive Affect-Negative Affect scale 55
Protection motivation theory 42

Questionnaire development (see scale
  development)

Rathus Assertiveness Inventory 90
Rational descision making 77, 261
Recall
  accuracy of 80
Religion 17, 26, 82, 94, 190, 235
Representativeness heuristic 170
Risk (see perceived risk)
Risk of HIV infection (see HIV infection,
  risk of)
Risk denial 70, 122, 131, 154, 155, 157,
  170, 195

Safer sexual behaviour (see also unsafe
  sexual behaviour)
Safer sex strategies
  adopted 259
  preferred 20, 195-197
Safer sexual behaviours
  determinants of 7, 17, 121, 145
  knowledge of 258
SAPA Project 257, 259, 261
Scale development 17, 169, 170, 172, 180
Self-effficacy

and health behaviour 136
Self-efficacy
  and perceived control 62, 137
  and prediction of behaviour 138
  and prediction of intention 138
  and theory of planned behaviour 135,
    150
  and theory of reasoned action 138
  effect on condom use 89
Self-efficacy theory 29, 38, 41, 43, 194
Self-report measures 24, 215
Serial monogamy 67
Sex education 78, 272
Sexual activity
  non-penetrative 2, 20, 159, 166, 192,
    196, 215, 216, 241, 272, 273
  penetrative 30, 33, 154, 192, 227
Sexual arousal 72, 74, 76, 77, 78, 84, 163,
  218, 229, 237, 239
Sexual initiation (see virginity loss)
Sexual orientation 20, 52, 91, 167, 190,
  220, 229, 235
Sexual partner
  communication with 232, 239
  roles of 49, 169, 188, 191, 272
  types of 20, 75, 227, 231, 233, 236,
    237, 241, 242, 256, 257, 272
Sexual risk taking 186, 227
Sexually transmitted diseases 32, 33, 35,
  55, 67, 81, 82, 85, 86, 87, 192
Skills training (see intervention
  programmes)
Social cognitive theory 135, 136, 139,
  147
Social construction theory 253, 255, 257
Social context 2, 29, 33, 45, 79, 80, 155,
  157, 161, 217, 220, 256, 262
Social process model 254
Social role 172
Social structures 254, 256, 257
Social theory of change 255
State-dependent learning 229
Stereotypes
  of drug use 157
  of homosexuality 157

reliance on 229, 234
Stigmatisation 35, 154, 189
STOP AIDS Project 187-188, 194
Subjective norm
  conceptualisation of 14, 21, 24
  determinants of 9, 14, 47, 211
  measurement of 15-16, 22, 27, 56, 58,
    62, 63, 64, 126, 128, 133, 146, 149,
    150, 272
  towards condom use 102, 107, 271

Theory of planned behaviour
  description of 25, 49
  flaws in 241
  methodology 27
  support for 26, 62
  test of 112
Theory of reasoned action
  description of 7, 9, 11, 12, 25, 97, 149
  flaws in 253, 257, 259
  metatheory 217-219, 274
  methodology 20, 45, 214, 272
  specificity of measures 10, 20, 45, 80,
    173, 217, 272
  support for 39, 40, 47, 62, 65, 110
  target populations 40
  test of 65, 71, 87, 112

University students 39, 52, 79, 125, 141,
  142, 163
Unprotected intercourse
  incidence of 228, 233, 237-239, 300
  justification for 227, 228
Unsafe sexual behaviour 86-87, 154, 156,
  159-161, 166, 170, 179, 180, 189, 197,
  227, 230, 231, 238, 239, 242, 258,
  272, 273

Vaginal intercourse (see sexual activity)
Value-expectancy theory 160
Virginity loss 65-67
Volitional behaviours 38, 216, 217
Volitional control 11, 12, 25, 39, 41, 45,
  49, 62, 79, 137, 207, 208, 216, 217